Understanding FDI-Assisted Economic Development

Contemporary thinking recognises that economic growth and development are highly dependent on improving not just the availability of capital, but also access to technological capabilities, infrastructure and resources. This thinking has gone hand-in-hand with an increasing economic liberalisation of most developing countries. The role of the MNE as a viable source of both capital and technology is one of the key features of this new openness. In the process of embracing FDI as a solution to the myriad of economic ills – something even the World Bank has begun to do – little attempt is made to understand the rationale and the costs associated with this policy stance. Simply put, FDI is not a condition *sine qua non* for development. Too much emphasis has been placed on attracting FDI, and not on understanding how to optimise the benefits for the host economy. This volume aims to address this issue and to encourage and promote related research.

This book was previously published as a Special Issue of *The European Journal of Development Research*.

Rajneesh Narula
Professor of International Business Regulation
University of Reading

Sanjaya Lall
Professor of Development Economics
Univeristy of Oxford

Understanding FDI-Assisted Economic Development

Edited By

Rajneesh Narula & Sanjaya Lall

Routledge
Taylor & Francis Group

LONDON AND NEW YORK

First published 2006 by Routledge
2 Park Square, Milton Park, Abingdon, Oxon, OX14 4RN

Simultaneously published in the USA and Canada
by Routledge
605 Third Avenue, New York, NY 10017

*Routledge is an imprint of the Taylor & Francis Group,
an informa business*

© 2006 Edited By Rajneesh Narula & Sanjaya Lall

Typeset in Times 10/12 pt by the Alden Group Oxford

British Library Cataloguing in Publication Data
A catalogue record for this book is available from the British Library

Library of Congress Cataloging in Publication Data
A catalog record for this book has been requested

Publisher's Note
The publisher has gone to great lengths to ensure the quality of this reprint but points out that some imperfections in the original may be apparent.

ISBN 13: 978-0-415-56837-1 (pbk)
ISBN 13: 978-0-415-34816-4 (hbk)

This book is dedicated to Sanjaya Lall
(1940–2005)

CONTENTS

1 Foreign Direct Investment and its Role in Economic
   Development: Do We Need a New Agenda?
   SANJAYA LALL and RAJNEESH NARULA   1

2 Learning, Upgrading, and Innovation in the South
   African Automotive Industry
   JOCHEN LORENTZEN and JUSTIN BARNES   19

3 Targeting Winners: Can Foreign Direct Investment
   Policy Help Developing Countries Industrialise?
   MICHAEL MORTIMORE and SEBASTIAN VERGARA   53

4 Using Foreign Investment Strategically for Innovation
   LYNN K. MYTELKA and LOU ANNE BARCLAY   85

5 Foreign Direct Investment, Linkage Formation and
   Supplier Development in Thailand during the 1990s:
   The Role of State Governance
   LAURIDS S. LAURIDSEN   115

6 Exports and Technological Capabilities: A Study of
   Foreign and Local Firms in the Electronics Industry
   in Malaysia, the Philippines and Thailand
   RAJAH RASIAH   141

7 Foreign Direct Investment: A Catalyst for Local Firm
   Development?
   JOANNA SCOTT-KENNEL   178

8 Where do Foreign Direct Investment-Related
   Technology Spillovers Come From in Emerging
   Economies? An Exploration in Argentina in the 1990s
   MARTIN BELL and ANABEL MARIN   207

vii

9   **Regulation of Foreign Investment in
     Historical Perspective**
     HA-JOON CHANG   241

10   **Will a Trade and Investment Link in the Global Trade
     Regime Be Good for Human Development?**
     KAMAL MALHOTRA   270

     Index   291

Foreign Direct Investment and its Role in Economic Development: Do We Need a New Agenda?

SANJAYA LALL and RAJNEESH NARULA

Despite globalisation, the essential role of foreign direct investment (FDI) in economic development has not changed. However, many mechanisms and dynamics of FDI-assisted development have changed: there is greater variation in the kinds of FDI, the benefits each offers, and the manner in which each interacts with the host economy. This introductory chapter attempts to place the discussions and issues raised in this volume within the wider literature on FDI and development. The various chapters analyse the role of multinational enterprises in industrial development in a 'learning system' perspective. They also analyse the policy tools available for using FDI for economic development in a liberalising, post-World Trade Organisation world, and the constraints to doing this. While this is a nascent debate, this volume points to a variety of 'soft' policy options that provide a pragmatic response to the complexities of globalisation.

Malgré la mondialisation, le rôle essentiel des investissements directs étrangers (IDE) pour le développement économique n'a pas changé. Cependant, de nombreux mécanismes et la dynamique du développement basé sur les IDE ont, eux, bien changé: les types d'IDE sont plus variés, de même les bénéfices offerts par chacun et la manière dont chaque type interagit avec l'économie locale. Cet chapter d'introduction tente de placer les discussions et les thèmes soulevés

Sanjaya Lall was formerly at the International Development Centre, University of Oxford, UK and Rajneesh Narula is at the Department of Economics, University of Reading Business School, UK. Earlier drafts of the chapters included in this volume were presented at a workshop organised by The Centre for Technology, Innovation and Culture (TIK) at the University of Oslo, *Understanding FDI-Assisted Economic Development*, from 22 to 25 May 2003. Sanjaya Lall and Rajneesh Narula gratefully acknowledge financial support from two Norwegian Research Council-funded projects, 'The North Versus the South in a Globalising World' and 'Globalisation as a Transformative Force'. They gratefully acknowledge the support of Helge Hveem, Brian Portelli and Christine Sole in organisational matters. This chapter has benefited greatly from comments and discussions of the various participants. Comments on an earlier draft by Brian Portelli, Tanja Sinozic and Paola Criscuolo have also contributed to this chapter.

dans ce numéro spécial du European Journal of Development Research *dans le contexte de la littérature sur les investissements directs étrangers et le développement. Les chapters analysent l'importance des entreprises multinationales (EMN) pour le développement industriel à partir d'une perspective de «système d'apprentissage». Ils analysent également les instruments politiques qui, dans un monde de plus en plus libéralisé et «post-Organisation Mondiale du Commerce», pourraient servir à utiliser les IDE dans le sens du développement économique; les contraintes existantes sont également relevées. Alors qu'il s'agit d'un débat naissant, ce numéro spécial relève un nombre d'options politiques modérées qui donnent une réponse pragmatique aux complexités de la mondialisation.*

I. INTRODUCTION

The past two or three decades have seen a significant policy shift in the developing world, from inward-looking import substitution to outward-looking, market determined strategies. The reasons for this shift are complex, but mainly have to do with the inefficiencies of import substitution, the growth of globalised production and the success of the export-oriented Asian newly industrialised economies (NIEs). One key feature of liberalisation has been greater openness to foreign direct investment (FDI) as a means of acquiring technologies, skills and access to international markets, and of entering dynamic trade and production systems internal to multinational enterprises (MNEs).

The role of the MNE as a source of capital and technology has grown over time, as other sources of capital have become scarcer or more volatile and technical change has accelerated. MNEs continue to dominate the creation of technology; indeed, with the rising costs and risks of innovation their importance has risen (with the exception of very new technology areas). They have also become more mobile, searching the world for lower cost, more efficient production sites and for new markets. The interaction of technical change (with its need for more and higher skills and better infrastructure) with greater FDI mobility has not reduced the need for local capabilities in developing countries. On the contrary, entry levels for attracting (non-resource-extracting) FDI have risen, and investors (especially in activities facing world competition) are focusing on countries with strong local capabilities. Mobile MNEs, in other words, seek strong complementary factors wherever they locate. There is no conflict over the long term between inward FDI and domestic capabilities.

With this realisation, and with the growing role of MNEs in economic life in most countries, most developing country governments have removed restrictions on FDI inflows. International donors and development agencies focus more on promoting private rather than public capital flows as catalysts of long-term development. The international 'rules of the game' reinforce these trends, setting up a legal framework for minimising policy interventions in FDI. The main actions so far cover national treatment for MNEs and the removal of performance requirements on them (for example, on local content, technology transfer or export obligations).

However, liberalisation has not always increased FDI inflows into host developing countries. The reason is simple. The removal of restrictions on FDI does not create the complementary factors that MNEs need; it only allows them to exploit existing capabilities more freely. Thus, FDI response tends to be most vigorous where local capabilities are strong when liberalisation takes place, and feeblest where they are weak (of course, excluding resource extraction). Similarly, over time, FDI inflows rise where local capabilities are strengthened and new capabilities are created; they stagnate or fall where they are not. This still has not, surprisingly, been internalised in policy recommendations on FDI in developing countries – much of this still proposes liberalisation not just as a necessary but also as a sufficient condition for attracting FDI and extracting most development benefits from it.

There is thus a need to look afresh at the role of MNEs and FDI policies in developing countries. This is the objective of this volume, and one which the current chapter seeks to highlight by placing these contributions within the context of the literature on FDI and development. The chapters here indicate that much of what we already know about FDI in economic development remains valid. It is clear, for instance, that the creation of linkages and the internalisation of spillovers from MNE activities still depend on local absorptive capacity. However, we know more now on how these mechanisms work. Complementary assets in the host country reflect its stage of development, in turn influenced by its history, geography and business systems. Some chapters in this issue increase our understanding of the nature of absorptive capacities in a 'systems of learning' perspective.

This volume also analyses the FDI policy tools, constraints and options for host countries in the face of the changing global economy. How do countries respond to the limitations on traditional policy tools placed by World Trade Organisation (WTO) protocols such as the Subsidies and Countervailing Measures Agreement (SCM), Trade-related Aspects of Intellectual Property Rights (TRIPS) and so on? Several chapters point to the 'soft' policy options that may provide an appropriate response to the complexities of globalisation.

II. DEVELOPMENT CONSTRAINTS AND OPPORTUNITIES OFFERED BY FDI

The Washington consensus holds, in broad terms, that markets for knowledge are efficient, and that FDI flows will – *ceteris paribus* – generate positive externalities for domestic firms. This presumes that all MNE activity offers similar spillovers and development benefits. Its focus is thus mainly on the *quantity* of FDI rather than its *quality*. There are four points here that we must qualify.

The Competence and Scope of Subsidiaries

The quality of FDI spillovers depends on the scope and competence of the subsidiary. These depend partly on factors internal to MNEs, including their internationalisation strategy, the role of particular affiliates in their global system and the motivation for their investment. Internal strategies interact with host country capabilities and resources [*Benito et al., 2003*]. Affiliates undertaking complex activities need high levels of local competence: advanced specialised skills, strong industrial and service firms and clusters, and strong support institutions. Where host countries cannot provide high level local assets, MNEs will not set up high quality affiliates. For instance, research and development activities concentrate in the few locations that can provide the advanced resources and institutions.

However, once MNEs establish operations in a country, affiliates often develop new capabilities: thus, the sophistication of affiliates also reflects how long they have been in operation, as documented for East Asia [*Rasiah, 1994, 1995*]. However, such upgrading is not automatic or universal: affiliates have to build upon advantages *that already exist* in the host economy – local capabilities matter [*Ritchie, 2002*]. Over time, the upgrading of affiliates has generally responded to improvements in domestic capabilities. Mortimore and Vergara find that the nature of a foreign investment depends initially on the host country's technological, human resource and supplier capabilities. They examine the case of Intel in Costa Rica and Toyota in Mexico and argue that in the case of Costa Rica both the lead MNE and the host country were able to achieve their respective objectives. Mexico, on the other hand, was not able to capitalise on the opportunities provided by Toyota's investment.

While the scope of affiliate activities can be modified rapidly, developing new capabilities takes time. Foreign investments in high value-added activities (needing high competence levels) tend to be 'location-sticky'. MNEs undertake sequential investments (and building of higher levels of competences) in locations that provide sub-optimal returns but where they have prior experience [*Hagedoorn and Narula, 2001*].

Blomstrom and Kokko [1997] suggest that host country characteristics that influence the extent of linkages are market size, local content regulations and the size and technological capability of local firms. They argue that linkages increase over time as the skill level of local entrepreneurs grows, new suppliers emerge and local content increases [*see also Driffield and Noor, 1999; McAleese and McDonald, 1978; Gorg and Ruane, 1998; Scott-Kennel and Enderwick, 2001*].

Nonetheless, there are many instances where upgrading, linkages and spillovers have not grown over time.

The Motive for the Investment

The motive for a foreign investment is crucial in determining how linkages and externalities develop. There are four main motives for investment: 1) seek natural resources; 2) seek new markets; 3) restructure existing foreign production; and 4) seek new strategic assets [*Narula and Dunning, 2000*]. These can be placed into two categories. The first category includes the first three motives: asset-exploiting, to generate economic rent by using existing firm-specific assets. The second category is the fourth motive: asset-augmenting, to acquire new assets that protect or enhance existing assets. In general, developing countries are unlikely to attract the second category of FDI; they primarily attract the first category.

The relative importance of each motive partly reflects the stage of economic development [*Narula and Dunning, 2000; Narula, 1996, 2004*]. Least developed countries would tend to have mainly resource-seeking FDI and countries at the catching-up stage mostly market-seeking FDI. Efficiency-seeking investments, with the most stringent capability needs, will tend to focus on the more industrialised developing economies (though three or four decades ago they went to countries with relatively low capabilities, e.g. the electronics industry in Southeast Asia in the 1970s).

Not all affiliates offer the same spillovers to host economies. A sales office, for instance, may have a high turnover and employ many people, but its technological spillovers will be limited relative to a manufacturing facility. Likewise, resource-seeking activities like mining tend to be capital intensive and provide fewer spillovers compared to market-seeking manufacturing FDI. During import substitution, most MNEs set up miniature replicas of their facilities at home, though many functions were not reproduced (they were 'truncated'). The extent of truncation, however, varied by host country. The most important determinants of truncation – and thus the scope of activities and competence of the subsidiary – were market size and local industrial capabilities [*Dunning and Narula, 2004*]. Countries with small markets and weak local industries had the most truncated subsidiaries, often only single-activity subsidiaries (sales and marketing or natural resource extraction). Larger countries with domestic technological capacity (such as Brazil and India) had the least truncated subsidiaries, often with research and development departments.

With liberalisation, MNE strategies on affiliate competence and scope have changed in four ways [*Dunning and Narula, 2004*]. First, there has been investment in *new affiliates*. Second, there has been *sequential investment* in upgrading existing subsidiaries. Third, there has been some *downgrading of subsidiaries*, whereby MNEs have divested in response to location advantages elsewhere or reduced the level of competence and scope of subsidiaries.

Fourth, there has been some *redistribution of ownership* as the result of privatisation or acquisitions of local private firms. In many, but certainly not all, cases this also led to a downgrading of activities.

MNEs are taking *advantage* of liberalisation to concentrate production capacity in a few locations, exploiting scale and agglomeration economies, favourable location and strong capabilities. Some miniature replicas have been downgraded to sales and marketing affiliates, with fewer opportunities for spillovers. Countries that receive FDI with the highest potential for capability development are, ironically, those with strong domestic absorptive capacities. The chapter by Lorentzen and Barnes on South Africa shows that domestic capacity – in the form of infrastructure or an efficient domestic industrial sector – is a primary determinant of high competence affiliates. They base their analysis on eight case studies in the South African automotive sector, and show that indigenous firms can compete with MNEs, and – given the appropriate domestic capabilities and infrastructure – can maintain and improve their competitive advantages through indigenous innovation.

Like South Africa, other countries have succeeded in attracting such FDI, notably Mexico and the Caribbean Basin [*ECLAC, 2000, 2001; Mortimore, 2000*]. In addition to providing a threshold level of domestic capabilities and infrastructure, these countries have invested in developing their knowledge base (although to a lesser extent in the case of Mexico). Mortimore [2000] argues that much of this FDI has created export platforms for MNEs with limited benefits for the host countries [*ECLAC, 2001*]. This is a point reiterated by Mytelka and Barclay here in the case of Trinidad, where FDI has not been leveraged to develop the skills and capabilities of local downstream and supporting firms. The state has largely failed to act as a facilitator to stimulate and support domestic absorptive capacities and linkages with MNE affiliates.

MNE Linkages

FDI transfers technology to local firms in four ways: backward linkages, labour turnover, horizontal linkages and international technology spillovers. Studies of backward linkages have identified various determinants, including those internal to MNEs and those associated with host economies. The ability of the host economy to benefit from MNE linkages has been found to depend crucially on the relative technological capabilities of recipient and transmitter: the greater the distance between them, the lower the intensity of linkages.

Again, MNE motives and strategies matter. Domestic market oriented affiliates generally purchase more locally than export-oriented firms because of lower quality requirements and technical specifications [*Reuber et al., 1973; Altenburg, 2000*]. MNE affiliates are more likely to be integrated with host countries where they source relatively simple inputs [*Ganiatsos, 2000; Carillo,*

2001]. Rodriguez-Clare [1996] argues that MNEs create more linkages when they use intermediate goods intensively, communication costs between parent and affiliate are high and the home and host markets are relatively similar in terms of intermediate goods. Affiliates established by mergers and acquisitions are likely to have stronger links with domestic suppliers than those established by greenfield investment [*UNCTAD, 2000; Scott-Kennel and Enderwick, 2001*], since the former may find established linkages that are likely to be retained if they are efficient. Linkages vary significantly by industry. In the primary sector, the scope for vertical linkages is often limited, due to the use of continuous production processes and the capital intensity of operations. In manufacturing, the potential for vertical linkages is broader, depending on the extent of intermediate inputs to total production and the type of production processes [*Lall, 1980*].

Scott-Kennel examines linkage formation between foreign affiliates and domestic firms, as well as the resource flows from the parent MNE to the affiliate. Although she studies New Zealand, her findings are relevant to developing countries. New Zealand is highly dependent on natural resources, has moved away from import substitution relatively recently and is a small peripheral economy. On the other hand, it has well-developed infrastructure and high skill levels. Her results confirm that there are considerable opportunities for linkage formation when location advantages are appropriate, the extent of linkages varying by the type of FDI.

Bell and Marin suggest some caution in applying results such as Scott-Kennel's to developing and intermediate countries. They argue that methodologies to measure and evaluate knowledge spillovers in advanced economies depend upon a concrete understanding of the interactions between processes, industrial structures, resource endowments and the like, and these have been stylised in the spillover literature with advanced economies in mind. Using data from Argentina, they argue that a well-established domestic sector which has evolved independently of MNEs may mean that the traditional view that spillovers are largely one-way is simplistic. Co-location of domestic and foreign firms in intermediate economies has benefits for both groups of firms, and productivity growth in the domestic sector may not necessarily derive from MNE spillovers. Indeed, as also observed by Katrak [*2002*] in the case of India, knowledge creation mechanisms of MNE subsidiaries and domestic firms are sometimes largely independent. Better methods to measure and understand the direction and flow of knowledge is required before the controversy regarding the benefits of FDI and spillovers is settled.

Nature of MNE Assets

Although it is a reasonable assumption that MNEs have superior firm-specific assets, the assets they transfer to particular host countries are not always those that the latter seek or are able to assimilate. MNE competitive advantages derive from three types of assets. The first is associated with technology (knowledge, capabilities or machinery and equipment). The second is associated with the conduct of transactions, based on superior intra-firm hierarchies within and across national borders. The third is multinationality itself, the advantages of 'common governance'. These are transaction assets – MNEs gain rent from their superior knowledge of markets and internal governance of transactions. Thus, MNEs may have similar technologies to domestic counterparts but still out-compete them. In such cases, technological spillovers will not occur, though other types of spillovers might occur (say, through employee mobility or vertical links to suppliers) [*Narula and Marin, 2003*].

Even where absorptive capacity exists, MNE assets may be very tacit and internal to the firms, as with transaction-type advantages. These assets cannot be acquired easily by local firms. This may go some way to explaining the findings of Bell and Marin and their persuasive discussion about the difficulties of measuring and evaluating spillovers. As they emphasise in their chapter, not all MNE subsidiaries in developing countries have the same capacity to act as *generators* of knowledge spillovers.

III. ABSORPTIVE CAPACITY

How does the nature of location advantages determine the ability of the domestic economy to absorb spillovers from FDI? As almost all the chapters in this volume illustrate, the presence of externalities does not mean either that the domestic economy can internalise them, or that the externalities are significant in quantity or quality. Absorptive capacity is significant for development because it allows domestic actors to capture knowledge that exists elsewhere. Where absorptive capacity is lacking in domestic firms, they may, instead of reaping technological benefits from FDI, be 'crowded out' [*Agosin and Mayer, 2000*].

Capabilities in the host country context matter for the magnitude and intensity of technological upgrading. As Portelli and Narula [*2004*] have shown in the case of Tanzania, FDI in activities that match the comparative advantage of the host country provides greater linkages. Wider technology gaps between domestic and foreign-owned activities tend to lead to fewer backward linkages and to lower technological content in the inputs sourced locally.

Several authors, such as Findlay [*1978*] and Perez and Soete [*1988*], have noted that a minimum level of scientific and technical knowledge is required to use innovation. Below this level, the cost of adoption can be prohibitive. This is particularly true for FDI. Borensztein *et al.* [*1998*] show that, at country level, a minimum threshold of absorptive capacity is necessary for FDI to contribute to higher productivity growth. At the firm level, Narula and Marin [*2003*] show that only firms with high absorptive capacity are likely to benefit from FDI spillovers. Xu [*2000*] also shows that a country needs to reach a minimum human capital threshold level in order to benefit from technology transfer.

While insufficient absorptive capacity tends to lead to the inefficient use of technology inflows, knowledge accumulation is much more rapid once the threshold level of absorptive capacity is crossed. Simply put, technology absorption is easier once countries have 'learned-to-learn' [*Criscuolo and Narula, 2002*]. The cost of imitation increases as the follower closes the gap with the leader and the number of technologies available for imitation falls. This implies that there are diminishing returns on marginal increases in absorptive capacity as firms approach the frontier of knowledge [*Narula, 2004*].

Kokko *et al.* [*2001*] highlight the role of past industrialisation experience as a precondition for technology transfer. The absence of such experience is concomitant to lack of local absorptive capacity [*Radosevic, 1999*]. For example, in sub-Saharan Africa, the conditions that stimulate technological assimilation (such as developed human capital, adequate physical infrastructure and a dynamic business climate) are absent. This constrains the ability of African countries to master foreign technology and to compete in international markets [*Mytelka, 1985; Lall and Pietrobelli, 2002*]. The development of capacities and capabilities is key both to attracting FDI as well as to increasing MNE technological spillovers.

Narula [*2004*] decomposes absorptive capacity into four constituent parts: firm-sector absorptive capacity, basic infrastructure, advanced infrastructure and formal and informal institutions. Each is indispensable and each has different costs and benefits at different stages of development. Increases in absorptive capacity at earlier stages of development are associated with 'generic' basic infrastructure and increases in technological capacity generally have positive welfare effects. For example, increases in the percentage of population with primary and secondary education have numerous welfare benefits, as does the provision of infrastructure. Investment in such resources has large multiplier effects.

IV. TAKING A SYSTEMS VIEW TO ABSORPTION AND INDUSTRIAL DEVELOPMENT

Several contributions here (Mytelka and Barclay, Lorentzen and Barnes, Bell and Marin, and Rasiah) stress that industrial development and absorptive capacity must be seen from a 'systems' view. By this we mean that while learning and absorption take place at the firm level, the success or failure of individual firms occurs within a 'system'.[1] Within a system, there exists a broad knowledge base outside industrial enterprises; this base is central to technological accumulation by industry. Learning and innovation involve complex interactions between firms and their environment. The environment consists of the firms' networks of direct customers and suppliers but it stretches much further. It also includes the broader factors shaping their behaviour and activities: the social and cultural context; the institutional and organisational framework; infrastructure; knowledge creating and diffusing institutions, and so on. This is the essence of the systems approach to technology.

'System' does not necessarily mean that the influences on industrial innovation are systematically organised [*Narula, 2003*]. To put it simply, 'system' means a regularly interacting or interdependent group forming a unified whole. A system is in most cases the serendipitous intertwining of institutions and economic actors that defines the stock of knowledge in a given location [*Etzkowitz and Leydesdorff, 2000*]. For instance, changes in the educational policies of the government are likely to affect other actors and institutions, and influence the process and extent of technological learning in the future.

In a system, the efficiency of economic actors – firm or non-firm – depends on how much and how efficiently they interact amongst themselves. The means by which interactions take place are referred to as 'institutions' in the economics literature, though sociologists prefer to speak of 'social capital'. Institutions are the 'sets of common habits, routines, established practices, rules, or laws that regulate the interaction between individuals and groups' [*Edquist and Johnson, 1997*]. Institutions create the milieu within which innovation is undertaken; they establish the ground rules for interaction between economic actors and represent a sort of 'culture'. Institutions are associated with public sector organisations, but are not exclusively so. It is not only the creation of new knowledge but also the diffusion of extant knowledge that determine the national knowledge stock and the accumulation of national absorptive capacity.

The role of formal institutions has traditionally been considered under the rubric of political economy and has been the focus of debate on the role of the state in establishing, promoting and sustaining learning. It is not our intention to review the debate on the role of industrial policy in industrial development, highlighted in a special issue of *Oxford Development Studies* (volume 31, number 1). The contributors to our volume largely believe that governments are essential to promoting inter-linkages between the elements of absorptive capacity and to creating the opportunities for economic actors to absorb and internalise spillovers.

The importance of building institutions cannot be overstated: Rodrik *et al.* [2002] argue that efficient institutions contribute more to economic growth than location or trade. Institutions can be formal or informal. Formal institutions include the intellectual property regime, competition policy, technical standards, taxation, incentives for innovation, education and the like. Informal institutions are more difficult to define, but are associated with creating and promoting links between the various actors. For example, the government may play a role in encouraging firms to collaborate with universities or in promoting entrepreneurship.

Developing countries have switched reluctantly from inward-looking strategies with a large role for the government to market-friendly strategies that force them to face a new multilateral milieu, one in which they have little experience and with which they are often poorly prepared to cope. Institutions continue to remain largely independent and national. While formal institutions can be legislated, modifying and developing informal institutions is a complex and slow process, since they cannot be created simply by government fiat. The developed countries have taken 50 years to liberalise and adjust, but even they have faced considerable inertia. They have, for instance, yet to reform their agricultural sectors.

V. INDUSTRIAL POLICY AND FDI-ASSISTED DEVELOPMENT

The chapters in this volume all point to a basic paradox: with weak local capabilities, industrialisation has to be more dependent on FDI. However, FDI cannot drive industrial growth without local capabilities. The neo-liberal approach favoured by the Washington consensus which leaves capability development to free market forces provides few realistic answers. It can result in slow and truncated technological development, with gaps between countries rising. Some upgrading does take place, but is slower and more limited than with the promotion of local capabilities. Given the speed at which technologies are changing and path-dependence and cumulativeness in capability building, it can lead to latecomers being mired in low growth traps.

The policy needs of capability building have not changed much. They are *direct* – the infant industry case to provide 'space' for enterprises to master new technologies without incurring enormous and unpredictable losses – and *indirect*, to ensure that skill, capital, technology and infrastructure markets meet their needs. There is also a need to *co-ordinate learning* across enterprises and activities, when these are linked in the production chain and imports cannot substitute effectively for local inputs. At the same time, technical change makes it necessary to *provide more access to international technology markets*; it also makes it more *difficult to anticipate which activities are likely to succeed*. The information needs of industrial policy rise in tandem with technological change and complexity. The greater complexity of technology does not make selectivity unfeasible. Detailed targeting of technologies, products or enterprises may be more difficult because of the pace of change, but targeting at higher levels is feasible and more necessary. Technological progress may actually make industrial policy easier in some respects: information on technological trends and markets is more readily available, more is known about the policies in successful countries and benchmarking is easier.

The spread of integrated production systems makes it more difficult and risky to take the route used by the East Asian NIEs. It is much easier for countries to attract segments of MNE activity and build upon these rather than to develop local capabilities independently. All the later entrants into globalised systems, from Malaysia to Mexico and Costa Rica, have gone the FDI route. However, as FDI regimes become more liberal, MNEs are also less willing to part with valuable technologies to independent firms.

Globalisation does not do away with the need for all selective industrial policies; it only reduces the scope and raises the potential cost of some. FDI is complementary to local enterprises and capabilities after a certain level of development. Strong local capabilities raise the possibility of attracting high value systems and of capturing skill and technology spillovers from them; these capabilities need selective policies. Moreover, attracting export-oriented FDI increasingly requires selective promotion and targeting; the most effective targeting is undertaken by advanced economies [Loewendahl, 2001].

Lall [1996, 1997a, 1997b, 2003] and Wade [1990] among others point to the need of a holistic approach to selecting and leveraging sectors for dynamic growth along with stable government, transparent policies and basic infrastructure and skills. The role of governments as a market facilitator and provider of complementary assets is more critical [Narula, 2003].

The provision of basic location advantages is perhaps most significant for pre-catching-up and catching-up economies, where firms rely on governments to provide public and quasi-public goods. As countries reach a threshold level of technological capabilities and start catching up in earnest, governments need to provide more active support. This means developing specific industries and technological trajectories, so that their location advantages grow less 'generic'. In other words, their role as market facilitator and provider of complementary location-specific advantages becomes more critical [Dunning, 1997; Stopford, 1997].

The chapter by Rasiah undertakes a comparative analysis of export performance and technological capabilities of foreign and local firms in three Asian countries. Rasiah suggests that the role of governments is critical to providing the necessary technology infrastructure, support for technology activity in the form of subsidies, training, and research and development organisations, and special programmes to foster firm–university relationships. By doing so, governments create a 'strong latent capacity to stimulate technology transfer' by MNEs.

While several chapters contribute to the discussion of the role of government in promoting FDI-assisted development, they do not point to an optimal set of policies. Lauridsen discusses the role of the state in Thailand. As he illustrates, it is one thing that appropriate policies are adopted; it is quite another whether they are effectively implemented. Political and social constraints can severely affect the outcome. A similar point is also made by Mytelka and Barclay, using the contrasting examples of Costa Rica and Trinidad. Mortimore and Vergara argue that it is important to have policies to induce MNEs to improve and upgrade capabilities to sustain more sophisticated industrial activities, not just by attracting the initial investment but also by encouraging MNEs to realise dynamic comparative advantages in the host economy.

Liberalisation provides the policy framework for globalisation. However, it often administers a major 'shock' to industries and institutions in most countries, not just introducing import competition and new actors (MNEs), but also calling for the restructuring of institutions (legal codes, political structures, policy orientation). Sudden exposure to the full force of international competition will not facilitate countries' institutional adjustment, as illustrated by the chaotic state of the ex-Soviet economies. FDI does not necessarily help institutional restructuring. As Kogut [2000: 34] notes:

> Institutions, however, do not travel by the arteries of multinational corporations. They reflect patterns of behaviour that are inscribed in legal codes and political and economic relationships. Outside the power of any one actor to change, institutions are social agreements that guide and coordinate the interdependent acts of economic actors in a country.

The lack of success of liberalisation in many countries reflects both the failure to integrate aspects of policy in a systemic way and the difficulty of changing inherited institutions. Most countries have attempted to graft the new model on to the remnants of the old one, because interest groups and institutions are resistant or expensive to change. While liberalisation has helped to correct many inefficiencies, improving macroeconomic fundamentals and reducing the excessive role of the state in industrial activity, it has also led to a rapid and overzealous reduction in the state's provision of the public and quasi-public goods that are necessary for industrial development [Ramos, 2000; Katz, 2001; Alcorta, 2000].

The debate on how best to respond to the industrial policy challenges in an interdependent world continues. The contribution by Chang emphasises the lack of an alternative model to infant industry protection, which he argues is a case of 'kicking away the ladder' by the rich countries. Chang acknowledges that a return to the import-substitution model is no longer feasible, because globalisation is largely irreversible, and that international competition does help reduce inefficiencies. Nonetheless, catch-up through infant industry promotion has always been the bedrock of industrial development [see also Chang, 2002 and Wood et al., 2003 for further discussion] and as yet no clear alternative has presented itself.

It is difficult to see how host countries that have FDI can tap its potential fully without such strategies as local content rules, incentives for deepening technologies and functions, inducements to export and so on. Performance requirements have been deployed inefficiently in many countries, but, as with protection, they have also been used very effectively by others. Catching up implies the absorption and mastery of existing technology, and this implies that there is knowledge *available* for imitation and that rules permit firms to imitate. Multilateral and bilateral agreements such as TRIPs, Trade-related Investment Measures (TRIMs) and SCM severely limit the potential for developing countries to use traditional policy instruments to protect learning and promote reverse engineering, so reducing opportunities to build domestic industrial capacity.

The chapter by Malhotra addresses the agenda of FDI and development from the perspective of supra-national agreements. He highlights the need to rethink agreements such as TRIMs and TRIPS in light of the human development agenda, rather than the current singular focus on economic growth. Malhotra also argues that multilateral and bilateral investment agreements have dubious benefits since they restrict the policy autonomy of developing countries, and may increase transaction costs, while simultaneously increasing opportunity costs.

Several chapters in this issue highlight that while policies such as local content requirements may no longer be feasible, a variety of 'soft' policies remain available to host countries to encourage MNEs to create linkages. Mortimore and Vergara recommend the targeting of lead MNEs as a means of creating clustering. They illustrate their argument with two contrasting cases, one of which achieved impressive results, and the other of which failed. The chapters by Lauridsen and by Mytelka and Barclay also present suggestions for the use of soft policy options.

The critical issue facing the development community in industrialisation is whether the degree of policy freedom left to developing countries is sufficient to promote FDI-assisted industrial development without strong policy intervention. WTO rules do not prohibit all selective interventions, only those that affect trade. However, other forces making for liberalisation are less formal and rule-based (structural adjustment programmes, bilateral trade and investment agreements and pressures by rich countries) and they are as powerful. Together they constitute a formidable web of constraints on governments mounting industrial policy. Some constraints may be useful and may prevent the more egregious forms of intervention that have led to inefficiency, rent-seeking and technological sloth. They are also beneficial to countries with strong capabilities developed behind protective barriers: India, Brazil or China should accelerate liberalisation if they can combine this with a strategy to restructure activities and enter promising new activities.

The permissible tools are probably not enough to foster the rapid development of technological capabilities. They may force poor countries with weak industrial bases to become over-dependent on FDI to drive industrial development. This cannot meet a major part of industrialisation needs. Even countries able to plug into global production systems can only do so as providers of low-level labour services; subsequent deepening may be held back by constrictions on capability development. For developing countries with a capability base the rules can deter diversification into new technologies and activities. In general, the rules threaten to freeze comparative advantage in areas where capabilities exist at the time of liberalisation, yielding a relatively short period of competitive growth before the stock is 'used up'. Subsequent upgrading of competitiveness is likely to be slower than if governments had the tools to intervene selectively.

VI. CONCLUDING REMARKS

Our objective in writing this introductory chapter has been to place the various contributions to this volume in the context of the broad range of inter-disciplinary research on FDI and development.

To return to the question posed in the title of this chapter, 'do we need a new agenda?', the chapters here suggest that although the mechanisms underlying FDI and development have not changed, the intricacies of these mechanisms need to be better understood if they are to prove beneficial. All the contributors here are also unanimous in their scepticism of the Washington consensus and the rather simplistic view taken by certain mainstream economists that FDI is a *sine qua non* for economic development. Market forces cannot substitute for the role of governments in developing and promoting a proactive industrial policy. MNEs and FDI may well lead to an increase in productivity and exports, but they do not necessarily result in increased competitiveness of the domestic sector or increased industrial capacity, which ultimately determines economic growth in the long run. FDI *per se* does not provide growth opportunities unless a domestic industrial sector exists which has the necessary technological capacity to profit from the externalities from MNE activity. This is well illustrated by the inability of many Asian countries that have relied on a passive FDI-dependent strategy to upgrade their industrial development.

At the same time, the findings in this volume also suggest that liberalisation and increasing cross-border economic activity associated with globalisation are largely irreversible, and have changed the 'rules of the game'. This implies that traditional policy tools are not as effective as they might have been in the past. However, it is still a matter of conjecture what the long-term developmental effects of many of the supra-national and bilateral agreements will be. In this regard, our contributors would suggest, we *do* need a new agenda if FDI is to be leveraged efficiently to promote development.

NOTE

1. These have been referred to as innovation systems [*see e.g., Lundvall, 1992; Edquist, 1997*] or learning systems [*Lall, 1992; Viotti, 2002*].

REFERENCES

Agosin, M. and R. Mayer, 2000, 'Foreign Investment in Developing Countries: Does it Crowd in Domestic Investment?', UNCTAD Discussion Papers No. 146.

Alcorta, L., 2000, 'New Economic Policies and the Diffusion of Machine Tools in Latin America', *World Development*, Vol.28, pp.1657–72.

Altenburg, T., 2000, 'Linkages and Spillovers between Transnational Corporations and Small and Medium-sized Enterprises in Developing Countries: Opportunities and Best Policies', in UNCTAD, TNC-SME Linkages for Development: Issues-Experiences-Best Practices, New York and Geneva: United Nations.

Benito, G., B. Grogaard and R. Narula, 2003, 'Environmental Influences on MNE Subsidiary Roles: Economic Integration and the Nordic Countries', *Journal of International Business Studies*, Vol.34, pp.443–56.

Blomstrom, M. and A. Kokko, 1997, 'How Foreign Investment Affects Host Countries', Policy Research Working Paper, The World Bank.

Borensztein, E., J. De Gregorio and J.W. Lee, 1998, 'How Does Foreign Direct Investment Affect Economic Growth?', *Journal of International Economics*, Vol.45, pp.115–35.

Carillo, J., 2001, *'Foreign Direct Investment and Local Linkages: Experiences and the Role of Policies. The Case of the Mexican Television Industry in Tijuana'*, Geneva: UNCTAD, mimeo.

Chang, Ha-Joon, 2002, *Kicking Away the Ladder: Development Strategies in Historical Perspective*, London: Anthem.

Criscuolo, P. and R. Narula, 2002, 'A Novel Approach to National Technological Accumulation and Absorptive Capacity: Aggregating Cohen and Levinthal', MERIT Research Memorandum 2002-16.

Driffield, N. and A.H. Mohd Noor, 1999, 'Foreign Direct Investment and Local Input Linkages in Malaysia', *Transnational Corporations*, Vol.8, No.3, pp.1–24.

Dunning, J.H., 1997, 'A Business Analytic Approach to Governments and Globalisation', in J.H. Dunning (eds.), *Governments, Globalisation and International Business*, Oxford: Oxford University Press, pp.114–31.

Dunning, J.H. and R. Narula, 2004, *Multinational and Industrial Competitiveness: A New Agenda*, Cheltenham: Edward Elgar.

ECLAC (Economic Commission for Latin America and the Caribbean), 2000, *Foreign Investment in the Latin American and the Caribbean 1999*, United Nations, Santiago.

ECLAC (Economic Commission for Latin America and the Caribbean), 2001, *Foreign Investment in the Latin American and the Caribbean 2000*, United Nations, Santiago.

Edquist, C., 1997, *Systems of Innovation: Technologies, Institutions and Organisations*, London and Washington: Pinter.

Edquist, C. and B. Johnson, 1997, 'Institutions and Organisations in Systems of Innovation', in C. Edquist (ed.), *Systems of Innovation: Technologies, Institutions and Organisations*, London and Washington: Pinter.

Etzkowitz, H. and L. Leydesdorff, 2000, 'The Dynamics of Innovation: From National Systems and "Mode Z" to Triple Helix of University–Industry–Government Relations', *Research Policy*, Vol.29, pp.109–23.

Findlay, R., 1978, 'Relative Backwardness, Direct Foreign Investment and the Transfer of Technology, A Simple Dynamic Model', *Quarterly Journal of Economics*, Vol.92, pp.1–16.

Ganiatsos, T., 2000. 'Global Component Outsourcing in Developing Countries' Electronics and Automotive Industries', Paper submitted to the UNCTAD Expert Meeting on the Relationship between SMEs and TNCs to Ensure the Competitiveness of SMEs, Geneva, 27–29 November, mimeo.

Gorg, H. and F. Ruane, 1998, 'Linkages between Multinationals and Indigenous Firms: Evidence for the Electronics Sector in Ireland', Trinity Economic Paper Series, Technical Paper No. 98/13.

Hagedoorn, J. and R. Narula, 2001, 'Evolutionary Understanding of Corporate Foreign Investment Behaviour: US Foreign Direct Investment in Europe', in R. Narula (ed.), *International Trade and Investment in a Globalising World*, New York: Pergamon.

Katrak, H., 2002, 'Does Economic Liberalisation Endanger Indigenous Technological Developments? An Analysis of the Indian Experience', *Research Policy*, Vol.31, pp.19–30.

Katz, J., 2001, 'Structural Reforms and Technological Behaviour. The Sources and Nature of Technological Change in Latin America in the 1990s', *Research Policy*, Vol.30, pp.1–19.

Kogut, B., 2000, 'The Transatlantic Exchange of Ideas and Practices: National Institutions and Diffusion', les notes de l'ifri No. 26.

Kokko, A., M. Zejan and R. Tansini, 2001, 'Trade Regimes and Spillover Effects of FDI: Evidence from Uruguay', *Welwirtschaftliches Archiv*, Vol.137, pp.124–49.

Lall, S., 1980, 'Vertical Inter-firm Linkages in LDCs: An Empirical Study', *Oxford Bulletin of Economics and Statistics*, pp.209–22, August.

Lall, S., 1992. 'Technological Capabilities and Industrialization', in *World Development*, Vol.2, No.2, pp.165–86.

Lall, S., 1996, *Learning from the Asian Tigers*, Basingstoke: Macmillan.

Lall, S., 1997a, 'East Asia', in J.H. Dunning (ed.), *Governments, Globalisation and International Business*, Oxford: Oxford University Press, pp.407–30.

Lall, S., 1997b, 'Policies for Industrial Competitiveness in Developing Countries: Learning from Asia', Report prepared for the Commonwealth Secretariat, Oxford.

Lall, S., 2003, 'Foreign Direct Investment, Technology Development and Competitiveness: Issues and Evidence', in S. Lall and S. Urata (eds.), *Competitiveness, FDI and Technological Activity in East Asia*, Cheltenham: Edward Elgar, pp.12–56.

Lall, S. and C. Pietrobelli, 2002, *Failing to Compete. Technology Development and Technology Systems in Africa*, Cheltenham: Edward Elgar.

Loewendahl, H., 2001, 'A Framework for FDI Promotion', *Transnational Corporations*, Vol.10, No.1, pp.1–42.

Lundvall, B. (ed.), 1992, *National Systems of Innovation: Towards a theory of Innovation and Interactive Learning*, London: Pinter.

McAleese, D. and D. McDonald, 1978, 'Employment Growth and the Development of Linkages in Foreign-owned and Domestic Manufacturing Enterprises', *Oxford Bulletin of Economics and Statistics*, Vol.40, pp.321–39.

Mortimore, M., 2000, 'Corporate Strategies for FDI in the Context of Latin America's New Economic Model', *World Development*, Vol.28, No.9, pp.1611–26.

Mytelka, Lynn, K., 1985, 'Stimulating Effective Technology Transfer: The Case of Textiles in Africa', in N. Rosenberg and C. Frischtak (eds.), *International Technology Transfer*, New York: Praeger.

Narula, R., 1996, *Multinational Investment and Economic Structure*, London: Routledge.

Narula, R., 2003, *Globalisation and Technology*, Cambridge: Polity Press.

Narula, R., 2004, 'Understanding Absorptive Capacities in an Innovation Systems Context: Consequences for Economic and Employment Growth', MERIT Research Memorandum 2004-003.

Narula, R. and J.H. Dunning, 2000, 'Industrial Development, Globalisation and Multinational Enterprises: New Realities for Developing Countries', *Oxford Development Studies*, Vol.28, No.2, pp.141–67.

Narula, R. and A. Marin, 2003, 'FDI Spillovers, Absorptive Capacities and Human Capital Development: Evidence from Argentina', MERIT Research Memorandum 2003–16.

Perez, C. and L. Soete, 1988, 'Catching-up in Technology: Entry Barriers and Windows of Opportunities', in G. Dosi, C. Freeman, R. Nelson, G. Silverberg and L. Soete (eds.), *Technical Change and Economic Theory*, New York: Columbia University Press.

Portelli, B. and R. Narula, 2004, 'Foreign Direct Investment though Acquisitions and Implications for Technological Upgrading. Case Evidence from Tanzania', Merit Research Memorandum 2004–008.

Radosevic, S., 1999, *International Technology Transfer and Catch-up in Economic Development*, Cheltenham: Edward Elgar.

Ramos, J., 2000, 'Policy Directions for the New Economic Model in Latin America', *World Development*, Vol.28, pp.1703–17.

Rasiah, R., 1994, 'Flexible Production Systems and Local Machine Tool Subcontracting: Electronics Component Multinationals in Malaysia', *Cambridge Journal of Economics*, Vol.18, pp.279–98.

Rasiah, R., 1995, *Foreign Capital and Industrialization in Malaysia*, London: Macmillan.

Reuber, G.L., H. Crookell, M. Emerson and G. Gallais-Hamonno, 1973, *Private Foreign Investment in Development*, Oxford: Clarendon Press.

Ritchie, B., 2002, 'Foreign Direct Investment and Intellectual Capital Formation in South East Asia', OECD Technical Papers No. 194.

Rodriguez-Clare, A., 1996, 'Multinationals, Linkages, and Economic Development', *American Economic Review*, Vol.85, pp.852–73.

Rodrik, D., A. Subramanian and A. Trebbi, 2002, 'Institutions Rule: The Primacy of Institutions over Geography and Integration in Economic Development', NBER Working Paper 9305.

Scott-Kennel, J. and P. Enderwick, 2001, 'Economic Upgrading and Foreign Direct Investment: Exploring the Black Box of the IDP', Mimeo, University of Waikato, New Zealand.

Stopford, J., 1997, 'Implications for National Governments', in J.H. Dunning (ed.), *Governments, Globalisation and International Business*, Oxford: Oxford University Press, pp.457–80.

UNCTAD, 2000, *World Investment Report 2000 – Cross-Border Mergers and Acquisitions and Development*, New York and Geneva: United Nations.

Viotti, E., 2002, 'National Learning Systems: A New Approach on Technological Change in Late Industrializing Economies and Evidences from the Cases of Brazil and South Korea', *Technological Forecasting and Social Change*, Vol.69, pp.653–80.

Wade, R., 1990, *Governing the Market: Economic Theory and the Role of Government in East Asian Industrialization*, Princeton, NJ: Princeton University Press.

Wood, R., J. Roberts, R. Wade and S. Lall, 2003, 'Symposium on Infant Industries', *Oxford Development Studies*, Vol.1, pp.3–20.

Xu, B., 2000, 'Multinational Enterprises, Technology Diffusion, and Host Country Productivity Growth', *Journal of Development Economics*, Vol.62, pp.477–93.

Learning, Upgrading, and Innovation in the South African Automotive Industry

JOCHEN LORENTZEN and JUSTIN BARNES

This chapter addresses the innovation activities of automotive component manufacturers in South Africa. It looks at the technological trajectory of a handful of firms that stand out from the crowd and analyses the results of their endeavours in the context of their interaction with foreign capital and their internal upgrading and research and development agenda. The analysis makes use of eight case studies and illustrates the conditions under which indigenous innovation in the automotive industries can happen in a developing country. This finding contradicts at least part of the conventional wisdom concerning the location of innovation activities in global car value chains. Questions that need further attention include among others the overall functioning of South Africa's national innovation system, and changes over time in the perception of local innovation potential by car assemblers.

Cet chapter est consacré aux activités d'innovation des manufactures de composantes automotrices en Afrique du Sud. Il suit la trajectoire technologique d'une poignée d'entreprises qui sortent du lot et analyse le résultat de leurs efforts dans le contexte de leur interaction avec le capital étranger, leur évolution interne et leur agenda de recherche et de développement. L'analyse se base sur huit études de cas et illustre les conditions dans lesquelles l'innovation indigène dans les industries automotrices est possible dans un pays en développement. Cette découverte contredit du moins en partie les thèses traditionnelles concernant la localisation des activités innovatrices à l'intérieur des chaînes mondiales de valeurs d'automobiles. Certaines questions ont

Jochen Lorentzen is at the Department of International Economics and Management, Copenhagen Business School, and the School of Development Studies (SODS), University of KwaZulu-Natal; Justin Barnes is Managing Director, B&M Analysts, Durban. The managers of a number of automotive component manufacturers who chose to remain anonymous generously made time available to answer many questions. Without their insights the authors would not have been able to write these case studies. Mike Morris and Imraan Valodia helped to clarify some ideas. Workshop participants in Copenhagen, Oslo, and Durban provided constructive comments. The authors are grateful to all of them, and to Rajneesh Narula for encouraging them to write this chapter in the first place. Any errors or omissions are the authors' own.

besoin d'être analysées davantage, entre autres le fonctionnement général du système national d'innovation en Afrique du Sud et les changements dans le temps des perceptions concernant l'innovation locale potentielle par les assembleurs d'automobiles.

I. INTRODUCTION

Technological innovation is to development what a blue sky is to the Sunday picnic: essential to its success but in many parts of the world hard to rely on. The conditions under which technological upgrading takes place are rather well understood in theory. In the context of developing countries, what matters is the availability of foreign capital and the presence of local capabilities to make good use of it. When foreign and local inputs match well, technology transfer and diffusion may take place and do the little trick of moving the developing country forward.

In practice, things are a lot messier. For a start, technological success stories are few and far between. Some firms, industries, and even entire countries have 'made it' but their number is dwarfed by those who stagnate or seem to be moving backward, relatively or absolutely. In addition, technology transfer and diffusion are empirically hard to operationalise. Studies of firms that overcome problems of intractability often conclude that multinational investments do not lead to spillovers in the host economies. Finally, in some industries the very structure of the value chain may militate against the technological upgrading of any firms that are not located in a core group of technology-leading countries.

This chapter addresses the innovation activities of automotive component manufacturers in South Africa and, hence, in the context of a continent often associated with the absence of technological activity *tout court*. More specifically, it looks at the technological trajectory of a handful of firms that stand out from the crowd in the sense that they pursue activities aimed at technological upgrading *and* innovation. It analyses the results of their endeavours in the context of foreign capital (through the global supply chains to which they deliver), of their internal agenda in terms of upgrading and research and development (R and D), and, to a lesser extent, of South Africa's national innovation system. Section II summarises the relevant literature. Most technological learning – namely the ability to make use of externally available knowledge – takes place in firms (Section II.a). In addition, public investment in education and training feeds into technological accumulation. Especially scale-intensive sectors such as the automotive industry necessitate technical and graduate engineering skills. This is part of the business environment – or the national innovation system – in which firms operate (Section II.b). Finally, the specific structure of the value chains within which firms find themselves influences the location of and the scope for innovation activity in global supply networks (Section II.c). Section III introduces key performance indicators of the South African automotive industry post-liberalisation, from both a macro and a micro perspective. Section IV discusses eight case studies and constitutes the principal analytical contribution of the chapter. Section V concludes with suggestions for further research.

II. INDIGENOUS TECHNOLOGICAL ACTIVITY IN DEVELOPING COUNTRIES: DETERMINANTS AND PROBLEMS

Local Firms: Productive Capacity, Technological Capability, and the Impact of Foreign Knowledge

Following the widespread liberalisation of trade and investment regimes in developing countries in the 1980s and 1990s, local firms are more exposed to competition from foreign firms and products. Hence indigenous technological activity interacts more than previously with imported knowledge, often in the form of foreign direct investment (FDI). This relationship is not straightforward. Inflows of superior foreign technology may enhance incentives for innovation because of the competitive climate they create. Alternatively, they may obviate the need for indigenous generation of technology through the creation of no-need-to-reinvent-the-wheel type situations. Firms who learn and upgrade – and this is not limited to new know-how in a narrow sense but includes operational techniques and managerial processes – are likely to be affected differently by foreign knowledge over time. Thus, for a technological newcomer, licensed technology may be the best bet to grow its competences. By contrast, once technologically more mature, the same firm may be in a position to take on more advanced knowledge embodied in FDI. Therefore, transfer modes influence the incentives for innovation.

How all this plays out for the local firm and the host economy more generally depends, *inter alia*, on capabilities at both the micro and the national level. Relevant firm competences include the search for new knowledge, skill development, and internal knowledge diffusion. Investments in education, information provision, and infrastucture more generally are key among host country characteristics [*Lall, 1993; Pack and Saggi, 1997*] (see also Narula and Dunning [*2000*] and Ozawa [*1992*] for stage arguments linking the relative development of the host economy to the kind and complexity of inward direct investment it attracts, or Birkinshaw and Morrison [1995] for the relation between the entrepreneurial ambition and capability of subsidiaries on the one hand, and intra-firm technology flows on the other).

In principle, technological spillovers may materialise because local firms manage to copy technology from a foreign subsidiary. This is significant insofar as the technologies brought by multinational enterprises (MNEs) will typically not be available in the market. Also, interacting with subsidiaries that use advanced technology may facilitate diffusion to local firms and reduce the risk from go-it-alone innovation. In practice, however, spillovers often prove elusive. Unfortunately, empirical research regularly fails to turn up strong evidence as to the exact nature and magnitude of spillovers [*see Blomström and Kokko, 1998, for a general survey, and Görg and Greenaway, 2002, for an analysis of transition economies*]. This is but one of the reasons why research on the conditions of indigenous innovation in developing countries is so important, independently of whether they do or do not attract FDI.

Whether diffusion – understood as the acquisition of technology by local firms who then engineer adaptations and modifications to suit local needs – leads to innovation depends on the quality of resources the acquiring firms control. At a more basic level firms produce industrial goods using known combinations of equipment, skills, specifications, and organisational systems. Yet while necessary, production capacity is not a sufficient condition for upgrading. To make the upgrading happen, firms must additionally possess the competences to incorporate new technology into their production capacity. These competences are also critical for continuous access to foreign technology in the context of moving closer to the global technology frontier which is of course itself a moving target.

This underlines the importance of learning for technological capability. The more complex technologies are, the more trial and error play a role in their improvement. Therefore product design, process and product engineering are all important sources of technical change even in the absence of direct links with R and D. R and D laboratories, design offices, and production engineering must feed off each other to facilitate learning by doing. In other words, innovation is rarely if ever a unidirectional step from R and D downwards to production, and upgrading is certainly possible in the absence of product innovation [*Bell and Pavitt, 1993a; see also Bell, 1997; Bell and Albu, 1999; Tidd et al., 1997*]. This is not to detract from the key role of R and D for learning [*Cohen and Levinthal, 1989*], but merely suggests that R and D spending alone is not a sufficient indicator for actual or potential innovation activity.

National Innovation Systems: Developing Countries and South Africa

The concept of national innovation systems (NISs) suggests that while firms are the main agents of technological learning, they interact more or less successfully with a host of other organisations and institutions. This interaction, in turn, influences where technical change comes from and how it is disseminated. The concept also proposes that countries are a meaningful unit of analysis insofar as distinctive national characteristics at least in part describe the differentiation of innovation activities across the world. High-income countries have been subject to very sophisticated and comprehensive analyses of both the evolution and the operation of their respective NIS [*for example, Edquist, 1997; Nelson, 1993; see also Freeman, 1994*]. A large body of work also exists that tries to explain differential rates of technological accumulation across developing countries [*for an overview, see Bell and Pavitt, 1993b, or Lall and Pietrobelli, 2002, for a treatment of sub-Saharan countries*]. On the whole, however, the links between the different constituents of the system, especially between firms and the tertiary education sector where advanced skills must be produced, are much less drawn out in developing country contexts. South Africa is no exception.

From the beginning of apartheid in the late 1940s to the regime change in 1994, South Africa had no coherent NIS. What elements of a system existed were informed by the needs of a privileged minority with a distinct supremacist agenda. This obviously stood in the way of an integrated framework [*Scerri, 1998*], but did not prevent the country from world-class performance in a number of technologies. Examples include coal-to-oil conversion, deep mining, clinical medicine and, prominently, information technology (IT) and armaments. The latter in particular exemplified both the achievements of mission-driven research (for example, in the development of nuclear weapons as well as biological and chemical warfare capabilities) and the ability to acquire, adopt, adapt, and extend foreign technologies.

In the face of international sanctions, the sort of imitation encouraged by import substitution only partially gave way to competitive innovation in select areas such as aerospace engineering where advanced technologies proved much harder to get on the open market. What the sanctions regime definitely did was to keep effectively rather indiscriminate import substitution alive beyond any sensible economic motivation. Except in the military sector, industry and universities did not collaborate much, but science was generously funded, replicating the dichotomy between pockets of excellence and severe deprivation that characterised the country at large [*Kahn and Reddy, 2001, see also Birdi et al., 2000*]. For example, offerings in natural sciences and technology were traditionally discouraged in the ten black universities. Their remit consisted primarily of teaching; research programmes remained the exclusive domain of the eleven white-governed universities. It is not clear how long it will take to redress this imbalance which is clearly dysfunctional in an inclusive society. What is clear is that innovation in South Africa at present suffers from this heritage.

Attempts to exploit best practices from national innovation systems elsewhere for a new science and technology policy led to the tabling of the first White Paper on Science and Technology in 1996. The ideas behind this initiative were an emphasis on co-operation between government, industry, and research institutions, along with a stronger focus on applications-based research. The White Paper spawned a number of policy initiatives. Of relevance to the present analysis is the Innovation Fund which promoted initiatives aimed at increasing competitiveness and at pushing collaboration between public Science, Engineering, and Technology Institutions (SETIs), the private sector, tertiary education, and civil society. This included the development of human resources generally and postgraduate training in particular through programmes such as the Technology for Human Resources Programme (THRIP). To date, there has been little systematic evaluation of the effectiveness of these initiatives [*but see Human Sciences Research Council, 2003, Kaplan, 2001*].

Critics charge that South African science and technology policy focuses too much on technology generation by the SETIs, and too little on technology diffusion [*Kaplan, 1999: 486*]. The situation is compounded by unemployment levels of over 40 per cent, low skill levels, and insufficient labour mobility that exacerbate the social costs of technological change *per se*. Moreover, the country's brain drain has affected the world-class aeronautical and IT industries (see Goldstein [2002] for a perceptive analysis of the difficulties of South Africa's aerospace industry in adapting to reduced government demand and increased international competition). At 1.2 per cent of gross domestic product (GDP), spending on higher education may be too low to reverse this trend [*Kahn and Reddy, 2001*]. Even alleged high-tech hubs such as the Midrand area in the Gauteng are based on manufacture and functional services instead of R and D, except in defence-related firms. The retrenchment of the public sector as a major contractor and the absence of a deep venture capital market combine in a vicious dynamic that knocks firms off their feet without providing them with an opportunity to struggle back up again [*Hodge, 1998; Rogerson, 1998*]. What remains is, as in the past, relatively isolated pockets of excellence [*e.g. Versi, 2001*].

Dynamics of Innovation in the Automotive Industry

Vehicle assemblers co-design new car models in co-operation with so-called 0.5 or 1st-tier suppliers who deliver complete systems or modules, rather than individual components. Outsourcing and long-term co-operation – for components that require relationship-specific investments – have increasingly replaced the high degree of vertical integration and arm's length contracts that traditionally characterised the industry. The car manufacturers' investment into the relationship with key suppliers culminates in the system sourcing concept pioneered among others by General Motors at its Gravatai plant in Brazil, where the entire plant layout was jointly developed with leading component manufacturers. However, the locus of R and D in the value chain has not really changed. Independent companies such as Delphi or Visteon, having been spun off by the car makers, have joined historically important component manufacturers such as Bosch or Allied Signals in delivering black-box parts to the specifications of the assemblers but based on their own design and technological solutions.

In other words, vertical disintegration has not affected the scope for innovation activities below the 1st tier. What has changed, apart from a certain dissipation of the technological core away from the exclusive control of the assemblers, is the degree of concentration in the component industry which was forced to consolidate in order to acquire the global reach and financial depth necessary to survive in a very competitive industry suffering from chronic overcapacity. Hence, automotive R and D is essentially performed by fewer and very large, powerful firms protected by considerable entry barriers. It is unsurprising then that the world's ten largest automotive component manufacturers each have annual sales in excess of US$8 billion.

In their attempts to reduce costs, car makers have begun to build a larger model variety on to fewer vehicle platforms. In addition, the idea of a 'world car' aspires to compensate rising development costs and shorter model turnover cycles on the one hand with larger model runs on the other. This means that locally adapted versions of essentially the same model are available worldwide. It also means that, in conjunction with the widespread liberalisation of investment and trade regimes over the past two decades, select car plants in developing or transition economies deliver top-of-the-range models to high-income countries. In practice, this has led to the harmonisation of quality standards across the world. For example, while in the past VW could get away with producing a substandard (old) Beetle in Mexico because it was mainly aimed at the domestic market, the new Beetle is primarily exported and must meet the same standards of quality and delivery as its model cousins manufactured in one of VW's European plants. Therefore, except for the remnants of genuinely local vehicles manufactured mostly for local markets such as the Russian Lada or the Malaysian Proton, cars produced by the major vehicle assemblers anywhere in the world must meet the same exacting quality standards.

Organisationally, the system of relations between vehicle assemblers and component and part suppliers is among the most complex in any industry. Not only have assemblers devolved substantial responsibilities in product development to upper-tier suppliers, the latter are also expected to guarantee quality standards and delivery schedules of their own lower-tier suppliers whose parts and components feed into their modules and systems. Lean production methods (just-in-time inventory systems, decentralised total quality management, bottom-up suggestions for process improvements) affect the entire value chain; for example, even a 3rd-tier supplier must in principle be in a position to accommodate engineering changes to be implemented in ongoing manufacturing processes [*MacDuffie and Helper, 1997*].

Car makers have responded to the devolution of control over detailed design and production processes by tightening overall control of the production cycle. The two key strategic tenets are 'follow design' (several countries share the same vehicle design) and 'follow sourcing' (the same manufacturer supplies parts in different locations). This guarantees the standardisation of vehicles and components within and across regions in the context of 'world car' designs. Follow source decreases monitoring costs for the car makers while guaranteeing homologation.

The structure and organisational configuration of the car industry and the strategic orientation of its key players militate against the involvement of upper-tier manufacturers from developing countries in design and of independent suppliers in global supply chains more generally. Currently it makes most sense for a vehicle manufacturer with an investment in a developing country to rely on the tested and trusted relationships with preferred suppliers that set up production close to wherever their customer goes. Consequently, a number of observers have concluded that developing country firms are likely to lose design and engineering capabilities, and that the auto industry will contribute little to the hoped for technological capability within manufacturing at large. Humphrey [2000] makes this argument for Brazil and India, Barnes and Kaplinsky [2000a, 2000b] for South Africa, and Rutherford [2000] comes to a similar conclusion with respect to Canada. At the same time there is emerging evidence that these downbeat assessments may overstate their case (for a contrasting analysis concerning Japanese automotive investments in the US, see Craig and DeGregori [2000], Humphrey and Memedovic [2003: 34–5] on product development capabilities in Mexico, Lung [2003, 18] on the new design pole in the Barcelona metropolitan area, or Lorentzen et al. [2003] on the experience in Eastern Europe). The present analysis is an attempt to shed light on this controversy.

The review of the literature makes clear that local automotive component manufacturers intent on engaging in innovation activities have the cards stacked against them. First, the presence of sophisticated local competences is no guarantee that technological spillovers will be forthcoming. Hence the role of foreign technology is ambiguous. Furthermore, there is a long way from improving production capacity to developing technological capability and, finally, to engaging in innovation true and proper. Second, although the mechanisms of the post-apartheid national innovation system are not well understood at present, it is uncontroversial that the system suffers from its apartheid-era legacy and also exhibits dysfunctionalities of more recent vintage. Third, innovation and design in global automotive production put a premium on core localities and traditional suppliers with global remits. This tends to jeopardise these activities in liberalised emerging markets such as South Africa both directly and indirectly.

Yet as the case studies below show, some firms do in fact engage in innovation activities. Before analysing how they defy the odds, it is important to understand the development of the South African automotive industry pre- and post-liberalisation.

III. MACRO AND MICRO PERSPECTIVES ON INNOVATION IN SOUTH AFRICA'S AUTOMOTIVE INDUSTRY

Although marginal by the standards of emerging markets with significant regional or global roles such as Mexico or Brazil, automotive production is an important industry in South Africa. It comprises eight producers of light vehicles, a number of specialist medium and heavy commercial vehicle makers, and some 250 dedicated component manufacturers, many of whom are subsidiaries of multinational firms. The industry employs over 100,000 people who are paid above-average wages. The 2002 turnover was close to ZAR 100 billion. In 2001, total automotive production was worth 5.7 per cent of GDP and accounted for 12 per cent of exports. The industry's relative share in manufacturing employment, sales, and production has increased over the 1990s and in 2001 reached 6, 13, and 9 per cent, respectively.

The Industry before 1995

Historically South African industry was heavily protected from outside competition. The car sector was no exception [*see Black, 2001 for an historical review*]. Nominal imports tariffs of up to 115 per cent ensured that domestic producers could profitably produce a broad portfolio of essentially outdated vehicles of questionable quality almost exclusively for the local market of, in the early 1990s, some 300,000–350,000 units annual sales. In contrast to the East Asian experience, where temporary infant industry protection against import competition was granted in parallel with enforcing tough competition among domestic producers, vehicle assemblers and component manufacturers in South Africa enjoyed the privilege of passing on the inefficiencies nurtured in an ossified import substitution model to the consumers. This obviously affected the scope for learning in automotive firms. For example, until 1989 the basic reference parameter of almost three decades of local content programmes had been weight rather than value. Thus firms received a premium for designing and producing heavy rather than light – or lean – products.

The Industry from 1995

In line with its broader macroeconomic liberalisation strategy, the new government launched the Motor Industry Development Programme (MIDP) in 1995, originally expected to run until 2002. The MIDP aimed at increasing the international competitiveness of firms in the industry [*for a detailed description, see Barnes and Black, 2003, and Black, 2001*]. It consisted of a package combining a series of incentives with substantial import liberalisation – for example immediately cutting the import tariff on completely built up vehicles (CBUs) from 115 per cent to 65 per cent. Two reviews, in 1999 and in 2002, extended the programme to 2007 and 2012, respectively. Import tariffs are scheduled to reach 25 per cent for CBUs and 20 per cent for completely knocked down components (CKD) by 2012.

Next to gradual tariff reductions and the abolition of local content provisions, the most important feature of the MIDP is the Import-Export Complementation Scheme (IEC). Under this scheme vehicle assemblers and component suppliers can earn Import Rebate Credit Certificates (IRCCs) from exporting. Based on the value of local raw materials and value added in the exported product, these duty credits are tradable and can be used to offset import duties on vehicles or components. In turn, this allows vehicle manufacturers to buy credits from component exporters to finance the import of completely assembled vehicles not produced locally, or of components they prefer to source abroad. In addition, car manufacturers can also draw on a duty-free allowance on component imports of 27 per cent of the wholesale value of the vehicle. Taken together, on the one hand this creates incentives for foreign assemblers to invest in production in South Africa for both the local and the export markets. It also makes sense for them to work with suppliers based in South Africa – though these need not be domestically owned. On the other hand the MIDP allows the car makers to retain their global supply networks.

The flip side of this arrangement is that domestic firms no longer have the luxury of domestic go-it-alone strategies and must confront the challenge of export success. This means that they either manage to join global supply chains or resign to bidding the automotive industry farewell.

The MIDP appears to have been successful in providing a framework conducive to the development of the industry though concerns persist how the gradual phasing out of export incentives will affect the sustainability of export expansion. For example, in 2002 total passenger vehicle production was 288,000 units, nearly 50 per cent more than the 193,000 vehicles produced in 1998. Almost a fifth of these were essentially outdated models, some of which with a slow phase-out period of up to three years. Over 40 per cent of total production was for export markets, up from 4 per cent in 1995 and 9 per cent in 1998. By contrast, sales of light commercial vehicles (LCVs) were 17 per cent lower in 2002 than in 1995, with only 8 per cent going abroad. Further, yearly real turnover of the components industry grew 7 per cent in 1997–2000. Exports prominently contributed to this, growing more than 20 per cent annually since 1995. This performance was based on increased levels of capital investment and manifested itself in higher profitability, especially from the late 1990s, for both assemblers and component manufacturers.

The automotive industry's trade balance continued to be negative through 2002. This is due to the reduction in effective protection and the use of IRCCs which increased the share of fully imported CBUs to 24 per cent of the domestic market, from 5.5 per cent in 1995, and reduced local content in locally assembled vehicles from 58 per cent to 50 per cent in 1997–2001. In 2000, only 5 per cent of component imports by value actually faced a duty [Black and Mitchell, 2002: 6]. Hence, South African based operations are progressively being integrated into global sourcing networks both upstream and downstream. This implies that they are much more subject to international competition than only a few years ago.

TABLE 1
AVERAGE COMPETITIVENESS IMPROVEMENTS RECORDED AT BENCHMARKING
CLUB MEMBERS

Indicator	Unit	1999	2002	Improvement (%)
Total inventory holding	Days	51.14	40.19	21.41
Customer return rate	Ppm	4,269	1,034	75.78
On time and in full delivery	%	91.73	92.17	0.48
Absenteeism	%	4.20	3.59	14.52

Source: KwaZulu-Natal/Eastern Cape/Gauteng Benchmarking Club database.

A number of competitiveness indicators for the industry improved. Labour productivity in 2001 was roughly a third higher than in 1998, and above the manufacturing average. Firm level data confirm that operationally much has been happening since the late 1990s (see Table 1). The information in Table 1 is taken from a benchmarking club database that comprises competitiveness and financial performance data from over 40 automotive component manufacturers located in South Africa. These firms belong to one of three regional benchmarking clubs in KwaZulu-Natal, Eastern Cape and Gauteng provinces. They represent roughly 25 per cent of the national automotive components industry by value. Each member is benchmarked against an international competitor based in Western Europe, Eastern Europe, Malaysia or Australia. Thus the database includes information from a set of international firms that broadly match the product profile of their South African counterparts.

How this compares to competitors in other developing, transition, and developed countries is evident from Table 2. South African based firms generally lag behind their competitors. Only the top performers generally match their international peers. How they manage to do that is discussed in detail in Section IV.

TABLE 2
RELATIVE PERFORMANCE OF BENCHMARKING CLUB MEMBERS

Indicator	Club member average	Club member upper quartile	Developing/transition economy average	Developed economy average
Total inventory holding	40.19	23.00	32.81	37.30
Customer return rate	1,034	23	529.71	785.22
On time and in full delivery	92.17	98.00	96.38	91.91
Absenteeism	3.59	2.00	4.35	5.67

Source: KwaZulu-Natal/Eastern Cape/Gauteng Benchmarking Club database.

TABLE 3
OWNERSHIP STATUS OF SOUTH AFRICAN BASED OEM SUPPLIERS ($N = 4$), %

Category	1997	2001	2003
Wholly owned subsidiaries of MNC auto component manufacturers	26.0	31.7	37.5
Joint ventures between SA companies and MNC auto component manufacturers	18.5	26.0	32.5
SA companies with technology agreements with MNC auto component manufacturers	29.8	24.3	20.0
SA companies with SA technologies	25.8	18.0	10.0
Total	100.0	100.0	100.0

Notes: Values for 2003 are projections. SA, South African.
Source: Interviews with purchasing directors of OEMs.

Also, the architecture of globalised automotive value chains has militated at least in part against domestic firms. A number of large, independent component manufacturers have had to leave their 1st-tier position for the 2nd tier, for example the Metair companies, Murray and Roberts, and the various subsidiaries of Dorbyl Automotive Technologies, all with turnover in excess of US$150 million. Others were forced to abandon the industry altogether. Table 3 shows a clear preference on the part of the South African based car makers to source their components from wholly owned subsidiaries of multinational component suppliers rather than from domestic companies with proprietary or licensed technologies.

Although local technology has thus come under pressure, a quarter of the firms in the Benchmarking Club database in 2002 invested only 17 per cent less, in relative terms, in R and D than the international firms (see Figure 1). Of course, the data do not show if this is residual expenditure left over from the previous era of localisation and local design for the local market, or if it indicates, on the part of these firms, a search for more high value adding and innovative roles in the new global environment. The empirical evidence from the Benchmarking Club database is inconclusive insofar as it shows no positive relationship between R and D expenditure on the one hand and the age profile of products or operational competitiveness on the other. The former is due in part to the significant presence of foreign-owned subsidiaries who do not invest in R and D at all but do produce the latest products. The latter is probably affected by the manner in which most firms fail to measure R and D aimed at process innovation. At this level of aggregation, then, it appears difficult to investigate upgrading and innovation. It seems clear, however, that in line with theoretical predictions independent product innovation is not a prerequisite for upgrading (see Section II.a). To unpack the nexus between upgrading and innovation and gain a more robust understanding of how firm activities in either are linked to the dynamics of global value chains and the national innovation system, our attention now turns to the case studies.

FIGURE I
RESEARCH AND DEVELOPMENT EXPENDITURE AS A PERCENTAGE OF TURNOVER

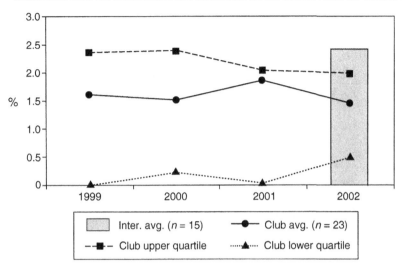

IV. CASE STUDIES

Data and Methodology

Managers of five firms contained in the database discussed in Section III plus of three firms from without the Benchmarking Club agreed to participate in a series of in-depth interviews with both authors. The interviewees held positions of managing director (seven), CEO (one), and technical director (one). They received the questionnaire (see the Appendix) prior to the meeting, and subsequently a written protocol for review. Because of the in part highly confidential nature of the data, anonymity was agreed. The interview explored questions derived from the theoretical discussion in Section II. Thus it conceptualised three levels of analysis, namely primarily the firm and the supply chain, but also the national innovation system. Note that in line with the exploratory character of the study, the sample has an intended selection bias in favour of firms with promising technological agendas.

The firms span the entire range of possible ownership constellations (see Table 4). Four are domestically owned (two privately and two by a large holding company), one is a domestic company owned by an international investor, and three are foreign-owned subsidiaries of European multinational companies (MNCs). We also interviewed a joint venture that is not fully reported here to protect confidentiality but that does inform the findings. Principal customers include the aftermarket (three), assemblers (five), and 1st-tier suppliers

TABLE 4
LEARNING, UPGRADING, AND INNOVATION IN EIGHT CASE STUDIES

Firm	Ownership	Product/market	Learning what?	From whom?	Upgrading what?	How?	Innovation of what?	How?	Why?
D1	Domestic	Vehicle electronics/ mainly aftermarket	Strategic insights	Industry dynamics, competition (own search)	Products	5% turnover on R&D; 80% of R&D toward new product development	Product	*Diversification sideways* → expansion to non-automotive products (GPS, GSM)	Target new markets (e.g. India) and new sectors to occupy new niches
			Advanced production techniques	Staff training in TQM in Japan	Production facilities, processes	Pull exerted by in-house product development	Product	*Adaptation* → 1st- and 2nd-tier supplier to Ford and VW for local models	Tap into remnant of vehicle designs available on local market only
D2	Domestic	Fuel tanks and fuel systems/ OEM supplier mainly for local market	Regulations in high-income markets	By doing Own search activity	Products	1.2% turnover on R&D; 85% of R&D on new product development	Process	*Diversification upwards* → rotational moulding for fuel tanks	Cost advantages for production runs up to 45,000 units
			Best practices in rotational moulding	Staff visits to rotational manufacturers overseas	Raw material inputs	Suppliers invested in R&D themselves	Process	*Diversification upwards* → new process to guarantee tank impermeability	Prospective Californian zero-emission standards
			Design (e.g. utility boxes)	OEM customer (e.g. Daimler-Chrysler)	Fuel tanks to fuel systems	Assume control over system and accept system liability Technological capability			
					Production capacity				

TABLE 4 *continued*

Firm	Ownership	Product/market	Learning what?	From whom?	Upgrading what?	How?	Innovation of what?	How?	Why?
D3	Domestic	Gearlocks, u-bolts, spare wheel carriers/OEM supplier mainly for local market	Production technology: reconcile efficiency with low volumes	Path dependence	Procedures	ISO 9001 in 1994; QS 9000 in late 1990s; tripling of engineering staff 1996–2003	Process	Input substitution	Cost advantages
					Products	85% of R&D on new product development; improve on existing licences	Process	Self-sufficiency in tooling, dyes etc.	Cost advantages
							Product	Own design for locally sold vehicles	Keep R&D and design capability
D4	Domestic	Lighting systems/OEM supplier mainly for local market; aftermarket	Specs of finished products (know-how but not know-why)	Re-engineering of complex designs	Process	Foreign staff and outside (but local) expertise in injection moulding	Process	Re-engineer expensive machine tools	Increase cost effectiveness; exploit flexibility; secure local production
					Products	2–3% turnover on R&D; TA partners assist with technical change	Product	*Adaptation*→ supply to OEMs for local models; specialty products for niche applications	Exploit remnants of local-only vehicle design

TABLE 4 continued

Firm	Ownership	Product/ market	Learning what?	From whom?	Upgrading what?	How?	Innovation of what?	How?	Why?
F1	Foreign	Trim, foam, foam mouldings/ OEM supplier	New production technology	Staff visits abroad to pick up best practices; JV partner/licensor set up production line from scratch, fix problems	Technological capability	Licence agreements (because firm must understand latest technology); 90% of R&D on new product development			
			Strategic direction	Web of technical agreements with competing MNCs	Core competence (problem: increased competitiveness upsets TA partners)	Reduction of product portfolio because of increased competition			
			Production technology	TA partners					
F2	Foreign	Heat transfer components, HVAC systems/OEM supplier	Innovation activity of parent before end of product cycle	Parent	Production technology	Staff training in-house and abroad	Product	*Re-engineering downwards* → e.g. combine different specifications in fewer products	Exploit aftermarket at beginning of replacement cycle
			Stock control	Parent	Manufacturing competence	Investment in operational performance	Product	*Re-engineering upwards* → dedicated A/C unit for Isuzu truck; follow design not so strict for LCVs	Enhance control over product and *vis-à-vis* customers

TABLE 4 *continued*

Firm	Ownership	Product/ market	Learning what?	From whom?	Upgrading what?	How?	Innovation of what?	How?	Why?
					Raw materials	Quality requirements of supply chain			
F3	Foreign	Catalytic conver-ters, exhaust systems and components/ OEM supplier	Dedicated solutions to specific company problems	Student interns from nearby technikon	Process (human capital)	Regular staff training, support for work-cum-study programmes, staff assignments abroad, support of local higher education institutions	Process	Draw on expertise of local machine and tooling manufacturers	Design better and cheaper process solutions than parent
F4	Foreign	Catalytic converters/ aftermarket + licensees	Design and testing	Parent (OEM partner)	Product	3–4% turnover on R&D; strategic alliance with customer	Product	Increase performance with lower maintenance costs; apply accumulated expertise to new cats for diesels and heavy vehicles	Keep technological edge

TABLE 4 *continued*

Firm	Ownership	Product/ market	Learning what?	From whom?	Upgrading what?	How?	Innovation of what?	How?	Why?
			New solutions problem-driven	In-house efforts				Identification of common characteristics of diverse OEM designs to simplify replacement models	Retain price competitiveness
			Emission regulations	Own search activity					

Notes: GSM, Global System for Mobile Communications; GPS, global positioning system; HVAC, heating, ventilation, air conditioning; JV, joint venture; TQM, total quality management.

(one) on both the local and the global market. In terms of size, the firms ranged from 100 to 800 employees and US$4 million to US$120 million turnover. Their export-to-sales ratio in 2002 was 0–80 per cent. The product portfolio includes relatively simple parts such as u-bolts, components such as alarm devices as well as complete fuel, exhaust and air conditioning systems.

Findings

The discussion of the case studies follows the structure of the literature review. The focus is first on how firms learn, upgrade, and innovate. We then discuss the innovation activities of the firms in conjunction with the national innovation system. Finally, we draw out the implications of the innovation activities for the firms' strategic positioning in the global automotive supply chain.

1. Learning

Learning is present in all firms. It covers production techniques, where the source of new insights was either the respective foreign partners (D1, D2, F1, F2), independent search activities (D1, D3, F3), or both; specifications of more complex finished products through re-engineering of existing designs (D4); design (D2, F2, F4), where in one instance a foreign customer involved a local firm in finding technical solutions to their specifications (D2) and where, in another, an original equipment manufacturer (OEM) set up a joint laboratory with a local firm (F4); and strategy (D1, D2, F1, F4), where the competitive environment or changing regulatory requirements in important markets challenged the local firms to respond to new situations. In an example of strategic alertness, D2 tried to abide by EU Regulation 34 on gas permeability even though at present only very few vehicles with D2's components are actually exported to OECD countries.

Five firms regularly send staff abroad to pick up best practices or receive on-site input from their foreign partners. The purpose of these missions can be both learning (D1, D2, F1) and upgrading (F2, F3). One (F3) supports further studies of select staff. Another (F2) absorbs the innovation activity of the parent company over the life cycle of the product to be able to re-engineer variants of the original equipment when it matures into the aftermarket. Finally, some firms purposefully monitor industry dynamics so as to build competences before market demand for new or modified products actually manifests itself.

2. Upgrading

All firms upgrade what they make (D1, D2, D3, D4, F1, F4) and how they make it (D1, D2, D3, D4, F2, F3), or both. F1 alluded to the quality revolution that accompanied the arrival of global sourcing. In the past, reject rates below 3 per cent were tolerated and rates around 0.5 per cent considered eminently acceptable. Until a few years ago 'ppm' (parts per million) was an unknown concept yet for the new Toyota Corolla export project F1 managed to meet the required target of no more than 50 ppm. R and D and solid engineering capabilities are behind the improvement in product profiles. Most R and D spending is targeted at new product development. In another case (D4), technical change is managed mostly through technology transfer from two licensors in Germany and Japan, respectively. For F3, the major challenge consists of translating the parent's innovations into its extended production system, ranging from material sourcing to the optimisation of its production layout.

R and D affects process improvements, too, along with a more broadly based technological and organisational facility to integrate individual parts and components into more complex products. D2 moved up the value chain by offering complete fuel systems instead of just fuel tanks. This implies accepting warranty obligations for parts and components, such as pumps or valves, that are sourced from abroad and that are thus more difficult to control. There are knock-on effects upstream and downstream in that the dynamics of the value chain pull up the quality at each tier (D2, F2). At D2 for example, rotational moulding benefited on the input side from the R and D activities of the polymer and fluorination producers whose product, because of their link with D2, assumed safety critical features. Upgrading may thus be both supplier- and customer-driven, as well as domestically and internationally linked, much as it presupposes a positive disposition for learning in the first place.

3. Innovation

Only two firms (F1, F3) categorically exclude self-driven product innovation activities. In the first case, research in acoustics control and noise reduction is so expensive and thus geographically concentrated that scope for decentralised activity does not really exist (F1). In the second, the design of OEM exhaust systems requires proximity to the vehicle assemblers which is why the foreign parent has R and D centres in both Europe and the US.

Two firms (D2 and D3) have come up with innovative processes where they employ radically new techniques, different input combinations, or specific tooling arrangements primarily to obtain cost advantages. In one case (D2) it is tougher regulatory requirements that drives the search for a new production technique. Also on the process side, D4 and F3 substituted processes developed in-house for much more capital-intensive toolings that would have been uneconomic for the much smaller production runs typical for South Africa. In one case (F3), the result was qualitatively so impressive – in terms of guaranteeing lower reject rates – that the US sister operation preferred it to the equipment used by the German parent. In acknowledgement of the local process engineering capabilities, the parent dropped the process support fee previously charged and granted complete process autonomy.

Three other firms (D1, F2, F4) have produced entirely new products for which they own the intellectual property. In one case (D1) this has taken the form of diversification sideways which aims at new markets, namely away from automotive products. In another (F2), downwards re-engineering (whereby fewer different components with wider applicability substitute a higher number of more specific components) aims at developing cost-effective components for the aftermarket, while diversification upwards tries to circumvent the strictures of follow design in marginal markets both locally and abroad. By contrast, F4 holds multiple international patents and in 1997 won the European Environmental Award for its innovations. It licenses its products to a major OEM assembler and a 1st-tier supplier.

F2 shows the limits to blue-sky developments compared to the past. The world car concept increasingly means that all capital-intensive R and D is centralised in Western Europe and North America, thus leaving little or no space for players that in terms of their innovation activities are marginal. By contrast, in the early 1990s the predecessor of the affiliate had 4–5 professional staff working on a leading materials technology it had developed. After the arrival of its new owner this was immediately discontinued in South Africa and for cost reasons moved to a more central location. Of course, the location for R and D need not remain in the home country of the MNC but to the extent that it does get relocated it is much more likely to move to another place in the Triad (the core car-producing regions of Europe, the US, and Japan), as happened when the new parent set up a technology centre in the US in proximity to the Big-Three auto companies, GM, Ford, and DaimlerChrysler.

This trend appears to be growing stronger as design and manufacturing for car makers are separated. For example, a MNC competitor is developing a system that the group to which this firm belongs will eventually make, meaning that even among 1st-tier suppliers core competences are more and more narrowly defined. In a global context, the local subsidiary does not occupy a position from which it could single-handedly promote ambitious innovation activities nor offer itself to customers who would like to outsource certain development tasks. This sort of subsidiary mandate could emerge only if the affiliate were assigned centre-of-excellence status because of a fortuitous combination of low labour costs and sophisticated engineering skills. In sum, with expensive, highly centralised R and D, technical agreements (TAs) are important for the local firm to keep up to date. But when R and D is centralised purely for organisational reasons, then TAs are instrumental only to guarantee follow-source contracts. Over time, the latter may be subject to change.

Ownership and market focus may have a bearing on how easily firms can exploit technological opportunities. Independent firms on the whole have obviously fewer resources than multinational groups. But they do not face the trade-off between access to resources and R and D concentration that characterises MNCs. For example, D2 engages in expensive innovation activities that it would not likely be allowed to undertake if it were a subsidiary in a larger group.

The example of F2 and F4 also shows that the aftermarket and the local OEM market are more permissive in terms of accepting solutions that deviate from the norm. But although F2 as a member of a group is kept on a much shorter leash than F4, they share a commitment to retaining technical competence, along with the ability to design and test solutions that in essence can be either minor adaptations of existing solutions or more radical departures from existing products or processes. Either way, this involves innovation, thus requiring staff (or at least to have access to service providers) who can design, test, create the necessary tooling, and so on.

These findings, albeit not representative, suggest some insights into the relationship between production capacity and technological capability on the one hand, and innovation activity on the other. The going wisdom in technology accumulation, namely the principles of a certain hierarchy of competences and linearity implied in the idea of a progression from process to product innovation, does shed light on select trajectories but is only part of the whole story. For example, prodded on by its parent, F2 has made significant improvements in stock control. Although inventory management is not a sufficient condition for innovation, it is necessary – firms that do not possess a world-class manufacturing competence are unlikely to get involved in successful innovation. This is because the knowledge accumulation associated with the former provides the ground for building technological capability. The gains for F2 from the relationship with the parent company imply that, in the absence of the foreign direct investment, F2 would have been relegated to the niche aftermarket.

But the problem with generalising this view is that it simply reverses the hierarchy of simpler and more complex competencies and the linearity of assimilation compared to innovation that emanates in top-down fashion from R and D proper. The cases show that exposure to the exacting requirements of lean production need have no bearing on the scope for R and D and design. For some components, R and D is geographically so concentrated that opportunities and incentives for technological learning are objectively limited so that lab activity bypasses all but the leading units or manufacturers and hence not just those in emerging markets. Industry or (sub-)sector characteristics therefore matter. Perhaps more importantly, sometimes technological capability informs production capacity rather than the other way round (e.g. D1, D2). And there is also learning-without-doing (D2). Hence the other part of the story is less intuitive. What seems clear is that when a firm's knowledge system is superior to its production system, the real bottleneck to bringing innovative ideas on stream lies on the shopfloor and not in the absence of cutting edge activities *per se*, nor for that matter in the logic of the supply chain as such.

4. Path Dependency and the National Innovation System

Import-substituting industrialisation and, later, sanctions turned South African manufacturing into a jack-of-all-trades. The former meant that there was a premium on local content. The latter necessitated designing technical solutions even when they were available on the open market simply because South Africa under apartheid was not an accepted customer. The principal challenge for innovation was to realise low volumes at acceptable cost. Drawbacks of this system included, as elsewhere, inefficiency and substandard quality except in areas deemed essential to the regime's survival.

What happened subsequent to the liberalisation of the economy was that increased competition disciplined manufacturers to reduce their product portfolio. The new focus on core competence, in connection with cheap, high-skilled labour and the knack of engineers for 'making do', meant that niche opportunities in global automotive supply became within reach. For example, through rearranging toolings produced in-house and through decreasing capital-to-labour ratios, local firms were able profitably to organise production runs of 60,000 units for phase-out vehicle models that producers in high-cost countries could only make at volumes of at least 300,000 units. At the extreme, F4 occasionally produces a dozen catalytic converters to order. Hence compared to the past, where in the absence of effective competition firms could get away with the inefficiencies that resulted from doing too many things themselves, including in-house tooling, tooling now deepens the firms' focus and no longer contributes to horizontal efficiency losses. It helps local firms to compensate for perhaps less-than-optimal production runs by designing alternative solutions at low engineering costs. This is a positive example of path dependency.

A negative example is the uncertain future of human capital in engineering. It appears in short that competences embedded in South Africa's old military industry have more successfully adapted to global market demands than the country's new education system. In the past, engineering competence was created for and absorbed by the military sector from where it fertilised other manufacturing sectors. A substantial part of R and D personnel and also many production engineers in the case firms had a military background. Most were middle-aged or older. With the retrenchment of the military complex, it is important that the tertiary education system produce technical specialists and engineering graduates to fill the thinning ranks of gradually retiring military engineers. Yet all firms report serious difficulties with hiring and retaining qualified staff; high-order skills appear in short supply in the industry.

Links with university career centres are underdeveloped. Only one firm (F3) underlined the value of its trainee programme in conjunction with the local technikon. At F2, recent graduates start earning their keep after about four years of in-house training. At D1, only one engineer is a recent university graduate and the company, despite being only 2 kilometres from a leading university, has had no contact with the engineering faculty in more than a decade. In addition, training has public good character and the problem is that qualified staff have ample incentives to leave the company in search of the highest bidder. This is particularly true for technically qualified black staff, due to strong affirmative action policies that prioritise the employment of black people. The disjuncture between tertiary education sector output and labour market demand, unless addressed with urgency, has the danger of lock-in into activities that are not aligned with the country's traditional competence and that are below its potential.

The business environment is deficient also with respect to institutions that support innovation activities. Almost all firms report difficulties with the national testing bureaus, the South African Bureau of Standards (SABS), the Council for Scientific and Industrial Research (CSIR) as well as university labs. For example, it was noted that CSIR staff are sometimes unfamiliar with international testing parameters. D3 reports that turnover time for testing products at the local CSIR office is six weeks. The firm has consequently resorted to sending samples to the Massachusetts Institute of Technology which guarantees the same service within one week. D4 has to have its more complex chemical analyses done in Japan because of an absence of suitable local facilities, although it does rely on a local university for simpler testing. The problem appears to be not so much quality *per se* as a lack of specialisation required to deal with the very precise requirements of the automotive industry. F4's foreign parent organises testing through universities in Europe. If it were not for the testing, F4 could in principle do away with the parent company's support. This suggests a mismatch between the technological capabilities and the innovation potential of some South African firms and the national support infrastructure.

5. Strategy

Local automotive suppliers must reckon with the constraints the global automotive supply chain imposes on them. But contrary to what some observers have argued, they need not resign themselves to the downplaying of their technological capabilities through the principles of follow source and follow design. Indeed, the firms analysed here quite definitely challenge the marginalisation of local design and development activity. Figure 2 sketches the strategic options available to developing-country producers from the perspective of local automotive supply manufacturers [for the OEM perspective, see for example, Sugiyama and Fujimoto, 2000].

The strategic positioning of automotive suppliers depends on the markets they are focused on; the customers they sell to; and the level of control they have over

FIGURE 2
STYLISED STRATEGIC POSITIONING OF AUTOMOTIVE SUPPLY FIRMS

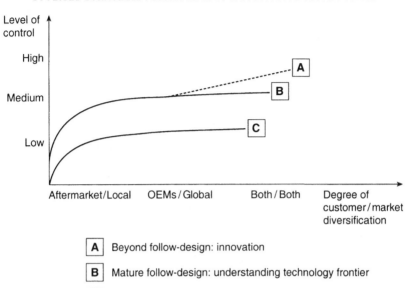

the product (see Figure 2). The control variable is the one most relevant to technological learning and innovation. High levels of control imply ownership of intellectual property. A firm affords medium levels of control if it has the capability to understand the technology developed by its technology partner or its competitors. Hence in principle it would be able to improve the product, diversify upwards, and claim ownership of a new design. Low levels of control denote firms with sufficient productive capacity but too low absorptive capacity to appreciate what is going on at the technology frontier. In terms of customers, firms may sell to the aftermarket or to assemblers and upper-tier suppliers, or both. Likewise, in terms of markets they may concentrate on the local market or also export to global markets, or serve only the latter.

The different combinations of control, customers, and markets affect the viability of strategic positioning. Firms on trajectory C that sell licensed or off-patent products only to the local aftermarket – denoted by the bottom left corner of Figure 2 – are more subject to the vagaries of demand than those that sell both locally and internationally, supply both OEMs and the aftermarket, and own or at least understand the technology embedded in their product (trajectories A and B). Clearly, firms that supply key components to OEMs that are difficult to source elsewhere because they have a combined cost/technology advantage, are less vulnerable to supplier substitution. By the same token, a global supply mandate based exclusively on cost advantages is dangerous in that it may last no longer than the next model change. The more fortuitous positionings thus lie in the top right areas of Figure 2.

Table 5 illustrates the stylised trajectories from Figure 2 in more detail. D1, D2, and F3 follow global niche strategies, and D4 may attempt to do so in the future. They target output levels that extend beyond the confines of local demand while settling for production runs that are too small to interest their global competitors. This reconciles their own capacity with market opportunity and affords them a relatively high degree of control. It also opens up the prospect of co-operative agreements with leading systems suppliers such as that envisaged between D1 and Visteon where the latter may see this as an opportunity to complement its product portfolio for volumes in which its own minimum efficient scale is too high. Global niche strategies may also grow out of local-only supply contracts, and this has implications for innovation activities. The LCV sector, which is more developed in South Africa than in many higher income economies, has traditionally more scope for indigenous R and D because it was mainly aimed at the local market and manufactured in smaller volumes. But when Ford soon starts exporting 18,000 units of the 4-litre Rancher truck to Australia, D2 is in a strong position to supply the export programme on top of production for the local market.

D3 competes for follow-design contracts to maintain its reputation with existing customers. At the same time it invests in its technological capability to retain the option of permit diversification – in terms of further developing the technology codified in existing licenses – so that it can claim more value added once it has become an acknowledged and trusted supply partner. The hoped for upshot is again more control. D4 and F3 are similar cases.

F1, F2, and F3 jockey for world mandates. F1 uses a combination of technical know-how gained from its joint venture partners, privileged access to raw materials, and its own competence in the manufacture of cost-effective toolings to try to emerge gradually from the shadow of the OEMs' preferred suppliers in their home countries. This would raise the attractiveness of the assets they command and, hence, afford them more control. The biggest organisational challenge consists of defending the firm's interest in a web of technical agreements of different nature with MNCs that compete against each other. By implication, F1 increasingly both co-operates with and competes against the very same partners in different contracts.

F2's main challenge has been how to graduate from a capable but also vulnerable supplier concentrated on the local market to a dynamic MNC subsidiary with multiple constituencies and promising product mandates. Thus it competes for group-wide contracts against other subsidiaries, much like F3. Parent strategy obviously matters, but so does the entrepreneurial instinct of

TABLE 5
PRINCIPAL STRATEGIC POSITIONING OF CASE FIRMS

Firm	What?	How?	Why?
D1	Niche	Volume targeted between global and local ('marginal' supplies to e.g. Visteon)	Reconcile limited financial and organisational capacity with technological and growth opportunity
D2	Niche	Volume targeted between global and local	(1) Enhance control over product and *vis-à-vis* customers (2) Vehicles targeted at local market more scope for local R&D
D3	Permit diversification	Negotiate relaxation of zero-modification requirements with OEMs	Enhance control over product and *vis-à-vis* customers
D4	Niche	Team up with licensors	Reduce reliance on local market
F1	World mandate	Combine technical assistance with preferred suppliers in source country, advantageous access to raw materials, and unique toolings	Enhance control over product and *vis-à-vis* customers
F2	(1) World mandate	(1) Achieve excellence within group	(1) Fend off competitive threat from group operations in China and Eastern Europe
	(2) Customer diversification	(2) Group supply + aftermarket + 3rd parties	(2) Insure against cost-based-only advantages vulnerable to model changes
F3	Niche + world mandate	Group supply + local OEM contracts for export CBUs	Compensate location disadvantage through manufacturing excellence and risk diversification
F4	Blue sky	Exploit new JVs for global distribution channels	Secure viability of SA location

the local managers. The main issue here is to secure the survival of the affiliate in the context of changing market demands and new supply opportunities through new affiliates in other emerging markets such as China that clearly are competitive threats. So the firm must have a spread of local vehicle assembler customers, a local aftermarket presence, plus significant export business.

F4 possesses a world mandate for the aftermarket. It licenses its technology to OEMs rather than selling to them directly. Retaining its technological edge is a key tenet of the company's strategy.

In sum, firms that pursue global niches, world mandates, or both possess world-class technological capability without which car makers would not even talk to them. And they possess or secure access to the resources that support global activities. This often involves a foreign partner, but need not. Technological capability is important also for firms who supply the aftermarket. As car makers raise and expand product specifications, they help create an advanced aftermarket that the supplier, through its own ongoing design and development activities, can exploit. D1 reported such dynamics from the market for retrofitting cars with ever more complex and intelligent security devices.

6. Summary

So where does the evidence from the eight firms leave us? Firms learn both through their own search activities and from others, notably foreign technology partners [*for a more cautious view, see Valodia, 1999*]. The object of their learning encompasses manufacturing processes, product specifications, as well as what goes on in their sector more broadly. The fruits of this learning manifest themselves in the upgrading of how they operate, what they make, and how they position themselves in the value chain to which they belong. Upgrading relies on individual and collective technological capabilities, namely those that the individual firm possesses as well as those present upstream and downstream with beneficial effects across tiers. The innovation activities of firms cover processes and products. Product innovation is strictly excluded only if R and D is so capital-intensive as to be prohibitively costly. Where it does happen, it takes the form of downwards (into the aftermarket) or upwards re-engineering, sideways diversification, and even blue-sky development (F4). Whether innovation trickles downward from R and D or grows upward from gradual assimilation of technologies and process improvements, differs from firm to firm and depends, more precisely, on the relative strengths of each firm in terms of productive capacity and technological capability. Innovation in aftermarket products is generally easier and helps retain technological competences.

Subsidiaries of multinational firms typically have easier access to superior technology compared to their domestic rivals. Yet the latter may marshal superior technological competence insofar as they can decide to invest in R and D while the subsidiary will often be sidelined by centralised innovation activities. This means that what militates against indigenous innovation in the automotive industry is not so much the strategic principles of follow design or follow source *per se*, but the presence, alongside foreign capital, of local technological competence. This should not be misconstrued as an argument against FDI but it suggests that FDI attraction alone will not do the trick of promoting technological innovation. By extension, the national innovation system, especially the subsystem of education and training, merits more attention because it is here that learning and upgrading – which are clearly promoted by foreign capital – can be translated into innovation.

Innovation activities are path-dependent insofar as current competitive strengths draw on engineering competences originally bred in the military sector that manifest themselves both in innovative product design and in process engineering capabilities, especially concerning technical solutions for niche demands, in highly flexible tooling environments [*for parallels in the history of Toyota, see Fujimoto, 1998*]. The gradual implosion of the military sector is thus a problem, as is the perhaps inappropriately focused or weak higher education system. This limits the potential to produce the human capital to fill the present gap and, more seriously, ensures future shortcomings. Firms also suffer from a deficient innovation infrastructure as far as advanced testing institutions are concerned.

Local firms, including foreign subsidiaries, insure themselves against uncertainty by diversifying their portfolio in terms of customers and markets and by trying to enhance control over how and what they produce. Harnessing their technological capability is a key means to this end. The latter point again underlines the significance of innovation as the means to gain ownership of intellectual assets. Firms follow four strategies. First, the global niche strategy attempts to leverage control over technological assets for more secure positions in the supply chain. Second, the (process or product) permit diversification strategy bets on gradual emancipation from follow source or follow design through offering either better or more efficient solutions to 1st-tier suppliers or assemblers. This may, but need not be limited to the local market. Third, the world mandate strategy exploits the cost advantages inherent in cheap, high-skilled human capital. Fourth, the blue-sky strategy defends its technological edge in the longer term through the judicious creation of strategic partnerships allowing for world mandate remits.

V. CONCLUSION

This analysis has illustrated the conditions under which indigenous innovation in the automotive industry can happen in a developing country. It has also explored what drives activities aimed at exploring innovation potential and what stands in the way of dynamic local firms in terms of bringing their endeavours to a successful completion, independent of whether they are of domestic, foreign, or mixed ownership. In one sentence, innovation builds on cumulative past capabilities mediated through learning and upgrading, with the aim for firms to position themselves strategically in global automotive supply chains. The case studies consciously singled out firms that stand out from the crowd in terms of their technological dynamism [*see Hobday, 1995, for a similar approach*]. This obviously biases the findings, which must not be read as a characterisation of South Africa's automotive sector at large or, for that matter, of the general relationship between productive capacities and technological capabilities on the one hand, and innovation on the other.

The results do not constitute a wholesale rebuttal of the pessimism that is evident in previous assessments of the potential contribution the automotive sector might make to technological development both in South Africa itself and in other developing countries. But it refutes two very deterministic arguments of that literature. First, it is simply not true that indigenous innovation does not happen. Second, there is no evidence that, over time, the structure of innovation in the automotive industry necessarily marginalises local innovation potential to the point of extinction.

The chapter admittedly leaves many questions unanswered. While it establishes the importance of firm capabilities in their dynamic interaction with the automotive supply chain and the national innovation system, it says nothing about the relative significance of these three levels of analysis. This is problematic especially insofar as the operation of the national innovation system and its bearings on individual manufacturing industries in South Africa have never been systematically researched. For those interested in science and technology policy (S & T), one of the most interesting questions is at what point the marginal benefits for the development of technological capability from learning-by-doing in ongoing manufacturing processes become so low as to require discretionary investment into new skills and knowledge, and if there is a danger of market failure. The present analysis hints that (some) domestic entrepreneurs will try to wrest control over technology embodied in foreign capital from the original owners. So the real worry may be hollowing-out from within. That is, managers and engineers may be able to move their operations up the supply chain. But they obviously cannot organise the education system on which they rely for their exploits. There is much to be gained from addressing South Africa's knowledge infrastructure – both its past anatomy and the changes it has been subject to – in a comprehensive study.

Another question that needs systematic analysis is the relationship between ownership and innovation. The cases show that while domestically owned firms at times seem to enjoy greater leeway than their foreign-owned counterparts in committing resources to R and D, the most innovative firm in the sample, although formerly South African, is now in foreign ownership. This throws up many questions, not least about the stickiness of competences based on tacit and thus location-bound knowledge.

Also, the firms analysed here, while offering rich insights, represent just 3 per cent of all automotive firms in South Africa. The database described in Section III suggests that up to a quarter of all firms have upward technological trajectories based on their internal innovation-related activities. It would clearly be desirable to include more of these firms in the analysis. Finally, the analysis does not directly engage with the car assemblers even though they are key for the strategic perspective of indigenous innovation. For example, given what we currently know it would appear difficult empirically to judge the dynamic trade-off between low monitoring costs thanks to follow source on the one hand and cost advantages from gradually incorporating more efficient and capable local firms into more advanced mandates of their supply chains on the other. In sum, watch this space.

APPENDIX

Notes for a semi-structured interview with select car component manufacturers, March 2003.

Premise

The purpose of these exploratory conversations is to probe the conditions for innovation activity in the automotive supply sector in South Africa. More specifically, the inquiry focuses on the relative dearth of product innovation since the opening of the sector to global competition and the arrival of foreign OEMs. Conceptually, we look at three different levels of analysis, namely the

• individual firm and its (dynamic) capabilities (including intra- and inter-firm relations)

• structure of global automotive supply chains

• national innovation system.

Section 1: The Firm Level

1.1 Do you aim at product innovation? (If 'no', why not?)

1.2 If 'yes', what do you target?

1.3 What type of resources do you commit to your innovation activity in terms of...?

   a) capital investment/equipment (specific R and D outlays):

   b) skills (operating and managerial know-how): (Is learning a by-product from doing or a purposeful search?)

    c) product and input specifications (How do you generate and manage technical change?)

    d) organisational systems (How do you combine activities of R and D labs, design offices, production engineering etc.?)

1.4 Do you believe that your involvement in quality control and production organisation has allowed (or will allow) you to generate activities in R and D, design, and production engineering (i.e. is there a progression from process to product innovation)?

Section 2: The Supply Chain Level

2.1 In general, do you feel that local design and development activity is increasing or decreasing?

2.2 In general, what is the more important impediment to acquiring global supply mandates...?

    a) your technological capability *per se*

    b) the financial, managerial and organisational resources required to develop global operations

    c) control by OEMs and/or parent company and/or JV partner and/or licensor and/or technical aid partner.

Section 3: The National Innovation System

3.1 Do technological opportunities on the domestic market differ from the demands of the global market?

3.2 Are technical and graduate engineering skills readily available to you? (If 'no', what are the key weaknesses?)

3.3 Do you feel that your scientists and/or engineers possess the problem-solving skills and the familiarity with research methodologies and instrumentation (and are they perhaps members in international networks of professional peers) to put your skill profile/technological capability at par with your global competitors? (If 'no', probe for reasons.)

REFERENCES

Barnes, Justin and Anthony Black, 2003, 'Motor Industry Development Programme: Review Report', in *Department of Trade and Industry*, Vol.24, Government of South Africa, February 2003 (mimeo).

Barnes, Justin and Raphael Kaplinsky, 2000a, 'Globalization and the Death of the Local Firm? The Automobile Components Sector in South Africa', *Regional Studies*, Vol.34, No.9, pp.797–812.

Barnes, Justin and Raphael Kaplinsky, 2000b, 'Globalisation and Trade Policy Reform: Whither the Automobile Components Sector in South Africa?', *Competition and Change*, Vol.4, No.2, pp.211–43.

Bell, Martin, 1997, 'Technology Transfer to Transition Countries: Are there Lessons from the Experience of the Post-War Industrializing Countries?', in Dyker A. David (ed.), *The Technology of Transition: Science and Technology Policies for Transition Countries*, Budapest: CEU Press, pp.63–94.

Bell, Martin and Michael Albu, 1999, 'Knowledge Systems and Technological Dynamism in Industrial Clusters in Developing Countries', *World Development*, Vol.27, No.9, pp.1715–34.

Bell, Martin and Keith Pavitt, 1993a, 'Accumulating Technological Capability in Developing Countries', Proceedings of the World Bank Annual Conference on Development Economics, 1992: Supplement to *The World Bank Economic Review* and *The World Bank Research Observer*, pp.257–81.

Bell, Martin and Keith Pavitt, 1993b, 'Technological Accumulation and Industrial Growth: Contrasts between Developed and Developing Countries', *Industrial and Corporate Change*, Vol.2, No.2, pp.157–210.

Birdi, Alvin, Paul Dunne and David S. Saal, 2000, 'The Impact of Arms Production on the South African Manufacturing Industry', *Defence and Peace Economics*, Vol.11, No.6, pp.597–613.

Birkinshaw, Julian M. and A. Morrison, 1995, 'Configurations of Strategy and Structure in Subsidiaries of Multinational Corporations', *Journal of International Business Studies*, Vol.26, No.4, pp.729–54.

Black, Anthony, 2001, 'Globalization and Restructuring in the South African Automotive Industry', *Journal of International Development*, Vol.13, pp.779–96.

Black, Anthony and Shannon Mitchell, 2002. 'Policy in the South African Motor Industry: Goals, Incentives, and Outcomes', Paper presented at the TIPS Annual Forum, www.tips.org.za.

Blomström, Magnus and Ari Kokko, 1998, 'Multinational Corporations and Spillovers', *Journal of Economic Surveys*, Vol.12, No.2, pp.1–31.

Cohen, Wesley M. and Daniel A. Levinthal, 1989, 'Innovation and Learning: The Two Faces of R&D', *Economic Journal*, Vol.99, pp.569–96 (September).

Craig, Steven, G. and Thomas R. DeGregori, 2000, 'The Forward and Backward Flow of Technology: the Relationship between Foreign Suppliers and Domestic Technological Advance', *Technovation*, Vol.20, pp.403–12.

Edquist, Charles, (ed.), 1997, 'Systems of Innovation: Technologies, Institutions, and Organizations', London: Pinter.

Freeman, Christopher, 1994, 'The Economics of Technical Change', *Cambridge Journal of Economics*, Vol.18, No.5, pp.463–514.

Fujimoto, Takahiro, 1998, 'Reinterpreting the Resource-Capability View of the Firm: A Case of the Development-Production Systems of the Japanese Auto-Makers', in Alfred D. Chandler, Jr., Peter Hagström and Örjan Sölvell (eds.), *The Dynamic Firm*, Oxford: Oxford University Press, pp.15–44.

Goldstein, Andrea, 2002, 'The Political Economy of High-Tech Industries in Developing Countries: Aerospace in Brazil, Indonesia and South Africa', *Cambridge Journal of Economics*, Vol.26, No.4, pp.521–38.

Görg, Holger and David Greenaway, 2002, 'Much Ado about Nothing? Do Domestic Firms Really Benefit from Foreign Investment?', London: Centre for Economic Policy Research, Discussion Paper no. 3485.

Hobday, Mike, 1995, 'East Asian Latecomer Firms: Learning the Technology of Electronics', *World Development*, Vol.23, No.7, pp.1171–93.

Hodge, James, 1998, 'The Midrand Area: An Emerging High-Technology Cluster?', *Development Southern Africa*, Vol.15, No.5, pp.851–73.

Human Sciences Research Council, 2003, Working Partnerships: Higher Education, Industry and Innovation, www.hsrcpublishers.ac.za.

Humphrey, John, 2000, 'Assembler-Supplier Relations in the Auto Industry: Globalisation and National Development', *Competition & Change*, Vol.4, pp.245–71.

Humphrey, John and Olga Memedovic, 2003, 'The Global Automotive Industry Value Chain: What Prospects for Upgrading by Developing Countries', in *UNIDO Sectoral Studies Series*, Vienna.

Kahn, Michael J. and B. Daya Reddy, 2001, 'Science and Technology in South Africa: Regional Innovation Hub or Passive Consumer?', *Daedalus*, Vol.130, No.1, pp.205–34.

Kaplan, D.E., 1999, 'On the Literature of the Economics of Technological Change. Science and Technology Policy in South Africa', *South African Journal of Economics*, Vol.67, No.4, pp.473–90.

Kaplan, David, 2001, 'Rethinking Government Support for Business Sector R&D in South Africa. The Case for Tax Incentives', *South African Journal of Economics*, Vol.69, No.1, pp.72–92.

Lall, Sanjaya, 1993, 'Promoting Technology Development: The Role of Technology Transfer and Indigenous Effort', *Third World Quarterly*, Vol.14, No.1, pp.95–108.

Lall, Sanjaya and Carlo Pietrobelli, 2002, *Failing to Compete: Technology Development and Technology Systems in Africa*, Cheltenham: Elgar.

Lorentzen, Jochen, Peter Møllgaard and Matija Rojec, 2003, 'Host-Country Absorption of Technology: Evidence from Automotive Supply Networks in Eastern Europe', *Industry and Innovation*, Vol.10, No.4, pp.415–32.

Lung, Yannick, 2003, 'The Changing Geography of the European Automobile System', Working Paper no.10, Groupement de Recherches Economiques et Sociales, www.gres-so.org.

MacDuffie, John Paul and Susan Helper, 1997, 'Creating Lean Suppliers: Diffusing Lean Production through the Supply Chain', *California Management Review*, Vol.39, No.4, pp.118–51.

Narula, Rajneesh and John H. Dunning, 2000, 'Industrial Development, Globalization and Multinational Enterprises: New Realities for Developing Countries', *Oxford Development Studies*, Vol.28, No.2, pp.141–67.

Nelson, Richard R., 1993, *National Systems of Innovation*, Oxford: Oxford University Press.

Ozawa, Terutomo, 1992, 'Foreign Direct Investment and Economic Development', *Transnational Corporations*, Vol.1, No.1, pp.27–54.

Pack, Howard and Kamal Saggi, 1997, 'Inflows of Foreign Technology and Indigenous Technological Development', *Review of Development Economics*, Vol.1, No.1, pp.81–98.

Rogerson, Christian, M., 1998, 'High-Technology Clusters and Infrastructure Development: International and South African Experiences', *Development Southern Africa*, Vol.15, No.5, pp.875–903.

Rutherford, T.D., 2000, 'Re-embedding, Japanese Investment and the Restructuring Buyer-Supplier Relations in the Canadian Automotive Components Industry during the 1990s', *Regional Studies*, Vol.34, No.8, pp.739–51.

Scerri, Mario, 1998, 'The Parameters of Science and Technology Policy Formulation in South Africa', *African Development*, Vol.10, No.1, pp.73–89.

Tidd, Joe, John Bessant and Keith Pavitt, 1997, *Managing Innovation*, Chichester: John Wiley and Sons.

Valodia, Imraan, 1999, 'Trade Policy, Productivity and Learning: Evidence in South Africa', *Development Southern Africa*, Vol.16, No.3, pp.531–46.

Versi, Anver, 2001, 'The Hidden Edge', *African Business*, July/August, pp.18–21.

Targeting Winners: Can Foreign Direct Investment Policy Help Developing Countries Industrialise?

MICHAEL MORTIMORE and SEBASTIAN VERGARA

The globalisation process provides opportunities for developing countries in the context of tighter international agreements that limit their policy instruments for promoting industrialisation. An option for governments in this new context is to 'target lead transnational corporations', whose corporate strategies are more attuned to their developmental circumstances and industrial aspirations, in order to locate nodules of their international systems of integrated production in their economy. This can have a clustering effect in the same host economy that can contribute significantly to the creation and consolidation of internationally competitive industries there. Here we examine the cases of two developing countries: one that achieved impressive results by following such a policy and another that missed a golden opportunity by not doing so.

Le processus de mondialisation offre de nouvelles chances pour les pays en développement dans un contexte de traités internationaux plus stricts qui limitent leurs instruments politiques destinés à promouvoir l'industrialisation. Dans ce nouveau contexte, les gouvernements ont la possibilité d'attirer des corporations internationales leader dont les stratégies corporatives sont plus en accord avec leur propre situation de développement et leurs ambitions industrielles, afin d'établir des nodules de leurs systèmes internationaux de production intégrée à l'intérieur de leur économie. Ceci peut entraîner un effet d'attraction à l'intérieur de l'economie nationale, qui peut contribuer à créer et à consolider des industries concurrentielles à niveau international dans le pays. Dans cet chapter, nous analysons les cas de deux pays en développement: l'un a obtenu des résultats impressionnants en suivant une telle politique, l'autre a manqué une chance unique de faire.

Michael Mortimore is Chief, Unit on Investment and Corporate Strategies, United Nations Economic Commission for Latin America and the Caribbean, Santiago, Chile and Sebastian Vergara is Consultant, Unit on Investment and Corporate Strategies, United Nations Economic Commission for Latin America and the Caribbean, Santiago, Chile.

I. INTRODUCTION

In a globalising world, host countries can attempt to use foreign direct investment (FDI) to advance their industrialisation process into new activities and deepen existing ones. FDI policy-makers can attract selected transnational corporations (TNCs) – especially leaders[1] – whose corporate strategies are more attuned to their developmental circumstances and industrial aspirations in order to locate nodules of their international systems of integrated production (ISIP) in their economy. This attempt to extend and deepen industrialisation by way of a clustering effect of numerous ISIP nodules in the same economy can contribute significantly to the creation and consolidation of internationally competitive industries. This is considerably different from the 'picking winners' strategy based on converting rising national champion companies into world-class exporters which proved so successful for some East Asian countries, such as Japan, Korea and Taiwan [*Amsden, 1989*; *Wade, 1990*; *Chang, 2001*]. The success of the 'targeting winners' strategy depends on the interaction of the leader TNCs' decisions to shift comparative advantage from one investment site to another in the framework of their ISIP and the national policy-makers' ability to take advantage of those decisions from a developmental perspective within the constraints of the new multilateral rules and the competitive situation of specific international product markets [*Mortimore et al., 2001*; *Lowendahl, 2001*].

The idea of governments actively targeting TNCs is, of course, heresy for economic policy traditionalists. To a large extent, the traditional view was founded on the original economic literature on foreign investment 'spillovers'. The spillovers concept suggests that after a certain threshold is reached in terms of the level of inflow of foreign direct investment to a host country, a number of benefits in the form of technology transfer, production linkages, the training of human resources and local entrepreneurial development, among others, 'spill over' into the host economy, much like a glass that overflows when filled past the brim. For a long time, this view of automatic and effective benefits on the host country was the dominant view. That is *not* the case any more. Critical reviews of the literature and new empirical findings suggest that the FDI spillovers literature is, at best, exaggerated, at worst, unsubstantiated [*Gorg and Greenaway, 2001*; *Mortimore, 2004*].

This chapter focuses on evidence from Latin America and analyses two examples of the entry of leader TNCs in the region taking into account their corporate strategies and how host country policies, manifest in trade and investment agreements, industrial and technology initiatives, and incentives, influence the TNCs' siting decisions. The first section indicates that Latin America has been a major recipient of FDI, however, the impact has been weaker and less positive than generally expected. The second section looks at two noteworthy examples of the interface of leader TNC strategies and national policies in the context of specific product markets: semiconductor leader Intel in Costa Rica, and automobile leader Toyota in Mexico. The final section provides conclusions that suggest that in the right circumstances the 'targeting winners' strategy can be quite successful, especially in comparison to previous strategies that simply passively depended on FDI inflows, rather than being actively co-ordinated with them.

II. LATIN AMERICA'S EXPERIENCE WITH FDI

The strong FDI inflows to Latin America and the Caribbean beginning in the 1990s have come to a screeching stop and that makes it a good time to evaluate the recent experience. Inflows to the region (excluding those to financial centres) rose from an annual average of $15.8 billion in 1990–94 to $60.6 billion in 1995–99 before collapsing from $88.2 billion in 1999 to just $44.4 billion in 2002 (all values here and throughout in US dollars). *Mexico, Central America* and *the Caribbean* more than doubled their average annual inflows from $6.8 billion in 1990–94 to $15.2 billion during 1995–99 and generally remained slightly above that average thereafter.[2] *South America* experienced more of a roller coaster ride when average annual inflows of about $9 billion during 1990–94 were multiplied by a factor of five to $45.4 billion during 1995–99 before declining steeply to $26.6 billion in 2002. These figures for South America hide two separate realities. On the one hand, the Andean Community tripled its average annual FDI inflows between the first and second period and more or less maintained that level thereafter. On the other hand, the Southern Cone (Mercosur plus Chile) experienced the roller coaster ride multiplying average annual inflows by six from $6.1 billion to $35.6 billion before seeing those inflows fall to below $20 billion in 2002. Thus, distinct subregional realities underlay the general picture described above.

The impact of FDI and TNC activities on Latin America has been dealt with in considerable detail elsewhere [*Mortimore, 2000; 2004*]. Table 1 interprets the logic of the corporate strategies driving FDI in the region. Here we concentrate on one particular corporate strategy that has been driving FDI during the recent period: the *efficiency-seeking* one [*UNCTAD, 2002*]. Effectively, this strategy has demonstrated more pronounced impacts on the recipient countries' productive structure, international competitiveness and industrial development than have the other principal strategies [*UNCTAD, 2000*].

The primary efficiency-seeking TNC activities in Latin America and the Caribbean are export platforms established to form part of international or regional systems of integrated production of the TNCs. These have attained a higher or more sophisticated level in the form of the automotive and electronics platforms in Mexico [*Mortimore, 1998a, 1998b; Dussel, 1999, 2000; Dussel et al., 2003*] and a lower or less sophisticated level in the form of the apparel

TABLE 1
THE PRINCIPAL FOCAL POINTS OF FDI IN LATIN AMERICA AND THE CARIBBEAN
ACCORDING TO THE CORPORATE STRATEGIES DRIVING THEM

Corporate strategy/ sector	Raw materials- seeking	Market (national or regional) access-seeking	Efficiency- seeking	Strategic element- seeking
Goods	*Petroleum/natural gas*: Andean Community, Argentina, Trinidad and Brazil *Minerals*: Chile, Argentina and Andean Community	*Auto industry*: Brazil and Argentina *Food, beverage and tobacco*: Argentina, Brazil and Mexico *Chemicals*: Brazil	*Auto industry*: Mexico *Electronics*: Mexico and Caribbean Basin *Apparel*: Caribbean Basin and Mexico	
Services		*Financial services*: Brazil, Mexico, Chile, Argentina, Venezuela, Colombia and Peru *Telecommunications*: Brazil, Argentina, Chile and Peru *Retail trade*: Brazil, Argentina, Mexico and Chile *Electricity*: Colombia, Brazil, Argentina, Chile and Central America *Gas distribution*: Argentina, Brazil, Chile and Colombia		

platforms in Central America and the Caribbean [*Mortimore, 1999, 2002c, 2003*]. The efficiency-seeking strategy often begins with simple cost reduction in each production site, however, the more successful ones evolve to include efficiency concerns with regards to the interrelationship of each production location with the regional or international system of integrated production of the TNC. It is relevant to distinguish these two kinds of export platform because their developmental impacts are quite distinct in the region.

In *Mexico*, the efficiency-seeking TNC activities relate primarily to greenfield investment in new export platforms, many began in the context of the *maquiladora* scheme for export assembly. Some of the favourable impacts of this FDI were to increase exports and improve export competitiveness to the extent that Mexico became one of the ten 'winner' countries associated with the new international systems of integrated production [*UNCTAD, 2002*]. These export platforms represent the dynamic part of the manufacturing sector, although the recent recession in the US market has taken some of the shine off it. The automotive cluster is particularly impressive, providing exports of $31.7 billion in 2001 (or 20 per cent of Mexico's total exports) and generating a favourable balance of payments in the order of $8.9 billion [*BANCOMEXT, 2002*] compared to exports of $10.8 billion in 1994 (and a deficit of $0.7 billion). Evidence on production impacts is quite limited; nevertheless, it seems probable that the configuration of the automotive cluster has produced significant upgrading of human resources and some production linkages, although the effects in terms of technology transfer or assimilation and enterprise development are less noteworthy [*Carrillo, 1995*; *Lara and Carrillo, 2003*; *Mortimore, 2004, 1998a, 1998b*; *Romo, 2003*; *Carrillo et al., 1998*]. Another positive impact is found in the apparel industry where the effect of the North American Free Trade Agreement (NAFTA) rules of origin is to generate new production linkages and facilitate some 'full package' providers [*Bair and Gereffi, 2003*; *Gereffi and Bair, 1998*].Thus, many of the export platforms in Mexico have produced very significant results, especially in terms of export competitiveness of the automotive and apparel industries.

Some negative impacts (or lack of positive ones) have also been attributed to the export platforms in Mexico. For example, the dynamism of the export sector has not been transmitted to the rest of the economy, suggesting that it is not well integrated into the economy as a whole [*Dussel, 2000*]. Exports grew at almost 18 per cent a year over the 1994–2002 period, while the gross domestic product (GDP) grew at only 3 per cent a year suggesting that the link between FDI inflows and GDP growth was not direct and the expected multiplier had not materialised. The electronics industry (dominated by Asian TNCs) possessed few of the positive production impacts – improved human resources, production linkages and enterprise development – associated with the automotive and clothing industries (dominated by US TNCs) and even the latter were mainly limited to foreign – not Mexican – suppliers [*Carrillo and Zarate, 2001*; *Contreras, 2001*; *Dutrenit and Vera-Cruz, 2001*; *Gomis, 2001*; *Gonzalez and Barrajas, 2001*; *Jaen and Leon, 2001*]. The NAFTA itself and many of the bilateral investment agreements signed by Mexico contained elements that put limitations on future policy choices to deal with some of these shortcomings.[3] Finally, the *maquiladora* format used by many exporters severely reduced the taxes paid by them, weakening the fiscal link between the export platforms and the National Treasury [*Dussel, 2001*]. One of the major shortcomings of the Mexican model is, then, that the huge export success is not reflected in the value added in the manufacturing sector [*UNCTAD, 2003*]. In other words, the export platform never evolves into a manufacturing cluster and, moreover, national policy is limited by bilateral, plurilateral and multilateral agreements.

In the case of *Central America and the Caribbean* (CAC) the benefits were even *more* limited. The apparel industry was the focus of TNCs operating in the subregion's export processing zones (EPZ), usually in the context the US production sharing mechanism (now known as US HTS 9802). The apparel industry produced over half of the exports of goods of many of these countries. A significant amount of new exports was generated by way of these TNC activities, both through FDI in new, more efficient plants and through buyers' contracts with foreign and local assemblers. The export competitiveness of the subregion demonstrated a marked improvement as a result. Other positive effects were the generation of new jobs (especially for women in non-urban settings), some upgrading of human resources, and some enterprise development as local companies bid for and won assembly contracts [*Buitelaar et al., 1999*; *Buitelaar and Padilla, 2000*; *Chacon, 2000*; *Gereffi and Memedovic, 2003*; *Mortimore et al., 1995*; *Mortimore and Zamora, 1998*; *Vicens et al., 1998*]. Thus, many of the export platforms in CAC generated a surge in exports from the apparel industry and this considerably improved the export competitiveness of the subregion.

Many negative impacts have been attributed to these export platforms. Unlike the situation in Asia where many EPZs often were converted into industrial zones and eventually became linked to science and technology parks [*UN-ESCAP, 1994*], the EPZs in CAC quickly got stuck in a rut. On the one hand, the US production sharing mechanism effectively limited the CAC contribution to an assembly stage of production utilising only US inputs since tariffs are applied to all value added outside of the US upon entry to the US market. This leads the TNC activities in this industry to focus primarily on low wages in CAC [*Mortimore, 1999, 2002c, 2003*]. On the other hand, the intense competition for plants and contracts in the context of US import quotas can lead to a 'race to the bottom' in terms of competitive devaluations, wage repression, and reduced social security benefits, and a 'race to the top' with respect to (over dimensioned) incentives, both of which severely reduce the national benefits deriving from such operations [*Oman, 2000*; *Mortimore and Peres, 1997, 1998*]. Extremely little in the way of production linkages or technology transfer and assimilation is forthcoming. CAC does not have the benefit of anything similar to the NAFTA rules of origin that work in favour of the further integration of the Mexican apparel industry.[4] To date, the CAC apparel export platforms have been limited to one market – the United States – and one function – simple assembly of US-made components. Any possible upgrading of these operations will have to take place very fast to be effective as the last part of the WTO Agreement on Textiles and Clothing will kick in as of 2005 and that will mean that CAC apparel producers will face a much harsher competitive environment in the US market owing to the increased presence of Asian, especially Chinese, competitors. Thus, the apparel export platforms enjoyed success with regard to export competitiveness, however, the effect on the overall production apparatus was truncated by the principal mechanism used to gain access to the US market. Recent alterations in bilateral and multilateral agreements appear not to be sufficiently comprehensive or rapid to make much of a difference.

This evaluation of the main efficiency-seeking TNC activities in Latin America – those in Mexico and CAC – suggests that the indicators of success in terms of new exports and export competitiveness are truly impressive and much superior to the rest of Latin America; nonetheless, this success does not square with the lack of progress in Mexico and CAC with regard to extending and upgrading their industrialisation process. Evidently, the impacts of the transmission belts associated with the transfer and assimilation of technology, the construction of production linkages, the upgrading of human resources and enterprise development have turned out to be much smaller or different from what is generally assumed [*Mortimore, 2004*]. It would appear that, in the absence of an explicit development strategy defining national industrial objectives, the benefits generated from these kinds of TNC activities based on efficiency-seeking strategies *accrue primarily to the TNCs themselves and not the host countries*. There is a clear role for national policy in this regard.

III. CAN HOST COUNTRY POLICY MAKE A DIFFERENCE?

The globalisation process, which incorporates the progressive liberalisation of trade and investment, obliges TNCs to co-ordinate and integrate their distinct production sites in order to compete better in all markets. Efficiency-seeking TNC strategies usually rely on increased specialisation on core activities to make better use of economies of scale and implement policies to increase outsourcing. This means that the TNCs are continually evaluating their existing and potential new production sites for their international systems of integrated production from an efficiency-seeking perspective. The more far-sighted TNCs increasingly look beyond static comparative advantages, such as existing wage levels, toward dynamic comparative advantages, such as potential technological capacities, human resource capabilities, supplier networks and cluster formation, and enterprise development.

This section will present two concrete cases of countries that attracted considerable amounts of efficiency-seeking FDI, one using a 'targeting winners' strategy and one not. Unsurprisingly, the former did appreciably better than the latter.

Case One: Costa Rica Captures a Nodule of Intel's ISIP

Costa Rica took advantage of Intel's announcement that it wanted to geographically diversify its ISIP to include a site in Latin America, by designing and implementing a focused, targeted and active FDI policy that emphasised the coincidence between Intel's corporate objectives and Costa Rica's development strategy. This becomes apparent by examining Intel's global expansion strategy and Costa Rica's national policy in the context of the competitive situation of the international semiconductor industry.

The Competitive Situation of the International Semiconductor Industry. The semiconductor industry is one of the principal economic activities in which efficiency-seeking TNCs are particularly active. It is the most important of the high-technology global production chains and is *technology*-driven [*UNCTAD, 2002*]. Semiconductors, broadly defined as SITC 7599, became the most dynamic products in world trade during 1985–2000 rising from 1.5 to 5 per cent of world imports. The demand for semiconductors is closely associated with the accelerated expansion of the information and communications technology (ICT) sector (computers, telecommunications and consumer electronics) and semiconductors accounted for 20 per cent of trade in high-technology non-resource based manufactures, which was the most dynamic category of world trade during 1985–2000.

The top ten semiconductor TNCs account for over 50 per cent of the total sales of the industry. The evolution of the semiconductor industry has been dramatic, with sales rising from $17 billion in 1983 to over $200 billion in 2000 before collapsing by 32 per cent as the recession took hold in the ICT industries. Intel was able to deepen its dominance of the industry, even during temporary meltdown of semiconductor sales in 2001. Intel alone accounted for 19 per cent of global semiconductor sales in 2001.

Intel's dominance of the semiconductor industry derives from very concrete competitive advantages of a technological nature. From its first microprocessor (4004) in 1971 to its Pentium 4 in 2000, Intel has been able to increase the speed of processing, pack more transistors on to each chip, squeeze more chips on to bigger wafers and raise the upper limit of its addressable memory. In November of 2003, Intel announced that it had developed a new material – high k – which would reduce leakage by 100 times over silicon dioxide chips (*New York Times,* 5 November 2003). This, naturally, gives it an immense lead over its rivals and allows Intel to innovate, based on the superior technological capacities of its products, to create new uses for its products and thereby increase demand. That lead was further strengthened by Intel's success in developing a brand name ('Intel Inside') that produced consumer loyalty, similar to that of Microsoft's 'Windows' operating system, and made Intel into a major stakeholder of the dominant 'Wintel' system, that is, the Microsoft operating system running on Intel microprocessors. Intel also has strengthened these competitive advantages by way of huge expenditures on research and development (equivalent to almost 15 per cent of sales in 2001) to maintain its technological lead, and by extending its ISIP to safe, qualified, lower cost production and assembly sites.

Intel's Global Expansion Strategy. Intel has consolidated its status as the global semiconductor leader by developing a global investment strategy to refocus its international system of integrated production. This is reflected in the fact that its annual average investment rose from less than $500 million a year in the 1980s to $1,700 million during the early 1990s to about $4,600 during 1996–2002. Intel's international system of integrated production complements its technological lead.

Intel's global expansion has been in response to a number of different factors. Three stand out: security, logistics and cost reduction. The first has in fact restricted Intel's global expansion in order to avoid any leakage of its principal competitive advantage – its technology – to competitors. For that reason, over two-thirds of Intel's employees work in its home country, the United States, even after its recent global expansion. Security also explains why Intel's production system consists entirely of fully owned subsidiaries. Intel therefore is extremely careful when it takes a decision to expand internationally. The second factor – logistics – encompasses speed to market and market access. Intel reckons that each new generation of microprocessors possesses at the most a six-month lead time over competitors. Therefore its production sites must minimise time to market, so that it can keep its competitors at bay. Other logistical factors, such as transportation costs are less important due to the extremely high value to weight ratio of its semiconductors. The third factor – cost reduction – is gaining increasing importance as Intel's competitors continue to expand internationally to take advantage of lower cost production sites. These three factors combine to produce the particular characteristics of the Intel ISIP: a few huge operations in a small number of countries outside of the United States (Table 2). Intel, as a result, has become the principal exporter in countries such as Ireland, the Philippines and Costa Rica.

Intel's ISIP encompasses two types of plants: (i) those where the wafers are manufactured and the integrated circuits etched on them, and (ii) assembly and testing plants (ATPs) where the wafers are thinned to reduce internal stress, then cut into anywhere from 300 to 500 individual chips or microprocessors. These chips are mounted on to a lead frame and attached to thin gold wires that will eventually connect them with other elements of the computer. They are then encapsulated, revised and tested. Intel's ISIP consists of 18 wafer manufacturing and fabricating plants in the United States (14), Ireland (two) and Israel (two), and 12 ATPs in the United States (one), Malaysia (four), Philippines (three), Costa Rica (two) and China (two).

Security factors account for the fact that most of the wafer plants – especially the most modern ones using the most advanced technology, such as the 0.13 micron process technology – are located in the United States, where the danger of war, terrorism, and technology filtration is more minor. Even though a new wafer plant today can easily cost over $1 billion and, therefore, represents a huge financial exposure, Intel decided to locate its first wafer plant outside of the United States in Israel in 1985. Another new plant was added in 1999. The other foreign site of wafer manufacture and fabrication is Ireland where a plant was established and upgraded during 1993–98 and another more modern one (300 mm wafers) is being constructed. European market access plays a role in that site selection. About 30 per cent of Intel's wafer manufacture and fabrication capacity is now located outside of the United States. In other words, other factors progressively became more important than the original security concerns for the siting of the capital-intensive wafer manufacture and fabrication plants.

Cost reduction is a primary factor in the siting of the labour-intensive ATPs. Intel's expansion in this regard began with the Manila plant in the Philippines in 1979, and was extended to incorporate the Penang plant in Malaysia (1988), the San José plant in Costa Rica (1997) and the Shanghai plant in China (1997).

TABLE 2
CHARACTERISTICS OF INTEL'S PRINCIPAL MANUFACTURING, ASSEMBLY AND TESTING PLANTS

Country/ region/year initiated	Functions/ products	Process technology (microns)	Wafer size (mm)	Programme post-2002 (microns)	Employeees
United States					44 164
Oregon					15 000
1978	Manufacture of motherboards	n.a.	n.a.	To be increased	
1992	Manufacture of logic and flash	0.25, 0.35	200	0.18, 0.13	
1996	Manufacture of logic	0.13	200	–	
1999	Manufacture of logic	0.13	300	0.10	
2003	Manufacture of logic (development)	n.a.	300	Under constr.	
Arizona					10 000
1996	Manufacture of logic	0.18	200	–	
1999	Assembly and testing	n.a.	n.a.	–	
2001	Manufacture of logic	0.13	200	–	
California 1988	Manufacture of logic, flash memory	0.13, 0.18	200	0.13 flash	8 500
New Mexico					5 500
1980	Manufacture of flash memory	0.35	150	Closing	
1993	Manufacture of logic and flash	0.18, 0.25	200	0.13	
2002	Manufacture of logic	0.13	300	Opening	

TABLE 2 *continued*

Country/ region/year initiated	Functions/ products	Process technology (microns)	Wafer size (mm)	Programme post-2002 (microns)	Employeees
Mass. 1994	Manufacture of logic	0.28, 0.35, 0.50	200	0.13	2 700
Washington 1996	Manufacture of production systems	n.a.	n.a.	–	1 400
Colorado 2001	Manufacture of flash memory	0.18	200	0.13	1 064
Israel					2 300
Jerusalem 1985	Manufacture of logic and flash	0.35, 0.50, 0.70, 1.0	150	–	
Qiryat Gat 1999	Manufacture of logic	0.18	200	–	
Ireland					3 400
Leixlip 1993–98	Manufacture of logic	0.18, 0.25	200	–	
Leixlip 2004	Manufacture of logic	n.a.	300	Under constr.	
Philippines					5 984
Manila 1979–95	Assembly and testing	Flash memory	50–200	–	
Cavite 1997	Assembly and testing	Logic	200	300	
Cavite 1998	Assembly and testing	Flash memory	200	–	
Malaysia					7 790
Penang 1988	Assembly and testing	Logic, comp. products	150–200	–	
Penang 1994	Assembly and testing	Logic, comp. products	150–200	–	
Kulim 1996–97	Assembly and testing, manuf. boards	Logic, comp. boards	200	Board design	
Penang 1997	Assembly and testing	–	200	300	
Costa Rica					1 845
San José 1997	Assembly and testing	Logic	200	300	
San José 1999	Assembly and testing	Logic	200	300	
China					1 227
Shanghai 1997	Assembly and testing	Flash memory	150–200	–	
Shanghai 2001	Assembly and testing	Logic	150–200	–	

Note: n.a., not applicable.
Source: based on http://www.intel.com and UNCTAD [*2002*].

Intel has deepened its presence in each of these sites by way of the construction of new ATPs to complement the original ones. In other words, one of the principal characteristics of the Intel ISIP is that it tends to grow in the few existing sites and that expansion to new sites is quite uncommon. The siting decisions usually are based on the availability of qualified technicians, construction costs, infrastructure quality, logistics, supplier capabilities and production costs. Thus, there exist important differences between the siting of wafer manufacture and fabrication plants and the siting of assembly and testing plants.

Intel's decision to invest in Costa Rica in the mid 1990s is remarkable when placed in the context of its existing ISIP [*Shiels, 2000*; *Spar, 1998*]. Intel's site selection team put together a long list of what they considered to be qualified sites,[5] including China, India, Indonesia, Singapore, Thailand, Argentina, Brazil, Chile, Costa Rica and Mexico. In the research and evaluation process that followed, Intel's interest in diversifying its geographic risk by extending its ISIP to Latin America began to play a more important role, reflected in the fact that the short list contained more Latin American (Brazil, Chile, Costa Rica and Mexico) than Asian (Indonesia, Thailand) countries. The on-site evaluation process eventually brought the choice down to two candidate countries: Costa Rica and Mexico. The latter possessed some very strong advantages, such as an existing and large electronics sector, labour availability, skills levels and cost, and proximity to the United States. Nevertheless, it was Costa Rica's well-organised and well-focused negotiating process in the context of its relevant competitive advantages[6] that most impressed the Intel site selection team.

Costa Rica's National Policy. The only country in Latin America in which the efficiency-seeking TNCs' activities are dominant and in which a new national developmental strategy explicitly defines the role of FDI is the exceptional case of Costa Rica [*Egloff, 2001b*]. This country had a developmental trajectory very similar to other countries of CAC in which the apparel export platform represented its principal link to the international economy [*Mortimore and Zamora, 1998*]. With the end of the civil wars in other parts of Central America, higher wage Costa Rica came under considerable competitive pressures. Instead of opting for the 'low road' to export competitiveness encompassing competitive devaluations, repressed wages, reduced social security benefits, and never-ending incentives, Costa Rica chose to design and implement a new development strategy based on attracting FDI to upgrade into more technologically sophisticated activities [*Robles, 2000*]. A considerable amount of success was achieved in electronics, medical devices and logistics by way of selective interventions using third generation FDI promotion techniques.[7]

Some of the major decisions that backed up the new focused developmental strategy were those related to improving domestic capabilities to attract FDI (i.e. investing heavily in education in the order of 6 per cent of GDP for decades and

emphasising technical and English language skills), designing and implementing
an active and targeted FDI policy reflecting national developmental priorities,
identifying the TNCs to be targeted and negotiating firm-level packages, and
designing and implementing industrial policies to deal with some of the problems
which arise from the TNC activities, especially weak technology transfer and
assimilation and limited productive linkages [*Egloff, 2001a*]. Of particular
importance was the explicit congruence among investment priorities, the package
of advantages offered and the overall development strategy [*Gonzalez, 2002*].
TNCs' activities are evaluated in that light. In this sense, Costa Rica's
development strategy possessed elements found in well-known success stories,
such as Singapore and Ireland [*Mortimore et al., 2001*].

With regards to its efforts to get the Intel ATP investment, Costa Rica put
together a negotiating team that included the foreign trade and investment
promotion agency CINDE, the Ministries of Energy and Environment,
Transportation, Finance, Science and Technology, and the Costa Rican
Technological Institute. It had a high-level co-ordinator and direct access to
the Costa Rican President, who took a direct interest in the negotiations, even
travelling to Intel headquarters in Arizona to press Costa Rica's case. From the
beginning, Costa Rica's message was to highlight the coincidence between
the government's developmental objectives and Intel's corporate goals for a
Latin American assembly and testing site. The practical problem-solving attitude
of the negotiating team was particularly appreciated by the Intel site selection,
legal, and tax teams that arrived to evaluate Costa Rica's 'fit' into Intel's ISIP.
Once the 'nitty-gritty' details were worked out, such as the provision of
electricity substations and several other infrastructural works (roads, etc.), more
frequent flights, lower electricity rates for high demand, new consulates in the
Philippines and Malaysia, and a dedicated call centre, among other things, Intel
decided to commit to build its first Latin American ATP in Costa Rica, near the
international airport in San José.

The impact of that decision on the Costa Rican economy was
extraordinary. The export stream generated represented almost 30 per cent of
the value of Costa Rica's exports to its principal market – the United States – in
2000, produced a trade surplus and represented the consolidation of the national
trade strategy to diversify out of apparel and natural resources toward electronics.
Furthermore, this huge investment produced a ripple effect throughout the
economy in terms of related activities, especially software.[8] Benefits in terms of
technology transfer and assimilation, production linkages, human resource
upgrading and enterprise development have been registered [*Larrain et. al.,
2001, Mytelka and Barclay, 2003*], in differing degrees, although it should be
kept in mind that the functional activity remains assembly and testing,
not manufacture, and the industrial cluster is in formation, it is not consolidated.
Intel later decided to establish a second plant to assemble and test another line

of microprocessors (for servers) in Costa Rica. The Intel investment also represented a kind of 'stamp of approval' for Costa Rica's developmental strategy and CINDE's active and targeted FDI attraction policy [*Rodriguez-Clare, 2001*].

Costa Rica stands out as an example of what can be achieved by coupling the correct policy framework – one that reflects the priorities of the national development strategy – to a leader TNC's global expansion strategy. The case of Intel in Costa Rica thus demonstrates how national policy goals and corporate strategy objectives can coincide and is a good example of a targeting winners strategy, that is, the use of national policy to further industrialise by attracting the right kind of TNC activities in the best conditions.

Case Two: Mexico Misses Becoming Part of Toyota's ISIP

Mexico missed an excellent opportunity for FDI targeting in its automobile industry by limiting its national policy purview to horizontal and generally passive instruments, as well as depending on US auto TNCs in the context of the NAFTA integration scheme. That is demonstrated by the analysis of Toyota's global expansion strategy and Mexico's national policy in the context of the competitive situation of the international automotive industry.

The Competitive Situation of the International Automotive Industry. The automobile industry is another of the principal economic activities – along with electronics and apparel – where efficiency-seeking strategies of TNCs are most active in establishing new nodules of their ISIPs. It is the most important of the medium-technology global production chains and is *production*-driven [*UNCTAD, 2002*]. The continuing shift from market-seeking to efficiency-seeking TNC strategies that has accompanied the globalisation process in the auto industry has led to a situation of extreme international competition, one characterised by excess capacity (about 20 million units a year, or 25 per cent of the total) as a result of over investment. Auto TNCs must take market share from their rivals to survive in mainly stagnant markets. It is estimated that 40 plants will have to close in the near future, 12 of them in North America [*USITC, 2002*].

The global automobile market is concentrated in the sense that the ten principal producers account for about three-quarters of world output. For the past 30 or so years, Japanese, and more recently, Korean, auto TNCs have been gaining market shares at the expense of North American and European auto TNCs and have been working their way up the list of principal producers. Technological and organisational innovations in the form of lean manufacturing based on higher productivity, improved quality and innovations in inventory management allowed Japanese auto manufacturers to produce better passenger vehicles at lower prices [*Mortimore, 1997*]. Faced with superior production technology, the US and European auto TNCs originally enlisted protectionist policies of their home governments to defend market shares in the face of surging imports from Asia. This obliged Asian auto TNCs to rely less on exports from their home base and more on extending their ISIPs, especially the new plants in the principal regional markets. While some of the Japanese (Nissan, Isuzu, Mazda, Subaru) and Korean (Daewoo, Samsung) auto TNCs faltered as a consequence of economic weaknesses in their domestic economies (and were wholly or partially acquired by US or European TNCs), the strongest continued their relentless advance on US and European market shares. Toyota's expansion in the US market is the best example of that.

The US automotive industry once again became the biggest in the world as the Japanese internal market shrank due to the financial bubble at the beginning of the 1990s; however, it produced a light vehicle trade deficit in the order of $114.4 billion in 2001 (exports of $75.4 billion minus imports of $189.8 billion) [*USITA, 2003*]. During 1997–2001 almost $25 billion was invested in new capacity and as a result US capacity has doubled since 1992. In 2001, production reached 11.4 million units while sales surpassed 17.5 million. The US market share of what are often referred to as the Big-3 US auto TNCs (General Motors, Ford and Chrysler – before Chrysler was acquired by Daimler Benz) has fallen from 95 per cent in 1965 to 72 per cent in 1986 to 61.3 per cent in 2002 and is expected to be in the range of 50 per cent within five years. That of the Japanese auto TNCs rose from 20.5 per cent in 1986 to 27.9 per cent in 2002 and is set to expand sharply due to the fact that they are fast moving into the last area of US domination: light trucks and sports utility vehicles. The Japanese share of US production has risen from 6 per cent in 1986 to 22 per cent in 2001, indicating that they rely increasingly on their North American plants than on exports from Japan. Overall, Japanese auto TNCs' brand sales from their plants in NAFTA countries rocketed from 11.8 to 67.4 per cent in 1996 (previous to the latest round of new plants which is predicted to raise their production capacity in the US to 4.7 million units). Evidently, the Japanese auto TNCs have been very successful in neutralising the NAFTA option of US auto TNCs (see below).

Toyota's Global Expansion Strategy. Toyota Motor Corporation (TMC) produced 6.3 million vehicles in 2003 and became the world's second largest auto TNC after General Motors (GM). It has a production system that consists of 12 manufacturing plants and 11 subsidiaries in Japan and 45 manufacturing plants in 26 other countries. It sells its products in 160 countries. TMC has managed to position itself as the technological and organisational leader of the automotive industry on the basis of the Toyota Production System. This lean production system helped TMC to elevate productivity, improve quality and motivate multifunctional work groups to such an extent that it became the heart of the 'Japanese challenge' to other auto TNCs [*Mortimore, 1997*]. Presently, Toyota's global expansion is extending these competitive advantages throughout its ISIP.

TMC production is still mainly in Japan (4.1 million units), although the foreign share is rising precipitously (2.2 million units). TMC's sales trend is more or less the opposite, that is, 2.2 million units in Japan and 4 million units in the rest of the world. Toyota exports 1.7 million vehicles from Japan.[9] Evidently, the dynamic part of the TMC system is now the international part.

TMC began to seriously develop its international system from the perspective of *integrated* production in the mid 1980s (Table 3). Previous to that it had established a significant number of market-seeking plants to serve national markets, such as Brazil (1959), Thailand (1964), Malaysia (1968), Portugal (1969), Indonesia (1970), Venezuela (1981), and Bangladesh (1982). As of 1985, Toyota developed a coherent strategy for establishing its competitive advantages within the most important regional markets, that is, first North America, then Europe (Figure 1). TMC grew its international production from 3.6 per cent of the total production in 1985 to 14 per cent in 1990, 28.3 per cent in 1995, and 38.2 per cent in 2002.

The North American market has been central to the TMC global expansion. Since 1971, TMC has possessed a plant for truck beds, catalytic converters and stamped parts; however, during 1984–88 its North American expansion began in earnest comprising the New United Motor Manufacturing Inc. (NUMMI) joint venture with GM, Toyota Motor Manufacturing Kentucky (TMMK) (Avalon and Camry models), Toyota Motor Manufacturing Indiana (TMMI) (Tundra, Sequoia and Sienna models) and Toyota Motor Manufacturing Canada Inc. (TMMC) (the Camry Solara, Corolla and Matrix models). A second round of major investments in components followed in the 1998–2003 period consisting of Toyota Motor Manufacturing West Virginia (TMMWV) (engines and transmissions) and Toyota Motor Manufacturing Alabama (TMMAL) (engines). Future investments include Toyota Motor Manufacturing Baja California (TMMBC) (truck beds for the Tacoma) and Toyota Motor Manufacturing Texas (TMMTX) (Tundra). Toyota is presently bringing forward its investment programme because of the success that it has enjoyed in the North American market.

Toyota's focus on and penetration of the North American market – originally based on exports from Japan – is now firmly founded on a local North American production system. The integrated production nodule in North America represents 21.4 per cent of TMC's global production capacity and accounts for 62 per cent of sales in that continent. TMC now undertakes significant research and development activities in that market. The Toyota Camry has been the best selling vehicle in the United States for a number of years. All this indicates the degree to which TMC has been able to lay down an effective regional production system in North America.[10]

In Europe TMC's presence began with a market-seeking operation in Portugal in 1968; however, the new nodule of its regional production system began to take form with Toyota Motor Manufacturing UK (TMUK)

TABLE 3

CHARACTERISTICS OF TOYOTA'S INTERNATIONAL SYSTEM OF PRODUCTION[a]

Sales (2003)/affiliate/year	Country	Models/products	Export market	Production 2002	Exports 2001
North American sales: 1 981 824				**1 205 500**	**156 045**
New United Motor Manufacturing Inc. (NUMMI) 1984	USA	Corolla, Tacoma	Canada, Puerto Rico	310 300	2 703
Toyota Motor Manufacturing, Kentucky (TMMK) 1988	USA	Avalon, Camry	Taiwan, Canada, Japan, Middle East	490 591	17 831
Toyota Motor Manufacturing, Indiana (TMMI) 1988	USA	Tundra, Sequoia, Sienna	Canada, Oceania	186 573	8 022
Toyota Motor Manufacturing Canada Inc. (TMMC) 1988	Canada	Camry Solara, Corolla, Matrix	USA, Puerto Rico, Mexico	218 018	127 489
Toyota Motor Manufacturing, West Virginia (TMMWV) 1998	USA	Engines, transmissions			
Toyota Motor Manufacturing Alabama Inc. (TMMAL) 2003	USA	Engines			
Toyota Motor Manufacturing, Texas (TMMTX) 2006	USA	Tundra			
Toyota M. Manufacturing Baja California (TMMBC) 2004	Mexico	Tacoma truck beds, Tacoma (2005)	North America		
European sales: 775 952				**344 600**	**168 113**
Salvador Caetano IMVT 1969	Portugal	Dyna, Hiace, Optimo	UK, Spain, Germany	3 587	87
Toyota Motor Manufacturing (UK) (TMUK) 1992	UK	Avensis, Corolla, engines	Europe, Africa, South America, Japan	209 016	120 636
Toyota Motor Manufacturing Turkey Inc. (TMMT) 2000	Turkey	Corolla	Europe, Middle East	39 039	

TABLE 3 continued

Sales (2003)/affiliate/year	Country	Models/products	Export market	Production 2002	Exports 2001
Toyota Motor Manufacturing France (TMMF) 2001	France	Yaris	Europe	135 406	47 390
Toyota Motor Manufacturing Poland (TMMP) 2002	Poland	Transmissions			
Toyota Motor Industries Poland (TMIP) 2005	Poland	Engines			
Toyota Peugeot Citroen Automobile Czech (TPCA) 2005	Czech Republic	New small car (2005)	Europe		
Asian sales (excl. Japan): 1 034 148				**497 368**	**130 284**
Toyota Motor Corp. Australia Ltd 1963	Australia	Camry, Corolla, Avalon	N. Zealand, Thailand, Oceania, Middle East	86 558	59 231
Toyota Motor Thailand (TMT) 1964	Thailand	Camry, Corolla, Hilux, Soluna	Pakistan, Philippines, Singapore, Australia	140 246	11 800
Assembly Services Sdn. Bhd. 1968	Malaysia	Avensis, Corolla, Dyna, Hiace		28 000	
P.T. Toyota-Astra Motor 1970	Indonesia	Camry, Corolla, TUV, Dyna Land Cruiser	Brunei, etc.	84 864	22
Aftab Automobles Ltd 1982	Bangladesh			319	
Kuozui Motors 1986	Taiwan	Camry, TUV, Hiace, Corolla, Vios		67 495	
Toyota Philippines Corp. 1989	Philippines	Camry, Corolla, TUV		21 269	
Siam Toyota Manufacturing 1989	Thailand	Engines			
Indus Motor Company 1993	Pakistan	Corolla, Hilux		9 887	
Toyota Motor Vietnam 1996	Vietnam	Corolla, Hiace, Camry, Land Cruiser, TUV, Vios		7 138	

TABLE 3 continued

Sales (2003)/affiliate/year	Country	Models/products	Export market	Production 2002	Exports 2001
Sichuan Toyota Motor Co. 2000	China	Coaster, Land Cruiser			
Tianjin Toyota Motor Eng. Co. 1998	China	Engines			
South American sales: 160 971				**28 100**	**16 899**
Toyota do Brasil Ltd 1959, 2002	Brazil	Corolla	Argentina	16 074	1 350
Toyota de Venezuela 1981, 2002	Venezuela	Corolla, Land Cruiser	Colombia, Ecuador	7 333	738
SOFASA 1992	Colombia	Hilux, Land Cruiser	Ecuador, Venezuela	7 823	8 159
Toyota Argentina SA 1997	Argentina	Hilux	Brazil, Uruguay	11 173	7 904
African sales: 65 665				**82 222**	**2 224**
Toyota south Africa Motors 1962	S. Africa	Corolla, Dyna, Hilux, Hiace, TUV		81 555	2 224
Sales outside Japan: 4 028 417				**4 138 873**	**1 749 041**
Sales in Japan: 2 21 7739					
Total sales: 6 246 156				**6 314 008**	

[a] The rows in italics indicate those parts of the Toyota ISP that can be identified with an efficiency-seeking motivation.
Source: Based on UNCTAD [2002] and http://www.toyota.com.

FIGURE 1

TOYOTA MOTOR CORPORATION: VEHICLE PRODUCTION IN AND IMPORTS TO
US MARKET, 1985–98 (NUMBER OF UNITS AND PER CENT)

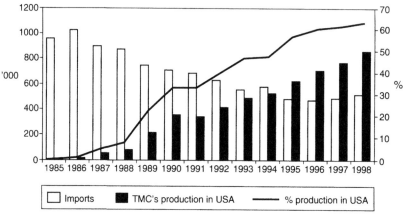

Source: based on www.toyota.com

(Avensis and Corolla models) in 1992, followed by Toyota Motor Manufacturing Turkey Inc. (TMMT) (Corolla) in 1994, Toyota Motor Manufacturing France (TMMF) (Yaris) in 2001 and Toyota Motor Manufacturing Poland (TMMP) (transmissions) in 2002. Future investments will be in Toyota Motor Industries Poland (TMIP) (engines) and a joint venture with PSA in Toyota Peugeot Citroen Automobile Czech (TPCA) (new small car) both of which will come on stream in 2005. Based on these investments in the European nodule of the TMC ISIP, Europe's share of TMC's total production is in the range of 6 per cent and its share of sales will be about 13 per cent. Thus, TMC's ISIP based on efficiency-seeking strategies in integrating markets of North America and Europe is gaining a larger presence within the overall Toyota international system, as the intra-regional exports from its Toyota Motor Manufacturing label subsidiaries there suggest.

There is clear evidence to suggest that TMC was centring its globalisation strategy on the North American and European markets and, in the former, Mexico could have played a significantly more important role. In North America, TMC undertook two rounds of significant expansion: the 1984–88 phase to establish the NUMMI, TMMK, TMMI and TMMC plants in the US and Canada and the 1998–2004 phase in which the TMMWV, TMMAL (and TMMBC and TMMTX) plants are being established in the US (and Mexico). The TMMBC plant as such represents somewhat of a curiosity in the sense that it is designed to assemble truck beds, later to be converted into a low volume (20,000–30,000 units a year) light truck producer. In other words, the TMMBC is *not* a significant element of TMC's

North American production system in spite of the fact that since 1994 the NAFTA has facilitated the incorporation of new Mexican plants in its regional production system in a similar way that the Canada–US Free Trade Agreement did for its plants in Canada. Given the competitive circumstances of the North American market and the clearly defined efficiency-seeking strategy of TMC to establish a North American nodule to its ISIP, the limited investment in Mexico stands out as an oddity, considering that the production capacity of the auto TNCs established in Mexico doubled between 1992 and 2002. Was it the lack of an active Mexican FDI policy that contributed to that mediocre outcome in the case of Toyota?

Mexico's National Policy. Mexico in the 1970s was somewhat of a prototype of the nationalistic developing country. Its bid in the mid 1980s to break with its previous development model based on overprotected import substituting industrialisation (ISI)[11] led it to implement a complete volte-face of its economic strategy and to adopt most of the central elements of the Washington consensus, that is, the reduction in the role and presence of the state, and the adoption of a more private sector-based orientation based on deregulation, privatisation and opening up to trade and investment. This new strategy included joining the General Agreement on Trade and Tariffs (GATT) and the Organisation of Economic Cooperation and Development (OECD) with all that this implied in terms of new and binding multilateral commitments. Mexico took it upon itself to negotiate a host of free trade agreements (FTAs) and bilateral investment treaties (BITs) to consolidate its internationalisation process. The principal FTAs were with Canada and the US in 1994 (NAFTA) and the European Union in 2002 but included over 30 countries altogether. The BITs covered over 20 countries. The policy framework supporting Mexico's new liberal strategy could be characterised as notably horizontal, in the sense of employing primarily across-the-board – not sectoral – policies, and exceptionally passive, from the perspective of the level of state participation or intervention in economic activities. It is relevant to focus on the changes in industrial policy in respect of the automotive industry and the influence of the new FDI policy.

The new horizontal and passive macroeconomic policy contrasted sharply with what had been the nature of industrial policy before the sea change in Mexican national economic policy and what continued to be for some time the situation in the automotive industry. It might be mentioned at the outset that the transformation of the Mexican automobile industry into an internationally competitive one is often considered to be one of the principal successes of Mexico's new economic policy, however, its success as an export platform actually began in the early 1980s. It was given a huge boost by NAFTA. During 1990–2000 alone the industry invested almost $15 billion and FDI inflows during 1994–2000 reached $8.4 billion, equivalent to 44 per cent of all FDI in the manufacturing sector. The Mexican automotive industry accounts for 2.8 per cent

TABLE 4

FUNCTIONAL ASPECTS OF THE MEXICAN AUTOMOTIVE DECREES AND NAFTA, 1962–2004

Aspect	1962	1972	1977	1983	1989	NAFTA
1. Import protection	Imports prohibited				Import tariff: 20%, only vehicle assemblers, within export and B of P limits	Import tariff: 1994: 9.9% 2003: 0% certain quotas apply
2. Local content or value added	60% local content; obligatory national components			Local content reduced to 30% for export lines (max. 25% domestic sales); for others: 50–60%	V/A for auto parts: 30%, for vehicles: 36%; obligatory national components eliminated	Auto parts: 1994–2003: 20% 2004: 0% vehicles: 1994: 34% 2003: 29% 2004: 0%
3. Trade balancing/foreign exchange budget	–	Imports must be offset: 1973 by 30%; 1976 by 60%	Annual foreign exchange budget restraints	Sliding scale according to export or local content performance	100% compensation; wider definition allows for FDI to be included	Compensation: 1994: 80% 2003: 55% 2004: 0%
4. % auto parts in vehicle producers' exports	–	40%	50%			
5. Ownership restrictions (auto parts)	60% Mexican 40% foreign	60% Mexican 40% foreign	60% Mexican 40% foreign	60% Mexican 40% foreign	Limits ignored	
6. Product line or make limits	Production quotas	New limits	Limits softened	Limits hardened	Limits eliminated	

TABLE 4 *continued*

Aspect	1962	1972	1977	1983	1989	NAFTA
7. *Maquiladora* inputs	–	–	–	Maximum of 20% trade balance to be used for foreign exchange budget	Sold in national market: max. 20%	Maximum sold in national market: 1994: 55% 2000: 85% 2001: 100%
8. Regional content	–	–	–	–	–	Minimum content from NAFTA: 1995: 50% 1997: 56% 2001: 62.5%
9. Focus	ISI	ISI	ISI/auto parts exports	Auto parts and vehicle exports	Vehicle exports	Consolidation of North American auto industry
10. Favoured groups	Auto parts	Auto parts	Auto parts/ vehicles	Vehicles/ *maquiladoras*	Vehicles/ *maquiladoras*	US Big Three auto TNCs

Sources: de Maria y Campos [*1994*]; Mortimore [*2004, 1998a, 1998b*]; BANCOMEXT [*2002*]; CEESP [*2001*].

of GDP, 16 per cent of manufacturing GDP, employs 613,000 persons (15 per cent of the total), and generates 20 per cent of exports. The industry consists of 20 assemblers and 875 auto parts companies (60 Tier 1 and 815 Tiers 2 and 3). In 2002, it produced 1,821,447 vehicles, exporting 1,329,375 of them, 94 per cent to North America. In 2001, Mexico provided 18.7 per cent of US auto imports, up from 9.5 per cent in 1994. However, the road to this success was a bumpy one.

Table 4 provides an idea of some of the principal functional aspects of the Mexican Automotive Decrees and the NAFTA rules for that industry. In general, the policy shifts, while not linear, consisted of moving from an ISI focus favouring the auto parts industry to one more focused on exports, especially exports of vehicles that, in the context of NAFTA, heavily favoured the Big-Three US auto TNCs. The shift was from sectoral policies with heavy government intervention to more liberal policies accommodating auto TNC strategies to create an export platform in Mexico, all in the context of perennial balance of payments difficulties.

The initial period favoured administrative controls in terms of import prohibitions and high tariff protection, high local content requirements and the obligatory production of certain components, limits on product lines and makes, trade balancing, the promotion of auto part exports via vehicle producers and restrictions on the foreign ownership of auto parts companies. That focus produced some notable results in terms of establishing new automotive activities, especially auto parts, however, it was not achieved in an international competitive manner and the industry came to account for 58 per cent of the trade deficit of the Mexican economy in 1981 [*de Maria y Campos, 1992*]. Thereafter, a progressive shift toward the promotion of vehicle exports took hold of Mexican automotive policy in the form of export models that required lower levels of national content or value added, making more flexible the foreign exchange budget obligations of vehicle assemblers, ceasing to oblige vehicle producers to export auto parts, allowing for the progressive incorporation of *maquiladora* inputs, ignoring the ownership restrictions on auto parts firms and, finally, facilitating the consolidation of the North American auto industry according to the criteria of the US Big-Three auto TNCs. These auto TNCs led the push to negotiate and implement the NAFTA in order to restructure and consolidate their continental operations to compete better in the US market versus Asian auto TNCs from Japan and Korea. In other words, the focus of the Mexican automobile policy moved from establishing a strategic national industry to facilitating the regional strategies of certain auto TNCs. From the perspective of the dimension and international competitiveness of the industry, the result is clearly astounding, even though it has been criticised for the lack of success in evolving the export assembly platform into an integrated manufacturing centre.

FDI policy also did a sharp about face. A radically different orientation came with the implementation of the new economic model that put FDI at its centre

[*Mortimore, 1998c*]. Although the FDI law did not formally change until the early 1990s, Mexico's new orientation became evident as of the 1980s. Mexico threw out the welcome mat for FDI. In terms of the right to enter and establish activities, National Treatment and Most Favoured Nation became the new norms and most of the sectoral prohibitions and restrictions were abolished unilaterally or by way of multilateral (GATT/GATS/TRIMs/TRIPs) or bilateral agreements – be they investment treaties or free trade agreements – or simply ignored in practice. The conflict resolution mechanism of choice became the investor-state alternative of the FTAs and BITs. As a new member of the OECD, Mexico undertook new obligations in this regard and became a leader in promoting a FDI-friendly economic policy. The horizontal and passive aspects of the FDI policy squared well with the new economic policy, but had their costs.

One significant cost was that the government was not ideologically or functionally capable of reacting to the opportunity that the Toyota global expansion represented in terms of designing and implementing a targeted and active FDI policy. It might be mentioned in this context that in 2002 the task of attracting FDI to Mexico was passed to the state foreign trade bank BANCOMEXT. That institution is presently training its staff – particularly its 45 foreign representatives – to adopt more active attraction policies [*BANC-OMEXT, 2003*]. Furthermore, this new policy initiative is being closely co-ordinated with the economic and industrial development offices of the different Mexican states. In other words, it would appear that a more targeted and active FDI policy is under consideration, however, it does not form part of a focused development strategy, as was the case in Costa Rica, rather it is an addition to the existing, basically horizontal, policy framework. Even so, this might prevent other 'Toyotas' from slipping through Mexico's fingers.

IV. CONCLUSIONS

Latin American countries have had rather poor industrialisation experiences with or without FDI in comparison to East and South East Asian industrialisers [*Lall et al., 2004*]. It would appear to be too late for them to attempt to follow the examples of Japan, South Korea and Taiwan in this regard as many of the policies that these countries employed are either no longer permissible under new multilateral rules or in some cases are no longer relevant for the more globalised international economy. Nor is it feasible to return to the Latin American style closed ISI model that generated few national champions and got the worst out of tariff-hopping, market-seeking TNCs. More recently, attempts to attract efficiency-seeking TNCs by way of horizontal and passive open economy policies have often produced the result that the TNCs obtain most of the benefits based on their use of the host countries' static comparative advantages. Latin American countries do not seem to be able to effectively use FDI to improve their industrial competitiveness. A UNCTAD/UN-ECLAC regional seminar on FDI policies in Latin America held in January of 2002 arrived at the conclusions that i) in terms of the amount of FDI received, the region had done rather well, ii) with regard to the developmental impact of those FDI inflows the record was mixed, and iii) in comparison to the more active and focused policies of Asia and Europe, the FDI policies of Latin America were considered to be clearly inadequate [*Lall, 2002a, 2002b; Loewendahl, 2002a, 2002b, 2002c; Mortimore, 2002a,2002b*]. Might the use of 'targeting winners' strategies in an open economy be the answer?

The two cases in this chapter suggest that success depends on the interaction of TNC siting decisions and the national policy-makers' ability to take advantage of them from a developmental perspective within the constraints of the new multilateral rules and the competitive situation of specific international product markets. In the absence of national policies, TNC siting strategies tend to focus on existing sites and, when they evaluate new sites, they tend to prioritise static not dynamic comparative advantages of potential host countries and this can lead to 'illusory' not authentic competitiveness [*Mortimore, 2003*].

In the first case, *both* the leader TNC and the host country seem to have achieved what they were looking for. Intel diversified its geographic risk and Costa Rica provided the advantages they sought. Costa Rica advanced toward strategic development goals, such as diversifying into electronics in an internationally competitive way and laying the foundation for cluster formation. Here, the targeting winners approach worked because FDI not only was attracted to Costa Rica but it also was an investment that had a good 'fit' with the host country's development strategy.

The second case is less clear but perhaps more representative of the more typical Latin American experience in the sense that it represents a lost opportunity. Automobile leader Toyota was consolidating the North American component of its ISIP by way of major investments in new plants located in the United States and Canada. The objective conditions for incorporating Mexico into its North American production base existed for Toyota just as was the case for the US Big-Three (as well as other firms operating in Mexico, such as Nissan and Volkswagen) in the context of the NAFTA. Mexico probably would have done better by building its automotive export platform around the industry leader rather than the TNCs that had moved production to Mexico solely to reduce costs and thereby compete better in the US market with the likes of Toyota. Even the recent (and minor) TMC investment in Tijuana seems to fit into a mentality based on taking advantage of static comparative advantages in Mexico rather than extending its regional production system to incorporate Mexico in significant manner. In this case, national policy was clearly not up to the challenge and missed a unique opportunity to strengthen its industrialisation process

[*Mortimore and Barron, 2004*]. A targeting strategy in this case probably would have worked.

This suggests that a targeting winners strategy to attract efficiency-seeking TNC leaders could very well assist able Latin American (and other) governments to achieve strategic development goals, such as extending and upgrading industry. Numerous examples of the redefinition of TNC siting decisions in the context of globalisation suggest that huge opportunities exist for a small number of well-organised host countries [*UNCTAD, 2002*]. Increasingly, factors more susceptible to host country policies (market access, human resources, infrastructure, logistics, supplier networks, cluster formation, regulatory frameworks, investment incentives, and institution) are coming to the fore in TNC decisions on siting FDI to extend or consolidate their international systems of integrated production.

To work, the targeting strategy must, on the one hand, reflect the congruence among key national institutions about the role of FDI within the context of an explicit development strategy that defines sectoral and other priorities, and, on the other, coincide in a concrete way with the decisions of efficiency-seeking TNC leaders to shift comparative advantage from one investment site to another in the framework of their ISIP. In other words, a sectoral strategy must be coherent with the national development strategy. The TNCs' initial investment is usually framed in the context of the host country's *existing* technological, human resource and supplier capabilities. The idea is to implement national policies that will convince, cajole or incentivise the TNC into improving and upgrading those capabilities to sustain more technologically sophisticated industrial activities, producing more benefits for domestic companies and employees in the process. Thus, success depends not only on attracting the investment but also on deepening its presence in the host economy on the basis of dynamic not static comparative advantages. For that reason, government policy must permanently evaluate the impact of TNC investments in order to measure the degree to which both TNC objectives and host country developmental priorities are being met. This chapter has suggested that, at a minimum, some concrete idea of improvements in technology transfer and assimilation, human resources, production linkages, and enterprise development is a requisite to defining how FDI assists in extending and upgrading national industry.

NOTES

1. These are large TNCs with a strong global presence that are the principal innovators in specific industries. Their presence in any host country often has a multiplier effect in terms of attracting other of the participants of the global value chain in which they operate.

2. The year 2001 was distorted by the atypical purchase of a Mexican bank by Citigroup for $12.5 billion [*UN-ECLAC, 2003*].

3. The opportunity afforded foreign investors to litigate against state policy of Mexico produced uncertainty about the effectiveness of national policy. Moreover, the number of performance requirements prohibited by NAFTA was much greater than the Trade Related Investment Measures (TRIMs) agreement of the World Trade Organisation (WTO) and represented a harsher environment for policy-makers dealing with production effects.

4. While physical inputs for exports to NAFTA countries by NAFTA members can originate – indiscriminately – from the US, Canada or Mexico, the US production sharing mechanism effectively dissuades non-US cloth and other inputs and processing from CAC countries. The Caribbean Basin Trade Partnership Act of 2000 attempted to face up to that problem by doing away with some quotas, allowing for the incorporation of a certain amount of locally produced cloth and permitting some further local processing (cutting, stone washing, etc.). Furthermore, it is hoped that the Central American Free Trade Agreement currently under negotiation will provide NAFTA-like rules of origin for the apparel industry; however, the US textile industry seems set on maintaining the existing restrictions.

5. The main selection criteria at this stage included stable economic and political conditions, human resource availability and labour conditions, the operational cost structure, a 'pro-business' environment, logistics and manufacturing lead-time and 'fast track' administrative permit processing [*Shiels, 2000*].

6. Such as low cost and good quality human resources (workers, technicians and managers) with English language capabilities, an open economy, low levels of corruption, political and economic stability, transparency, a solid legal tradition and relevant incentives.

7. First generation FDI promotion usually does not go beyond opening up the economy to FDI. Second generation promotion is based on the active marketing of a location, usually by way of an investment promotion agency. Third generation FDI promotion incorporates a more focused promotion strategy centred on a defined subset of TNCs rather than FDI in general [*UNCTAD, 2002*]. The more successful countries have used a targeted approach to improve their chances of attracting the type of FDI more likely to assist them to advance towards defined industrial priorities and overall development objectives.

8. A significant number of Intel 'satellites' have set up in Costa Rica. These companies usually have few employees and contribute relatively little to the local cluster formation, however, they demonstrate Intel's attractiveness and reach.

9. See: http://www.japanauto.com/statistics.

10. TMC's regional production system was made consistent with the initiatives of the US automotive TNCs with regards to the Canada–US Free Trade Agreement in the sense that Canada became a significant part of the North American production system. That was not the case with the NAFTA, however, as Mexico does not play a role in any way similar to that of Canada within its regional production system.

11. A questionnaire administered to 63 of the largest 100 foreign manufacturing firms in Mexico in 1990 produced the opinion of 56 of the 63 that the success of the ISI model during 1973–82 was 'scarce' [*Mortimore and Huss, 1991*].

REFERENCES

Amsden, A., 1989, *Asia's Next Giant: South Korea and Late Industrialization*, New York: Oxford University Press.

Bair, J. and G. Gereffi, 2003, 'Los conglomerados locales en las cadenas globales: causas y consecuencias del dinamismo en las exportaciones de la industria maquiladora de pantalones de mezclilla en Torreón', *Comercio Exterior* (BANCOMEXT, México City), Vol.53, No.4, pp.338–55.

BANCOMEXT (Banco Mexicano de Comercio Exterior), 2002, 'La industria automotriz de México, 2002', Power Point presentation available at http://www.bancomext.com

BANCOMEXT, 2003, 'Programa de actualización para la promoción de la inversión extranjera para promotores estatales y consejeros comerciales', CENCACI, Mexico City, 3 April, available at http://www.bancomext.com

Buitelaar, R. and R. Padilla, 2000, 'Maquila, Economic Reform and Corporate Strategies', *World Development*, Vol.28, No.9, pp.1627–42.

Buitelaar, R., R. Padilla and R. Urrutia, 1999, 'Centroamérica, México y República Dominicana: maquila y transformación productiva', *Cuadernos de la CEPAL* (Santiago), No.85, July.

Carrillo, J., 1995, 'Flexible Production in the Auto Sector: the Industrial Organization at Ford-Mexico', *World Development*, Vol.23, No.2, pp.87–101.

Carrillo, J. and R. Zarate, 2001, 'Proveedores en la industria electrónica en Baja California', presentation to CUCSH/COLEF seminar 'Challenges and Perspectives of the Mexican maquiladoras: Local Settings and Global Processes', University Center for Social Sciences and Humanities (CUCSH) and the College of the Northern Frontier (COLEF), Guadalajara, Jalisco, 30–31 October.

Carrillo, J., M. Mortimore and J. Alonso, 1998, *Competitividad y Mercado de Trabajo: empresas de autopartes y televisores en México*, Ed. Plaza y Valdes, Mexico City, June.

CEESP (Centro de Estudios Economicos del Sector Privado), 2001, 'La industria nacional de autpartes', *Actividad economica*, No.233, July.

Chacon, F., 2000, 'Comercio internacional de los textiles y el vestido: reestructuración global de las fuentes de oferta de EE.UU. durante la década de los noventa', *Integración y Comercio*, BID-INTAL, Buenos Aires, Year 4, No. 11.

Chang, H.-J., 2001, 'Rethinking East Asian Industrial Policy – Past Records and Future Prospects', in P.-K. Wong and C.-Y. Ng (eds.), *Industrial Policy, Innovation and Economic Growth: The Experience of Japan and the Asian NIEs*, Singapore: Singapore University Press.

Contreras, O., 2001, 'Empleo, estructura ocupacional y salarios en las maquiladoras del televisor', presentation to CUCSH/COLEF seminar 'Challenges and Perspectives of the Mexican maquiladoras: Local Settings and Global Processes', University Center for Social Sciences and Humanities (CUCSH) and the College of the Northern Frontier (COLEF), Guadalajara, Jalisco, 30–31 October.

De Maria y Campos, 1992, 'Reestructuración y desarrollo de la industria automotriz mexicana en los años ochenta: evolución y perspectivas', *Estudios e Informes de la CEPAL UN-ECLAC* (Santiago), No.83, August.

Dussel, E., 1999, 'La subcontratación como proceso de aprendizaje: el caso de la electrónica en Jalisco (México) en la decada de los noventa', serie Desarrollo Productivo, No.55, Santiago: UN-ECLAC.

Dussel, E., 2000, *Polarizing Mexico: the Impact of Liberalization Strategy*, Boulder: Lynne Rienner Publishers.

Dussel, E., 2001, 'Ser maquila o no ser maquila, ¿Es esa la pregunta? Una reflexión', presentation to CUCSH/COLEF seminar 'Challenges and Perspectives of the Mexican maquiladoras: Local Settings and Global Processes', University Center for Social Sciences and Humanities (CUCSH) and the College of the Northern Frontier (COLEF), Guadalajara, Jalisco, 30–31 October.

Dussel, E., M.L. Galindo and E. Loría, 2003, *Condiciones y efectos de la inversión extranjera directa y del proceso de integración regionalen México durante los noventa: una perspectiva macro, meso y micro*, Mexico City: Plaza y Valdes (in association with BID-INTAL and UNAM).

Dutrenit, G. and A. Vera-Cruz, 2001, 'Las PYMEs antes las redes de proveedores de la maquila ¿reto o utopía?', presentation to CUCSH/COLEF seminar 'Challenges and Perspectives of the Mexican maquiladoras: Local Settings and Global Processes', University Center for Social Sciences and Humanities (CUCSH) and the College of the Northern Frontier (COLEF), Guadalajara, Jalisco, 30–31 October.

Egloff, E., 2001a, 'La inversión de Intel y políticas micro para fortelecer la competitividad en Costa Rica', presentation at UN-ECLAC/IDB seminar on 'Camino a la competitividad: el nivel meso y microeconómico', Santiago, Chile, 15–16 March.

Egloff, E., 2001b, 'CINDE. Costa Rican Investment and Development Board', presentation at the UNCTAD 'Expert Meeting on the Impact of FDI Policies on Industrialization, Local Entrepreneurship and the Development of the Supply Chain', Geneva, 5–7 November.

Gereffi, G. and J. Bair, 1998, 'US Companies Eye NAFTA's Prize', *Bobbin* (San Francisco), Vol.39, No.7.

Gereffi, G. and O. Memedovic, 2003, 'The Global Apparel Value Chain: What Prospects for Upgrading by Developing Countries', *Sectoral Studies Series*, Vienna: UNIDO.

Gomis, R., 2001, 'La generación de ventajas competitivas a partir de la adopción y la aplicación de las tecnologías de la información: el sector de la electrónica de la industria de maquiladora de exportación en Tijuana', presentation to CUCSH/COLEF seminar 'Challenges and Perspectives of the Mexican maquiladoras: Local Settings and Global Processes', University Center for Social Sciences and Humanities (CUCSH) and the College of the Northern Frontier (COLEF), Guadalajara, Jalisco, 30–31 October.

Gonzalez, A., 2002, 'The Case of Costa Rica', UNCTAD-ECLAC regional seminar 'FDI Policies in Latin America', Santiago, Chile, 7–9 January.

Gonzalez, G. and M. Barrajas, 2001, 'Los procesos de aprendizaje en la industria electrónica maquiladora, ¿Una senda predefinida?', presentation to CUCSH/COLEF seminar 'Challenges and Perspectives of the Mexican maquiladoras: Local Settings and Global Processes', University Center for Social Sciences and Humanities (CUCSH) and the College of the Northern Frontier (COLEF), Guadalajara, Jalisco, 30–31 October.

Gorg, H. and D. Greenaway, 2001, 'Foreign Direct Investment and Intra-industry Spillovers', UNECE/EBRD 'Expert Meeting on Financing for Development: Enhancing the Benefits of FDI and Improving the Flow of Corporate Finance in the Transition Economies', Geneva, December.

Jaén Jimenez, B. and Leon M. Sánchez, 2001, 'Escalamiento industrial de la industria electrónica de Jalisco en la decada de los noventa: el papel de IBM', presentation to CUCSH/COLEF seminar 'Challenges and Perspectives of the Mexican maquiladoras: Local Settings and Global Processes', University Center for Social Sciences and Humanities (CUCSH) and the College of the Northern Frontier (COLEF), Guadalajara, Jalisco, 30–31 October.

Lall, S., 2002a, 'Asian Success Stories: Improving Industrial Competitiveness with and without FDI', UNCTAD-ECLAC regional seminar 'FDI Policies in Latin America', Santiago, Chile, 7–9 January.

Lall, S., 2002b, 'Leveraging FDI to Make the National Economy More Competitive', UNCTAD-ECLAC regional seminar 'FDI Policies in Latin America', Santiago, Chile, 7–9 January.

Lall, S., M. Albaladejo and M. Moreira, 2004, 'Latin American Industrial Competitiveness and the Challenge of Globalization', Inter-American Development Bank, INTAL-ITD Occasional Paper SITI-05.

Lara, A. and J. Carrillo, 2003, 'Globalización tecnológica y coordinación intra-empresa en el sector automotriz: el caso Delphi-México', *Comercio Exterior* (BANCOMEXT, Mexico City), Vol. 53, No. 5 (May), pp.604–16.

Larraín, F., F. López-Calva and A. Rodriguez-Clare, 2001, 'Intel: a Case Study of Foreign Direct Investment in Central America', in Felipe Larraín (ed.), *Economic Development in Central America*, Growth and Internationalization, Vol. I, Cambridge, MA: Harvard University Press, chapter 6.

Lowendahl, H., 2001, 'A Framework for FDI Promotion', *Transnational Corporations*, Vol.10, No.1 (January), pp.1–42.

Lowendahl, H., 2002a, 'Comparative FDI Trends in Latin America and Caribbean: Evidence from FDI Project Data', UNCTAD-ECLAC regional seminar 'FDI Policies in Latin America', Santiago, Chile, 7–9 January.

Lowendahl, H., 2002b, 'The FDI Experience of Western Europe: Lessons for Emerging Markets', UNCTAD-ECLAC regional seminar 'FDI Policies in Latin America', Santiago, Chile, 7–9 January.

Lowendahl, H., 2002c, 'Targeting As a Means to Increase the Impact of National FDI Policy', UNCTAD-ECLAC regional seminar 'FDI Policies in Latin America', Santiago, Chile, 7–9 January.

Mortimore, M., 1997, 'The Asian Challenge to the World Automobile Industry', *Economia Contemporanea*, Vol.2, Economics Institute of the Federal University of Rio de Janeiro, Brazil, pp.67–92.

Mortimore, M., 1998a, 'Corporate Strategies and Regional Integration Schemes Involving Developing Countries: the NAFTA and MERCOSUR Automobile Industries', *Science, Technology and Development* (University of Strathclyde, Glasgow), Vol.6, No.2, pp.1–31.

Mortimore, M., 1998b, 'Getting a Lift: Modernizing Industry by Way of Latin American Integration Schemes. The Example of Automobiles', *Transnational Corporations*, Vol.7, No.2, pp.97–136.

Mortimore, M., 1998c, 'Mexico's TNC-centric Industrialization Process', in R. Kozul-Wright and R. Rowthorn (eds.), *Transnational Corporations and the Global Economy*, London: Macmillan Press.

Mortimore, M., 1999, 'Threadbare: Apparel-based Industrialization in the Caribbean Basin', *CEPAL Review* (Santiago), Vol.67, April, pp.119–36.

Mortimore, M., 2000, 'Corporate Strategies for FDI in the Context of the New Economic Model', *World Development*, Vol.28, No.9, pp.1611–26.

Mortimore, M., 2002a, 'Is Latin America on the FDI Policy Map?', UNCTAD-ECLAC regional seminar 'FDI Policies in Latin America', Santiago, Chile, 7–9 January.

Mortimore, M., 2002b, 'Is There a FDI Policy Goal Trade-Off Between Improved International Competitiveness and Deepened Industrialization? Reasons for Promoting Linkages', UNCTAD-ECLAC regional seminar 'FDI Policies in Latin America', Santiago, Chile, 7–9 January.

Mortimore, M., 2002c, 'When Does Apparel Become a Peril? On the Nature of Industrialization in the Caribbean Basin', in G. Gereffi, D. Spener and J. Bair (eds.), *Free Trade and Uneven Development: the North America Apparel Industry after NAFTA*, Temple University Press.

Mortimore, M., 2003, 'Competitividad ilusoria: el modelo de ensamblaje de prendas de vestir en la cuenca del Caribe', *Comercio Exterior* (Mexico), Vol.53, No.4 (April), pp.306–17.

Mortimore, M., 2004, 'The Impact of TNC Activities on the Development of Latin America and the Caribbean', in D.W. te Velde (ed.), *Foreign Direct Investment, Income Inequality and Poverty. Experiences and Policy Implications*, London: Overseas Development Institute, forthcoming.

Mortimore, M. and F. Barron, 2004, 'Informe sobre la industria automotriz mexicana', *Revista Mexicana de Economía y Finanzas*, forthcoming.

Mortimore, M. and Torben Huss, 1991, 'Encuesta industrial en Mexico', *Comercio Exterior* (BANCOMEXT, Mexico City), Vol.41, No.7 (July), pp.694–703.

Mortimore, M. and W. Peres, 1997, 'Policy Competition for Foreign Direct Investment in the Caribbean Basin: Costa Rica, Jamaica and the Dominican Republic', OECD Project 'Policy Competition and FDI', Paris: OECD Development Center.

Mortimore, M. and W. Peres, 1998, 'Empresas transnacionales e industrialización en economías pequeñas y abiertas: Costa Rica y República Dominicana', in G. Stumpo (ed.), *Empresas transnacionales, procesos de reestructuración industrial y políticas económicas en América Latina*, Buenos Aires: Alianza Editorial Argentina.

Mortimore, M. and Ronney Zamora, 1998, 'La competitividad internacional de la industria de prendas de vestir en Costa Rica', *Desarrollo Productivo*, Vol.46, (LC/G1979).

Mortimore, M., H. Duthoo and J.A. Guerrero, 1995, 'Informe sobre la competitividad internacional de las zonas francas en la República Dominicana', *Desarrollo Productivo*, Vol.42 (LC/G.1866), August.

Mortimore, M., S. Vergara and J. Katz, 2001, 'La competitividad internacional y la política nacional: implicancias para la política de de IED en América Latina', *Desarrollo Productivo*, Vol.107, (LC/L.1586-P), July.

Mytelka, L. and L. Barclay, 2003, 'Using Foreign Investment Strategically for Innovation', Paper presented to the Conference on Understanding FDI-Assisted Economic Development, University of Oslo, 22–25 May.

Oman, C., 2000, *Policy Competition for Foreign Direct Investment: a Study of Competition among Governments to Attract FDI*, Paris: OECD Development Center.

Robles, E., 2000, 'Política de atracción de inversión extranjera directa en Costa Rica', SP/FIEALC/Di No.11-2000, June.

Rodriguez-Clare, A., 2001, 'Costa Rica's Development Strategy based on Human Capital and Technology: How It Got There, the Impact of Intel, and Lessons for other Countries', input for the *Human Development Report of 2001*, New York: UNDP.

Romo, D., 2003, 'Derrames tecnológicas de la inversión extranjera en la industria mexicana', *Comercio Exterior* (BANCOMEXT, Mexico City), Vol.53, No.3 (March), pp.230–43.

Segerstrom, P., 2001, 'Intel Economics', Working Paper, Stockholm School of Economics.

Shiels, D., 2000, 'Site Selection for Intel's Assembly and Test Plant #6', presentation at the MIGA meeting 'South America Investment Promotion Strategy for Heads of Investment Promotion Agencies', Rio de Janeiro, 6–7 May.

Spar, D., 1998, 'Attracting High Technology Investment: Intel's Costa Rica Plant', *FIAS Occasional Paper*, No.11, Washington: World Bank.

UN-ECLAC (United Nations Economic Commission for Latin America and the Caribbean), 2003, *Foreign Investment in Latin America and the Caribbean, 2002*, Santiago: United Nations.

UN-ESCAP (United Nations Economic Commission for Asia and the Pacific), 1994, *Transnational Corporations and Technology Transfer in Export Processing Zones and Science Parks*, New York: UN-ESCAP.

UNCTAD (United Nations Conference on Trade and Development), 2000, *The Competitiveness Challenge: Transnational Corporations and Industry Restructuring in Developing Countries*, New York and Geneva: UNCTAD.

UNCTAD, 2002, *World Investment Report 2002 – TNCs and Export Competitiveness*, Geneva: UNCTAD.

UNCTAD, 2003, *Trade and Development Report*, Geneva: UNCTAD.

USITA, 2003, 'The Road Ahead for the U.S. Auto Industry', International Trade Administration, Washington, DC: U.S. Department of Commerce.

USITC, 2002, 'Industry and Trade Summary: Motor Vehicles', International Trade Commission, Washington, DC: Office of Industries, USITC Publication 3545.

Vicens, L., M. Mortimore and Eddy Martínez, 1998, 'La competitividad internacional de la industria de prendas de vestir de la República Dominicana', *Desarrollo Productivo*, No.45, (LC/G1973).

Wade, R., 1990, *Governing the Market: Economic Theory and the Role of Government in East Asian Industrialization*, Princeton, New Jersey: Princeton University Press.

Using Foreign Investment Strategically for Innovation

LYNN K. MYTELKA and LOU ANNE BARCLAY

The impact of foreign direct investment (FDI) on future opportunities for catching up by developing countries is much greater than its importance as a source of capital. Indeed, transnational corporations presently set the pace for technological change and shape the distribution of production globally. Their influence on the opportunities for learning and innovations and thus growth and development in developing countries is unparalleled. This chapter explores these issues by presenting case studies, which attempt to analyse the manner in which two countries, Trinidad and Tobago and Costa Rica, have been able to use FDI strategically for innovation. It examines the manner in which their governments have situated FDI in a long-term development process whose goals go beyond technological capability building within a single enterprise to the much broader aim of strengthening local innovation capabilities system-wide.

Les répercussions des investissements directs étrangers (IDE) sur les capacités des pays en développement à rattraper leur retard sont de loin supérieures à leur importance en tant que source de capital. En fait, les corporations transnationales indiquent actuellement le rythme du changement technologique et définissent l'ampleur de la distribution de la production à échelle mondiale. Leur influence sur les possiblités d'apprentissage et d'innovation, et donc sur la croissance et le développement dans les pays en développement , est énorme. Cet chapter explore ces thèmes en présentant des études de cas, qui tentent d'analyser la manière dont deux pays, Trinidad et Tobago et Costa Rica, ont réussi à utiliser stratégiquement les IDE dans le sens de l'innovation. Il examine la manière dont leurs gouvernements ont intégré les IDE dans un processus de développement à long terme dont les objectif vont au-delà de l'avance technologique à l'intérieur d'une seule entreprise, pour renforcer les capacités locales d'innovation au sein du système complet.

Lynn K. Mytelka is at the United Nations University, Institute for New Technologies, Maastricht, and Lou Anne Barclay is at the University of the West Indies, Mona, Jamaica. The authors wish to thank Frederique Sachwald and Michael Mortimore for their very helpful comments on an earlier draft of this chapter.

I. INTRODUCTION

Since the 1960s, relationships between states and transnational corporations (TNCs) have alternated between attraction and animosity. The most recent phase began in the 1980s and has been characterised by the progressive liberalisation of investment policies and the extensive use of incentives to attract investors. In a world in which countries, regions and even cities now compete with each other to attract foreign direct investment (FDI), simply having the 'right' 'investment' environment, however, is no longer sufficient. Nor can most developing countries compete successfully in locational tournaments. Competition globally, moreover, is increasingly knowledge-based and driven by a complex matrix of price and innovation factors. The global strategies of foreign investors shape that matrix and the benefits it generates for recipients at different moments in time and across industrial sectors. This combination of factors makes the purposeful attraction of foreign investment and its use for strategic purposes a far more important, though highly uncertain endeavour, especially if measured against long-term, dynamic development goals. One set of such goals to which this chapter pays particular attention are those related to the strengthening of local innovation capabilities system-wide and not merely the incremental process of technological capability building within a single enterprise.

Section II of the chapter charts the difficulties developing countries face in competing for FDI despite the increased openness of national economies to FDI, and it analyses the opportunities and constraints that developing countries have encountered in pursuing traditional catch-up strategies as production became more knowledge-intensive across all economic sectors and innovation-based competition diffused around the world. Section III relates these changes to the growing need for a more systemic framework within which to design development strategies and situate an innovation-oriented approach to foreign direct investment. Sections IV and V apply this framework to analyse the evolution of a natural gas cluster in Trinidad and Tobago and an electronics cluster in Costa Rica. The concluding section summarises these findings and offers guidelines to further stimulate the use of foreign investment strategically to strengthen the national system of innovation.

II. COMPETING FOR FOREIGN DIRECT INVESTMENT

During the 1960s, with the exception of countries that were members of the socialist bloc, foreign direct investment was widely welcomed. Many of the newly independent countries of the Caribbean and Africa, in particular, embraced the views of W. Arthur Lewis on the need to woo foreign investors whose role in industrial development for the domestic market was regarded as central [*Barclay, 2003; Mytelka, 1989*]. The focus of strategies for the attraction of FDI was on 'production' and in that context employment and output were critical indicators of success. In rare cases, small market developing countries, such as Singapore, with an historical tradition as a commercial hub in its region, sought to attract TNCs with an export orientation [*Wong, 2001*].

The dominant position of foreign firms in 'strategic' sectors, their impact on the ability of local firms to compete and the high cost of technology transfer through the TNC led to a brief period in which more restrictive policies towards foreign direct investment were introduced and firms in key sectors were nationalised. But balance of payments problems persisted and the debt crises of the 1970s and 1980s led to the imposition of austerity measures under structural adjustment programmes, the progressive liberalisation of investment policies to bring in new capital and the extensive use of incentives to attract export-oriented investors.

As Table 1 illustrates, from the mid 1980s onward, an increasing number of countries introduced ever more numerous changes favourable to foreign investors. Many of these changes involved incentives.

Developed country governments were particularly active in the use of fiscal incentives for foreign investors. Data covering 26 OECD member countries over the period from the mid 1980s to the early 1990s showed that more of these countries were using a reduction of standard income tax rates, tax holidays, accelerated depreciation, investment/reinvestment allowances and deductions from social security contributions than in the past and many of them had increased the range and importance of such incentives [*UNCTAD, 1995: 292*].

Locational tournaments in which states, provinces and cities competed to attract foreign investors became the rule in automobiles, electronics and other manufacturing and service sectors. In the competition for a Mercedes-Benz plant in the state of Alabama in 1993, for example, some 170 cities and regions across two continents were initially in the running (*Wall Street Journal*, 25 November 1993). Iterative bargaining has also pushed 'attraction prices' up. Automobiles are a case in point. In Brazil, locational tournaments over a three-year period led to incentive packages amounting to an estimated US$54,000 to US$94,000 per job created for VW in 1995 and US$133,000 for Renault and US$340,000 for

TABLE 1
CHANGES IN INVESTMENT REGIMES: 1991–2001 (NUMBER)

	1991	1992	1993	1994	1995	1996	1997	1998	1999	2000	2001
Total countries introducing changes	35	43	57	49	64	65	76	60	63	69	71
Total changes introduced	82	79	102	110	112	114	151	145	140	150	208
Changes more favourable to FDI	80	79	101	108	106	98	135	136	131	147	194
Changes less favourable to FDI	2	–	1	2	6	16	16	9	9	3	14

Source: UNCTAD [*2002: 7*].

Daimler-Benz in 1996. In the same year, Daimler-Benz was attracted to the United States with an incentive package of US$100,000 per job created. Similarly in 1997 Ford received US$420,000 in incentives per job created in India but only US$138,000 per job created in the UK in 1998 [*Mytelka, 1999, 2000; Molot, 2003*]. Such sums make it difficult, if not impossible, for the vast majority of developing countries to compete in this game. Worse still, we have no well-developed methodology to assess the impact of incentive-based investment promotion, including incentives on FDI flow, or the net benefits from such locational tournaments in the host country in terms of economic welfare and development.

Although developing countries are increasingly 'open for business', their attractive potential is nowhere near as great as that of their competitors in the industrialised world. Nor can most developing countries compete with the small number of countries that consistently top the list of FDI host countries in the developing world. From the mid 1980s onward their situation worsened. Between 1986 and 1991, average annual FDI flows amounted to US$159,331 million, only 18.3 per cent of which went to developing countries. Moreover, 48 per cent of this amount went to just five developing countries: Singapore, China, Mexico, Hong Kong and Malaysia while a mere 0.5 per cent went to the least developed countries, a share that has remained fairly constant over the years. In the period 1992–96, the share of developing countries in annual average total FDI inflows of US$261,027 million rose to 34.8 per cent, but so, too, did concentration in a handful of developing countries, the top five of which (China, Mexico, Singapore, Malaysia and Brazil) received 58.2 per cent of the FDI going to developing countries. In the period 1997–2001, average annual FDI flows reached US$897,576 million but the developing country share fell to 23.3 per cent and the top five recipients, China, Hong Kong, Brazil, Mexico and Argentina, garnered 58.8 per cent of this. As the share of reinvested earning and of mergers and acquisitions in FDI inflows rises and TNCs increasingly resort to domestic borrowing, FDI's role in development needs to be rethought [*UNCTAD, 1995, 1997, 1999, 2001, 2002*].

III. INNOVATION, COMPETITIVENESS AND DEVELOPMENT

The inability to compete in attracting foreign investment is matched by the difficulties most developing countries face in using foreign investment strategically for innovation. The need to do so became increasingly more important as the knowledge intensity of production dramatically increased in the last quarter of the twentieth century and innovation-based competition diffused rapidly around the globe. Investments not only in research and development (R and D) but also in other intangibles such as software, design, engineering, training, marketing and management thus came to play a greater role in the production of goods and services. Much of this involved tacit rather than codified knowledge and technological transfer thus increasingly required a conscious effort at learning by doing, by using, by searching and by interacting – a process pioneered in Japanese catch-up strategies and successfully adapted in the first tier newly industrialising economies of South Korea, Taiwan, Hong Kong and Singapore [*Mytelka, 2000*].

The pressure on developing countries just beginning to catch up, however, grew as the knowledge intensity of production gradually extended beyond the high-technology sectors to reshape a broad spectrum of traditional industries from the shrimp and salmon fisheries in the Philippines and Chile, the forestry and flower enterprises in Kenya and Colombia, to the furniture, textile and clothing firms of Taiwan and Thailand. Sustainability of comparative advantage based solely on the existence of location-specific raw materials or cheap labour began to erode and competitive advantages changed rapidly [*Ernst et al., 1998*]. Despite the historical record in the newly industrialised countries which shows that importing foreign technology and creating it locally are not alternatives but complements, most developing countries have not kept up in building the knowledge-based capabilities needed to compete. Learning through reverse engineering, domestic content requirements and procurement rules that had proved so useful in earlier catch-up strategies, moreover, was increasingly compromised by efforts to adopt uniform global rules governing trade, investment and intellectual property.

This created a new challenge for developing country firms that had caught up, to keep up as competitive conditions changed. The need to strengthen knowledge and information flows by building linkages within the domestic innovation system and with partners abroad now became evident. These changes gave rise to a growing interest in the application of an innovation system framework to development planning and policy-making.

A system of innovation can be defined as a network of economic agents, together with the institutions and policies that influence their innovative behaviour and performance [*Nelson, 1993; Nelson and Winter, 1982, Lundvall, 1992*]. Underlying the system of innovation approach is an understanding of innovation as an interactive process in which enterprises in interaction with each other and supported by institutions and a wide range of organisations play a key role in bringing new products, new processes and new forms of organisation into economic use. Conceptually, the innovation system approach acknowledges the role of policies, whether tacit or explicit, in setting the parameters within which these actors make decisions about learning and innovation and it distinguishes 'organisations' such as universities, public sector research bodies, science councils and firms, from 'institutions', understood as 'sets of common habits, routines, established practices, rules or laws that regulate the relations and interactions between individuals and groups' [*Edquist, 1997: 7*].

These '...prescribe behavioral roles, constrain activity and shape expectations' [*Storper, 1998: 24*].

The utility of this distinction is threefold. First, it draws attention to the fact that simply identifying the existence of key actors co-located within a geographical space, does not predict their interaction. Actor competences, habits and practices with respect to three of the key elements that underlie an innovation process – linkages, investment and learning – are critical in determining the nature and extensiveness of their interactions [*Mytelka, 2000*].

Second, from a policy perspective, the distinction between organisations and institutions builds awareness of the need to look more carefully at the historical specificities of these habits, practices and institutions, their learned nature and the possibility that at least some of these will become less relevant as conditions change over time. Continuous monitoring of policy dynamics generated by the interaction between policies and the varied habits and practices of actors in the system, will thus be of importance in fine-tuning policies for maximum impact. So, too, will learning and unlearning on the part of all actors, firms and policy-makers, if a system is to evolve in response to new challenges.

Third, it redirects attention towards the flows of knowledge and information that are at the heart of an innovation system. Although these may, on occasion, move along a linear path from the 'supply' of research to products in the market, more often they are multidirectional and link a wider set of actors than those located along the value chain. Which actors other than suppliers and clients will be critical to a given innovation process cannot always be known a priori and they are likely to be sector specific. So, while it is important to have an overview of the 'national' system of innovation, sector specificity – in industrial structure and technological terms – and the particular habits and practices of actors in that sector will be major factors in shaping policy dynamics and policy impacts. From an innovation system approach, perhaps the greatest contribution that FDI can make to development, therefore, is less the capital, than the knowledge that it brings and the role it plays in networking and interacting within the local system. Government's vision, its ability to situate FDI within the context of the country's development goals and target the right TNCs are thus essential.

But simply attracting a TNC to locate within the geographical confines of a particular country does not lead to an automatic flow of knowledge. TNC affiliates are, after all, parts of a very different network and their behaviour is shaped by other institutional referents and strategies. Innovative policy-making, however, has a role to play in reshaping the parameters within which the decisions of foreign affiliates are made. Similarly, while there may be an educational threshold below which the ability of local firms to absorb and use new information and knowledge is rendered more difficult, as a recent OECD study concluded, the overall benefits of FDI critically depend upon host country policies [*OECD, 2002: 9*]. In a developing country context, therefore, along with strategic targeting, complementary policies aimed at strengthening the linkages and knowledge flows that support a process of innovation will be needed. In so doing, a basis is laid both for cluster growth and for the progressive transformation of a cluster of co-located actors into an innovation system.

To a large extent analyses of foreign direct investment and its impact on development have not kept pace with the growing importance attributed in the innovation literature to learning to learn, to innovate and to collaborate. In the dominant approach, derived from the pioneering work of Bloomstrom, Caves and Globerman, among others, technological change is narrowly conceptualised in terms of production rather than innovation and measures technological spillover as growth in labour productivity, often derived simply from investments in new machinery and equipment that are not necessarily labour augmenting, and less frequently measured as increases in domestic value added or in labour skills. With rare exceptions, the production-oriented approach viewed FDI from a short-term perspective, initially as an addition to employment and output and later as the principal channel for manufactured exports. This approach, captured in the notion of 'FDI Assisted Development', is passive and capability building, and, when it is mentioned at all, is dealt with in static terms as codified knowledge and routine operating practices within a firm.

In a similar vein, much of the literature dealing with the attraction of FDI in the initial period of liberalisation, focused simply on maximising the quantity of foreign investment received by developing countries in the throes of debt crises and its role in the privatisation of 'inefficient state owned firms' and in exports. Assessments of the contributions sought from foreign investors have continued to be made primarily in terms of capital, employment and exports with only an occasional reference to the role of TNCs in international technology transfer [*Lall, 2002: 52*]. Even here, however, the 'learning' component from a dynamic systems perspective is missing and the approach taken remains short term and production-oriented.

At the regional level, FDI attraction strategies have overwhelmingly emphasised the potential employment benefits and only recently has attention been focused on the way in which supply-chain development contributes to this process [*Phelps et al., 1998; Mytelka, 2000; UNCTAD, 2001*]. This literature adds to earlier quantitative approaches to direct foreign investment targeted efforts to attract quality investment, where the latter is understood in two senses: investment that induces employment creation through local linkages and investment in high-tech industries. Once again, however, learning and innovation are not among the explicit goals of FDI promotion policies.

Neither production-oriented nor export-oriented FDI strategies and the policies that flow from them are sufficient today. Still less so is the categorisation of investment policies in terms of three generations – opening up to FDI, active marketing of a location to FDI through an investment promotion agency (IPA) and a more focused programme of targeting only a subset of TNCs – developed by UNCTAD [2002]. Missing from such approaches is a strategic development dimension as well as the need for continuous system-wide learning, linkages and skills upgrading to facilitate adaptation and innovation as competitive conditions change. In this chapter, therefore, we argue for a reconceptualisation of FDI within a more dynamic development perspective focused on learning, linkages and innovation. In this conceptualisation, government plays a more pro-active role than merely 'targeting' firms for short-term job creation or exports. Instead FDI is situated within a longer term development strategy whose objectives go beyond the building of technological capability within a single enterprise or the narrow view of 'technological spillovers' in terms of productivity growth and to the broader goal of strengthening local innovation capabilities system-wide. Table 2 summarises the above discussion and provides a schematic representation of the conceptual bases of the strategies, policy objectives and capability-building focus that differentiate production-oriented, export-oriented and innovation-oriented approaches to FDI.

The next two sections will address these issues through case studies of the evolution of a natural gas cluster in Trinidad and Tobago and an electronics cluster

TABLE 2
DIFFERENTIATING INNOVATION-ORIENTED FDI STRATEGIES AND POLICIES

	Production-oriented	Export-oriented	Innovation-oriented
FDI strategy	Passive, 'open for business', adoption of a favourable investment regime; promotional incentives to 'attract' but not 'orient' FDI	Targeted attraction strategy: targeting companies for export potential; high level of pre-investment and after care service	FDI as part of a broader development strategy. Pro-active: balancing of targeting and complementary policies designed to stimulate learning, upgrading and technology spillover
FDI policy objectives	Focus on short-term goals of increasing domestic manufacturing output and employment	Focus on short-term goals of increasing employment through exports; little attention to technological change processes in keeping-up as competitive conditions change	Longer term dynamic perspective on learning and innovation within the firm and broader technology spillover across the sector
Capability building	Learning to operate plants and production processes; static focus on codified knowledge and routine practices	Learning to meet quality standards and delivery times. Develop the flexibility and skills to deal with product and process changes	Learning to innovate by creating linkages to the local knowledge base and partnerships for continuous upgrading

in Costa Rica. These two sectors have attracted considerable foreign investment to developing countries in the 1990s. Both are believed to offer opportunities for the growth of clusters through sub-contracting and service provision as well as the stimulus for knowledge-flows and skills upgrading which support the strengthening of local innovation practices and processes. As core activities in these sectors are capital intensive and based on proprietary knowledge, there are particular advantages for innovation system building to be gained by targeting appropriate anchor investors. But it is important to recognise that natural gas, its compression, liquefaction and many of its downstream usages, are more amenable to site specificity and longevity than the semiconductor industry, which is the anchor investment in the emerging electronics cluster in Costa Rica.

Both Trinidad and Tobago and Costa Rica are small, stable, developing countries with relatively well-educated populations, and quite similar levels of gross domestic product (GDP) per capita and manufactured exports (Table 3). Inflows of foreign direct investment, however, have grown more rapidly in Trinidad and Tobago over the 1990s than in Costa Rica, despite the latter's success in attracting Intel in this period. The stock of FDI, which stood at US$2,093 million in 1990 had thus risen to US$7,825 million in 2001 in Trinidad and Tobago and FDI flows as a per cent of gross fixed capital formation (GFCF), which had annually averaged 33.8 per cent in the period 1990–95 rose to 48.3 per cent in 1996–2000. In contrast, although the stock of FDI in Costa Rica, amounting to US$1,447 million in 1990, rose to US$5,654 million in 2001, there has been only a small increase in average annual FDI flows as a per cent of GFCF: 14.8 per cent in the years 1996–2000, up from 13.8 per cent in the previous five-year period (Table 3).

TABLE 3

SIZE AND STRUCTURE OF THE ECONOMY IN TRINIDAD AND TOBAGO AND COSTA RICA

Indicators	Trinidad and Tobago	Costa Rica
1. Population (1999)	1.3 million	3.9 million
2. Urban population (%) 1999	73.6	47.6
3. GDP (1999) (US$)	6.9 billion	15.1 billion
4. GDP per capita (1999) (US$)	8176	8860
5. Manufactured exports as a % of merchandise exports	27	27
6. Public education expenditure as a % of GNP (1995–97)	4.4	5.4
7. Adult literacy (15 years and above) (1999)	93.5	95.5
8. Tertiary education as a % of total (1995–97)	13.3	28.3
9. Human Development Index	49 (medium)	41 (high)
10. FDI flows: average 1990–95 (US$)	269 million	241 million
11. FDI flows: average 1996–2001 (US$)	705 million	487 million

Sources: Indicators 1–9, UNDP [*2001: 10, 11*]; UNCTAD [*2002*].

IV. TRINIDAD AND TOBAGO'S NATURAL GAS CLUSTER

FDI has played a strategic role in the economic development of Trinidad and Tobago since the immediate post independence period (1958–73). During this early period, the government implemented a strategy of passively relying on FDI for industrialisation, which led to little economic transformation. However, in response to the socio-economic and political crisis of the early 1970s, it reversed its earlier approach to foreign investment and sought to become the prime mover in the economy. This policy reversal came at an opportune moment. The unprecedented increases in oil prices in 1973/74 and again in 1979/80 coincided with significant discoveries of oil off Trinidad's east coast.

Awash with oil windfalls, the government, in its new role as prime mover in the economy, expanded the social and economic infrastructure and established a foundation for industries that were intensive in their use of natural gas. Five gas-based projects in iron and steel, ammonia, methanol and urea were established in the period from 1977 to 1984. All were located in the government-built Point Lisas Industrial Estate,[1] and all were export-oriented.

The oil boom years were a golden opportunity for Trinidad and Tobago to use the foreign investment attracted to this new sector to build a system of innovation in the natural gas sector, but this was not done. Economic, technological management and institutional factors contributed to this failure.

Planning and implementation of these five export-oriented industrial projects were entrusted to a newly created, *ad hoc* body, the Coordinating Task Force (CTF), which possessed a meagre complement of five staff members and a five-member board.[2] Apart from the organisational inefficiency arising from the small size of such an important body, the CTF co-ordinated little with Trinidad and Tobago's main industrial promotion agency, the Industrial Development Corporation (IDC). The IDC, which had been created in 1958 to administer the government's system of industrial incentives, thus persisted in nurturing the development of import-substituting activities; expending more than 50 per cent of its incentives on consumer durables, and developing few industries based on the downstream activities of the energy-intensive projects. Domestic institutions such as the Caribbean Industrial Research Institute (CARIRI) and the National Institute for Higher Education (NIHERST), moreover, maintained their existing focus on small-scale research exercises in animal feed and plant breeding, and the provision of testing and information services for the agro industry [*Barclay, 1990*].

Opportunities were also missed for strengthening competencies in a natural gas-based innovation system over the project cycle. Despite the apparent awareness of planners of the need for technological skills upgrading at the project planning and later stages, no detailed, comprehensive approach to technology policy planning was attempted. Thus, for example, neither the local university nor the local technical and vocational institutes offered special training programmes for this industry. Instead most of the local work-force employed in methanol and ammonia production were drawn from the oil industry and the US-owned fertiliser company, Federation Chemicals, that was operating in the country at this time. Further, little attempt was made to carefully define the areas in which such capability needed to be built over the long term, and within this context, the specific technologies that the foreign firms could contribute [*Farrell, 1987*].

Over the following years, the demand and price forecasts on which several of these investment decisions were made, notably in the case of ammonia, proved to be unrealistic. Technical problems related to plant operations, including poor maintenance of machinery and equipment, together with substantial time and cost overruns, moreover, meant that three years post start-up, the steel plant was not yet producing at design capacity. Further, its initial exports to the United States were hit with anti-dumping charges. The collapse of the international oil market, the decline in domestic oil production, coupled with economic mismanagement then pushed the economy into a recession that lasted for seven years.

It was during this recessionary period that the government was compelled to approach the international lending agencies for financing. As part of its loan conditionalities, it entered into stabilisation and structural adjustment programmes. The state's role in economic development was now redefined as one of policy-maker and regulator, with the private sector given the task of economic transformation.

Currently, Trinidad and Tobago is in a new phase of its relationship with transnational firms. It is described as one of the most sought out locations for energy-related activities in the Western hemisphere, and investments in this sector have risen dramatically. It presently has 18 foreign firms involved in primary production in its natural gas industry (see Appendix One).

Significantly, none of the earlier institutions created for industrialisation are at present actively involved in formulating and implementing policy for the natural gas industry.[3] Instead four bodies, to varying degrees, fulfil this function. The Natural Gas Export Task Force, created in 2002 as a subcommittee of the Energy Committee chaired by the Prime Minister, has responsibility for the liquefied natural gas (LNG) projects, the gas pipeline to the Caribbean and the possible introduction of new gas technologies into the country. The Ministry of Energy itself grants licenses for oil and gas exploration. The Tourism and Industrial Development Corporation (TIDCO), created in 1994 from the merger of the IDC, the Export Development Corporation, and the Tourism Development Association, plays an indirect role in the natural gas industry. It processes applications for investment incentives offered to the foreign investors. Lastly, the National Gas Company (NGC), created in 1975, is the main state institution involved in the purchase, transportation and sale of natural gas. It is also the main institution that carries out the targeted promotion of the gas industry to the foreign investor, short-listing firms that have expressed interest in projects developed by its Business Development Division.

Foreign firms operating in this industry enjoy a fairly standardised package of investment incentives, including special incentives for highly capital-intensive enterprises. They also benefit from the innovative gas-pricing regime offered by the NGC since 1989. The price of gas offered to the firm varies with the market price for its product. Thus, when the product market price is depressed, the natural gas price automatically declines. Conversely, when the market price increases, the natural gas price rises [Barclay, 2000]. This gas-pricing regime has been especially beneficial to the ammonia and methanol producers, which are producing commodities. It allows them to earn profits even in depressed market conditions.

While the government has a clear strategy for attracting targeted firms to its natural gas industry, there appears to be no clearly articulated policies for the role that these firms can and will play in enhancing the natural gas-based innovation system. This is largely a result of the discontinuities in institutional building, which have plagued Trinidad and Tobago since its immediate post independence period. The discontinuities in institutional building have resulted in a failure to provide for the systemic thinking, policy consistency and long-term goal setting which make it possible to envisage the differential policy and policy sequencing that are tailored to the local natural gas industry. Nonetheless, there appear to be two policies that may serve to potentially allow the foreign firm to play a greater role in the development of the natural gas-based system of innovation.

One is the imposition of local content requirements. This policy is implemented on a contract-by-contract basis. However, evidence of its use or of the existence of institutions that monitor the foreign firm's adherence to local content requirements on an ongoing basis is spotty. Local content concerns were addressed, for example, during the construction phase of the LNG and methanol projects. In the former, no firm targets seem to have been established and the team of officials appointed to monitor local requirements has already been disbanded. However, in the present World Trade Organisation-inspired environment, policy-makers have shifted to addressing this issue by attempting to increase the capabilities of local engineering and construction firms. Indeed, it seems that plans are afoot to enhance the capabilities of local firms not only at the civil engineering stage, but also inter alia at the pre- and post-construction stage. Yet, there seems to be no clearly articulated role for the foreign firm in these plans.

The second policy with a potential role in strengthening a natural gas-based system of innovation is in human resource development. Two new training institutes were expressly created to deal with what was regarded as a critical skill shortage. These are the National Energy Skills Centre (NESC), a non-profit foundation for craft training, incorporated in 1997 and its counterpart organisation, the Trinidad and Tobago Institute of Technology (TTIT) established in 2001 to build skills at the middle and upper levels of the industry. The latter operates as a corporate university and offers a one-year Certificate course in Process Operations, a two-year Diploma in Technology with a focus on industrial engineering disciplines, and a four-year Bachelor of Applied Technology. The NESC has graduated more than 2000 craftsmen and the TTIT currently has an enrolment of more than 1,200 students. Both of these institutes have been funded, in part, by the private and public firms operating in Trinidad's natural gas industry. These funds are provided on a voluntary basis. Foreign firms have also provided equipment, conducted training and participated in curriculum development at these institutes, and they employ the students from the TTIT under its apprenticeship programme.

All of the firms interviewed for this study have intensively used the training programmes offered by the TTIT. In addition, they have also attempted to enhance the skills of their local work-force by offering comprehensive training programmes that are conducted locally and abroad. It should be noted, however, that courses at the TTIT and those given elsewhere are overwhelmingly aimed at developing the skills needed to manage and operate process plants such as ammonia, methanol and LNG. Yet, Trinidad and Tobago already possesses a cadre of workers who have the capability to operate and manage these process plants. Many of these are technical and professional personnel trained in the comprehensive training programmes offered at the petrochemical firms in Trinidad when these were still state owned, or graduates from the apprenticeship programmes offered by the oil multinationals, Shell and Texaco, which formerly operated in the country [Barclay, 2000; Energy Correspondent, 2002b]. Hence, in this respect, the TTIT and the foreign firms are not extending the range of technical and managerial capabilities that exist in the natural gas industry of Trinidad and Tobago.

The range of activities carried out in Trinidad's energy sector, however, is much greater than operating and managing process plants. The increase in investments in the natural gas industry has been accompanied by a surge in gas and oil exploration. Thus, the development of skills in marine exploration and production technologies urgently needs to be addressed [Energy Correspondent, 2002a]. Further, the country needs to develop the capabilities to carry out activities at the pre-construction phase such as plant and engineering design (equipment selection and specification, use of advanced simulation and optimisation design software); planning and managing large-scale projects during the engineering, procurement and construction (EPC) phase; and at the post-construction phase including retrofit design (for plant upgrade in terms of increased productivity, de-bottlenecking and trouble shooting) and international commodity marketing and shipping logistics [Furlonge, 2002].

Indeed, the foreign firms in tandem with the TTIT are developing what has been described as a 'static technological capability' in the gas-based industry. These are the skills required for the maintenance of a given system. The nationals possess the technologies that permit them to successfully carry out certain routine tasks in a more or less fixed fashion and with more or less given equipment. They are not developing a 'dynamic technological capability' which consists of the skills needed for the long-term development of the industry. The nationals do not possess the complex set of technologies (identified above) that are needed to run the industry successfully over time, innovating when necessary to solve its problems [*Farrell, 1987*].

It is thus ironic that the country appears to be losing critical capabilities in petrochemical marketing. Trinidad has developed a nascent ability to market petrochemicals. Locals performed this function at the former state-owned petrochemical companies. However, when the Petrochemical Company of Saskatchewan (PCS) acquired the privatised ammonia and urea companies from its first owner, Arcadian Company, in 1995, it moved the marketing activities to its sister company, PCS Sales. Some of the nationals who worked in this department were also relocated to this company in Chicago, but several were made redundant.

With regard to the building of industrial research capabilities in the natural gas industry, currently Trinidad and Tobago has only two candidates: CARIRI, whose initial research focus was agriculture, and the Engineering Institute of the Faculty of Engineering. Over the past five years, the former has developed substantial capabilities in metallurgic testing for all materials used in the construction of the LNG, methanol and ammonia plants, and testing capabilities for the quality of the gas in petrochemical plants. The quality of their work is recognised by their clients, but the range of their service is limited and their ability to work quickly has been criticised. Since 1986, CARIRI has increasingly been required to finance its operational costs and in the small local market, this has been a problem. With low salary levels, CARIRI has thus been unable to hire and retain qualified and experienced staff and staff levels are currently one-half of what they were in 1984. Funding difficulties extend to the hiring of personnel with specialised skills in areas such as metallurgy or microbiology and to the purchase of state-of-the art equipment.[4] Given the tendency of TNCs to locate higher value-added activities such as research and development in advanced, developed countries that possess *inter alia* the requisite science and technology infrastructure, the government's present posture towards financing the operations of CARIRI appears to be short-sighted.

Trinidad and Tobago's only other candidate for R and D activities of relevance to the natural gas industry is the Engineering Institute, established in 1994 with initial funding from the NGC. Only one of its departments, however, has undertaken research of relevance to the needs of the natural gas industry, and only three of its listed clients are drawn from that sector. More importantly, it seems that the Institute suffers from a problem of visibility since few of the managers interviewed were aware of its existence. The technologies used for the production of petrochemicals such as ammonia, methanol and, to some extent, LNG are relatively mature, codified, widely disseminated and with well-defined property rights. More sophisticated downstream products are not currently being produced in Trinidad and Tobago, thus limiting the incentive for R and D by organisations such as the Engineering Institute in these areas.

The only research activity undertaken by firms in this country is the tailoring of the licensed technology and the plant to make them more compatible with local conditions. It seems that the local firm CL Financial is actively engaged in this process. Its engineers are involved at the start of the project, working with the British engineering and construction company Davy Corporation and the US construction firm Kellogg Brown & Root. They incorporate those safety and operability elements into the firm's methanol plants, which demonstrably have worked well in the Trinidadian environment. This competence, acquired over the past ten years, has significantly enhanced the capabilities of the local firm. However, it has not been transformed into an industry-wide capability. There are two reasons for this. First, the other methanol plants – Titan Methanol and Atlas Methanol – use a different process technology from the plants owned by CL Financial. These facilities employ the low-pressure process technology licensed from the German firm Lurgi Oel Gas Chemie GmbH, while the plants owned by CL Financial use the licensed ICI low-pressure process technology. The second point relates to the level of 'technological underdevelopment' of the local science and technological institutions [*Girvan, 1979*]. As noted earlier, these institutions have limited links with firms operating in this industry. As a result, they are totally left out of this process of technological adaptation. They are thus unable to capture and disseminate the positive externalities arising from CL Financial's activities.

At the core of an innovation system is the supplier–client relationship. In Trinidad and Tobago's natural gas industry, there are eight primary downstream firms producing ammonia, methanol and LNG. In the liquefaction process of LNG production, and in the liquid removal process of gas processing done by Phoenix Park Gas Processors Limited, two natural gas liquids – propane and butane – are produced. These natural gas liquids, together with the three identified above, are exported. However, a wide range of products such as caprolactam, vinyl acetate and polyethylene could be made from these petrochemicals. Nonetheless, further downstream activity in the petrochemical industry of Trinidad and Tobago is negligible. There is only one firm involved in the downstream processing of methanol produced in CL Financial's plants. This is the state-owned oil company, the Petroleum Company of Trinidad and Tobago

Limited (PETROTRIN), which began the production of methyl tertiary butyl ether (MTBE) in 1997.

Several factors limit the further development of the downstream industry in the country. First is that of costs. The petrochemical industry is characterised by large, lumpy investments with long gestation periods. Moreover, the majority of the costs are incurred at the start of the project planning and plant construction. The size of the initial investment costs and the lumpiness of this investment thus limit the extent to which small domestic firms could participate in the industry [*Mytelka, 1979*]. Further, in some cases, economic considerations weigh against the local development of certain types of downstream activity. For example, the production of caprolactam – used for the manufacturing of nylon – is usually made from more than one major primary product, namely ammonia and cyclohexane; the latter is not produced locally. The investor will thus have to import cyclohexane, which could affect the viability of the investment. In addition, in the case of ethylene, which is a critical chemical building block, there is an insufficient quantity of ethane produced locally for a world-scale, economically sized plant.[5] Finally, the corporate strategy of the foreign firms operating in this industry limits the development of further downstream activity. The primary motive for foreign petrochemical firms locating production in Trinidad is its competitively priced natural gas. These firms are producing bulk commodities for which they are able to achieve economies of scale in shipping. However, it is difficult for them to achieve economies of scale in the shipment of certain secondary products. It is cheaper to produce these downstream products closer to their end-consumer market or in other processing facilities [*Furlonge, 2002: 14*].

Given the above, it is unsurprising that both the local and foreign investor are not actively engaged in further downstream activity in Trinidad and Tobago. Several commentators note that this activity will only emerge if the government assumes a more pro-active role in its development [*e.g.,Furlonge, 2002*]. It was suggested that the government should modify its existing investment incentive programme to better target foreign firms to these activities. In addition, it is believed that government could catalyse the growth of these activities by making equity investments. Indeed, the emergence of the primary petrochemical industry was a result of such investments. Hopes are now being pinned on the introduction of an ethylene plant in the country, which would foster the further growth of the local plastics industry.

Although Trinidad's downstream activity is practically non-existent, it still possesses a small number of firms that provide supporting services for the primary producers in the natural gas industry. The Point Lisas Industrial Estate houses roughly 75 such firms. The services offered by these companies range from the instrumentation for maintenance and repair of electronic equipment to janitorial services. A group of these firms provide support services to the primary petrochemical firms on an ongoing basis and this study examined four of these. Two are engineering firms and the others managers and operators of process plants.

The engineering firms have been operating in Trinidad and Tobago for the past 30 years. One is a mechanical engineering company, which has a staff of 300, of whom 200 are craftsmen. This firm offers low-tier project management services. Its core activities include the design, fabrication and installation of storage tanks, pressure vessels, structural steel and piping. It is also involved in the fabrication and laying of sub-terrain and undersea pipelines, and the installation of process plants. The other firm boasts a staff complement of 350 workers, 70 per cent of whom are engineers, technicians and craftsmen. This structural engineering company specialises in the design, fabrication and erection of steel structures and other structural components.

By contrast, the other two firms studied are of a more recent vintage. Interestingly enough, the impetus for their development came from executives at the local firm CL Financial. They actively encouraged the development of the first locally owned company in the country that provides plant management services to firms in the petrochemical industry. This is the Process Plant Services Company, established in 1992. This company initially operated and managed all of CL Financial's methanol plants. With a staff of 75, it now operates and manages the Titan Methanol plant. The other firm, which is a joint venture between CL Financial and a local company, was incorporated in 1999. This company, Industrial Plant Services Limited, has a staff of 344. It offers a range of services to potential clients, which includes project management, pre-feasibility studies, front-end engineering, and plant commissioning. This company presently manages and operates all the petrochemical plants owned by CL Financial in Trinidad and Tobago.

The local support firms receive little technical or managerial assistance from the foreign primary petrochemical producers but have close links to foreign construction and engineering firms with which they have formed a variety of alliances to secure technological expertise in areas in which they are deficient. For example, the mechanical engineering firm formed an alliance with one foreign firm during the construction of the three LNG plants to access specialised technology needed for pipe and equipment installation. Similarly, there seem to be informal arrangements for the training of workers in new techniques. The mechanical engineering firm benefited from a welding programme conducted by a US construction firm during the construction of the ammonia plant.

Likewise, the engineering firms appeared to receive only limited support from foreign firms in enhancing their capabilities in plant maintenance. Only one primary producer, PCS Nitrogen, provides training related to the safety and repair of machinery to these firms on a continuous basis. Thus, local support firms are only involved in routine maintenance of plant and equipment, while more specialised maintenance activities are performed by foreign equipment vendors. Some of the primary petrochemical producers, moreover, appear to be internalising more of the maintenance functions. Atlantic LNG, for example, has developed a specially trained 'maintenance in-house team'.

Given the limited support that the local support firms, specifically the local engineering firms, receive from the primary petrochemical producers and other foreign firms operating in the country, it is surprising that the government has no active policies for their development. The only incentive that is provided to these firms is the general investment incentive regime, which is offered to all local manufacturing firms. However, the duty-free concession on imported equipment that was traditionally enjoyed by these firms, has since become obsolete with the recent implementation of trade liberalisation.

There appear to be recent moves to reformulate the policies that guide the development of the natural gas industry in Trinidad and Tobago. As part of their rethinking of local content regulations, policy-makers are focusing not only on pre-construction, but also on construction and post-construction activities; and TIDCO, the local investment promotion agency, is examining its investment incentive regime with the aim of developing one that is more effective in promoting local engineering capabilities. In a similar vein, the NGC is attempting to stimulate the development of engineering firms by, for example, fabricating and installing a marine platform. It is believed that this activity will have a demonstration effect on local support firms. Although these policies are still at their embryonic stage, it is noticeable that they have not attempted to address the role of the foreign firm in the development of the country's natural gas-based innovation system. Indeed, despite over 20 years of production in the natural gas industry, the foreign investors neither on their own nor stimulated by a coherent set of development policies, can be said to have contributed in a significant way to building a natural gas-based system of innovation in Trinidad and Tobago.

V. COSTA RICA'S ELECTRONICS CLUSTER

Costa Rica has a relatively long history of political stability,[6] high educational attainment, environmental protection[7] and public health care.[8] Over the past three decades, these factors contributed to shaping a policy process that is characterised by a long-term, strategic vision, notably with respect to its natural environment, the use of targeted state intervention to enhance social welfare and stimulate the application of technology in agriculture and industrial production and more recently a conscious process of learning through linkages to foreign firms and to foreign and local universities. These policy-making practices, 'institutions' in our systems sense, have a bearing on the approach that diverse Costa Rican governments have taken towards foreign investment, notably with regard to goal setting, to learning and to technological capacity-building and upgrading.

This does not mean that Costa Rica has mastered the art of using foreign investment strategically for innovation, but, more than others, Costa Rican policy-makers seem to understand the need for doing so and in a number of small ways have attempted to move down this path.

In 1989, Costa Rica began its first foray into high-tech diversification[9] with the creation of INBio, the National Biodiversity Institute, a non-governmental, non-profit association, whose mission was to 'promote awareness of the value of biodiversity and thereby achieve its conservation and use it to improve the quality of life'. In 1991, INBio developed the concept and practice of 'bioprospecting' as 'one of the answers to the need of using, in a sustainable way, Costa Rican biodiversity to benefit society' [Cabrera, 2001]. The forest sector was thus reconceptualised as a 'system' of production – with backward linkages to the identification of inputs into pharmaceuticals and agriculture and to training in science and sustainability and forward linkages to ecotourism – if not yet fully as a system of innovation.

Since then, through a large number of partnerships with transnational corporations, local and foreign universities, INBio has learned to take a long-term strategic planning perspective, to negotiate effectively with its foreign partners and to build capacity in bioprospecting, notably in taxonomy, ecology, ecochemistry, molecular biology and the isolation and characterisation of genes. In 1999 INBio signed an agreement with the Inter-American Development Bank for technical co-operation to support the development of the use of biodiversity by small local firms and six projects were identified. This may be the beginning of a transformation of the forest-based system of production into a broader and more dynamic biopharmaceutical innovation system. There is still a long way to go, however, before a full innovation system is in place that permits the identification of promising substances in nature, their complete analysis and testing (through enzymatic bioassays, for example), their reproduction through chemical synthesis or genetic engineering and their production as a drug. Nonetheless, the INBio experience has influenced Costa Rican views with regard to strategic, long-term goal setting and to learning from foreign partners and investors.

It is within this context that the Costa Rican government decided to undertake a second process of high-tech diversification, this time into electronics. From the outset, the sector was broadly reconceptualised in terms of a wider system of production that could become competitive and cost effective, if not innovative, over time. CINDE, the Coalicion Costarricense de Iniciativas para el Desarrollo, a quasi private, non-profit organisation, is both the principal agency co-ordinating investment promotion activities in Costa Rica and an actor in the local development initiatives. 'In the late 1980s CINDE had explicitly decided to follow a focused strategy of attraction, marketing itself to a specific group of potential investors rather than spreading its fairly limited resources across a hodgepodge of ambiguous leads' [Spar, 1998: 8]. Initially it focused mainly on textiles and clothing but, as wage levels rose, by the early 1990s, it had shifted to targeting electronics firms. Ten such firms,[10] mostly American owned, were thus already in Costa Rica when CINDE decided to target Intel and a number of these, RICR (Reliability) and Motorola, for example, have since established links with that firm while others have expanded production.

Many believe that a small country does not have the created assets, market size or incentive clout to attract a large anchor investor in this field, but Costa Rica proved otherwise. Most critical in doing so were the persistence of CINDE in working to attract Intel and then to overcome perceived obstacles[11] to the making of a major investment in a small country. The latter was accomplished through close and co-ordinated links with government though few resources were dedicated exclusively to Intel and all changes made to tax policies, educational programmes or infrastructure were generalised to other foreign investors and in some cases to local firms as well.[12]

In November 1996, Intel announced that it would invest US$300 million in an assembly and testing plant for Pentium II chips. By December 1999 it had invested close to US$390 million. The additional investment resulted from a decision to upgrade to the next generation product, Pentium III. Intel's investment transformed the composition and value of Costa Rica's exports,[13] added several points to the Costa Rican growth rate in 1998 and 1999 and contributed 2,217 jobs in direct employment [*UNCTAD, 2002: 167–8; UNDP, 2001: 81*]. Several of the electronics firms that had located in Costa Rica prior to the arrival of Intel saw their sales and employment grow dramatically [*Monge, 2003: 10*].

Beyond these classic 'contributions' and in contrast to the case of Trinidad and Tobago, there are also some signs that the Intel investment has had a small but positive impact on cluster growth, learning and innovation.

In an industry known for its short product life cycle, the rapid upgrading to a new product generation reflects well on the careful targeting of an investor known to put down roots and to reinvest. This meant that Costa Rica might be able to use an Intel investment as the core of a new cluster, provided that a number of complementary policies were put in place to develop local capabilities.

One set of capabilities lay in the educational and training area. Here close linkages between Intel and the Instituto Tecnologico de Costa Rica (ITCR) in the field of engineering and technical training were particularly important. The ITCR was granted 'Intel Associate' status which provided it with opportunities to seek financial support from Intel in the development of new programmes for technical training and the expansion in the number of places for engineering students. This boosted enrolment in engineering 'from 577 in the first quarter of 1997 to 874 in the year 2000' [*Larrain et al., 2000: 23*] thus avoiding the problem of heightened competition for scarce knowledge resources encountered by local firms in other small countries and regions.

Linkage capabilities as a vehicle for learning is also a leitmotif of the innovation school. During its first two years of operation, Intel attracted more than ten new electronics companies and is believed to have developed a network of more than 200 domestic suppliers. Appendix Two provides a list of Intel's main suppliers of electronics and other products and services [*Monge, 2003*]. In this connection, it should be remembered that logistical factors such as speed to market, market access and transportation costs were important considerations in Intel's decision to expand abroad. Normally these functions are performed by Intel's preferred suppliers. In Costa Rica, however, a 'local customs broker and airfreight forwarder firm – with a regional position in the market – established alliances with another local firm and a worldwide provider ... to manage high speed inventory, deliver sales orders to Intel customers and support ... distribution-related services' [*Monge, 2003: 17*].

As in the Trinidad and Tobago case, most of these are low-skilled manufacturing and service activities. Many of these are locally owned. In addition, however, Intel is reported to have stated that 63 of these firms are important suppliers of inputs [*Larrain et al., 2000: 24*]. Many of these are foreign owned. A number of traditional Intel suppliers, such as Photocircuits (circuit boards), Pycon (test boards) and Aetec (media cleaning and recycling), for example, were attracted to co-locate in Costa Rica [*Hershberg and Monge, 2001: 18–19*]. These were greenfield investments and not mergers and acquisition and their presence thus enlarged the size of the electronics cluster which today includes a core of about 30 electronics and information technology-related firms (Appendix Two). More interestingly, from an innovation perspective is the growing number of linkages emerging amongst these firms as some of Intel's suppliers are beginning to supply a range of clients and not only Intel; Cyperpack for example supplies thermo-form plastic packaging to Intel and to DSC, and others such as Motorola, a firm located in Costa Rica before the arrival of Intel, are now establishing linkages to Intel.

Even more interesting is the way in which a US firm that had been a provider of quality inspection at the end of the process, upon the expiration of its contract with Intel in 1999 decided to continue operations in Costa Rica, upgrading its activities to tooling, where printed circuit boards are designed using computer-assisted design (CAD) software – an activity at the higher end of the value chain.

> This change meant, at the time of contract ending, to reduce its workforce from 300 to 10 workers and at the same time the upgrade of personnel profiles and requirements, from an essentially *maquila* activity to one more technologically sophisticated with design skills required. From the inception of these new activities the firm grew quickly to 250 employees in 2001. [*Monge, 2003: 16–17*]

Another important element in the emergence of a dynamic cluster, if not yet an innovation system, is the development of skills training by Intel for its suppliers. A recent survey of supplier firms[14] revealed that some 35 per cent of the service providers had received training from Intel with some 80 per cent of the training taking place at Intel's plant [*Larrain et al., 2000: 26*]. Among providers of goods, many of which carry out the production process inside Costa Rica, 17 per cent had received training by Intel [*Larrain et al., 2000: 26*]. Working with and being trained by Intel has led to some innovative activity within these firms. Of the 43 suppliers of goods participating in this survey 'around 18% ... stated that they had changed their organizational practices due to their activities with Intel. Around 8% of the providers of goods and 9% of the providers of services reported some changes in their product variety due to Intel ...' [*Larrain et al., 2000: 26*].

One other example of a small move towards greater learning and innovation lies in a recent Intel investment in local software development. This is in keeping with new strategic initiatives by Intel and its venture capital arm, Intel Capital, around the world.[15] Today, Costa Rica is said to export

> more software per capita than any other Latin American country. Two recent decisions by Intel have contributed to the development of the domestic industry. First, Intel decided to invest in a centre to develop software for the company and to contribute to semiconductor design, moving beyond the limits of an older assembly and testing plant. Second, through its venture capital fund, Intel invested in one of the country's most promising software companies. [*UNDP, 2001: 81*]

The emergence of knowledge-intensive activities within the cluster and the growth in the cluster's size in such a short period of time is thus impressive. Yet the cluster still lacks a strong knowledge base, R and D activities, and type of interactions and knowledge flows that characterise a dynamic innovation system. A number of problems, moreover, remain and their solutions are not self-evident. There is the problem, for example, of reliance on a single anchor firm in an industry marked by dramatic fluctuations in demand and the accompanying shifts in strategy. There is also the problem of attracting dedicated Intel supplier firms that do not upgrade. This has already occurred in one instance when Intel moved from the six-layer circuit boards required for Pentium II processors to the 12-layer circuit boards used for the Pentium III [*Hershberg and Monge, 2001: 17*]. The happy ending in this case was a rather unusual outcome.

Several other problems can only be addressed through new policies and programmes. The future impact of current inequalities in the tax structure is a case in point. These result from the tax holidays granted to dynamic foreign firms and the growing tax burden that will over time be shouldered by smaller, local firms in less dynamic sectors. This could lead to declining government tax revenues and to difficult political choices in the not too distant future.

There is also the need to address the imbalance in incentives and support programmes offered to local firms as compared to their foreign competitors. One small step in dealing with this problem was the creation, in 2001, of the CAATEC Foundation, that brings individuals from the private sector and the academic community together to enhance competitiveness in high-technology sectors. 'As part of Costa-Rica's "e-readiness" programme, CAATEC seeks to provide online financial services to SMEs and … enhance their ability to participate in the knowledge-based economy' [*UNCTAD, 2001: 232*]. Programmes to upgrade supplier capacity and stimulate linkages undertaken by CINDE and PROCOMER, Costa Rica's export promotion agency, with the support of the Inter-American Development Bank were discussed as early as 1997 but only started up in 2000 [*Larrain, 2000: 28*]. Clearly CINDE and its government partners will need to play a more pro-active role in developing support mechanisms and policies to meet the needs of local firms and thus create a truly indigenous innovation and growth dynamic.

VI. CONCLUSIONS

Given its shaping potential, the impact of foreign direct investment on future opportunities for catching up by developing countries is much greater than its importance as a source of capital. Indeed, the 'capital flow' element in FDI is hardly its most significant attribute, nor from a dynamic perspective is it the major contribution that FDI might make to development in the context of knowledge-intensive production whether it is based on a natural resource, such as oil and gas, or on so-called high-tech sectors, such as electronics.

Through in-house R and D, intense patenting activity, a wide range of R and D linkages and investments in production at home and abroad, TNCs set the pace of technological change and shape the pattern in the distribution of production and trade around the globe. Their impact on opportunities and constraints for learning and innovation and thus for growth and development in the developing world is unparalleled and developing countries everywhere have had to work within this context. To what extent have they been able to do so in a dynamic, innovation-related way? The two case studies presented provide a closer look at the limits of such an approach. Despite the 'attractiveness' of both countries to foreign investors, foreign investment has made only a minimal contribution to strengthening local innovation systems in these countries and one might question whether such expectations are not misplaced.

The case of Trinidad and Tobago is illustrative here. FDI inflows into the natural gas sector have had a tremendous economic impact. During the years 1997 to 2001, oil and natural gas accounted for 25 per cent of the country's GDP, 90 per cent of its export earnings, and 46 per cent of its investment. The natural gas sector alone contributed more than 60 per cent of the government's energy revenues in 2001 [*Energy Correspondent, 2002c*]. Yet, FDI in this sector has played only a small role in enhancing the national system of innovation, limited mainly to the training of nationals in the operation and maintenance of processing plants. It has not been fully involved in the development of a deeper and wider range of technical skills or in enhancing the capabilities of the local downstream and supporting firms. Its failure to play a greater role in the development of the national system of innovation, however, lies partly with the state. Since the mid 1980s, inspired by the World Bank and International Monetary Fund orthodoxy, the government in Trinidad and Tobago has conceptualised its role in development as that of facilitator, while the task of economic development and transformation has been left to the private sector, mainly the foreign firms. While eschewing selective intervention policies, the government has failed even in its role as facilitator, to provide the kind of policy environment needed to stimulate and support the emergence of an innovation system, including market failures in capital markets, gaps in knowledge and information and the absence or weakness of critical organisations.

The result has been that local firms possess only static production-related technological capabilities; few local downstream and supporting firms have emerged, and weaknesses remain in the local science and technological institutions and their linkage to the productive sector. In addition, there is a serious lack of strategic policy-making in defining the areas in which technological capabilities need to be built in the long term and, within this context, the specific technologies that the foreign firms could contribute.

The post 1980 surge in FDI in Trinidad and Tobago's natural gas industry has provided the country with a second opportunity to achieve economic transformation. However, as this chapter shows, the FDI-facilitated development of this country cannot be left solely to foreign firms. The government clearly needs to reassess its role in this development process in order to catalyse an FDI-facilitated development process.

In contrast to the situation in Trinidad, Costa Rica appears to have taken a number of small steps towards learning, innovation and linkages in an emerging electronics cluster. This we would argue has much to do with the more pro-active stance taken by government in Costa Rica and the more strategic reconceptualisations that have characterised its relationships with foreign firms in the recent period. Several of these have been particularly important and give rise to broader generalisations.

Reconceptualising foreign direct investment as part of a broader development process and a recognition that this process required close attention to learning, linkages and innovation was the critical point of departure for the choice of a targeting strategy and the complementary policies and support activities that were put in place. Without this fundamental reconceptualisation of FDI and its potential contribution to the growth of a cluster and of an innovation process within it, the speed with which new firms have either been drawn into the cluster from abroad or been created locally to provide goods and services within the cluster, given the experience of other clusters in both developing and developed countries, would not have been possible.

Reconceptualising investment promotion agencies as development agencies is a critical step in the ability of IPAs to play a more effective role in attracting foreign investment that might contribute to the strengthening of local systems of innovation. Costa Rica's CINDE has moved in this direction as have Forfar in Ireland and a number of other IPAs.

Reconceptualising 'sectors' as 'systems' and moving beyond the view of systems in static 'production' terms to the notion of dynamic 'innovation systems' is another key insight that is yet to be realised by most policy-makers, let alone IPAs. The European Union has created a variety of channels for dialogue and information exchange of this sort and a number of programmes to promote such reconceptualisations and engage in technology foresight, policies to support the strengthening of innovation systems and policy benchmarking indicators to enable closer monitoring of change. These bear further study by IPAs with a view to assessing their applicability in other contexts.

Lastly there is a need to rethink the notion of FDI-assisted development in light of the strategies and interests of both TNCs and host governments. From a policy perspective this will require the conscious development of a dual-use focus, on both domestic needs and markets and on exports, and not merely on exports, and on policies to promote learning and innovation in local firms as well as policies to attract foreign firms and encourage technology spillover. The latter presupposes a move away from the conventional 'within firm' approach to technological upgrading in terms of higher value-added products, to a wider focus on upgrading as a process of innovation in sector-based systems as a whole and efforts to upgrade within the system and across innovation systems in a concerted manner.

IPAs as development agencies have many roles to play in overcoming the narrowness of the FDI-assisted development approach. In addition to current efforts to identify potential suppliers, such agencies can form 'industry-wide and system-wide working groups' to build trust amongst all actors and provide a forum for co-ordinated upgrading within a sector-based system. Inter-sectoral upgrading could also be addressed more pro-actively by IPAs cum development agencies in preparing the terrain by stimulating awareness through technology foresight activities and monitoring and by involving a broad range of potential stakeholders in participatory agenda-setting processes that build bridges and broker partnerships across all actors in the system, thus ensuring local buy-in to a process of change, facilitating co-ordination and collaboration amongst clients and suppliers and coherence in the setting of policy parameters within which such innovation-related decisions are taken.

APPENDIX ONE

THE EVOLUTION OF THE NATURAL GAS SECTOR OF TRINIDAD AND TOBAGO

Year of establishment	Name of company	Product
1959	Hydro Agri Trinidad (originally owned by WR Grace)	Ammonia
1977	Trinidad Nitrogen (Tringen 1) (originally owned by the government and WR Grace)	Ammonia
1980	Caribbean Ispat Ltd (originally owned by the government)	Direct reduced iron, steel billets and wire rods
1981	PCS Nitrogen (originally owned by the government and Amoco)	Ammonia
1984	PCS Nitrogen II (originally owned by the government and Amoco)	Ammonia
1984	PCS Nitrogen II (originally owned by the government and Amoco)	Urea
1984	Methanol Holdings Trinidad Limited (originally owned by the government)	Methanol
1991	Phoenix Gas Processors Limited	Propane, butane and natural gas
1993	Caribbean Methanol Company	Methanol
1996	Trinidad & Tobago Methanol Company II (originally owned by the government)	Methanol
1996	PCS Nitrogen III	Ammonia
1997	PETROTRIN MTBE	Methyl tertiary butyl ether
1998	PCS Nitrogen IV	Ammonia
1998	Farmland/MissChem	Ammonia
1998	Methanol IV Company	Methanol
1999	Ispat DRI	Direct reduced iron
1999	Atlantic LNG Company of Trinidad and Tobago	Liquefied natural gas
2000	Titan Methanol	Methanol
2002	Caribbean Nitrogen Company	Ammonia
2002	Atlantic LNG 2/3 Company of Trinidad and Tobago	Liquefied natural gas

APPENDIX TWO

INTEL COSTA RICA SUPPLIERS IN 2002

	Activity
High-tech providers	
Aetec Intl.	Circuit board production, media cleaning process (trays)
Agilent – HP	Instrumentation, measurement and semiconductor equipment
AK Precision	Material injection, trays for pick and place equipment (moulds)
Alphasem	Fully automatic die attach and die sort systems
Anixter	Data communications products and electrical wire and cable
DEK Printing Machines Ltd	Precision screen printing systems and pre-placement solutions
EMC Technology, Inc.	Electronic components for satellite telecommunications (microwave)
Entex	E-business consulting and management of LAN/WAN/desktop
Fema	fixtures for pick and place equipment and magazine walls
LKT	Automatic loading systems
Mecsoft	Software and design involved in trays for pick and place equipment
OPM Microprecision	Microprecision products for pick and place equipment (moulds)
Panduit Corporation	Cable tying and accessories, electronic components, labelling
Photocircuits	Circuit boards
Pycon	Electronic boards calibration, test during burn-in systems
Reliability	DC to DC converters and burn-in and test equipment
Robotic Vision Systems Inc.	Automated inspection, packages, machine-vision-based scrutiny
Sawtek	Radio and intermediate frequency, filters for digital wireless phones
Schlumberger	Systems and services for testing semiconductor devices
Sykes	Call centre/support services
Tiros Thermal Solutions	Design and manufacture automated curing system, vertical cure ovens
Other providers	
Electroplast	Plastic products
Corbel	Boxes, corrugated boxes
Econopak	Wood boxes
PRAXAIR de Costa Rica	Nitrogen
Capris	Hardware store, industrial equipment and machinery
Universal	Office supplies
Wackenhut	Security services for facilities
InHealth	Food
CORMAR – AEI-Danzas	Transportation/custom service
Metro Servicios	Occupational safety and health products
Metrologia Consultores	Equipment calibration
ICE	Electric power
Vargas Mejia y Asociados	Security services

Source: Monge [*2003: 13–14*].

NOTES

1. The creation of the Point Lisas Industrial Estate dates back to the early initiatives of the South Trinidad Chamber of Industry and Commerce, which sought to develop an industrial port that would be a magnet for proposed, export-oriented industries. However, it was not until the late 1970s that this site was used as the location for the government's establishment of an industrial estate to house its new export-oriented, gas-intensive industries.
2. The CTF was also responsible for the co-ordination of other projects (such as cement expansion, furfural, power plant installation, the development of water supply systems, Point Lisas Marine Facilities, Point Lisas Industrial Estate, liquefied natural gas, refractory brick, and paper and pulp) that were undertaken or being considered during this time.
3. In 1979, the Coordinating Task Force was transformed into the National Energy Corporation (NEC). Until 1991, the NEC was responsible for planning and implementing policy for the natural gas industry. It also managed the then state-owned methanol and ammonia companies. In 1991, the NEC was merged with the National Gas Corporation, and given the responsibility of managing the infrastructure of the Point Lisas Industrial Estate. However, in 1998, this merger was dissolved, with the NEC emerging as an independent subsidiary engaged solely in the management of the estate and marine infrastructure of the Point Lisas Industrial Estate.
4. Indeed, British Petroleum Trinidad and Tobago (bpTT) purchased the equipment CARIRI uses to analyse the quality of gas used in the LNG plants. BpTT willing made this investment because of the difficulties in transporting the gas overseas and the frequency with which these tests need to be conducted.
5. The completion of the four LNG trains will result in Trinidad having sufficient ethane to support an economically sized cracker. In anticipation of this, the NGC has implemented an ethylene strategy. This strategy seeks to stimulate the interests of local industry in a proposed ethane plant. The NGC is presently co-ordinating its promotional activities with those of the local investment promotion agency, TIDCO. The objective here is 'develop and expand the local plastics industry along the lines of the resins targeted for production locally, even ahead of the actual cracker implementation' [*Baisden, 2002: 6*].
6. During the 1930s, a style of government involving the development of institutions to mediate social relations and provide some measure of social security emerged in Costa Rica. This model broke down in the 1940s and a civil war led to a banning of the Communist Party and the exile of its leaders. Since the 1950s, Costa Rican governments have attempted to integrate social and entrepreneurial functions with varying degrees of success.
7. Costa Rica began protecting land in 1890 and in 1987, under President Oscar Arias Sanchez, created the first commission to develop a strategic plan to protect its biodiversity and ensure sustainable development.
8. A public health care system emerged in the 1940s.
9. From an economy based on exports of coffee and bananas, Costa Rica undertook its first diversification process in the development of textiles and clothing.
10. These included: Motorola, DSC (circuit boards), Bourns-Trimpot (PC board assembly and testing), RICR (Reliability), Espion – an affiliate of C&K (transformers and mini-switches), Protedck (electronic components), Cortek (coils), Suttle (telephone connectors), Altor (transformers) and Sawtek (frequency filters) [*UNCTAD, 2002: 232*], Square D and Tico Pride Electronics [*Hershberg and Monge, 2001: 16*].
11. For Intel these include, the frequency of flights into San José (government agreed to grant more licences to foreign carriers) [*Spar, 1998*], concern that the educational system would not generate enough trained graduates (links to the local Instituto Tecnologico de Costa Rica have eliminated this problem), fear that Intel would absorb more than 30% of Costa Rica's power capacity. This was later reduced to 5%, but the plant would need its own substation. Intel contributed the land from its site to the power commission and arranged a loan to fund this and a substation to serve a neighbouring industrial park [*Spar, 1998: 19*]. In exchange, they and other 'large' users were assured of lower electricity prices.

12. This applied to educational programmes, some infrastructure and tax incentives such as duty-free imports.
13. In its first year of operations, 1998, Componentes Intel de Costa Rica's exports represented 18% of national exports [Monge, 2003: 7].
14. This included 43 suppliers of goods and 37 suppliers of services [Larrain et al., 2000: 24].
15. See, for example, Sam Nagarajan, 2002, 'Intel Capital to Boost Investment in Companies with Local Focus', Bloomberg News Archive, Technology News at http://quote.bloomberg.com.

REFERENCES

Baisden, C., 2002, 'New Horizons for Ethylene – The Challenge of Implementing a Local Ethylene Cracker', Gasco News, Vol.15, No.2, pp.5–8.
L.A.Barclay, 1990, 'Industrial Planning in Trinidad & Tobago: A Critical Appraisal', M.Sc. Thesis, Department of Economics, University of the West Indies, St. Augustine, Trinidad.
Barclay, L.A., 2000, Foreign Direct Investment in Emerging Economies. Corporate Strategy and Investment Behaviour in the Caribbean, London and New York: Routledge.
Barclay, L.A., 2003, 'FDI-facilitated Development: The Case of the Natural Gas Industry in Trinidad and Tobago', UNU-INTECH Discussion Paper 2003-7, September 2003.
Cabrera Medaglia, J., 2001, 'The Legal Framework and Public Policy on Access to Genetic Resources and Benefit-sharing: The Case of Costa Rica', University of Costa Rica, Faculty of Law, mimeo.
Edquist, C. (ed.), Systems of Innovation: Technologies, Institutions and Organizations, London: Pinter/Cassell Academic.
Energy Correspondent, 2002a, 'Skills Shortage Looms in the Energy Sector', Business Express, 2 October.
Energy Correspondent, 2002b, 'Education and Training in the Energy Sector', Business Express, 6 March.
Energy Correspondent, 2002c, 'Back to Reality', Business Express, 4 September.
Ernst, D., T. Ganiatsos and L.K. Mytelka (eds.), 1998, Technological Capabilities and Export Success in Asia, London: Routledge.
Farrell, T.M.A., 1987, 'Worship on the Golden Calf. An Oil Exporter's Industrial Strategy, Technology Policy and Project Planning during the Boom Years', Department of Economics, The University of the West Indies, St. Augustine, Trinidad, mimeo.
Furlonge, H.L., 2002, 'The Business of Developing an Integrated Gas Industry in Trinidad and Tobago', Gasco News, Vol.15, No.2, pp.9–16.
Girvan, N., 1979, 'The Approach to Technology Policy Studies', Social and Economic Studies, Vol.28, No.1, pp.1–53.
Hershberg, E. and J. Monge, 'Industrial Upgrading, Employment and Equity in Costa Rica: Implications of an Emerging Chain in Electronics', Paper presented at the SSRC-CODETI-FLACSO Workshop 'Combining Industrial Upgrading and Equity', San Jose, Costa Rica, 12–14 October 2000 and second draft, July 2001.
Lall, S., 2002, 'Linking FDI and Technology Development for Capacity Building and Strategic Competitiveness', Transnational Corporations, Vol.11, No.3, pp.39–88 (December).
Larrain, B.F., L. Lopez-Calva and A. Rodriguez-Clare, 2000, 'Intel: A Case Study of Foreign Direct Investment in Central America', Cambridge, MA: Harvard University, Center for International Development, Working Paper No. 58.
Lundvall, B.-A., 1992, National Systems of Innovation, London: Pinter Publishers.
Molot, M.A., 2003, 'Location Incentives: The Cost of Playing the Autos Game', Paper presented to the Auto21 Conference, Ottawa, April.
Monge, J., 2003, 'Building SMEs Competitiveness: Business Development Services and the Case of Intel Investment in Costa Rica', Paper presented at a UNU/INTECH conference.
Mytelka, Lynn K., 1979, Regional Development in a Global Economy The Multinational Corporation, Technology and Andean Integration, New Haven: Yale University Press.
Mytelka, Lynn K., 1989, 'The Unfulfilled Promise of African Industrialization', African Studies Review, Vol.32, No.3, pp.77–137.

Mytelka, Lynn K., 1999, 'Locational Tournaments for FDI: Inward Investment into Europe in a Global World', in Neil Hood and Stephen Young (eds.), *The Globalization of Multinational Enterprise Activity and Economic Development*, UK: Macmillan Press, pp.278–303.

Mytelka, Lynn K., 2000, 'Local Systems of Innovation in a Globalized World Economy', *Industry and Innovation*, Vol.77, No.1, pp.15–32 (June).

Nelson, R. (ed.), 1993, *National Innovation Systems: A Comparative Analysis*, New York: Oxford University Press.

Nelson, R. and S. Winter, 1982, *An Evolutionary Theory of Economic Change*, Cambridge, MA: Harvard University Press.

OECD, 2002, *Global forum on International Investment: New Horizons for Foreign Direct Investment*, Paris: OECD.

Phelps, N., J. Lovering and K. Morgan, 1998, 'Tying the Firm to the Region or Tying the Region to the Firm? Early Observations on the Case of LG in South Wales', *European Urban and Regional Studies*, Vol.5, No.2, pp.199–237.

Spar, D., 1998, 'Attracting High Technology Investment Intel's Costa Rican Plant', Washington, DC: The World Bank, Foreign Investment Advisory Service.

Storper, M., 1998, 'Industrial Policy for Latecomers: Products, Conventions, and Learning', in M. Storper, T. Thomadakis and L. Tsipouri (eds.), *Latecomers in the Global Economy*, London: Routledge, pp.13–39.

UNCTAD, 1995, *World Investment Report 1995*, New York and Geneva: United Nations.

UNCTAD, 1997, *World Investment Report 1997*, New York and Geneva: United Nations.

UNCTAD, 1999, *World Investment Report 1999*, New York and Geneva: United Nations.

UNCTAD, 2001, *World Investment Report 2001*, New York and Geneva: United Nations.

UNCTAD, 2002, *World Investment Report 2002*, New York and Geneva: United Nations.

UNDP, 2001, *Human Development Report*, New York: United Nations.

Wong, Poh-Kam, 2001, 'The Role of the State in Singapore's Industrial Development', in Poh-Kam Wong and Chee-Yuen Ng (eds.), *Industrial Policy, Innovation and Economic Growth*, Singapore: University of Singapore Press, pp.503–79.

Foreign Direct Investment, Linkage Formation and Supplier Development in Thailand during the 1990s: The Role of State Governance

LAURIDS S. LAURIDSEN

During the 1990s inbound foreign direct investment (FDI) became a significant factor in Thailand's industrial transformation. At the same time there were increasing concerns about whether the new transnational comporation (TNC)-driven export industries actually contributed to the long-term competitiveness and a sustainable pattern of industrialisation in Thailand. This led in turn to the formulation of TNC – small and medium-scale enterprise (SME) linkage policies as well as a set of broader SME and supporting industry policies to supplement unfolding liberalisation of trade and investment policies. The chapter is concerned with the extent to which the Thai government was able to formulate and in particular implement a credible and adequate set of linkage and supplier development policies. It is generally argued that the Thai governments failed to implement such policies and thereby missed an early opportunity of supporting upgrading among Thai-owned parts producers. Mistaken policies were mainly due to a range of politico-institutional constraints that may be in the process of changing under the present Thaksin government.

Pendant les années quatre-vingt-dix, les nouveaux investissements directs étrangers (IDE) devinrent un facteur essentiel de la transformation industrielle en Thaïlande. En même temps, des doutes surgirent quant à la question si les nouvelles industries d'exportations initiées par les corporations transnationales (CTN) contribuaient vraiment à la compétitivité à long terme et à un modèle d'industrialisation soutenable en Thaïlande. En conséquence, on formula des mesures politiques ayant pour but d'associer les CTN et les petites et moyennes entreprises (PME), ainsi qu'une série de mesures politiques plus larges à l'égard des PME et de l'aide à l'industrie, afin d'équilibrer la libéralisation du commerce en cours et la politique des investissements. L'article analyse dans quelle mesure le

Laurids S. Lauridsen is at International Development Studies, Roskilde University Centre, Denmark.

gouvernement thaïlandais a réussi à formuler et surtout à mettre en œuvre une série crédible et adéquate de mesures politiques de développement soutenant les fournisseurs. On dit généralement que le gouvernement thaïlandais échoua dans sa tâche de mettre en œuvre de telles mesures politiques et manqua donc une première occasion de soutenir le développement parmi les producteurs de composantes thaïlandais. Les mesures politiques erronées étaient généralement dues à une série de contraintes institutionnelles et politiques qui pourraient bien changer sous le gouvernement actuel de Thaksin.

I. INTRODUCTION

At the international academic and policy-making scene the attitudes towards foreign direct investments (FDIs) and transnational corporations (TNCs) have changed considerably during the past two decades of intensified internationalisation or globalisation. Gone are earlier discussions – on restrictive business practices, transfer pricing, crowding out of local business, technological dependence, unequal development and loss of sovereignty – that prevailed during the 1970s. Instead, there is a renewed confidence in the positive benefits of FDI/TNC. In contrast to the volatile short-term capital flows that may trigger financial crises, direct foreign investments are considered as fairly stable. In contrast to the fading flows of foreign aid, FDI now appears to be an expanding source of capital. In contrast to protected and 'rent seeking' domestic business groups, TNCs are looked upon as providers of new types of technology and modern forms of organisation – both through their foreign affiliates and through their wider impact upon local enterprises.

In parallel with this discursive shift, managers of foreign-owned plants in developing countries show an increasing willingness to expand 'local sourcing' of inputs and enter into tighter relationships with domestic small and medium-scale enterprises (SMEs). This is particularly the case in a range of low-tech processes where labour costs are crucial or in mid-tech items where transport costs are important. Concurrently, TNCs are in the process of modernising their supplier base and of reducing the number of suppliers on which they depend. They now buy from the most competitive suppliers on a worldwide basis and often induce their established home-based or global suppliers to follow them to new locations. As a consequence, local suppliers in developing countries compete against both overseas suppliers and global suppliers that have invested in the country in question. The previous lower domestic market supplier standards in developing countries have been replaced by international standards, putting a strong pressure on suppliers of parts and components to approach the new standards of price, quality and timely delivery. If the local SMEs do not move fast in the upgrading direction or if the barriers of entry are insurmountable such suppliers will be replaced by imports or by the global-in-place suppliers mentioned above.

Under pressure from these challenges and opportunities, host governments in developing countries are forced to reconsider and to adjust their policy portfolio to the new reality. It should be emphasised that the issues at stake vary significantly from country to country, very much depending on the capacity of the state. There is extremely little that we can expect weak – or predatory – states can do to influence TNC activities or assist local suppliers. The issue involved in foreign investment, as seen from the perspective of government officials in such states, is simply to extract the greatest personal share from whatever wealth or income that might be generated by private actors. Intermediate and strong developmental states, on the other hand, may be capable of influencing and shaping TNC behaviour [*Evans, 1995*]. These states are not just aggregates of individual maximisers but organisations capable of pursuing collective goals. Here, it becomes meaningful to discuss problems of host government policy in general and, more specifically, how policy interventions may influence technology transfer and spillovers. This may be done by attracting more foreign investment; by ensuring an appropriate selection of TNC investments; and by developing local capabilities and absorptive capacities, so that the local firms can take advantage of the links with foreign investors.

The Thai state is chosen as the focus in this chapter because it belongs to the category intermediate states, and because it has been in the forefront of designing TNC linkage policies. By the mid 1990s, it looked as if Thailand was on the threshold of becoming the Fifth Tiger in Asia. Thailand's macro-level economic performance had for decades been quite impressive. The country had recorded rapid and sustained growth rates, it had diversified both its agriculture and industrial sector, and it had the fastest growing export of manufactures among Asian economies during the 1985–96 period. At the same time there were increasing concerns about whether it was a sustainable pattern of industrialisation and in particular whether the new TNC-driven export industries actually contributed to the long-term competitiveness of the country. This led in turn to the formulation of TNC-SME linkage policies as well as a set of broader SME and supporting industry policies to supplement unfolding liberalisation of trade and investment policies.

The present chapter is concerned with the extent to which the Thai government was able to formulate and in particular implement a credible and adequate set of linkage and supplier development policies. It is generally argued that the Thai governments failed to implement such a policy and thereby missed an early opportunity of supporting upgrading among Thai-owned parts producers.

The following section deals theoretically with FDI, linkages and supplier development. The third section discusses the role of linkage and supplier development policies. The fourth section addresses the issue of policy formulation and state capacity in relation to the chosen policy domain. The subsequent section looks at investment promotion, industrialisation strategies and inbound FDI in Thailand. The sixth section addresses design and implementation of linkage development policy in Thailand during the 1990s. Then follows a section that analyses supporting industry and SME policies during the same period. The eighth section summarises the findings, while an 'addition' refers to some recent policy developments.

II. FDI, LINKAGES AND SUPPLIER DEVELOPMENT

In this chapter, we are concerned with the indirect effects of FDIs in developing countries (Thailand). Such spillovers can occur through four main channels: 'demonstration effects', 'competition effects', training of local employees of TNC affiliates and finally through linkages between TNCs and local firms. We focus on one type of linkage – backward linkages – which refers to 'inter-firm relationships in which a company purchases goods and services as its production inputs on a regular basis from one or more other companies in the production chain' [Battat et al., 1996: 4]. More specifically, we are concerned with the purchasing of inputs (parts, components, raw materials and services) from domestically owned suppliers by foreign affiliates. Thus we exclude arm's length and one-off relations where TNCs simply buy existing products 'off-the shelf' and focus on more regular inter-firm relations. Similarly, we do not include backward linkages to other foreign affiliates. Though such linkages can contribute in 'rooting' foreign investors, linkages between foreign affiliates and domestically owned enterprise are of particular interest to developing countries.

The following analysis is based on the assumption that successful linkage formation between TNCs and local SMEs is a cost-effective and viable way of fostering long-term economic development.[1] It should be noticed that this is not a self-evident statement. First, some of the East Asian newly industrialising countries (NICs) did actually adopt a more autonomous strategy and relied primarily on local firms and externalised forms of technology transfer in their process of catching up [e.g.Lall, 1995]. Second, global commodity chain scholars have argued that FDI-based, producer-driven commodity chains (run by TNCs) generally have a limited developmental impact. In contrast, they contend that local producers have good prospects of benefiting from trade-based, buyer-driven commodity chains. While local suppliers mostly are involved in simple assembly of imported inputs in producer-driven networks, new lead firms such as retailers and marketers need (full-package) suppliers with the ability to make finished products and by themselves organise their own supplier network [Gereffi, 1999].

Nevertheless, we will deal only with FDI-based, producer-driven commodity chains and concentrate on how domestic suppliers and host developing countries can benefit from linkages with foreign affiliates. The benefits take the form of: increasing domestic production and employment, rising local value added of foreign investments, improvements in the current account balance, and higher technological-managerial capabilities of local enterprises.

Inbound FDI flows do not automatically result in dense backward linkages. The decision to source locally from domestic suppliers depends on a variety of factors. First, the presence of reliable and flexible local suppliers that can meet the requirements of buyers (cost, quality and timely delivery) is of crucial importance for linkage formation. The technological and managerial gap between foreign firms and local supplier enterprises is often referred to as the main obstacle for efficient backward linkage formation in developing countries. Second, even when efficient local suppliers are not present, foreign affiliates may look for potential domestic suppliers and assist them in improving their capabilities. Third, some industries have a larger linkage potential than others. Linkages are typically low in process industries and high in industries where the production process is divisible into multi-stage activities using a variety of materials, components and parts. Fourth, market position and technological sophistication are important. TNCs in price-sensitive market segments are more footloose and thus less likely to 'invest' in local embeddedness. Similarly, affiliates producing very specialised and advanced products have fewer processes and products to outsource in a developing country context. Fifth, corporate strategies matter. TNCs in the same industry may source their inputs differently. Domestic-market-oriented affiliates have generally more local links to suppliers than export-oriented affiliates but the links between the latter and local suppliers may be more efficient and competitive. Further local sourcing varies according to the home country and corporate culture, so that European, American and Japanese TNCs display differences in their sourcing behaviour. There may even be considerable differences among affiliates from the same country. Finally, local procurement also seems to be influenced by the size of affiliates, by the degree of affiliate autonomy, by the length of operation in the host country and by regional trade agreements [*Battat et al., 1996; Dicken, 1998; UNCTAD, 2001; Altenburg, 2002*].

Mutual self-interest and strong commitment of both parties as well as time may lead to formation of developmental linkages if the capability gaps are not too wide. Yet, policy and institutional support are needed to foster a wide base of capable suppliers, and policies can affect both the terms of local procurement and the willingness of TNCs to transfer knowledge and skills to local suppliers. In the next two sections, we will conceptualise the policy content and the policy process, respectively.

III. LINKAGE AND SUPPLIER DEVELOPMENT POLICIES

The policies that are under consideration here are those that promote the creation of new backward linkages as well as the deepening and upgrading of existing linkages with the ultimate aim of upgrading the capabilities of local suppliers [*UNCTAD, 2001*]. They consist in fostering and supporting dense networks of suppliers who can reliably deliver high-quality, low-cost parts and components. By doing this they can 'deepen' formerly import-intensive import-substitution industrialisation (ISI)-assembly industries as well 'deepen' import-intensive export-oriented industrialisation (EOI)-assembly industries. Owing to the shift to export-oriented industrialisation and the opening of the economies in many developing countries, the focus is increasingly on SMEs that serve as suppliers to export-oriented assemblers. Such policies must also address information and co-ordination problems, because it is not obvious that individual assembly companies (often TNC subsidiaries or joint ventures) by themselves organise local procurement networks encompassing domestic suppliers.

Linkage and supplier development policies must be seen in combination with related policy fields, in particular FDI promotion policies and SME development policies. The objective of linkage and supplier development policies is to promote willing TNCs, capable SMEs and effective linkages between them. First, a country needs to attract foreign investors and in particular investors that have a large linkage potential and/or it needs to upgrade existing TNC activities so that they are more conducive to linkage formation. Second, policies should aim at expanding the local supplier base by preparing them for partnerships and by supporting potential domestic supplier firms in such areas as technology upgrading, training and financing so that they can exploit such partnerships to their own advantage. Third, policies can enhance linkages and support technology transfer from affiliates to local suppliers [*Altenburg, 2002: 18–19*].

Policy-makers may develop specific linkage policies by using 'harder' command and control measures or by using 'softer' policy instruments giving particular incentives or promoting co-operation efforts. The traditional linkage policies were mostly of the former mandatory kind. Thus, many developing countries have set high tariffs on imports on parts and components, and imposed local content requirements (LCRs) on foreign affiliates with the aim of expanding local procurement and strengthening domestic supplier industries. However, these measures did not necessarily promote local procurement because foreign affiliates could also choose to internalise input production or source input from foreign suppliers located in the host country. In addition, more liberal investment rules and restrictions on the trade-related investment measures have undermined the LCR instrument [*Battat et al., 1996: 13–15*; *UNCTAD, 2001: 167–71*].

As backward linkages no longer can be forced upon transnational companies, 'softer' policy instruments have taken over. Promotion of co-operation is an often-used policy instrument. Many countries have introduced information provision and matchmaking services. The former consist of various kinds of data banks, listing potential partners for subcontracting, while the latter goes a step further organising seminars, factory visits and follow-up initiatives. Such matchmaking services are conducted either by public officials or by consultants from private firms/private associations. Moreover, industrial estate policies may be organised so as to cluster supporting enterprises near large-scale assemblers. Finally, there is a range of policy measures that rest on economic incentives for foreign affiliates. Some countries have introduced tax incentives to promote backward linkages. Others utilise special credit and guarantee schemes, subsidies or privileged public procurement to induce TNCs to give special training and technical assistance to their suppliers.

The above mentioned policy measures focus predominantly on the extent of linkages, are technical in orientation and tend to present linkages in a benign manner – reciprocity and co-operation. However, linkages are also about asymmetry, stratification and power. This aspect has been forcefully addressed in the TNC debate. Besides studying the circumstances under which one can expect TNCs to utilise local sourcing of inputs rather than import, TNC critiques have pointed to the quality of such linkages. One criticism being that TNCs tend to procure only inferior or low-level inputs (packing, simple components, cleaning services etc.) from domestic suppliers. Another being that subcontracting may have more or less beneficial effects on the supplier firm (in relation to earnings, risk sharing, continuity in orders, and transfer of product and process know-how) depending on the rationale behind subcontracting and the power relations between suppliers and principals. Therefore, linkage policy must also encompass the quality of supplier linkages.

IV. FROM POLICY FORMULATION TO POLICY IMPLEMENTATION

Policy content and policy instruments are one matter, policy choice, policy design and policy implementation are another. Policy choice is constrained by the structural power of leading social groups and the organisational structure of the state but is also the result of the play of political forces and interests. Formulation of a coherent policy and the translation of policy objectives effectively into policy outputs and further on to outcomes is a complicated matter. In the following, we will concentrate on the process from policy formulation over policy implementation to policy impact with specific reference to linkage and supplier development policies [*we will draw upon Meyanathan and Munter, 1994; Levy et al., 1994; Battat et al., 1996; UNCTAD, 2001; Altenburg, 2002; Wattanapruttipaisan, 2002*].

First, it should be acknowledged that though the space for policy intervention has become more limited with the introduction of a new international policy framework (trade-related investment measures, TRIMs), there is still scope for pro-active linkage policies if policy-makers manage to use the options allowed within this framework. Specific linkage policy is one such measure. To be effective there must be 'a vision' about supplier development through backward linkages, and this vision should be built upon a strong political commitment and be shared among all stakeholders. Further, it should be based on a clear, realistic and detailed understanding of the level of supplier development in the country, of the needs of foreign affiliates, of the scope of the windows of opportunity, and of the policy measures that will work in the particular context. In order to create stakeholder credibility, a medium/long-term policy perspective is required. Therefore, constantly shifting policy priorities may constitute a problem.

Second, and related, policies have to take into account *the broader development strategies, the economic environment and the institutional setting* in the country. As far as policy coherence is concerned, linkage and supplier development policies have to be consistent with broader policies, such as FDI policies, technology policies, skill development policies and competition policies. FDI policies are of special importance; those which attract 'developmental' foreign investors with a high linkage potential or which affect upgrading of existing affiliates have direct relations with linkage formation. Finally, the broader economic policies and incentive environment must not undermine the strategic use of backward linkages for supplier upgrading or work to the detriment of SMEs. If policies generally discriminate against SMEs; if tax policies include sales taxes that are levied on the full value of the products so that they have a cascading effect (not found in value added taxing systems); if investment promotion policies favour global suppliers, or if the overall business and incentive environment work against supplier development, it will be extremely difficult to successfully implement linkage policies or SME development policies more broadly.

Third, and related, there is generally a strong need *for well-conceived and co-ordinated linkage policies.* Such policies must take into consideration the following: selecting a target group with a realistic potential for becoming suppliers; focusing on the most capable and committed domestic enterprises; avoiding support to suppliers that are assisted by large-scale assemblers anyway or supporting only additional assistance from the principal; avoiding assistance to SMEs that are unaware of their problems – and thus unprepared for changing their business; and avoiding assistance to principal-subcontractor arrangements of a highly asymmetric and short-term nature.

Fourth, *the institutional framework* for policy formulation and implementation must be in place. Though semi-public organisations may perform much of the practical implementation, a relatively autonomous and strong co-ordinating agency is an important prerequisite for co-ordinated programming. When more ministries and agencies are involved contradictory initiatives arise, just as functional duplication and conflicting lines of authority often result in 'blocking', inconsistency in implementation or 'side-tracking' during the process of implementation. For that reason and because a range of intermediate supporting institutions are involved there will thus be a strong call for co-ordination both at the level of programming and at the level of actual service delivery. Furthermore, policy failure tends to prevail if weak, low-status agencies staffed with a few, poorly paid and inexperienced officials are responsible for the actual implementation.

Fifth, *public-private networks* are needed in the process of policy design as well as in policy implementation. Linkage and supplier development is a complicated process, and in order to be effective in influencing the pace and direction of this process, the state must strongly involve the two other partners in the 'linkage triangle'. In relation to the TNCs, the point of departure must be that they only participate if there are tangible or other benefits for them and if a close collaboration is established. In relation to the suppliers, high awareness and certain capabilities must be in place or be created. Suppliers may more easily be approached if they have organised themselves collectively and this may also strengthen their bargaining position *vis-à-vis* foreign affiliates (cf. the asymmetric power issue). In relation to SMEs as would-be suppliers, the involved agencies must – in order to understand clients' changing needs and provide relevant services – maintain a close contact with clients (individual firms/networking firms).

Finally, in relation to the *policy impact*, it should be noted that even well-designed and well-implemented policy and institutional support might not have the expected impact. A global downturn, new modes of organisation of the TNC business or better investment opportunities and cheaper suppliers elsewhere may work against linkage formation, just as, for example, tax evasion considerations may keep potential suppliers (SMEs) at a certain distance from the state and its support agencies. It may also be that even with supplier development support or SME assistance programmes most/many SME suppliers (e.g. former domestic-market-oriented SME suppliers) cannot live up to the required lower prices, higher standards, higher product quality and faster delivery. Therefore, because of structural forces they are – despite policy initiatives – replaced by import and/or foreign suppliers located in the host country.

In the following, we are concerned with linkage and supplier development policies in Thailand. During the 1990s, the Thai authorities launched several such policy schemes. Before examining them, we will in the following section briefly look at FDI and the shifting industrialisation strategies.

V. INBOUND FDI, INVESTMENT PROMOTION, AND PATTERN OF INDUSTRIALISATION IN THAILAND

Pre 1986, liberal investment promotion policies and restrictive trade policies were the main instruments utilised by the Thai government in stimulating local investments as well as attracting FDI. Compared to investment in countries such as Singapore and Malaysia, investment in Thailand was based more on domestic resource mobilisation and less on FDI. Furthermore, foreign investments in the manufacturing industry mainly took the form of joint ventures (J/Vs) with an emphasis on assembly of final goods for the domestic market, while both capital goods industries and parts producing industries remained relatively under-developed. Apart from the general high level of trade protection and the LCRs used most pervasively in the automobile industry, there were no specific policies to induce local parts production, local spin-offs and inter-industry linkages. The tariff system actually worked against local parts production. Thus, tariffs of ready-made parts used by assemblers were lower than tariffs on raw materials used by parts producers. Discouragement of local supply industries was further aggravated by the negative impact of the business tax system. Until the introduction of the value added tax in 1992, a sales tax was imposed on gross revenue and therefore had a cascading effect that was particular painful in industries where the product ran through many phases of processing before emerging as a final product.

Concerning FDI and import dependence, Tambunlertchai and Ramstetter nonetheless found that the ratio of imports to total input purchases of foreign firms actually fell from 65 per cent in 1974 to 49 per cent in 1986. Though this finding does not indicate whether local content increased due to in-house production or through subcontracting, it demonstrates that the potential for local procurement was growing [*Tambunlertchai Somsak, 1991: 98*]. In both the automobile and electrical appliance industry, TNCs actually used localised suppliers – both related J/V suppliers and fully Thai-owned suppliers (typically with foreign technology contracts). The important point is here that in the case of Thailand, a group of domestic supplier firms were actually present as potential clients for linkage and supplier development initiatives and the scope for new suppliers was widening.

From 1986 and onwards, Thailand experienced an economic growth boom that to a considerable extent was linked to exceptionally high growth rates in manufacturing export. The annual growth rate in manufactured export from 1986 to 1996 was almost 25 per cent – making Thailand the fastest growing exporter among leading developing countries [*Lall, 1999*]. There was also an enormous increase in the rate of accumulation and the investment-savings gap widened. The fairly large gap was filled by external finance, part of which was non-debt-creating flows – direct and portfolio investments. As can be seen in Table 1,

TABLE 1
FDI INFLOWS IN THAILAND 1986–2002

Year	FDI inflows (million US$)	FDI inflows as a percentage of gross fixed capital formation (%)
1986–91 annual average	1,325	5.5
1992	2,114	4.8
1993	1,730	3.6
1994	1,322	2.3
1995	2,004	2.9
1996	2,271	3.0
1997	3,882	7.6
1998	7,491	29.9
1999	6,091	23.8
2000	3,350	12.4
2001	3,813	14.4
2002	1,068	3.7

Source: UNCTAD [*1998, 2001, 2003*].

Thailand suddenly attracted on the average US$1.3 billion of net FDI inflows per year during the 1986–91 period. These investments amounted to 5.5 per cent of the gross fixed capital formation in Thailand. The country became a 'hot spot' for foreign investors and Thailand almost doubled its share of net foreign investments in the Association of South East Asian Nations (ASEAN) [*Dixon, 1999: 129*].

A significant amount of these inflows went to export industries, to industries that provided intermediate inputs such as electronic parts and components, to other intermediate industries or to transport equipment industries. FDIs were pushed by the post-Plaza accord currency appreciation in Japan, South Korea and Taiwan. They were pulled by cheap labour, cheap land and export-oriented policies introduced in the second half of the 1980s. (Another surge of FDI came after the onset of the financial and economic crisis in 1997.)

The post-1985 boom in foreign investments resulted in increased competition in various industries, in increasing land and labour costs and in an overstrained infrastructure. The local business community did express some concern about the new FDI-driven manufacturing and protested against rules that favoured foreign investors (e.g. the Board of Investment promotion of wholly owned subsidiaries). Nevertheless, in the wake of the liberal reforms in the early 1990s and because of the boom in the economy, they shifted to a more benign view on foreign investments [*Felkner, 2001: 142–3, 163–4*].

Thailand's export performance looked very impressive during the 1986–1996 period. One aspect was the high growth rates mentioned previously. Another was a significant change in the structure of export towards a range of new high-tech products (especially computers and parts, electrical equipment and integrated circuits). However, much of Thailand's high-tech export was in reality manufactured through rather simple, labour-intensive assembly of high-tech components imported from advanced industrialised countries (including the Asian NICs). As a consequence, there was in reality no significant movement away from the light, final goods industry bias that prevailed during the former ISI-period.

The export boom, and the prevailing 'export fetishism', concealed not just the upcoming problems of competition, but also the missing linkages to local Thai enterprises and the import-dependent nature of this new mode of industrialis-ation. Measured as a share of gross domestic product (GDP), imports went up from 22 per cent in 1986 to 38 per cent in 1994. The share of intermediate goods and raw materials went up from 7.7 per cent to 11.0 per cent while that of capital goods increased from 7.2 per cent to 17 per cent [*Jansen, 1997: 42 table 2.7*]. Though the increase in the latter share partly was explicable by the high level of investment, it was also reflecting growing imports of components to the electronics and information industry. Electronic and electrical industries became the major export industry in Thailand, accounting for more than one-quarter of the total export in the mid 1990s, but at the same time a very import-intensive industry accounting for more than 23 per cent of Thailand's import. The automotive industry was not export driven and accounted for around 1 per cent of Thai export. On the import side, automotive and vehicles accounted for 6–7 per cent of the total import. Together these two industries – electronics and automotive – stood for a substantial trade deficit of 157 billion baht in 1995 or 44 per cent of the total [*calculated from Bank of Thailand, 1996, 1998*].

According to the calculations of Karel Jansen, the increase in the import/GDP ratio was mainly due to a rapid rise in the import dependency. In turn, this was probably a result of the growing role of FDI, partly because it led to expansion in more import-intensive sectors and partly because more imported inputs were utilised in production to export markets compared to production for the domestic market [*Jansen, 1997: 179–81*]. Comparing 1985 with 1998, Tambunlertchai found that local content ratio had increased in the automobile industry, while the electronics goods industry relied on imported components and was characterised by 'very low backward linkages' [*Tambunlertchai, 2002: 99–100*].

Thus, the shift towards FDI-driven, high-tech, export-oriented industrialis-ation seems to have reproduced and aggravated the problems of weak linkages and high import content. The lack of strong import-replacing linkages in the new export industries led to considerable loss of value added to foreign input manufacturers – just as Thailand bypassed potential diffusion and improvements of technology through such linkages. To the extent that backward linkages were established between foreign assembly firms and global suppliers located in

Thailand, the local content increased but subsequent linkages from these suppliers may be oriented towards foreign input manufacturers rather than second-tier local Thai suppliers. Against this background, it is understandable that part of the political and bureaucratic elite in Thailand became worried about the shallow nature of the Thai industrialisation, and that linkage and supplier development initiatives were launched. These initiatives were driven by two agencies – The Board of Investment (BoI) and the Ministry of Industry (MoI). The policies came into being during a period in which a process of financial, investment and trade liberalisation was initiated.

VI. LINKAGE DEVELOPMENT POLICY IN THAILAND DURING THE 1990s – THE BOARD OF INVESTMENT

The BoI had generally relied on a relatively passive and liberal approach to investment promotion. Thailand had a welcoming FDI regime and when targeting was on the agenda, the focus had been on either exporting or its decentralised geographical location, while linkages, skill upgrading and technological development played a marginal, if any role in actual implementation of the BoI's investment incentives. Instead, a separate unit – the BoI Unit for Industrial Linkage Development (BUILD) – was in 1991 set up to promote backward linkages from existing TNCs. The main objectives of the BUILD programme were: to encourage the development of supporting industries and promote the deepening of Thailand's industrial structure; to strengthen linkages between final product producers and companies producing components and parts or supplying technical services; to assist small and medium supplier companies in improving efficiency, productivity and quality; to foster co-operation between foreign investors, Thai supplier manufacturers, and related government agencies; and to remove impediments to subcontracting and improve backward linkage development [*BoI, 1994*]. The BoI was given a dual role. At the macro level it should act as an intra-bureaucratic 'broker', and promote the general environment for market-oriented backward linkages among other things by having a national database of potential suppliers, and by removing impediments to such linkages. At the micro level, the BUILD unit of the BoI was intended to promote and facilitate particular linkage projects by having a matchmaker and sometimes troubleshooter function.

In the process of implementation, the scope was almost narrowed down to matchmaking and information provision just as the work was subcontracted to local research institutes and consulting firms. During the first phase, the activities focused on electronics, automotive parts, and metal-working and machinery industries. The main activities were: development of an information base to support matchmaking in the form of ten investment opportunity studies inside the three industries and a database of suppliers as well as principals;

dissemination of information; arrangement of regional seminars with potential suppliers/principals; and upgrading of suppliers through seven training courses (in production management, ISO 9000, inventory management etc.). Then followed a pro-active phase (starting September 1993) with matchmaking undertaken by one of the consulting firms – SEAMICO. SEAMICO selected 15 major assemblers for pro-active matchmaking activities in which BUILD teams visited these assemblers, provided them with information on potential suppliers, listed parts and components being sought by these assemblers and worked with them to develop these relationships. However, during the following phase (starting June 1994) – which was run by two new consulting firms – matchmaking and related activities were de-selected, while database development and computerised information on subcontracting opportunities in Thailand were developed further. During the fourth phase (May 1996 to May 1997) the project was subcontracted to leading industrial trade association the Federation of Thai Industries (FTI) and missions, trade fairs and general seminar activities became the primary focus [BoI Investment Review, 1994: 9; Brimble and Pattanun, 1994].

From this short overview it appears that the BUILD programme already had lost steam by 1994–95 and that site visits to TNC assemblers had been abandoned. It turned out that the new more export-oriented TNCs were less interested in forming backward linkages to the local suppliers than the older TNCs and large domestic enterprises [Felkner, 2001: 172].Though publicly advocated by the Secretary General of the BoI, there was not similar strong organisational support. In principle, the BUILD team was made up of BUILD officers and staff from the BOI Planning and Development Division plus staff from sector and regional divisions. In reality, BUILD had problems in bringing the ordinary BoI staff's sectoral knowledge into the backward linkages support activities. During the whole period, the BUILD unit was staffed with a few officers from the Planning and Development Division but rather than building-up (and utilising) in-house expertise, BUILD activities were from the very early beginning contracted-out to shifting consortiums of consulting firms. Apart from the problems of being able to consistently follow matchmaking through, BUILD was also handicapped by not having the authority and capacity to enhance the capabilities and competence of domestic suppliers (information provided by the BUILD Unit, November 1996).

In order to circumvent that problem, the BoI in 1994 proposed to develop an internationally competitive base of supplier SMEs in Thailand through a comprehensive supplier development programme – the National Supplier Development Programme (NSDP). It was planned as a multi-agency effort in which the Board of Investment and the Ministry of Industry should divide the overall responsibilities but it did also encompass a range of other ministries, agencies and associations [Brimble and Sripaipan, 1994]. Though a steering committee was set up, the initiative failed to materialise, in part because the MoI did not in reality commit itself to the programme.

Besides the specific linkage initiatives mentioned above, the BoI had in 1993–94 decided to give special investment incentives to 14 (later 19) supporting industries. Following the controversial 1991 decision to allow 100 per cent foreign-owned firms to sell up to 20 per cent of their output on the domestic market, it was decided that in supporting industries such investors could sell all output at the domestic market. During 1996, the BoI speeded up a large campaign running from 1995 to 1997 to attract more investments from Japanese SME parts producers, hoping to attract as much as 1,500 SMEs to serve the automobile and motorcycle industries alone. Therefore, rather than supporting domestic suppliers the BoI actually gave priority to getting in particular Japanese SMEs to follow their principals to Thailand [*BoI Investment Review, 1996: 2*; *Economist Intelligence Unit, 1996: 2, 21*]. This met little if any organised protest from the local business community, in part because parts producers and SMEs were weakly organised. 'The Federation of Thai Industries voiced no specific objection to the promotion of FDI by foreign suppliers firms. Indeed, final goods assemblers, for whom the entry of foreign component suppliers posed no competitive threat, dominated the representative associations' [*Felkner, 2001: 173*].

The financial crisis and later the abolishment of LCRs made the situation extremely difficult for SMEs and domestic suppliers. The BoI revitalised its BUILD programme and expanded it in 1997 to include the ASEAN Supporting Industry Database (ASID) and the Vendors Meet Customers (VMC) programme. ASID provided information on more than 12,000 manufacturers in the ASEAN area, including about 7,000 firms in Thailand. The VMC programme was established to introduce local automotive and electronics parts suppliers to potential buyers. In this programme, the BoI acts as a broker to match assemblers (buyers) and suppliers (vendors). By September 1999, a total of 17, and two years later 50, assemblers had been visited by potential part suppliers. The BoI was also undertaking so-called 'local-to-local meetings' introducing Thai SMEs to counterparts in Japan, hoping for technology transfer and other possible alliances. Finally, BUILD started expanding its activities from local assemblers to overseas buyers (BUILD homepage[2]; *Bangkok Post*, 19 June 1999 and 5 November 1999) [*UNCTAD, 2001: 202–203*].

Altogether, though staffed with eight full-time staff and an average annual budget of five million baht, BoI/BUILD remained constrained by the scope of its mission, mandate and expertise. The activities were in the field of information and increasingly again in matchmaking, while the agency was not able to provide direct technical, financial and managerial support to Thai suppliers. Furthermore, by inviting foreign suppliers to invest in wholly foreign-owned firms, the BoI tended to give priority to upgrading of the TNC sector rather than to linkage formation and upgrading of Thai suppliers. However, the trend towards promotion of strategic alliances between Thai SMEs and reputable foreign suppliers ('local-to-local meetings') may strengthen the position of the former if effectively assisted.

VII. SUPPORTING INDUSTRIES AND SME POLICY IN THAILAND DURING THE 1990s – THE MINISTRY OF INDUSTRY

The Ministry of Industry's first policy initiative in relation to supplier development was the Master Plan for the Development of Supporting Industries in Thailand (1995). During the early 1990s, Japan became increasingly interested in protecting its investments in the ASEAN and in developing local supporting industries to promote the competitiveness of Japanese affiliates in the region. Through the Japan Ministry of International Trade and Industry (MITI) and the Japan International Cooperation Agency (JICA) it advanced 'the supporting industry' idea. In the Thai context, the Japanese were particularly interested in two supporting industries: auto parts and electrical/electronics parts. The Department of Industrial Promotion (DIP) agreed with JICA on a so-called comprehensive 'Study on Industrial Sector Development – Supporting Industries in the Kingdom of Thailand'. The overall objective of the study would be to formulate a master plan for supporting industries covering just two supporting industries: auto parts and electrical and electronic parts [*JICA-DIP, 1995: Annex A, p. A-10–2*].

The conclusions and recommendations in the study report were organised around six elements which together added up to a very comprehensive programme: policy and legislation, market development, technology upgrading, financial support, upgrading of management and investment promotion. Under the heading of 'policy and legislation', the report suggested a basic law of SME development as well as a law of subcontracting promotion. Market development support referred to promotion of subcontracting business. At the organisational level, the study advocated a reorganisation of the MoI in order to make the DIP into a 'pilot agency' for SME development. In relation to backward linkages, it included on the one hand an expansion of BUILD's intermediary activities and the units transfer to a new reorganised DIP in the MoI, and on the other hand a full-scale subcontracting assistance programme for those pairs of buyers and suppliers who wanted to enter into linkage arrangements to be promoted in the future by a new DIP unit [*JICA-DIP, 1995: 11-1-14 ff, 11-3-1ff, 11-4-3*].

The Master Plan for Supporting Industries was approved by the Cabinet in May 1996. There was an implementation period of six years (1996–2001). However, the plan met resistance inside the MoI where the industrial planning unit (OIE) pushed for inclusion also of 'non-metallic industries'. Similarly, the BoI tended to favour its own broader definition of supporting industries.

By the end of 1996, no particular budget had been established for the Master Plan, so the DIP would have to apply to the Budget Bureau on a yearly basis. The implementation process started inside the DIP with the formation of a Bureau of Supporting Industries Development (BSID), but any signs of implementation outside DIP jurisdiction were not visible.

During 1997, shallowness problems in the manufacturing sector were surpassed by problems in the real estate and financial sector. The Chuan II government in co-operation with the Bretton Woods institutions gave priority to macroeconomic policies and financial sector reforms, while SME/supplier problems were not addressed. In late 1998, this changed almost overnight. When it became obvious that the large conglomerates would be struggling with their debt problems for a long time and would eventually probably let foreign investors take over (or increase their stakes), the SME sector was suddenly presented as the 'rescue boat' for Thailand.

Leading Thai politicians suddenly presented themselves as strong devotees of SME programmes, too. The Thai Rak Thai Party, headed by Thaksin Shinawatra, suggested assistance to particular export-oriented SMEs using local technology. Chart Pattana Party, and its *de facto* leader Industry Minister Suwat Liptapallop, suggested a more broad-based support to SMEs, including those in rural areas. Finally, the Democrat Party, headed by Prime Minister Chuan Leekpai, supported the idea of channelling low interest loans to SMEs through state agencies. At the bureaucratic level, the Director-General of the Department of Industrial Promotion, Manu Leopairote was pushing for a comprehensive SME support package, encompassing a SME basic law. The BoI was in favour of support to Thai-owned suppliers. The Japanese agencies (JETRO and JICA) used their financial leverage to push for their supporting industry model, and were eager to see a new assistance agency (with technical support from Japan) heading these efforts. Finally, the World Bank was also in favour of SME support but not of cheap (non-market based) loans to SMEs (*Bangkok Post*, 6 November 1998, 9 November 1998, 11 December 1998).

In contrast to the pre-crisis period, there appeared to be a coalition of agents that had expressed their strong interest in assisting SMEs in exporting industries or in sectors supplying such industries. There was also a clear awareness that the SMEs were hit hard by the economic downturn. The weaker baht had made imported inputs more costly. Therefore, and in order to be able to manufacture according to the just-in-time principles, foreign (Japanese) assemblers were increasingly keen to have more localised supply of parts. Financial assistance through the Miyazawa plan brought the Japanese strongly back in SME policy. From March to August 1999, JICA conducted a 'Follow-up Study on Supporting Industries Development' that presented a framework for what was now called a 'Master Plan for SME Promotion' based on the Japanese experience. The plan had six strategies (again with the DIP as the lead implementing agency): strengthening SME financing, upgrading of technological and managerial capability of SMEs (including a subprogramme on technology transfer from large enterprises (LEs) to SMEs), development of human resources for SMEs, securing SME markets, and improvement of the business environment for SMEs, and promotion of three supporting industries [*JICA-DIP, 1999*]. At the same time, an ex-MITI Director-General, Mr Mizutani, was dispatched to Thailand as an advisor to the MoI and Ministry of Finance from November 1998 to July 1999.

In December 1998, the Cabinet endorsed the draft of a SME Promotion Act proposed by the Ministry of Industry. After a lengthy parliamentary process it was finally adopted in January 2000. In order to insure coherence and co-ordinated efforts, the new legislation created a SME Promotion Committee and an Executive Committee. Further, it was decided to establish a semi-autonomous SME Promotion Office (SMEPO) and a SME Promotion Fund. Finally, it was decided to create an Institute of SME Development (ISMED) focusing on entrepreneurial development and to draw up a SME Promotion Action Plan covering 18 areas, of which promotion of linkages between SMEs and LEs was one [*DIP, 2000a*].

In the meantime a comprehensive 'SME Master Plan (1999–2004)' was drawn up by the MoI/DIP with financial and personnel support from Japan (Mizutani). The plan was approved by the Cabinet in April 2000 and encompassed seven strategies: upgrade technological and management capabilities of SMEs; development of entrepreneurs and human resources of SMEs; enhance SMEs' access to markets; strengthen the financial support system for SMEs; provide a conducive business environment; develop microenterprises and community enterprises; and develop networking of SMEs and clusters. The third strategy included a programme to promote subcontracting and linkage formation with large enterprises plus development of a buyer-supplier database and information network. Apart from the cluster and microenterprise strategies which stemmed mainly from inputs by the United Nations Industrial Development Organisation (UNIDO) and the International Labour Organisation, the plan basically copied the programme elements already presented in the Japanese 'Follow-up Study on Supporting Industries Development' [*DIP, 2000b*].

In April 2000, Thailand had finally a comprehensive SME policy in place. However, the policy process was top-down and had been driven by a mixture of local political entrepreneurship and strong donor involvement. In contrast, local SMEs/suppliers played a limited if any role. The Federation of Thai Industries (which represented mostly large enterprises and assemblers) was involved but was not particularly interested in SME policy.

The implementation process was not always well co-ordinated. Thanks to the Miyazawa funds and after the model of the Japanese Institute for Small

Business Management and Technology (JSBC), ISMED was set up in April 1999. ISMED became an autonomous agency under the MoI and it was planned as a centre point for assisting new and existing SMEs through training, counselling and information services [*ISMED, 2001*]. ISMED was located at the Thammasat University Rangsit campus and consisted of a network of ten universities which may not be the optimal agent for approaching the target group – SME owners and middle management of SMEs [*Sevilla and Kusol, 2000: 41*]. Furthermore, the division of labour between and co-operation with the sectoral institutes under a parallel industrial restructuring programme was not clear [*Régnier, 2000: 85*]. Problems of targeting and co-ordination were also observed in relation to the SME Financing Advisory Centre (SFAC) set up in October 1999. SFAC had its main office in Bangkok but the 24 nationwide centres were located at accounting and management departments at the provincial universities [*Régnier, 2000: 82*] (*Bangkok Post*, 11 August 2000). Finally, by January 2001, the DIP still served as an interim SME promotion office and was in the process of formulating detailed projects under the seven strategies (interview with DIP official, January 2001).

In short, a fairly coherent SME policy was designed during 1998–1999. This was less a result of collective organised SME entrepreneurs and more due to an alliance between donor agencies distributing Japanese aid and the Ministry of Industry. The latter was headed by a Minister who managed to use the SME issue as a policy platform, and he had by then a leadership team in its Department of Industrial Promotion that had long tried to advance SME and supporting industry policies. However, implementation of a credible and well co-ordinated SME policy with a supplier development potential had not taken off by early 2001.

VIII. CONCLUSION ON LINKAGE, SUPPLIER AND SME POLICIES DURING THE 1990s

Promotion of backward linkages and complementary supplier development/SME policies came onto the policy agenda in Thailand during the 1990s. For a long time policy incentives had given priority to large end-product manufacturers and to vertical integration but some policies did also create space for a segment of locally owned producers of parts and components. However, the new environment of trade liberalisation (including abolishment of LCRs), export orientation and regional restructuring of TNC activities increasingly put this policy approach under pressure.

It was against this background that linkage and supplier development policies evolved in Thailand from 1991 onwards. Foreign donors and selected Thai officials became increasingly aware of the need for structural changes and industrial deepening in the manufacturing industry. They were especially preoccupied with how to develop low-level assembly processing towards the production of higher-value added items involving a greater use of locally made inputs. At the overall level, the introduction of a value added tax in 1992 undoubtedly changed the incentive structure in favour of more vertical disintegration. Moreover, promotion of backward linkages and supplier development with an emphasis on small scale enterprises were integrated into the overall national planning and adopted by the leading industrial policy agencies – the BoI and MoI – during the early 1990s.

The BoI developed two comprehensive linkage and supplier development programmes – the BUILD programme and the NSDP. The latter was a multi-agency effort that failed to obtain support outside the NSDP, and it did not reach the final stage of Cabinet decision-making. The BUILD programme started in 1992 but when implemented the scope of the activity was narrowed down. From being originally interested in linking local Thai parts producers to foreign assembly companies, the main BoI strategy ended up being that of encouraging foreign (Japanese) suppliers to follow their principals to Thailand.

Prior to the financial crisis, the Ministry of Industry never agreed internally on the content of a supplier industry strategy. One section – the Department of Industrial Promotion – took advantage of its departmental autonomy and Japan's 'extended industrial policy'. It advanced a Master Plan for the Development of Supporting Industries, which was approved by the Cabinet in 1996, but budgets were not allocated to the plan, so implementation was constrained. The comprehensive programme was reintroduced in the wake of the economic crisis of 1997–98, now in the form of a Master Plan for SME Development. The Miyazawa fund was a strong motivating factor and the plan was broadly speaking worked out along the lines suggested by a Japanese consultancy firm.

Compared with the flourishing policy initiatives in relation to linkage and supplier/SME development, programming was not co-ordinated across agencies and actual implementation was poor. The reason was fourfold. First, at the level of policy design, we observed that linkage and supplier development policies were not always consistent with or supported by broader policies. FDI policies were not adjusted so as to support a 'linkage triangle' with strong local (SME) suppliers. This was also the case with trade policy where tariffs favoured end-product manufacturers and where exporters were not induced to use local suppliers.

Second, and related, there was not strong high-level political support for linkage and supplier development policies. Prior to the crisis macroeconomic policies were the main concern. There was an 'implicit development strategy' to attract foreign capital as the principal motor of development [*Putzel, 2000: 183*]. There was much attention towards how foreign capital (portfolio capital, commercial loans and FDI) could cover the rising deficit on the current account, and little attention was given to the effects of the real appreciation of the baht for competitiveness as well as for the purchasing pattern of inputs. Generally, microeconomic policies were given low priority during the first two years of the crisis. The sudden interest in the SME issue during late 1998 was likely more a policy adjustment to small business criticism that a genuine shift in policy. Further, it was probably to an even larger extent designed to comply with aid requirements than to reflect a prioritised and focused set of problems that the Thai authorities could realistically cope with.

Third, there was inter-ministerial rivalry and a lack of a relatively autonomous and strong co-ordinating agency. Both unstable coalition governments and 'party ownership' to particular ministries worked to the detriment of comprehensive policies. Old plans tended to be scrapped before implemented when incoming governments brought new ones forward. Further, in the coalition governments, individual parties had a preference for particular ministries, and cabinet members (and their respective parties) focused exclusively on their own ministries, showing little interest in general economic policies and strategies. A final reason for the lack of co-ordination was the long tradition of departmental parochialism, leading to fragmentation, functional duplication and overlap inside ministries.

A fourth constraining factor was the lack of dense and effective institutionalised public-private sector links. This was partly because the FTI did not represent the interests of SMEs, partly because the particularistic links between politicians and business remained the dominant form of public-private sector interaction, and partly because priority (in the policy design phase) was given to extraverted policy networks. As a consequence, the policy initiatives were mostly government driven and there was little private sector involvement in implementation.

In short, we argue that because of a range of politico-institutional constraints an effective linkage and supplier development policy did not come into being in Thailand during the 1990s. Still one may ask whether mistaken policy and poor policy implementation were really major problems, that is whether even well-designed and well-implemented policies would have made any difference. This is a complicated matter because the structural forces were of a contradictory nature. On the one hand, managers of foreign-owned plant in developing countries show an increasing willingness to expand 'local sourcing' of inputs and enter into tighter relationships with domestic SMEs. That opens new opportunities for local suppliers in Thailand as did the financial crisis in 1997–98. Devaluation of the Thai baht made the export sector more competitive but imported inputs became more expensive, too. Therefore, foreign assemblers became increasingly interested in using local suppliers rather than importing their parts and components. On the other hand, TNCs are in the process of modernising their supplier base and of reducing the number of suppliers on which they depend. They now buy from the most competitive suppliers on a worldwide basis and often induce their established home-based or global suppliers to follow them to new locations. As a consequence, local suppliers in developing countries compete with global suppliers capable of providing 'full package supply services'. The global suppliers thus may crowd-out the local suppliers and that may reduce the propensity of TNC assemblers to co-operate with local part producers and to transfer know-how to them. In the Thai case, we observed a stronger presence of global suppliers and 'follow sourcing' during the 1990s. In addition, the domestic market for local parts producers during the crisis dropped to half of the pre-crisis level and as assemblers focused more on foreign markets local part producers were required to shorten delivery time and improve product quality to meet global standards. There can be little doubt that crowding-out and marginalisation were strong forces during the 1990s and in particular in the second half of the decade. Nevertheless, local Thai part producers would have been in a better position if effective linkage, supplier development and SME policies had supported upgrading of existing firms and developed a range of potential new suppliers. Though they may not have been able to hold a first-tier position they could by approaching the new standards of price, quality and timely delivery have stabilised themselves as second- or third-tier suppliers. In that sense, the 1990s turned out to be a period of lost opportunities for introducing the necessary upgrading of existing local Thai suppliers.

IX. ADDITION: POLICIES OF COMPETITIVENESS, SME CLUSTERS AND ENTREPRENEURSHIP UNDER THE THAKSIN GOVERNMENT

In February 2001, Thaksin's Thai Rak Thai Party (TRT) came to power. During the electoral campaign it had promised the (rural) poor debt relief and development funds, while the urban middle classes were promised recovery through a management approach to public policy. There was also a nationalist streak in economic policy and Thaksin argued that the movement into the 'knowledge-based economy' should rely more on the domestic market, local resource capacities and local entrepreneurship [TRT, 2001]. In contrast, there should be less emphasis on exports and FDI. The nationalist-populist platform was actually implemented in the form of an aggressive fiscal stimulus programme. Thaksin moved quickly to fulfil the promised populist programmes for the rural poor. Similarly, the new administration channelled new credits to SMEs. During the financial years 2002 and 2003, it provided funds that equalled 2.7–2.8 per cent of GDP [World Bank, 2003b: 36].

The new SME policies encompassed low interest loans channelled through commercial banks and a new SME Development Bank, and improvement of the functioning of SME-related agencies in order to improve training, technological assistance and marketing support [*MoF-NESDB, 2001*]. In relation to linkage policies, there was now less emphasis on vertical linkages to TNCs and more emphasis on horizontal networks, through the notion of cluster-based development of SMEs – adopted by the MoI as one its new policies. In the meantime, the composition of Thai export moved towards high-tech labour-intensive components and parts, while the share of traditional labour-intensive manufactures declined. According to the World Bank this shift was 'supported mainly by the foreign-invested enterprises that are part of the well-integrated production network in the region and elsewhere. There is however limited linkage of these firms with the small and medium Thai firms' [*World Bank, 2003b: 2*].

The economic strategy was further developed by the formation of a high-level National Competitiveness Committee (NCC) – under the National Economic and Social Development Board (NESDB) – in the spring of 2002. The new national competitiveness approach led to a change in BoI policy. A new BoI investment promotion strategy was launched in late 2002 which focused on the quality rather than the quantity of investments; that relaxed zoning rules in order to promote cluster development; and that gave special attention to investment services in five target industries. However, persistent poor funding of the BUILD programme was an indicator of the low priority given to vertical linkage formation [*World Bank, 2003a: 14; BoI Investment Review, 2002; Altenburg et al., 2004: 38*].

The BoI was also involved in the public governance reform that was accelerated when the Thaksin administration took over. Overseen by a Public Sector Development Commission and with strong donor support, an ambitious five-year bureaucratic reform programme was initiated in late 2002. The two new key acts were the Ministerial Restructuring Act (MRA) and the Public Administration Act (PAA). The former reorganised the existing 14 ministries in order to minimise functional duplication and established six new ministries. In this process, the BoI was transferred from being an agency under the Office of the Prime Minister to becoming a part of the MoI. The MRA provided guidelines for comprehensive overhauls of bureaucratic procedures.

Though aiming at higher efficiency, the bureaucratic reform should also be seen in the broader context of political power and control. The centre of industrial policy-making moved from ministries to the NESDB and Thaksin's party team, which controls all the important portfolios. TRT has consolidated its grip on Thai politics by absorbing other parties, so that Thailand seems to be moving towards a two-party system. Further, Thaksin has extended his growing dominance from the parliament and the bureaucracy to include the military and the media. Finally, organised business has been given access to policy-making through the representation of apex business associations (including the Federation of Thai Industries) in the NCC.

Political centralisation and bureaucratic streamlining may lead to effective industrial policy-making in general and effective linkage and SME/supplier development policies in particular. However, two key questions remain. One is whether the reform agenda is sustainable or whether patronage politics will take over. The creation of six new ministries and several new departments may be seen as a measure of increased patronage politics (i.e. more positions available for Thaksin supporters) rather than a measure of genuine public sector reform [*Mutebi, 2003*]. A second question is whether the Thaksin government will actually be able to implement the comprehensive and ambitious policy and institutional reform programmes. A crucial issue here is that while institutionalised links to big business have been established, similar institutional links to local SME suppliers have still not emerged.

NOTES

1. Here and in the following the term local enterprise or domestic supplier refers to an enterprise that is owned or controlled by host-country nationals (Thais).
2. BUILD homepage on: http://www.boi.go.th/english/build/index.html.

REFERENCES

Altenburg, Tilman, 2002, 'Transnational Corporation and the Development of Local Firms', Proceedings of the 2002 Conference of the Association of Development Researchers in Denmark (FAU), Copenhagen.

Altenburg, Tilman, Michaela Gennes, Arzu Hatakoy, Mirko Herberg, Jutta Link and Sabine Schoengen, 2004, 'Strengthening Knowledge-based Competitive Advantages in Thailand', German Development Institute (GDI), Reports and Working Papers 1.

Bank of Thailand, 1996, *Quarterly Bulletin*, June.

Bank of Thailand, 1998, *Quarterly Bulletin*, October.

Battat Joseph, Isaiah Frank and Xiaofang Shen, 1996, 'Suppliers to Multinationals. Linkage Programs to Strengthen Local Companies in Developing Countries', Foreign Investment Advisory Service (FIAS) Occasional Paper 6.

Brimble, Peter and Chatri Sripaipan, 1994, 'Science and Technology Issues in Thailand's Industrial Sector. The Key to the Future', prepared for the Asian Development Bank, June 1994, Annex 7, The National Supplier Development Programme – Concepts and Programs.

Brimble, Peter and Pattanun Woodtikarn, 1994, 'The Build Phase II Project. A Report on Supporting Industries Development', SEAMICO Business Information & Research Co., Ltd, a Report made for the Board of Investment (BoI), Thailand.

Board of Investment (BoI), 1994, 'Towards Developing Thailand's Supporting Industries. BUILD, BOI for Industrial Linkage Development', Office of the Prime Minister, Royal Thai Government.

Board of Investment (BoI), 1997, 'BOI Unit for Industrial Linkage Development. Your Key to Thailand's Supplier Industries', Office of the Prime Minister, Royal Thai Government.

BoI Investment Review, 1994, Vol.3, No.1, Bangkok: Board of Investment.

BoI Investment Review, 1996, Vol.5, No.3, Bangkok: Board of Investment, 30 September.

BoI Investment Review, 2002, Vol.11, No.4, Bangkok: Board of Investment, December.

Department of Industrial Promotion (DIP), 2000a, 14 December, http://www.dip.go.th/policy/epolicy2.htm.

Department of Industrial Promotion (DIP), 2000b, 14 December, http://www.dip.go.th/policy/epolicy6.htm.

Dicken, Peter, 1998, *Global Shift. Transforming the World Economy*, third edition, London: Paul Chapman/SAGE.

Dixon, Chris, 1999, *The Thai Economy. Uneven Development and Internationalisation*, London and New York: Routledge.

Economist Intelligence Unit, 1996, *Country Report Thailand*, Vol.2, p.12.

Evans, Peter, 1995, *Embedded Autonomy. States and Industrial Transformation*, Princeton, NJ: Princeton University Press.

Felkner, Greg, 2001, 'Politics of Industrial Investment Policy Reform in Malaysia and Thailand', in K.S. Jomo (ed.), *Southeast Asia's Industrialization. Industrial Policy, Capabilities and Sustainability*, Houndmills, Basingstoke: Palgrave.

Gereffi Gary, 1999, 'International Trade and Industrial Upgrading in the Apparel Commodity Chain', *Journal of International Economies*, Vol.48, pp.37–70.

ISMED (Institute of SME Development), 2001, brochure.

Jansen, Karel, 1997, *External Finance in Thailand's Development. An Interpretation of Thailand's Growth Boom*, London: Macmillan.

Japan International Cooperation Agency (JICA) and Department of Industrial Promotion (DIP), Ministry of Industry, Thailand, 1995, *The Study on Industrial Sector Development – Supporting Industries in the Kingdom of Thailand*, Tokyo: UNICO International Corporation, International Development Center, September.

Japan International Cooperation Agency (JICA) and Department of Industrial Promotion (DIP), Ministry of Industry, Thailand, 1999, *The Follow-up Study on Supporting Industries Development in the Kingdom of Thailand*, Tokyo: UNICO International Corporation.

Lall, Sanjaya, 1995, 'Industrial Strategy and Policies on Foreign Direct Investment in East Asia', *Transnational Corporations*, Vol.4, No.3, pp.1–26, December.

Lall, Sanjaya, 1999, 'Raising Competitiveness in the Thai Economy. Country Employment Policy', Review for the International Labour Office, June (first draft).

Levy, Brian with Albert Berry, Motoshige Itoh, Linsu Kim, Jeffrey Nugent and Shujiro Urata, 1994, 'Technical and Marketing Support Systems for Successful Small and Medium-Size Enterprises in Four Countries', Policy Research Working Paper 1400, Washington, DC: The World Bank.

Meyanathan, Saha Dhevan and Roger Munter, 1994, 'Industrial Structures and the Development of Small and Medium Enterprises Linkages: An Overview', in Saha Dhevan Meyanathan (ed.), *Industrial Structures and the Development of Small and Medium Enterprise Linkages. Examples from East Asia*, Washington, DC: The World Bank, Economic Development Institute (EDI) Series.

MoF-NESDB, 2001, *Strategy Plan Framework. Toward Quality and Sustainability of Thailand Economic Development*, Bangkok: Ministry of Finance and National Economic and Social Development Board, July.

Mutebi, Alex M., 2003, 'Thailand in 2002. Political Consolidation and Economic Uncertainties', *Asian Survey*, Vol.43, No.1, pp.100–12.

Putzel, James, 2000, 'Developmental States and Crony Capitalists', in Pietro Masina (ed.), *Rethinking Development in East Asia. From Illusory Miracle to Economic Crisis*, Richmond, Surrey: Curzon.

Régnier, Philippe, 2000, *Small and Medium Enterprises in Distress. Thailand, The East Asian Crisis and Beyond*, Vermont: Gower.

Sevilla, Ramon, C. and Kusol Soonthornthada, 2000, 'SME Policy in Thailand: Vision and Challenges. Institute for Population and Social Research', IPSR Publication No.251, Thailand: Mahidol University.

Tambunlertchai Somsak, 2002, *Tracking Manufacturing Performance*, UNIDO Integrated Programme for Thailand – Component 6 (unpublished).

Tambunlertchai Somsak and Eric D. Ramstetter, 1991, 'Foreign Firms in Promoted Industries and Structural Change in Thailand', in Eric D. Ramstetter (ed.), *Direct Foreign Investment in Asia's Developing Economies and Structural Change in the Asia-Pacific Region, Boulder*, San Francisco and Oxford: Westview Press.

Thai Rak Thai (TRT), 2001, 'The Standpoint on the Policy of the SME and the Establishment of the New Entrepreneurs', 3 May, http://www.thairakthai.or.th/.

Wattanapruttipaisan, Thitapha, 2002, 'SME Subcontracting as Bridgehead to Competitiveness: An Assessment of Supply-side Capabilities and Demand-side Requirements', *Asia-Pacific Development Journal*, Vol.9, No.1, pp.65–87.

World Bank, 2003a, *Thailand Economic Monitor*, May, The World Bank, The World Bank Office Bangkok, http://www.worldbank.or.th/monitor.

World Bank, 2003b, *Thailand Economic Monitor*, October, The World Bank, The World Bank Office Bangkok, http://www.worldbank.or.th/monitor.

UNCTAD, 1998, *World Investment Report 1998. Trends and Determinants*, New York and Geneva: UNCTAD.

UNCTAD, 2001, *World Investment Report (2001). Promoting Linkages*, New York and Geneva: UNCTAD.

UNCTAD, 2003, *World Investment Report (2003). FDI Policies for Development: National and International Perspectives*, New York and Geneva: UNCTAD.

Exports and Technological Capabilities: A Study of Foreign and Local Firms in the Electronics Industry in Malaysia, the Philippines and Thailand

RAJAH RASIAH

This chapter seeks to compare the export incidence and technological capabilities of foreign and local electronics firms in Malaysia, the Philippines and Thailand, and to explain their determinants. Foreign firms generally produced higher human resource and process technology capabilities than local firms in Malaysia and Thailand. Although foreign firms were generally endowed with higher research and development (R and D) capabilities in Malaysia and Thailand, local firms enjoyed higher technological capabilities than foreign firms in the Philippines. Statistically, only process technology, human resources, and R and D (indirectly through links with process technology) were linked with exports. Owing to low intensity levels, R and D enjoyed little relationship with the other explanatory variables. Foreign ownership was strongly correlated with exports, but its statistical link with process technology, human resources and R and D capabilities was not significant, which is likely to be a cause of the need to use cutting edge human resource and process technologies in order to export. Weak high-tech infrastructure seems to have restricted firms' participation in high value added activities such as R and D, but sufficient network cohesion in export processing zones has facilitated expansion in low value added exports.

Cet chapter cherche à comparer les effets sur les exportations et les capacités technologiques d'entreprises électroniques étrangères et locales en Malaisie, aux Philippines et en Thaïlande, et à en expliquer les causes déterminantes. En général, les entreprises étrangères produisent des capacités en ressources humaines et en technologie de processus

Rajah Rasiah is Senior Research Fellow at the United Nations University, Institute for New Technologies, Maastricht. The main empirical data used in this chapter on the Philippines and Thailand were drawn from the Asian Development Bank survey carried out in 2000–2002, and on Malaysia from the INTECH-DCT survey carried out in 2001–2002. Comments from workshop participants at 'Understanding FDI-Assisted Economic Development', TIK Center, University of Oslo, 22–25 May 2003 are gratefully acknowledged.

supérieures à celles des entreprises locales en Malaisie et en Thaïlande. Bien que les entreprises étrangères soient généralement dotées de capacités supérieures en Recherche et Développement en Malaisie et en Thaïlande, les entreprises locales font preuve de capacités techniques supérieures à celles des entreprises étrangères aux Philippines. Statistiquement parlant, seuls la technologie de processus, les ressources humaines et la Recherche et le Développement (indirectement à travers des liens avec la technologie de processus) sont liés aux exportations. Etant donné un bas niveau d'intensité, la Recherche et le Développement ont peu de liens avec les autres variables explicatives. La propriété étrangère est étroitement liée aux exportations, mais son lien statistique avec la technologie de processus, les ressources humaines et la Recherche et le Développement n'est pas significative, ce qui est probablement une des causes de la nécessité d'utiliser des ressources humaines et des technologies de processus de haut niveau afin d'exporter. Apparemment, une faible infrastructure de haute technologie réduit la participation des entreprises aux activités à haute valeur ajoutée, comme la Recherche et le Développement, mais la cohésion des réseaux dans les zones qui se dédient à l'exportation facilite l'expansion des exportations à basse valeur ajoutée.

I. INTRODUCTION

Latecomer economies typically access technology through learning – via a combination of imports and domestic development. The cumulative dimension of technology offers firms the opportunity to learn from already developed technologies. Countries such as Japan, South Korea and Taiwan generally imported foreign technology through imitation and licensing from transnational corporations (TNCs). Others such as Singapore and Ireland have relied extensively on transnationals' foreign direct investment (FDI) to stimulate learning and innovation. While the role of transnational corporations in the appropriation of knowledge, learning and innovation is growing in significance, little consensus exists on their impact on local firms. Scattered works – both anecdotal and analytical – detail spillovers of tacit and experiential knowledge embodied in human capital in the creation of local firms [*e.g. Rasiah, 1994, 2002a*].

However, transnational-driven technological capability development does not evolve in a vacuum. Domestic institutions through policy instruments and intermediation between firms, and firms and institutions have been critical in stimulating learning and innovation. Network cohesion is critical to raise the fluidity of interaction and systems synergies. This chapter attempts to one, compare the mean export and technological capabilities of foreign and local firms, and two, analyse the statistical relationship between these key variables and ownership, labour market and institutional and systemic variables in Malaysia, the Philippines and Thailand, where TNC-driven electronics exports dominate manufactured exports.

Malaysia is the most experienced of the three with the first major wave of electronics TNCs – dominated by component assembly - relocating operations from the early 1970s. Subsequent influxes of electronics firms led by consumer electronics (1980s) and disk drives, computer peripherals and computers (late 1980s and early 1990s) have made especially its western corridor dominated by export-oriented TNCs. Thailand experienced its first major wave of electronics firms from the second half of the 1980s – characterised particularly by American and Japanese firms seeking alternatives away from Malaysia when incentives expired and production costs rose in Malaysia. In particular, labour-intensive disk drive and computer component firms relocated operations to Thailand on a large scale. The Philippines competed with Malaysia in the early 1970s to attract electronics TNCs, but the insurgency under the Marcos rule raised political risks and hence restricted relocation until the late 1980s. Some firms such as Intel retained assembly operations in Manila and began to expand assembly and test or memory chips once the Philippines was able to offer stability and security in the export processing zones. TNCs relocated on a large scale in the 1990s to take advantage of the large reserves of literate labour there and because of rising production costs in Malaysia and Thailand. All three countries also benefited from an exodus of TNCs from Japan and the Asian newly industrialised countries following the Plaza Accord of 1985.

The chapter is organised as follows. Sections II and III present the analytic and methodological frameworks to examine the nexus between exports and firm-level and systemic capabilities. Section II examines the theoretical underpinnings of the conceptual framework. Section III presents the methodology and the data used. Sections IV and V discuss the results and econometric analysis. Section VI finishes with the conclusions and policy implications.

II. ANALYTIC FRAMEWORK

The literature on estimating aggregate spillovers is extensive, but little exhaustive work exists on its direct measurement. Caves [*1974, 1982*] presented arguably the first systematic production function estimation of spillovers, which led to a plethora of works extending the framework [*e.g. Blomstrom and Persson, 1983; Blomstrom and Wolff, 1994*]. Urata [*2001*] examined the nexus between investment and exports in Asia. Haddad and Harrison [*1993*], Aitken and Harrison [*1999*] and Gachino and Rasiah [*2003*], *inter alia*, took this approach to a new dimension by refining the methodology to address locational, industry-type, scale and demonstration effect variables. These works helped improve the original instruments that Caves had used to extend the understanding of spillovers. However, there has been growing debate over whether the relationships traced through such methodologies can be equated with actual spillovers. Given that technological external economies are often difficult to picture exhaustively, it is not wrong to contend that spillovers cannot be measured completely.

In light of the problems associated with measuring spillovers, an alternative framework was developed to examine capabilities between foreign and local firms. Antecedents to this framework can be traced to Lall [*1992*], Rasiah [*1995, 2003*], Lall and Wignaraja [*1995*], Bell and Pavit, 1995, Westphal *et al.* [*1990*], Ernst *et al.* [*1998*] and Wignaraja [*2002*]. This framework has its limitations as some capabilities measured may have been drawn from other firms, and the acquisitions involved may have been at the expense of high economic costs. The normalising formula used does not attach particular weights to a given set of proxies and hence may introduce biases. In addition, some capability measures require subjective assessments by companies thereby attracting biases. Nevertheless, since the measurements use estimations of data drawn wholly from firms, these biases are outside the control of analysts. It can be subsumed under the usual problem associated with data collection in general. Importantly it allows to some extent the estimation of latent spillovers, the extent of realisation of which will depend, *inter alia*, on the absorptive capacity of the domestic environment.

This chapter takes the implicit argument from Smith [*1776*] and Young [*1928*] that market size and capabilities stimulate each other. Smith made the observation – which was lucidly articulated later by Young – that causation involving the division of labour and the size of the market works both ways. Put simply, the scale and 'gales of creative destruction'[1] effects of external markets and competition respectively influence capability building, while improvements in capability building help sustain exports. This argument is also consistent with Hirschman's [*1958*] dynamic analysis calling for export orientation as the basis for stimulating backward linkages. Although this chapter does not deal with backward linkages extensively as measurement is confined to firm-level capabilities, it captures a significant part of its potential. Capabilities rise with the location of firms in the technology trajectory [*see Dosi, 1982; Pavitt, 1984*]. Firms engaged in product and process technology development require strong high-tech infrastructure (e.g. research and development (R&D) support).

Since a firm's performance is a function of its own endowments and conduct, and interactions with related economic agents, it can be examined from the taxonomy shown in Table 1. Industrial organisation typically expounds that a firm's performance is determined by the structure (or environment, including other economic agents in factor and final markets) in which the firm is located and by its conduct [*see Bain, 1968; Scherer, 1973, 1980; Greer, 1992*]. Two overlapping literatures – national innovation systems (NISs) and industrial policy (IP) – discuss the policy and institutional environment necessary to stimulate upgrading,

TABLE 1
TAXONOMY OF CAPABILITIES AND PERFORMANCE

Environment systemic	Structure	Conduct	Firm-level capabilities	Performance
Basic nfrastructure, labcur supply, socic-political and economic environment, high-tech support and network cohesion	Organisational structure of firms – vertically or horizontally integrated, domestic oriented or internationalised, ownership and firm size	Human resource development and process and product technologies, and financial strategies	Human resource, process technology, process technology R and D, product technology, product technology R and D, financial capability	Export, value added, return on investment

Note: The NIS viewed from the lenses of firms.
Source: Adapted from Rasiah [2002a].

innovations and firm-level performance. The earliest IP arguments can be traced to Smith [*1776*], Hamilton [*1791*], Mills [*1848*] and List, 1885. NIS examines knowledge production – flows and diffusion involving learning and innovations – which provides a systemic dimension to a firm's conduct and performance [*Freeman, 1989; Lundvall, 1992; Nelson, 1993; Nelson and Winter, 1982a, 1982b; Dosi, 1982; Pavitt, 1984*]. IP typically prescribes trade environment to nurture infant firms to competitive status [*see Lewis, 1955; Myrdal, 1957; Kaldor, 1957*].

Institutional and systemic effects are examined using the proxies of basic infrastructure and high-tech infrastructure and network cohesion. The first and last is particularly important for firms to keep costs and defects low and to meet tight delivery times. High-tech infrastructure becomes essential for firms to participate in higher value added activities. Neo-classical literature typically calls for government intervention to be limited to the provision of basic infrastructure. The NIS and IP literature actively supports active government intervention to overcome market failures associated with firms' participation in especially R and D activities, and the range of related activities such as human resource training beyond schooling, and process technology acquisition and development. Hence, the NIS and IP advocate interventions for building the high-tech infrastructure necessary to stimulate innovations in firms.

While a cluster may have a considerable density of firms and the requisite institutions, it may not enjoy strong connecting bonds between them. The role of systemic instruments in driving cluster cohesion has been important in the development of dynamic industrial districts. Inter-firm pecuniary relations through sales and purchases is only one channel of inter-firm interactions [*Rasiah, 1995*]. Knowledge flows – rubbing-off effects from the interaction between workers [*Marshall, 1890*], and the movement of tacit and experiential skills embodied in human capital – raise systems synergies [*Polanyi, 1997; Penrose, 1959*]. Open dynamic clusters encourage inter-firm movement of tacit and experiential knowledge embodied in human capital, which, *inter alia*, distinguishes dynamic from truncated clusters [*see Best, 2001; Rasiah, 2001*]. New firms benefited from gaining managerial and technical personnel from older firms in Silicon Valley irrespective of national ownership. American-owned Intel, Dell and Solectron, and Japanese-owned firms hired technical and managerial personnel from old firms in Silicon Valley [*see Rasiah, 2002a*]. Mature firms gain new ideas and processes to ensure continuous organisational change as some old employees are replaced to make way for fresh ones with new ideas, while new firms benefit from the entrepreneurial and technical – tacit and experiential – knowledge to start new firms [*Rasiah, 2001, 2002a*]. Saxenian [*1994, 1999*] offered an impressive documentation of inter-firm movement of human capital, which helped support new firm creation capabilities in Silicon Valley. Rasiah [*1999*], Doner [*2001*] and Aoki [*2001*] have argued the important role intermediary organisations play in strengthening network cohesion – including co-ordinating demand–supply relations between government, firms and institutions.

The role of government is generally only received positively universally when involving the provision of basic infrastructure (e.g. primary schooling, health and sanitation, road and telecommunications and basic utilities). Neo-classical economists consider private ownership should be the basis for the provision of high-tech infrastructure. IP and NIS exponents disagree here and are quick to emphasise the public goods characteristics of high-tech infrastructure such as R and D, training and information and communications technology (ICT). Institutions associated with human resource development and R and D often face collective action problems. Private agents are unlikely to participate in market-driven activities when the risks involved are not matched by returns. Schumpeter [*1934*], Kaldor [*1957*] and Arrow [*1962*] had argued that interventions in markets are necessary to stimulate participation in welfare-enhancing public goods activities.[2] Training and R and D institutions involve considerable acquisition and diffusion of knowledge, which is a public good in that its consumption by one does not exclude consumption by others. Hence, knowledge-producing institutions such as universities, R and D laboratories and technical schools come under the category of public goods. It is well recognised that strong government support initiated technological progress in the Western economies and Japan [*see Gerschenkron, 1962; Kaldor, 1962; Johnson, 1982*].

Given the public good characteristics of training and R and D, it can be argued that strong government is essential to stimulate firms to engage extensively in human resource training and R and D activities. Government support can take the form of financial incentives or subsidies, launching of training and R and D organisations, and special programmes to build firm – university and firm – public training and R and D relationships. However, within the trajectory of technology development, firms hardly participate in R and D activities initially. All three countries under consideration here are expected to be entrenched at the lower rungs of the technology ladder in the electronics industry, though Malaysia has enjoyed considerable development of institutions from the late 1980s. Hence, it is argued in the chapter that product R and D capability will be low in these countries, with little coherent statistical link with the explanatory variables. Also, given the eclectic nature of government intervention in these countries, apart from laying the groundwork to attract foreign direct investment (FDI) government support is unlikely to be correlated positively with even human resource and process technology capabilities. Nevertheless, network cohesion is essential to facilitate firms' efforts to internalise much of the related transactions and co-ordinate their operations competitively.

Labour market conditions often influence export competitiveness, including the relocation of labour-intensive low value added activities. Hence, it is vital to

TABLE 2
OWNERSHIP STRUCTURE OF FIRMS, 2001

	Malaysia	Philippines	Thailand	Total
Local	10	9	7	26
Foreign	36	18	18	72
Responding firms	46	27	25	98

Source: ADB [2002]; INTECH-DCT [2002].

examine wages and participation of trade unions. Given the problems associated with the reliability of firm-level data on labour market conditions and the conditioning domestic environment on the limited room enjoyed, trade unions are not necessarily effective instruments for ensuring strong labour conditions. Nevertheless, union incidence does reflect a certain minimum floor for labour welfare in the selected economies. Sabel [1989], Sengenberger and Pyke [1991] and Wilkinson and You [1995] offered lucid accounts of the high road to industrialisation where good labour conditions were instrumental in stimulating long-term competitiveness and the converse involving the low road to industrialisation. The difference can also be presented as flexible casualisation involving poor labour conditions [see Deyo, 1987] and flexible specialisation involving good labour market conditions. However, given the low incidence of union affiliation in the industry globally, and high reserves of surplus labour in the Philippines – including the supply of labour with at least secondary school education - and labour shortage problems in Malaysia, wages are likely to show a mixed relationship with exports and the technological capability variables. Given the high levels of literacy and technical knowledge required of electronics workers – especially in semiconductor assembly – exports are likely to show positive correlation with wages. The same may not hold for the technological capability variables as firms are required to have similar levels of capabilities in related stages and types of production to compete in an industry where technology evolves quickly. The Philippines in particular offers much lower wages and yet enjoys the highest share of literacy among secondary students among the three countries [see Rasiah, 2002b: Table 2]. Given the low levels of unionisation in the industry globally, union affiliation is unlikely to enjoy strong positive correlation with exports and the technological capability variables. R and D capability may provide an exception as the main focus on process R and D in these countries could have influenced the greater involvement of workers in creative decision-making.

There is a long debate on the importance of size on firms' export competitiveness. Typical industrial organisation arguments posit that firms achieve competitiveness with a certain minimum efficiency scale (MES), which varies with industries [see Scherer, 1973, 1991; Pratten, 1971]. Industries such as steel, automobiles and tankers are considered to enjoy scale economies and hence require higher MES unit production to achieve low marginal unit costs. Where scale is not considered important – e.g. small-batch machine tools and plastic components – scope rather than scale is considered important [*Piore and Sabel, 1984; Rasiah, 1995*]. Audretsch [*2002*] offered a persuasive analysis of US data to dispel arguments related to the significance of large size in efficiency and innovative activities. The increasing decomposition and dispersal of production involving information technology industries has made small size very efficient. Given the controversy over the role of size in economic performance and the claims of industrial organisation exponents over MES differences in industries, a neutral hypothesis was framed – simply that size has a bearing on export competitiveness.

Having established the key hypothesis of the paper, i.e. that FDIs originating from superior NISs – with the exception of R and D – are generally endowed with higher export, human resource and process technology capabilities than local firms, and hence offer developing economies strong latent capacity to stimulate technology transfer. However, the main source of data does not enable an assessment of technology transfer statistically. Because participation in product R and D activities requires superior domestic institution R and D support infrastructure, foreign firms typically retain such activities at home sites, and hence are likely to demonstrate inferior product R and D capabilities than local firms. Nevertheless, firms are expected to utilise host-site personnel to participate strongly in process R and D activities, and some levels of product diversification and proliferation activities where at least a minimal amount of R and D infrastructure exists.

III. METHODOLOGY

Capability indexes constitute the main pillar of the methodology used to examine export performance in this chapter. The use of capability indexes in examining the capacity of firms to compete can be traced to Lall [*1992*], Bell and Pavit [*1995*], Westphal et al. [*1990*] and Wignaraja [*2000*]. Wignaraja adapted the Ernst et al. [*2000*] taxonomy of capabilities to fit the narrow range of data available to examine upgrading in firms in Mauritius. The methodology developed here extracts elements from all the above but refines it further to obtain a broader understanding of learning, innovation and export performance in the four industries and three countries selected.

Exports: Proxy for Performance

Owing to the high export incidence among the firms in the sample – especially in the Philippines and Thailand where all firms enjoyed export experience, a more discriminatory proxy was chosen to represent exports. The logarithm of exports (in millions of US dollars) was preferred over just export incidence to transform the relationship between the dependent and independent variables from a quadratic to a linear one.

Firm-level Capabilities and Variables

Firm-level dynamics include minor processes such as the introduction of inventory control systems to human resource training and R and D strategies. Since a number of characteristics and strategies have overlapping objectives and effects, it is methodologically better to integrate related proxies into a composition of indexes. This will not only help minimise double counting, but also avert some amount of multi-collinearity problems in statistical analysis. Because there are no a priori reasons to attach greater significance to any of the proxies used, the normalisation procedure was not weighted. In addition, the proxies were chosen carefully to prevent the integration of endowments (e.g. R and D scientists and engineers, and share of technical human capital) acquired or poached from other firms, which will have direct bearing on capability. However, the indirect effects of these proxies would still remain as the hiring of key R and D scientists or engineers by one firm from another would inevitably have a bearing on its R and D capability. The following broad capabilities and related composition of proxies were used.

Human resource capability (HRD) was measured as:

$$HRD = \frac{1}{3}[TM, TE, CHR] \tag{1}$$

Where TM, TE and CHR refer to training mode (multinomial logit variable of 1 when only external staff are used to train employees, 2 when staff with training responsibilities are on payroll, 3 when a separate training department is used, 4 when a separate training centre is used and 0 when no formal training is undertaken) and training expense as a share of payroll and cutting edge human resource practices used. CHR was measured by a score of 1 for each of the practices and divided by the total number of practices. The firms were asked if it was their policy to encourage teamworking, small group activities to improve company performance, multi-skilling, interaction with marketing, customer service and R and D departments, lifelong learning and upward mobility.

Process Technology Capability. Data on four proxies facilitated the computation of process technology capability (PT), which was calculated using the formula:

$$PT = \frac{1}{4}[E, M, ICT, QC] \tag{2}$$

Where E, M, ICT and QC refer to equipment, machinery, information technology components and quality control instruments. E and M were computed as multinomial logistic variables with average age of over 5 years = 0, 3–5 years = 1, 2 to less than 3 years = 2 and less than 2 years = 3. Likert scale scores ranging from 1 to 5 (least to strong) were used to measure ICT. QC was measured as a dummy variable (QC = 1 if cutting edge methods were used, QC = 0 otherwise). Formula (3) below was used to normalise the scores in (1).

$$\text{Normalisation score} = (X_i - X_{min})/(X_{max} - X_{min}) \tag{3}$$

Where X_i, X_{min} and X_{max} refer to the ith, minimum and maximum values, respectively, of the proxy X.

Research and Development. The learning process leads firms to eventually participate in new product development. While beginners only learn and absorb, firms typically learn and develop new products. With the exception of funding of public laboratories and universities, firms seldom participate in basic research. Hence, firm-level R and D is largely focused on process technology and product development – especially diversification of use and proliferation.

The data collected have enabled the computation of three R and D proxies. The first relates to whether firms undertake in-house process R and D and is measured as:

$$\text{IPRD} = 1 \text{ if yes}, \quad \text{IPRD} = 0 \text{ otherwise}$$

The second deals with R and D expenditure incurred by firms to undertake R and D. It was not possible from the sample data to disentangle investment advanced between process and product R and D, and hence this proxy was measured to relate to both product and process R and D and was measured as:

$$\text{RDE} = (R \text{ and } D \text{ expenditure}/\text{sales}) \times 100 \text{ per cent} \tag{4}$$

The third measure deals with the resources firms' advance to undertake R and D activities and it was measured as:

$$\text{RD} = \frac{1}{2}[\text{RDE}, \text{RDM}] \tag{5}$$

Where RDE is derived from (4) and RDM refers to mode of R and D activity. RDM is a multinomial logistic variable equal to 4 if a separate centre, 3 if a separate department, 2 if staff with product R and D responsibility, 1 if engaged in contract R and D with firms, institutions or individuals located outside firms, and 0 if none of the above is involved. Formula (3) above is used to normalise the proxies for adding and averaging. This variable was used.

Labour Market Conditions

Two proxies were used to pick up labour market conditions, viz., wages and unions.

Wages. Average monthly wages were used. Since it is difficult to obtain wages of just workers, the figure was drawn up by dividing the total salaries and remuneration of each company with the number of their work-force and converted to US dollars. Average wages was used in regressions when HRD, PT and RD were run as dependent variables, and the logarithm of wages was used when X was used as the dependent variable. The latter was taken to make the exports and wages in the same denomination.

W = average wage = total payroll/(number of employees)

W1 = logarithm of average wage = logarithm of total payroll/(number of employees)

Union. A dummy variable equal to 1 if the firm's workers are unionised and 0 otherwise. Union = 1 if some or all workers were unionised; Union = 0 otherwise.

Other Critical Firm-level Variables

Two other important firm-level structural variables were included in the analysis, viz., ownership and size. Ownership was used as a separate variable as well as separate regressions by foreign- and locally controlled firms.

Ownership. Two definitions of foreign ownership (FO) were used and were measured as:

FO = 1 if foreign equity ownership was 50 per cent, or more; FO = 0 otherwise.

FO1 = 1 if foreign equity ownership exceeded 10 per cent, FO1 = 0 otherwise.

Size. In light of the controversy involving the defining criterion for different sizes, number of employees was used as the proxy for size. Originally four categories were used, viz.:

Micro = 50 and less
Small => 50–200
Medium => 200–500
Large => 500.

With the exception of micro firms, which did not produce statistically significant results in most regressions, the results of the remaining regressions did not change much when the categories were reduced to two, and hence the results presented use:

SMI = 500 and less

Large => 500

Institutional and Systemic Variables

Capabilities exogenous to firms under the systemic category include basic and high-tech infrastructure, the role of government and network cohesion. Since the supply of both basic and high-tech infrastructure often varies within countries – especially those involving large poor and middle-income economies, e.g. China and Thailand – a range of proxies were used to estimate the indexes. Basic and high-tech infrastructure was adjusted, with the national figures providing the supply of such services.

Basic Infrastructure. The basic infrastructure index (BI) is measured using the formula:

$$BI = \left\{ \frac{1}{3}[T, PS, H] \frac{1}{8}[TS, WS, TCI, HF, LI, FS, BE] \right\}^{\frac{1}{2}} \qquad (6)$$

Where T, PS, H, TS, WS, TCI, HF, LI, FS and BE refer to telecommunications, primary schooling, health, power supply, water supply, telecommunication infrastructure, health facilities, legal infrastructure, financial infrastructure and basic education, respectively. The variables of T, PS and H were represented by the proxies of main telephone lines per thousand people, primary school enrolment ratios and doctors per thousand people respectively. Since the supply of these endowments is nationwide actual national figures were used. The proxies were limited to three owing to lack of recent data on other proxies. Values of all variables were normalised using formula (3) before being added. Likert scale scores of 1–5 were used with range rising with strength of the institutions involved to estimate firms' rating of TS, PS, WS, TCI, HF, LI, FS and BE.

High-tech Infrastructure. The high-tech infrastructure (HI) index is measured using the formula:

$$HI = \left\{ \frac{1}{2}[RDI, RDSE] \frac{1}{7}[I(RDO), I(STC), I(STI), I(ICT), I(STU), I(IPR), I(VC)] \right\}^{1/2} \qquad (7)$$

Where RDI, RDSE, I, RDO, STC, STI, ICT, STU, IPR and VC refer to R and D investment in gross national investment, R and D scientists and engineers per million people, a dummy (1 if the institution/instrument exists or 0 otherwise), research and development organisations, science and technology human capital, science and technology incentives, information and communication technology infrastructure, science and technology programmes in universities, intellectual property rights infrastructure and venture capital. The proxies of RDI and RDSE were used to represent the supply of high-tech infrastructure. Values of all variables were normalised using formula (3) before being added. Other proxies were not used owing to the lack of data. Likert scale scores ranging from 1 to 5 were used (1 for least to 5 for the strongest) to estimate firms' rating of RDO, STC, STI, ICT, STU, IPR and VC.

Role of Government. Because of the varied nature of the role of government, an adjusted variable was used. Likert scale scores ranging from 1 to 5 (rising with firms' recognition of importance) were given for the individual roles played by the government. The scores from the different proxies are then summed and averaged.

$$GHR = \frac{1}{2}[HRI(HRA), HRO(HRB)] \tag{8}$$

Where HRI refers to human resource incentives (yes $= 1, 0$ otherwise). HRA $=$ Likert scale average scores involving the firms' rating of government training incentives. HRO refers to government-owned or -sponsored institutions and government-owned training institutions, vocational institutions, polytechnics and universities (yes $= 1, 0$ otherwise). HRB $=$ Likert scale average scores involving firms' rating of government-owned human resource and training organisations, vocational and technical schools, and universities.

$$GPT = \frac{1}{2}[PTI(PTA), PTO(PTB)] \tag{9}$$

Where PTI refers to process technology incentives such as duty drawback on import of new equipment and tax deductions on process innovation (yes $= 1, 0$ otherwise). PTA $=$ Likert scale average scores involving firms' rating of government process technology incentives. PTO refers to government-owned or -sponsored institutions engaged in assisting with firms' process technology upgrading (including quality and standards organisations, and the training of related personnel) (yes $= 1, 0$ otherwise). PTB $=$ Likert scale average scores involving firms' rating of government-owned organisations engaged in process technology assistance.

$$GRD = \frac{1}{2}[RDI(RDA), RDO(RDB)] \tag{10}$$

Where RDI refers to R and D incentives and grants (yes $= 1, 0$ otherwise). RDA $=$ Likert scale average scores involving firms' rating of government incentives, grants and -owned institutions engaged in R and D (including universities). RDO refers to government-owned or -sponsored R and D institutions or related institutions (yes $= 1, 0$ otherwise). RDB $=$ Likert scale average scores involving firms' rating of government-owned R and D and related organisations.

$$GFC = IOI(IOA) \qquad (11)$$

Where IOI $= 1$ if organisations or incentives to promote intermediary roles exist, 0 otherwise. IOA $=$ Likert scale average scores involving firms' rating of government organisations and incentives promoting firm-level capabilities.

$$Gov = \frac{1}{3}[GHR, GRD, GFC] \qquad (12)$$

Where Gov refers to the overall strength of government's role as rated by firms. This variable was dropped from the equations eventually owing to its composition in the cluster cohesion variable and multi-collinearity problems. Nevertheless, its role is captured separately.

GRD was used alternatively to examine government support for R and D activities. Separate regressions involving GHR, GRD and GFC were not run to avoid multi-collinearity problems.

Network Cohesion. Firms were asked to rate the strength of their connections and co-ordination with basic and high-tech infrastructure institutions, with related government organisations and between each other. Likert scale scores ranging from 1 to 5 were used and averaged with the number of proxies used. The network cohesion index (NC) was measured using the formula:

$$NC = \frac{1}{4}[BI, HI, GIR, SN] \qquad (13)$$

Where BI, HI, GIR and SN refer to links between firms and: relevant basic infrastructure institutions such as medical service, and road and transport authority; high-tech institutions such as training, university and R and D institutions; relevant government bodies such as licensing authority, incentives unit, customs and R and D laboratories; and buyer and supplier firms respectively. NC is constructed using Likert scale average scores of firms' ratings of BI, HI, GIR and SN (inter-firm supplier links). Since it is the firms' ratings of connections and co-ordination with support institutions and other firms that are important, the individual scores used are different from the ones used to measure BI, HI, GIR and SN above. Given the lack of a priori arguments to differentiate the significance of these proxies, no weights were attached.

Regressions were run with and without country dummies because of the use of institutional and systemic variables. Since all the countries studied are in

Southeast Asia the argument for using gravitational effects on the basis of regional trade and investment synergies does not arise.

Determinants of Capabilities

The following basic model was specified to estimate the statistical determinants of export capability. Ordinary least squares (OLS) regressions were preferred here with the *t*-ratios drawn using robust standard errors. The model was run with and without country dummies:

$$X = \alpha + \beta 1 \, \text{HRD} + \beta 2 \, \text{PT} + \beta 3 \, \text{RD} + \beta 4 \, \text{BI} + \beta 5 \, \text{HI} + \beta 6 \, \text{FO} + \beta 7 \, \text{W1}$$

$$+ \, \beta 8 \, \text{Union} + \beta 9 \, \text{NC} + \beta 10 \, \text{Gov} + \mu \tag{14}$$

The determinants of three important firm-level capabilities were estimated using Tobit regressions. Tobit regressions were preferred over OLS because the dependent variables are all censored. The models were run with and without country dummies:

$$\text{HRD} = \alpha + \beta 1 \, \text{X} + \beta 2 \, \text{PT} + \beta 3 \, \text{RD} + \beta 4 \, \text{BI} + \beta 5 \, \text{HI} + \beta 6 \, \text{FO}$$

$$+ \, \beta 7 \, \text{SMI} + \beta 8 \, \text{W} + \beta 9 \, \text{Union} + \beta 10 \, \text{NC} + \beta 11 \, \text{Gov} + \mu \tag{15}$$

$$\text{PT} = \alpha + \beta 1 \, \text{X} + \beta 2 \, \text{HRD} + \beta 3 \, \text{RD} + \beta 4 \, \text{BI} + \beta 5 \, \text{HI} + \beta 6 \, \text{FO}$$

$$+ \, \beta 7 \, \text{SMI} + \beta 8 \, \text{W} + \beta 9 \, \text{Union} + \beta 10 \, \text{NC} + \beta 11 \, \text{Gov} + \mu \tag{16}$$

$$\text{RD} = \alpha + \beta 1 \, \text{X} + \beta 2 \, \text{HRD} + \beta 3 \, \text{BI} + \beta 4 \, \text{HI} + \beta 5 \, \text{FO} + \beta 6 \, \text{PT}$$

$$+ \, \beta 7 \, \text{SMI} + \beta 8 \, \text{W} + \beta 9 \, \text{Union} + \beta 10 \, \text{NC} + \beta 11 \, \text{Gov} + \mu \tag{17}$$

Specific industry-level questionnaires were designed, pilot tested, translated into local languages and mailed to all firms listed in official government statistics records in Malaysia, the Philippines and Thailand. Case studies of at least three firms in each industry were undertaken by national consultants to help extract industry-type characteristics before the questionnaires were finalised. The survey and the case studies constitute the basis for the results and analysis in the study.

IV. DATA AND RESULTS

The survey produced 98 responses with the relevant data for the econometric analysis.[3] The breakdown is shown in Table 2. The complete response firms were used here so as to be consistent with the econometric analysis undertaken later. While the measurement of capabilities has enabled comparisons by ownership,

TABLE 3
FIRMS WITH EXPORT EXPERIENCE

	Malaysia	Philippines	Thailand	Total
No	3	0	0	3
Yes	43	27	25	95
Total	46	27	25	98

Source: ADB [2002]; INTECH-DCT [2002].

the lack of information on diffusion has prevented an assessment of technology transfer. Interviews in all three countries produced anecdotal evidence to suggest considerable transfer of technology from foreign to local firms.[4] In addition, Rasiah [1994, 1996, 2002a,b] produced substantial evidence to demonstrate FDI-rooted local capability development in the state of Penang, Malaysia. None of the independent variables shows serious problems of multi-collinearity (see Appendix). The highest correlation coefficient recorded between SMI and PT did not affect significantly the statistical significance, nor did the coefficients of the independent variables in equations (15) and (17), which was tested with separate regressions.

The electronics industry in Southeast Asia is dominated by foreign ownership. Foreign firms clearly outnumbered local firms in Malaysia, the Philippines and Thailand, which is reflective of the national ownership data for the electronics industry (see Table 2).

The electronics industry in Southeast Asia is essentially an export-oriented industry with the value chain dispersed across borders [Rasiah, 2003]. Even inward-oriented firms in the industry operate primarily as suppliers to exporting firms. With the exception of thee firms in Malaysia, the remaining electronics firms enjoyed export experience (see Table 3). Local ownership accounted for the three firms in Malaysia that did not export at all.

Foreign firms dominated exports in all three countries involving all four sub-industries (see Figure 1). With the exception of computers and peripherals where local firms enjoyed a higher export mean figure in Thailand, the foreign firms' share exceeded 80 per cent in all other industries in all three countries. There were no firms at all in the Thai sample and no local firms in the Filipino sample of the consumer electronics industry. There were also no foreign firms in the Filipino sample of the printed circuit board (PCB) and related industry.

Apart from product R and D capability, foreign firms generally enjoyed higher technological capabilities than local firms in all the countries except for the Philippines (see Table 4). Foreign firms on average enjoyed higher HRD capabilities in Malaysia and Thailand. The margin of difference was small in Malaysia and Thailand, while the index was the same for the Philippines. Foreign firms enjoyed higher PT capability in Malaysia and Thailand. Only in

FIGURE 1
FOREIGN FIRMS' SHARE OF MEAN EXPORTS, 2001

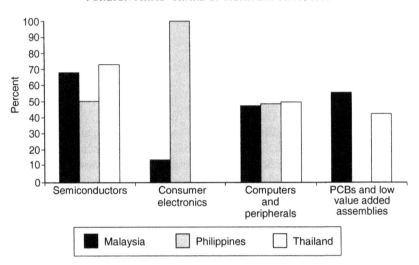

the Philippines was the local firms' PT index much higher than that of foreign firms. The picture was different though with RD capability where only in Malaysia was the index for foreign firms higher than that for local firms. Given the underdeveloped state of institutional support facilities at host sites in the Philippines and Thailand, foreign firms' use of superior R and D support facilities at their home sites is the main reason for this result. Malaysia is an exception where incentives since the late 1980s and specialised institutions have encouraged a limited amount of process R and D and developmental product R and D operations [*see Rasiah, 1996, 2002b*].

Given industry differences in the technologies, capabilities were disentangled into four sub-industries. Comparisons were not possible involving the consumer industry in the Philippines as there were no local firms, or in Thailand where there

TABLE 4
TECHNOLOGICAL CAPABILITY INDEXES, 2001

	HRD		PT		RD	
	Local	Foreign	Local	Foreign	Local	Foreign
Malaysia	0.44	0.47	0.47	0.67	0.03	0.10
Philippines	0.64	0.64	0.72	0.56	0.01	0.01
Thailand	0.56	0.58	0.48	0.55	0.06	0.04

Source: ADB [*2002*]; INTECH-DCT [*2002*].

FIGURE 2
FOREIGN FIRMS' SHARE OF MEAN HRD INDEX, 2001

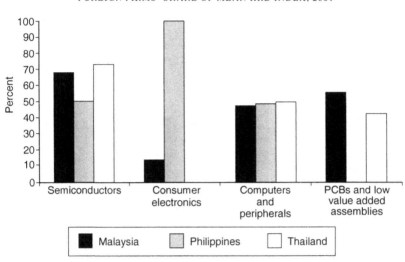

were no firms at all in the sample. There were also no foreign firms in the Filipino sample of the PCB and related industry. Foreign firms enjoyed a big advantage in HRD capability over local firms in the semiconductor industry in Malaysia and Thailand (see Figure 2). There were generally only slight variations on the basis of ownership controlling for sub-industries. Within the industry, foreign firms enjoyed an advantage in semiconductors and local firms had higher intensities in consumer electronics. This was expected generally since firms have to have similar levels of HRD capabilities to compete in export markets.

The picture was similar with PT capability, though foreign firms enjoyed even higher advantage than local firms in Malaysia and Thailand in semiconductors and PCBs and other low value added items (see Figure 3). Given that HRD capability is critical to operate and maintain the machinery and equipment and undertake organisational changes, the similar pattern is to be expected.

Three different proxies were used to estimate the RD index, viz., R and D personnel, R and D expenditure in sales, and incidence of process R and D activity. RD capability in all three countries was extremely low (see Table 4 and Figures 4, 5, 6 and 7). Within this highly limited participation, with the exception of semiconductor firms in Malaysia and Thailand, local firms generally carried out more product development activities than foreign firms. However, apart from the Philippines where local firms' share of firms equipped with in-house process R and D operations was higher than that of foreign firms involving semiconductors, the converse was the case with consumer electronics, computers and peripherals

FIGURE 3
FOREIGN FIRMS' SHARE IN MEAN PT INDEX, 2001

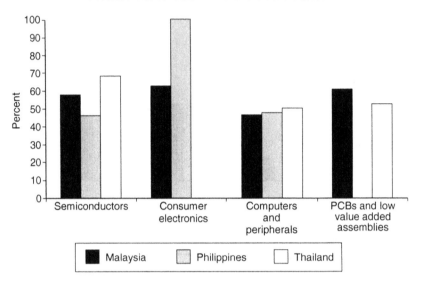

FIGURE 4
FOREIGN FIRMS' SHARE OF MEAN R AND D PERSONNEL, 2001

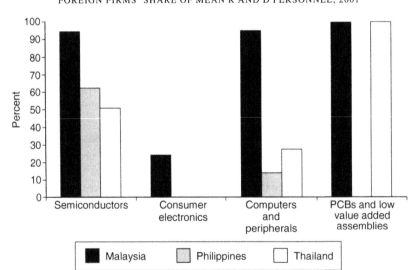

FIGURE 5
FOREIGN FIRMS' SHARE OF MEAN R AND D EXPENDITURE, 2001

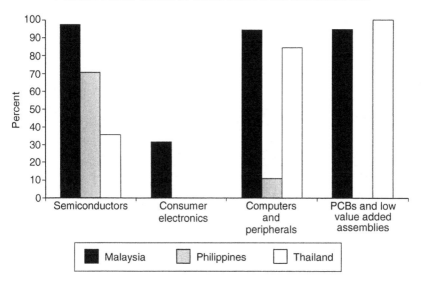

FIGURE 6
FOREIGN FIRMS' SHARE OF IN-HOUSE PROCESS R AND D, 2001

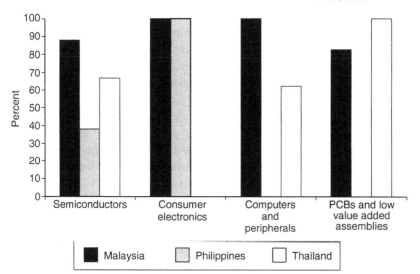

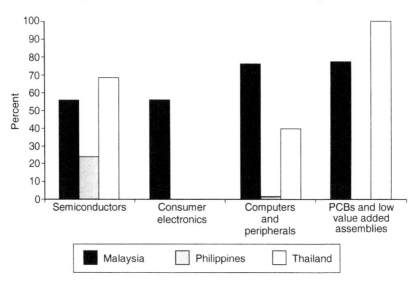

FIGURE 7
FOREIGN FIRMS' SHARE OF MEAN R AND D INDEX, 2001

and PCBs and other low value added activities (see Figure 6). In other words foreign firms were far more engaged in in-house process R and D operations than local firms. Given the significance of *kaizen* in particular foreign firms, this is to be expected as they continuously seek to raise throughput efficiency levels.

The patterns were different when R and D personnel were analysed (see Figure 4). Foreign firms enjoyed an advantage in all the countries in the semiconductor industry, though the difference was marginal in Thailand. In consumer electronics, local firms dominated in Malaysia – but they were all incurred in product development. The foreign firms in the Filipino sample had no R and D personnel.

In computers and peripherals, foreign firms dominated in Malaysia but the opposite was the case in the Philippines and Thailand. Dell stated that Penang, Malaysia was a major location for the development of Asia-based customisation of computer products.[5] Only foreign firms had R and D personnel in Malaysia and Thailand in the PCB and related low value added industries. The local firms in Philippines did not hire any R and D personnel in this industry.

Foreign firms dominated the limited R and D expenditure in sales incurred by semiconductor firms in Malaysia and Philippines. Local firms enjoyed higher R and D expenditures in sales in Thailand (see Figure 5). Foreign firms dominated in the computer and peripherals and in the PCB and related low value added industries in Malaysia and Thailand. Local firms enjoyed a much higher share in the computer and peripherals industry in the Philippines.

Foreign firms' share of the overall R and D index (RD) was higher in Malaysia and Thailand in semiconductors, in Malaysia in consumer and computer and related industries, and in Malaysia and Thailand in PCB assembly and related low value added activities (see Figure 7). Local firms enjoyed a lead in the Philippines in semiconductors and computers and peripherals. Hence, overall, despite their preference for carrying out much of their R and D activities in subsidiaries located in superior NISs, foreign firms still generally enjoyed higher capabilities than local firms. However, R and D was still little developed in these countries.

While capabilities differ with industrial specificity and the type of technology, three points can be summed up from this section. First, HRD capability was fairly even between foreign and local firms in all three countries. Second, apart from in the Philippines, foreign firms generally enjoyed higher PT capability than local firms – though the pattern was similar to HRD. Third, with the exceptions of the Philippines and computers and peripherals involving Thailand, foreign firms generally enjoyed higher – though extremely limited - overall R and D capability. Overall, three important conclusions emerge from this section. First, because the industry is largely export oriented and hence exposed to international competition, the disaggregated indicators of technological capabilities show that HRD did not vary significantly between foreign and local firms. Second, local firms in the Philippines enjoy the highest relative technological capability in relation to foreign firms among the three countries. Third, product R and D activities are generally very low in all three countries. Within the low levels, foreign firms still enjoyed higher RD capabilities than local firms, but largely because of their involvement in process development activities.

V. ECONOMETRIC ANALYSIS

The econometric analysis undertaken in this section is focused on establishing correlations rather than causation, which was avoided owing to the lack of panel data. The main objective of the analysis is to examine the statistical relationship between technological capabilities and other explanatory variables. As explained earlier, alternative regressions using FO with FDI of at least 50 per cent of equity, and FO1 with FDI exceeding 10 per cent of equity respectively were run.

Export Capability

The econometric exercise using OLS models – regressing firm-level technological capability and other explanatory and control variables on

TABLE 5
DETERMINANTS OF EXPORTS, 2001
$X = \alpha + FO + BI + HI + Gov + NC + PT + RD + HRD + SMI + W1 + Union + \varepsilon$

X	FO		FO1	
HRD	0.072	0.780	−0.216	0.580
	(0.07)	(0.79)	(−0.19)	(0.56)
NC	0.585	0.616	0.564	0.596
	(2.07)**	(2.14)**	(1.91)***	(1.97)**
BI	−0.452	−0.730	−0.241	−0.540
	(−0.48)	(−0.84)	(−0.24)	(−0.58)
HI	0.273	−1.029	0.177	−1.382
	(0.15)	(−1.00)	(0.10)	(−1.32)
Gov	−0.421	−0.254	−0.487	−0.289
	(−1.44)	(−0.99)	(−1.68)***	(−1.12)
FO	1.103	1.138	1.066	1.047
	(2.41)**	(2.53)*	(2.26)**	(2.21)**
RD	1.150	0.874	1.228	0.942
	(1.05)	(0.80)	(1.10)	(0.85)
PT	3.373	3.158	3.274	3.048
	(3.30)*	(2.99)*	(3.25)*	(2.93)*
Union	0.163	0.009	0.305	0.145
	(0.28)	(0.02)	(0.55)	(0.26)
W1	0.591	0.455	0.685	0.540
	(3.02)*	(2.32)**	(3.62)*	(2.81)*
$Countd_2$	−0.861	–	−0.509	–
	(−1.32)		(−0.79)	
$Countd_3$	−1.885	–	−1.930	–
	(−1.28)		(−1.31)	
Ind_2	−0.412	−0.277	−0.120	−0.277
	(−0.50)	(−0.33)	(−0.15)	(−0.33)
Ind_3	0.062	−0.070	0.201	−0.070
	(0.14)	(−0.16)	(0.43)	(−0.16)
Ind_4	−0.164	−0.246	0.019	−0.246
	(−0.26)	(−0.39)	(0.03)	(−0.39)
Constant	0.372	−0.204	0.652	−0.205
	(0.32)	(−0.18)	(0.53)	(−0.18)
N	98	98	98	98
F	7.32*	6.43*	6.75*	6.43*
R^2	0.427	0.399	0.421	0.399

Note: Country dummies were introduced and dropped; regressions easily passed the Cook–Weisberg
test for heteroskedasticity; values in parentheses refer to t statistics. *, Significant at 1% level;
, significant at 5% level; *, significant at 10% level.
Source: ADB [2002]; INTECH-DCT [2002].

exports – produced some interesting statistical results (see Table 5). Robust
standard errors were used to compute the t-ratios although the results easily
passed the Cook-Weisberg test for heteroskedasticity.

The OLS regressions produced statistically significant results between
exports and NC, FO, PT and W variables (see Table 5). FO was highly significant

and its coefficient strong and positive (exceeding 1), which shows that foreign firms are much more export oriented than local firms. This is consistent with the share of the mean export figure where foreign firms enjoyed a massive lead over local firms, discussed earlier (see Figure 1). Greater grip in export markets obviously means that foreign firms offer the domestic economy much more room for learning and backward linkages. Panel data are necessary to confirm this Hirschman [*1958, 1977, 1984*] thesis.

PT capability was statistically highly significant and its coefficient extremely strong (exceeding 3) and positive. Obviously exports were strongly correlated with process technology. Firms with newer machinery and equipment, quality control methods and ICT tended to export much more. Given the rapid rate of technological obsolescence in the industry [*see Rasiah, 1994*], this is inevitable.

The systemic variable of NC was statistically significant and its coefficient positive and strong. In the absence of a statistically significant relationship involving the institutional variables of BI, HI and Gov, network cohesion seems critical in ensuring that firms enjoyed sufficient production and export co-ordination to export with minimal transactions costs. Exporting firms located in export processing zones have been able to access factor supply (labour, machinery and equipment, basic utilities and custom co-ordination) and export markets smoothly because of special arrangements provided in all three countries. While improvements to basic infrastructure especially in the Philippines and Thailand will help the spread of firms' activities spatially, the creation and deepening of high-tech infrastructure will stimulate firms' participation in higher value added export-oriented activities.

The labour market variable of W1 was statistically highly significant, and its coefficient fairly strong and positive. The high positive correlation between exports and wages suggest a strong positive influence of export markets on wages. It is also a reflection of the higher wages needed to hire technically qualified knowledge workers within the three economies. Union affiliation was not statistically significant, which was expected as the global electronics industry has remained strongly opposed to unionisation. The incidences of unionisation in the 2001 sample in foreign and local firms respectively in Malaysia, the Philippines and Thailand were 10.0 and 13.8 per cent, 0 and 27.8 per cent, and 14.3 and 22.2 per cent respectively.

Human Resource Capability

The Tobit regression results involving HRD were statistically significant to enable economic analysis (see Table 6). The size variable was included in the regressions.

Foreign ownership under both classifications – FO and FO1 – was statistically insignificant suggesting that firms irrespective of ownership

TABLE 6

HUMAN RESOURCE CAPABILITY, 2001

$$HRD = \alpha + X + FO + BI + HI + Gov + NC + PT + RD + HRD + SMI + W + Union + \varepsilon$$

HRD	FO		FO1	
X	−0.005	−0.005	−0.007	−0.006
	(−0.69)	(−0.60)	(−0.88)	(−0.76)
NC	0.019	0.027	0.021	0.029
	(0.95)	(1.28)	(1.04)	(1.36)
BI	0.171	0.155	0.166	0.151
	(2.94)*	(2.57)*	(2.87)*	(2.52)*
HI	0.011	−0.148	0.013	−0.144
	(0.12)	(−2.23)**	(0.14)	(−2.18)**
Gov	−0.031	−0.014	−0.031	−0.015
	(−1.80)***	(−0.89)	(−1.79)***	(−0.90)
FO	−0.019	−0.017	−0.003	−0.003
	(−0.64)	(−0.53)	(−0.11)	(−0.08)
SMI	−0.067	−0.094	−0.071	−0.097
	(−1.91)***	(−2.69)*	(−2.04)**	(−2.80)*
RD	0.090	0.063	0.090	0.063
	(1.30)	(0.89)	(1.30)	(0.89)
PT	0.161	0.131	0.159	0.130
	(2.41)**	(1.95)***	(2.38)**	(1.93)***
Union	0.044	0.032	0.040	0.029
	(1.21)	(0.86)	(1.12)	(0.78)
W	−0.005	−0.009	−0.005	−0.009
	(−1.28)	(−2.52)*	(−1.41)	(−2.63)*
Countd$_2$	−0.089	–	−0.089	–
	(−2.27)**		(−2.28)**	
Countd$_3$	−0.209	–	−0.206	–
	(−2.62)*		(−2.58)*	
Ind$_2$	−0.149	−0.166	−0.153	−0.169
	(−3.09)*	(−3.35)*	(−3.19)*	(−3.43)*
Ind$_3$	−0.003	−0.027	−0.003	−0.027
	(−0.10)	(−0.85)	(−0.10)	(−0.85)
Ind$_4$	−0.011	−0.039	−0.011	−0.038
	(−0.30)	(−1.03)	(−0.28)	(−1.00)
Constant	0.502	0.482	0.499	0.479
	(5.92)*	(5.48)*	(5.83)*	(5.40)*
N	98	98	98	98
X^2	51.39*	44.05*	51.00*	43.78*

Note: Country dummies were introduced and dropped; values in parentheses refer to t statistics.
    *, significant at 1% level; **, significant at 5% level; ***, significant at 10% level.
Source: ADB [*2002*]; INTECH-DCT [*2002*].

have to install similar levels of HRD capability to be able to compete. Interestingly as discussed earlier the mean differences in HRD capability levels between foreign and local firms in all three countries were fairly even in Figure 2.

PT capability was highly significant statistically, and its coefficient fairly strong and positive in all the regressions. It seems obvious that higher input of ICT components and use of cutting edge quality control and newer machinery and equipment requires the use of high HRD capabilities. The country dummies of Thailand (Countd$_2$) but especially Malaysia (Countd$_3$) were statistically significant and negative, reflecting the longer experience and slightly higher PT index enjoyed by firms in these countries.

The relationship between HRD and the institutional and systemic variables was mixed. The institutional variable of BI was statistically highly significant and its coefficients positive in all the regressions. Given that all the coefficients in the regression are small, the influence of basic infrastructure on human resource capability seems very strong. Firms are likely to be endowed with a higher HRD index when the basic infrastructure offered is strong – access to training institutions and labour force with at least secondary education.

The relationship between HRD and HI was inverse when country dummies were dropped. Given that HI constitutes R and D support infrastructure and because electronics firms in all three countries participate little on R and D, little training obviously relates to such activities. Hence, this negative relationship can be considered as spurious. Filipino firms enjoyed the highest HRD capability (owing to its large reserves of labour with at least secondary and technical education), but had the lowest mean RD index (see Table 4).

The statistically insignificant relationship involving NC and the negative relationship with HI support the anecdotal evidence advanced by Rasiah [2002b], Brimble [2003] and Abrenica and Tecson [2003] that institutional and systemic synergies in all three countries are limited. Firms' efforts to upgrade their HRD will only rise if these deficiencies are overcome.

The size variable of SMI was statistically significant and its coefficient negative, demonstrating that larger firms invest more and enjoy higher levels of human resource capability than small and medium firms. The coefficients were stronger and statistically highly significant when country dummies were dropped.

The labour market variable of wages was significant when country dummies were dropped. The coefficient was negative but very small. It is interesting to find wages highly and positively correlated with exports, but negatively correlated with HRD capability. Given that the latter is only the case when country dummies were dropped and both country dummies of Malaysia and Thailand were negative and statistically significant, the availability of cheaper but literate and technical labour in the Philippines explains this. Indeed, the average daily salary in the Philippines sample was only US$1.5 when it was US$3.2 and US$9.6 in the Thailand and Malaysia samples respectively in 2001.

TABLE 7
PROCESS TECHNOLOGY CAPABILITY, 2001
$$PT = \alpha + X + FO + BI + HI + RD + HRD + SMI + W + Union + NC + Gov + \varepsilon$$

PT	FO		FO1	
X	0.020	0.020	0.021	0.021
	(1.50)	(1.51)	(1.65)***	(1.59)
HRD	0.382	0.316	0.378	0.314
	(2.30)**	(1.88)***	(2.28)**	(1.87)***
	0.006	−0.004	0.004	−0.005
	(0.17)	(−0.11)	(0.11)	(−0.14)
BI	−0.095	−0.063	−0.089	−0.060
	(−0.96)	(−0.62)	(−0.90)	(−0.59)
HI	−0.147	0.146	−0.150	0.142
	(−0.96)	(1.30)	(−0.97)	(1.27)
Gov	0.060	0.027	0.059	0.027
	(2.06)**	(1.00)	(2.04)**	(0.99)
FO	0.027	0.016	0.010	0.009
	(0.54)	(0.31)	(0.19)	(0.18)
SMI	−0.191	−0.165	−0.187	−0.164
	(−3.40)*	(−2.88)*	(−3.35)*	(−2.87)*
RD	0.134	0.167	0.135	0.167
	(1.17)	(1.44)	(1.18)	(1.44)
Union	−0.092	−0.075	−0.088	−0.073
	(−1.56)	(−1.23)	(−1.50)	(−1.20)
W	−0.002	0.005	−0.001	0.005
	(−0.31)	(0.80)	(−0.23)	(0.85)
Countd$_2$	0.056	–	0.056	–
	(0.85)		(0.85)	
Countd$_3$	0.333	–	0.329	–
	(2.50)*		(2.47)**	
Ind$_2$	−0.030	−0.011	−0.025	−0.009
	(−0.36)	(−0.13)	(−0.30)	(−0.11)
Ind$_3$	−0.070	−0.067	−0.070	−0.067
	(−1.32)	(−1.29)	(−1.31)	(−1.27)
Ind$_4$	−0.080	−0.073	−0.080	−0.072
	(−1.27)	(−1.16)	(−1.25)	(−1.12)
Constant	0.239	0.326	0.245	0.327
	(1.47)	(1.99)**	(1.49)	(1.99)**
N	98	98	98	98
X^2	59.15*	52.37*	58.90*	52.31*

Note: Country dummies were introduced and dropped; values in parentheses refer to t statistics.
   *, significant at 1% level; **, significant at 5% level; ***, significant at 10% level.
Source: Computed from ADB [*2002*]; INTECH-DCT [*2002*].

Process Technology Capability

All four Tobit regressions involving PT capability were significant statistically (see Table 7). Country dummy 3 was statistically highly significant, and its coefficient positive – which was expected as Malaysia has had the longest experience with export-oriented electronics manufacturing and hence its process technology can be considered the most sophisticated. Reversing the regression between PT and exports reduced the statistical significance of the relationship. Nevertheless, using FO1, the logarithm of exports was statistically significant at 10 per cent level.

Although the coefficients were positive, foreign ownership (FO and FO1) was statistically insignificant, which again demonstrates the need for electronics firms – irrespective of ownership – to install cutting edge equipment and control systems to be able to compete. Panel data will be necessary to confirm this observation.

HRD was statistically significant and its coefficient was positive and strong. Reversing the relationship between HRD and PT produced similar results suggesting the interdependence of these variables. High human resource capability is necessary to drive the machinery and equipment and sustain high levels of process technology, while strong process technology ensures expenditure and use of high levels of HRD capability.

The institutional and systemic variables of BI, HI and NC were statistically insignificant, suggesting that domestic institutions and systemics have had little direct influence in supporting changes in process technology in electronics firms. Nevertheless, the government variable was statistically significant, and its coefficient positive when country dummies were used. Duty reliefs on the import of machinery and equipment, preferential interest rates involving the acquisition of new equipment in Malaysia and quick customs co-ordination by government authorities seem to have helped slightly the acquisition and deployment of high PT capabilities. One important implication that can be drawn is that process technology can be strongly strengthened if strong supply networks and basic and high-tech infrastructure can be improved.

The SMI variable was generally statistically highly significant and its coefficient was strong and negative demonstrating the higher levels of process technology capability enjoyed by large firms. It seems that larger firms enjoy much more resources to install cutting edge machinery, equipment and process changes than small and medium firms. Given that all the firms are export oriented and enjoy fairly tariff-free environments in all three countries, the difference cannot be explained by higher protection rents enjoyed by large firms.

The statistically significant coefficients were slightly higher when country dummies were used, which is because of particularly higher PT capability levels enjoyed especially in Malaysia. The Malaysian country dummy (Countd$_3$) was positive and statistically strong and significant.

Both labour market variables were statistically insignificant in all four regressions. The cost of labour and union affiliation obviously seems to enjoy no statistically meaningful relationship with process technology. This was expected

TABLE 8
R AND D CAPABILITY, 2001
$$RD = \alpha + X + FO + BI + HI + PT + HRD + SMI + W + Union + NC + Gov + \varepsilon$$

RD	FO			FO1
X	0.017	0.018	0.018	0.019
	(1.09)	(1.13)	(1.17)	(1.21)
HRD	0.152	0.083	0.152	0.084
	(0.72)	(0.39)	(0.72)	(0.40)
NC	0.057	0.039	0.057	0.039
	(1.40)	(1.02)	(1.41)	(1.03)
BI	− 0.130	− 0.128	− 0.129	− 0.127
	(− 1.11)	(− 1.07)	(− 1.10)	(− 1.07)
HI	0.072	0.250	0.073	0.250
	(0.38)	(1.93)***	(0.39)	(1.94)***
RDI	0.081	0.103	0.080	0.101
	(0.84)	(1.11)	(0.82)	(1.09)
FO	− 0.009	− 0.011	− 0.025	− 0.029
	(− 0.15)	(− 0.17)	(− 0.40)	(− 0.45)
SMI	0.021	0.048	0.023	0.050
	(0.28)	(0.66)	(0.30)	(0.69)
PT	0.285	0.325	0.286	0.326
	(2.05)**	(2.34)**	(2.06)**	(2.35)**
Union	0.147	0.162	0.148	0.164
	(2.06)**	(2.25)**	(2.11)**	(2.30)**
W	− 0.002	0.002	− 0.002	0.002
	(− 0.27)	(0.29)	(− 0.26)	(0.30)
$Countd_2$	0.123	–	0.122	–
	(1.47)		(1.47)	
$Countd_3$	0.220	–	0.219	–
	(1.47)		(1.46)	
Ind_2	− 0.093	− 0.098	− 0.093	− 0.098
	(− 0.87)	(− 0.91)	(− 0.88)	(− 0.92)
Ind_3	− 0.095	− 0.071	− 0.096	− 0.073
	(− 1.48)	(− 1.13)	(− 1.51)	(− 1.16)
Ind_4	− 0.146	− 0.119	− 0.150	− 0.124
	(− 1.90)***	(− 1.57)	(− 1.94)***	(− 1.61)
Constant	− 0.312	− 0.254	− 0.303	− 0.245
	(− 1.52)	(− 1.25)	(− 1.47)	(− 1.20)
N	98	98	98	98
X^2	35.53*	32.82*	35.67*	32.99*

Note: Country dummies were introduced and dropped; values in parentheses refer to t statistics.
*, significant at 1% level; **, significant at 5% level; ***, significant at 10% level.
Source: Computed from ADB [*2002*]; INTECH-DCT [*2002*].

since the electronics industry is knowledge intensive and hence will be driven by the demands of technical precision rather than wages.

Research and Development Capability

The regressions involving R and D capability were generally weak owing to the extremely low incidence of firms' participation in such activities (see Table 8).

The relationship was even weaker with product R and D and hence the regressions were dropped – none of the coefficients was statistically significant when country dummies were used.

The relationship between RD and FO (and FO1) was statistically insignificant. This was expected given the arguments made earlier in the chapter, though foreign firms showed higher RD capability levels in Malaysia and Thailand within the extremely low index computed.

RD was statistically correlated with PT capability, and the coefficient was positive and strong suggesting that much of the limited R and D carried out by electronics firms in the three countries is related to process technology. This was expected as explained earlier as modifications to machinery and equipment and reorganisation of plant layouts dominated much of the R and D activities. A handful of local consumer electronics firms and computers and peripherals firms carried out new product development. Foreign firms in the sample undertook some amount of product development – but none related to new products.

Among institutional and systemic variables, only HI was significant at 10 per cent and only when country dummies were dropped. Firms are likely to participate in some amount of R and D activities when they enjoy access to high-tech infrastructure – especially RD incentives and support from university personnel in Malaysia and Thailand where specific incentives existed to promote RD.

The labour market variable of union affiliation was statistically significant, and its coefficient positive. Two possible reasons explain this relationship. First, the few firms that undertake R and D may have allowed greater say among workers to stimulate total participation in process technology development in firms. Small group activities engaged in generating ideas to support continuous improvement (*kaizen*) dominate these firms. The second reason may be that the relationship is just spurious given the low union incidence levels among the firms.

The econometric analysis produced a strong statistical link between exports and FO (and FO1), PT and NC in all four OLS regressions. PT was statistically strongly and positively correlated with exports, suggesting that cutting edge machinery and equipment and organisation is important to drive exports. HRD was strongly correlated with PT, suggesting a strong indirect link with exports. The lack of a direct statistically significant relationship between exports and HRD is likely to be the result of differences in wage rates involving particularly knowledge and technical workers between the three countries. Wages were statistically highly significant and their coefficient strong and positive. The Philippines enjoyed higher HRD capabilities than Malaysia and Thailand, but wages in the Philippines were much lower because of the large supply of literate and technical labour available. Process technology appears to be the key driver of exports, HRD capability and even the limited amount of R and D undertaken. Only RD was weakly correlated with the institutional and systemic variables, though it enjoyed some relationship with HI. Only NC was statistically and positively correlated with exports among the institutional and systemic variables, and BI was strongly correlated with HRD capabilities. Despite government failure and the lack of basic infrastructure in the Philippines, the creation of special industrial zones seems to have helped firms reduce transaction costs to bypass some of the general problems associated with export-oriented activities. Thus, NC has become a key variable in co-ordinating low value added exports. The lack of a consistent statistical relationship between firm-level technological capability variables and the institutional and systemic variables suggests that these economies need to improve institutional and systemic variables to stimulate firms' transition to higher value added activities.

VI. CONCLUSIONS

Overall, firms with export experience clearly outnumbered those that just sold in the domestic markets, which is consistent with the general orientation of the electronics industry in the sample countries. Foreign firms enjoyed greater export orientation than local firms. Ownership was not statistically significant involving the firm-level capability variables.

With the exception of the Philippines, foreign firms generally enjoyed higher HRD, PT and RD capabilities than local firms in the remaining countries. Local firms were generally better endowed with product RD capabilities – though foreign firms in Malaysia enjoyed a lead over local firms. However, R and D activities were extremely low in all three countries. Within the low levels, local firms tend to enjoy higher RD endowments than foreign firms, but such activities appear uncorrelated with exports and other firm-level technological capabilities. Only in semiconductors, computers and peripherals, and PCB assembly in Malaysia and PCB assembly in Thailand were foreign firms better endowed with product R and D operations – owing to long learning experience that had been achieved.

The econometric analysis produced a strong statistical link between exports and PT capability, and NC. While these relationships were direct, PT was statistically strongly and positively correlated with HRD and RD, suggesting a strong indirect link with exports. As expected RD was generally weakly correlated with the other explanatory variables. A combination of production infancy in the Philippines and problems of government failure meant that government instruments enjoyed no direct statistical relationship with exports, HRD or RD. Only PT enjoyed a positive relationship with Gov – access to special customs co-ordination instruments and duty reliefs on the import of equipment and machinery seem to have helped firms.

Size mattered in the provision of HRD and PT capabilities. Larger firms enjoyed the scale and the resources to acquire higher human resource and process technology capabilities. Size did not produce a statistically significant relationship with RD capability owing to its extremely low levels of participation.

The labour market variable of wages enjoyed a statistically highly significant and positive relationship with exports, despite the low incidence of union affiliation, and this is caused by the need for firms to hire literate and technically qualified workers to drive the knowledge-based industry. The link between wages and the firm-level technological capability variables was statistically insignificant – owing largely to the presence of qualified skilled and technical but cheaper workers in Thailand and especially the Philippines.

FO was strongly significant when involving exports. Despite government failure involving basic infrastructure, especially in the Philippines, the creation of special industrial zones seems to have helped firms to reduce transaction costs and overcome some of the general problems associated with export-oriented activities. Thus, NC has become a key variable in co-ordinating exports. Quite clearly the degree of cohesion between institutions and firms, rather than just their co-location, has been critical in driving export synergies. Varying degrees of inter-firm and institutional connections and co-ordination for firms located in the export processing zones in the Philippines, Indonesia and Thailand have helped successful exporters overcome systemic constraints.

Although the results did not allow a direct assessment of technological spillovers, given that foreign firms are largely export oriented and have generated more HRD and PT capabilities, it could be intuitively argued that their participation has at least produced latent technological capabilities for absorption by local firms. Panel data involving inter-firm links are necessary to confirm this. In the absence of such data, foreign firms' participation and the high levels of HRD and PT capabilities generated have at least transformed the local environment to facilitate export manufacturing in these countries involving a high-tech industry. It is interesting to note that the connections and co-ordination appropriated from the creation of export processing zones has helped firms – especially foreign firms – internalise transactions to overcome problems of infrastructure and government policy. Government policy must focus especially on improving the institutional and systemic variables to encourage learning and innovation in both foreign and local firms – to stimulate movement to higher value added activities.

APPENDIX

See Table A1.

TABLE A1
COEFFICIENT MATRIX

	HR	RD	PT	W	X	BI	HI	NC	FO	SMI	Union
HR	1.000										
RD	0.087	1.000									
PT	0.322	0.306	1.000								
W	-0.206	0.226	0.229	1.000							
X	0.087	0.130	0.286	0.168	1.000						
BI	0.034	0.044	-0.089	0.103	0.074	1.000					
HI	-0.072	0.178	0.055	0.329	0.029	0.290	1.000				
NC	0.063	0.198	0.159	0.246	0.162	0.232	0.172	1.000			
FO	-0.056	0.123	0.108	0.236	0.130	0.140	0.007	0.049	1.000		
SMI	-0.332	0.136	-0.441	-0.130	-0.371	0.098	-0.097	-0.061	-0.009	1.000	
Union	0.052	0.190	-0.091	-0.194	-0.042	0.021	-0.022	0.174	0.140	0.055	1.000

Source: Computed from ADB [2002].

NOTES

1. The role of competition was articulated extensively by Smith [*1776*], Marx [*1964*] and Schumpeter [*1934*]. Marx had contended that competition drives firms to replace old modes of technology with new ones.
2. Abramovitz [*1956*] produced a similar argument about increasing returns. New growth economists such as Romer [*1986*] and Lucas [*1988*] demonstrated these ideas using elegant models. See Scherer [*1992, 1999*] for a lucid account.
3. While the data were collected randomly by the national consultants, no sampling frame was followed to enable an extrapolation of the data for national representation.
4. Interviews carried out by the author in 2001 and 2002.
5. Interview by the author in 2001.

REFERENCES

Abramovitz, M., 1956, 'Resource and Output Trends in the United States since 1870', *American Economic Review*, Vol.46, pp.5–23.
Abrenica, J.V. and G.R. Tecson, 2003, 'Can the Philippines ever Catch Up?', in S. Lall and S. Urata (eds.), *Competitiveness, FDI and Technological Activity in East Asia*, Cheltenham: Edward Elgar.
ADB, 2002, 'Survey Data on Asian Industrial Firms' Competitiveness', compiled by Asian Development Bank, Manila.
Aitken, B.J. and A.E. Harrison, 1999, 'Do Domestic Firms Benefit from Direct Foreign Investment?: Evidence from Venezuela', *American Economic Review*, Vol.89, No.3, pp.103–32.
Aoki, M., 2001, *Toward a Comparative Institutional Analysis*, Cambridge, MA: MIT Press.
Arrow, K., 1962, 'The economic significance of learning by doing', *Review of Economic Studies*, Vol. 29, pp.155–73.
Audretsch, D., 2002, 'The Dynamic Role of Small Firms: Evidence from U.S.', *Small Business Economics*, Vol. 18, No. 1–3, pp.13–40.
Bain, J., 1968, *Industrial Organization*, New York: John Wiley and Sons..
Bell, M. and K. Pavit, 1995, 'The Development of Technological Capabilities', in I.U. Haque (ed.), *Trade, Technology and International Competitiveness*, Washington, DC: World Bank.
Best, M., 2001, *The New Competitive Advantage*, Oxford: Oxford University Press.
Blomström, M. and H. Persson, 1983, 'Foreign Investment and Spillover Efficiency in an Underdeveloped Economy: Evidence from the Mexican Manufacturing Industry', *World Development*, Vol.11, No.6, pp.493–501.
Blomstrom, M. and E. Wolff, 1994, 'Multinational Corporations and Productivity Convergence in Mexico', in W. Baumol, R. Nelson and E. Wolff (eds.), *Convergence of Produtivity: Cross-National Studies and Historical Evidence*, Oxford: Oxford University Press.
Brimble, P., 2003, 'Foreign Direct Investment, Technology and Competitiveness in Thailand', in S. Lall and S. Urata (eds.), *Competitiveness, FDI and Technological Activity in East Asia*, Cheltenham: Edward Elgar.
Caves, R., 1974, 'Multinational Firms, Competition and Productivity in Host-country Industries', *Economica*, Vol.41, pp.176–93.
Caves, R., 1982, *Multinational Enterprise and Economic Analysis*, Cambridge: Cambridge University Press.
Deyo, F.C. (ed.),1987, *The Political Economy of the New Asian Industrialism*, Ithaca: Cornell University Press.
Doner, R. 2001, 'Institutions and the tasks of economic upgrading', Paper prepared for delivery at the 2001 Annual Meeting of the American Political Science Association, San Francisco, 30 August–2 September.
Dosi, G., 1982, 'Technological Paradigms and Technological Trajectories', *Research Policy*, Vol. 11, No.3, pp.141–62.
Ernst, D., T. Ganiatsos and L. Mytelka, (eds.),1998, *Technological Capabilities and Export Success: Lessons from East Asia, London*, London: Routledge.

Freeman, C., 1989, 'New Technology and Catching-Up', *European Journal of Development Research*, Vol. 1, No. 1, pp.85–99.

Gachino, G. and R. Rasiah, 2003, 'FDI, Exports and Productivity: Evidence from Kenyan Manufacturing', Paper prepared for the conference 'FDI-Assisted Development', Oslo, 22-24 May.

Gerschenkron, A., 1962, *Economic Backwardness in Historical Perspective*, Cambridge, MA: Harvard University Press.

Greer, D., 1992, *Industrial Organization and Public Policy*, New York: Macmillan.

Haddad, M. and A. Harrison, 1993, 'Are There Positive Spillovers from Direct Foreign Investment? Evidence from Panel Data for Mexico', *Journal of Development Economics*, Vol. 42, pp.51–74.

Hamilton, A., 1791, 'Report on manufactures', in H.C. Syrett (ed.), *The Papers of Alexander Hamilton, Volume 1*, New York: Columbia University Press.

Hirschman, A., 1958, *Strategy of Economic Development*, New Haven: Yale University Press.

Hirschman, A., 1977, 'A Generalized Linkage Approach to Development with Special Reference to Staples', *Economic Development and Cultural Change*, Vol. 25, pp.67–98.

Hirschman, A., 1984, 'A Dissenter's Confession: The Strategy of Economic Development Revisited', in G.M. Meier and D. Seers (eds.), *Pioneers in Development*, New York: Oxford University Press.

INTECH-DCT, 2002, 'Survey Data on Malaysian Industrial Firms', compiled by the Institute for New Technologies (INTECH) and DCT, Penang, Malaysia.

Johnson, C., 1982, *MITI and The Japanese Miracle*, Stanford: Stanford University Press.

Kaldor, N., 1957, 'A Model of Economic Growth', *Economic Journal*, Vol. 67, pp.591–624.

Kaldor, N., 1962, 'Equilibrium Theory and Growth Theory', in M.J. Boskin (ed.), *Economics of Human Welfare: Essays in Honour of Tibor Scitovsky*, New York: Academic Press.

Kaldor, N., 1967, *Strategic Factors in Economic Development*, Ithaca: Cornell University Press.

Lall, S., 1992, 'Technological Capabilities and Industrialisation', *World Development*, Vol. 20, No. 2, pp.165–86.

Lall, S., Teitel, N.S. and Wignaraja, G., 1995, 'Skills and Capabilities: Ghana's Industrial Competitiveness', in M. Godfrey (ed.), *Skill Development for International Competitiveness*, Cheltenham: Edward Elgar.

Lewis, A., 1955, *The Theory of Economic Growth*, London: Allen and Unwin.

List, F., 1885, *The National System of Political Economy*, London: Longmans, Green and Co..

Lucas, R.E., 1988, 'On the Mechanics of Economic Development', *Journal of Monetary Economics*, Vol. 22, pp.3–22.

Lundvall, B.A., 1992, *National Systems of Innovation: Towards a Theory of Innovation and Interactive Learning*, London: Frances Pinter.

Marshall, A., 1890, *Principles of Economics*, London: Macmillan.

Marx, K., 1964, *Pre-capitalist Economic Formations*, London: Lawrence and Wishart.

Mills, J.S., 1848, *Principles of Political Economy with some of their Applications to Social Policy*, London: John Parker and West Strand.

Myrdal, G., 1957, *Economic Theory and Underdeveloped Regions*, New York: Methuen.

Nelson, R., (ed.) 1993, *National Innovation Systems*, New York: Oxford University Press.

Nelson, R.R. and S.G. Winter, 1982a, 'The Schumpeterian Tradeoff Revisited', *American Economic Review*, Vol. 72, pp.114–32.

Nelson, R.R. and S.G. Winter, 1982b, *An Evolutionary Theory of Economic Change*, Cambridge, MA: Harvard University Press.

Pavitt, K., 1984, 'Sectoral Patterns of Technical Change: Towards a Taxonomy and a Theory', *Research Policy*, Vol. 13, No. 6, pp.343–73.

Penrose, E., 1959, *The Theory of the Growth of the Firm*, Oxford: Basil Blackwell.

Piore, M. and C. Sabel, 1984, *The Second Industrial Divide: Prospects for Prosperity*, New York: Basic Books.

Polanyi, M., 1997, 'Tacit Knowledge', in L. Prusak (ed.), *Knowledge in Organizations*, Boston: Butterworth-Heinemann.

Pratten, C., 1971, *Economies of Scale in Manufacturing Industry*, Cambridge: Cambridge University Press.

Rasiah, R., 1994, 'Flexible Production Systems and Local Machine Tool Subcontracting: Electronics Transnationals in Malaysia', *Cambridge Journal of Economics*, Vol. 18, No. 3, pp.279–98.

Rasiah, R., 1995, *Foreign Capital and Industrialization in Malaysia*, Basingstoke: Macmillan.

Rasiah, R., 1996, 'Institutions and Innovations: Moving Towards the Technology Frontier in the Electronics Industry in Malaysia', *Industry and Innovation*, Vol. 3, No. 2, pp.79–102.

Rasiah, R., 1999, 'Malaysia's National Innovation System', in K.S. Jomo and G. Felker (eds), *Technology, Competitiveness and the State: Malaysia's Industrial Technology Policies*, London: Routledge.

Rasiah, R., 2001, 'Market, Government and Malaysia's New Economic Policy', *Cambridge Journal of Economics*, Vol.25, No. 1.

Rasiah, R., 2002a, 'Government-Business Coordination and Local Machine Too Linkages in Malaysia', *Small Business Economics*, Vol. 11, pp.1–3.

Rasiah, R., 2002b, 'Systemic Coordination and the Knowledge Economy: Human Capital Development in MNC-driven Electronics Clusters in Malaysia', *Transnational Corporations*, Vol. 11, No. 3, pp.89–129.

Rasiah, R., 2003, 'Foreign Ownership, Exports and Technological Capabilities in the Electronics Firms in Malaysia and Thailand', *Journal of Asian Economics*, Vol. 14, No. 5, pp.786–811.

Romer, P.M., 1986, 'Increasing Returns and Long Run Growth', *Journal of Political Economy*, Vol. 94, pp.1002–37.

Sabel, C., 1989, 'Flexible Specialization and the Re-emergence of Regional Economies', in P. Hirst and J. Zeitlin (eds.), *Reversing Industrial Declines?: Industrial Structure and Policy in Britain and Her Competitors*, Oxford: Berg Publishers.

Saxenian, A.L., 1994, *The Regional Advantage*, Cambridge, MA: Harvard University Press.

Saxenian, A.L., 1999, *Silicon Valley's New Immigrant Entrepreneurs*, San Francisco: Public Policy Institute of California.

Scherer, F., 1973, 'The Determinants of Industry Plant Sizes in Six Nations', *Review of Economics and Statistics*, Vol. 55, No. 2, pp.135–75.

Scherer, F.M., 1980, *Industrial Market Structure and Economic Performance*, Chicago: Rand McNally.

Scherer, F., 1991, 'Changing Perspectives on the Firm Size Problem', in Z.J. Acs and D.B. Audretsch (eds.), *Innovation and Technological Change: An International Comparison*, Ann Arbor: University of Michigan Press.

Scherer, F., 1992, *International High Technology Competition*, Cambridge, MA: Harvard University Press.

Schumpeter, J.A., 1934, *The Theory of Economic Development*, Cambridge, MA: MIT Press.

Sengenberger, W. and F. Pyke, 1991, 'Small firms, industrial districts and local economic regeneration', *Labour and Society*, Vol. 16, No. 1, pp.1–24.

Smith, A., 1776, *The Wealth of the Nations*, London: Strahan and Cadell.

Urata, S., 2001, 'Emergence of An FDI-Trade Nexus and Economic Growth in East Asia', in J. Stiglitz and Yusof Shahid (eds.), *Rethinking the East Asian Miracle*, New York: Oxford University Press.

Westphal, L.E., K. Kritayakirana, K. Petchsuwan, H. Sutabutr and Y. Yuthavong, 1990, 'The Development of Technological Capability in Manufacturing: A Macroscopic Approach to Policy Research', in R.E. Evenson and G. Ranis (eds.), *Science and Technology: Lessons for Development Policy*, London: Intermediate Technology Publications.

Wignaraja, G., 2002, 'Firm size, Technological Capabilities and Market-oriented Policies in Mauritius', *Oxford Development Studies*, Vol. 30, No. 1, pp.87–104.

Wilkinson, F. and J.I. You, 1995, 'Competition and cooperation: towards an understanding of the industrial district', *Review of Political Economy*, Vol. 6, pp.259–78.

Young, A., 1928, 'Increasing Returns and Economic Progress', *Economic Journal*, Vol. 38, No. 152, pp.527–42.

Foreign Direct Investment: A Catalyst for Local Firm Development?

JOANNA SCOTT-KENNEL

Foreign direct investment (FDI) is recognised as a mechanism by which a host country can upgrade the competitiveness of its resources and capabilities. In the extant literature, empirical assessment of the impact of FDI on development has tended to focus on the aggregate effects associated with capital, employment and technology transfer, without a corresponding emphasis on the longer-term impacts on firm upgrading. In this chapter, we investigate the effects of inward FDI at the level of the firm, within the context of a small, developed country. Statistical analysis highlights key relationships between resource flows from parent to affiliate, and a) competitive advantage of the affiliate, and b) resource transfer to local firms via linkages. The findings provide evidence that local firm development occurs as a result of direct resource transfer, both within the multinational enterprise and between the affiliate and host country firms.

Les investissements directs étrangers (IDE) sont reconnus comme étant un mécanisme utilisé par le pays d'accueil pour améliorer la compétitivité de ses ressources et capacités. Dans la littérature existante, les estimations empiriques concernant l'impact des IDE sur le développement se concentraient jusqu'à présent avant tout sur les effets secondaires liés au capital, à l'emploi et au transfert technologique, sans prendre en compte les effets à long terme sur le développement des entreprises. Dans cet chapter, nous analysons les effets des IDE internes au niveau des entreprises, dans le contexte d'un petit pays développé. L'analyse statistique démontre qu'il existe un lien essentiel entre les flux de ressources du centre aux filiales et a) les avantages concurrentiels des filiales et b) le transfert de ressources vers des entreprises locales à travers des liens particuliers. Les résultats de la recherche démontrent que le développement d'entreprises locales est une conséquence du transfert direct de ressources, autant à l'intérieur de l'entreprise multinationale qu'entre les filiales et les entreprises du pays d'accueil.

Joanna Scott-Kennel is at the School of Marketing and International Business, Victoria University of Wellington, New Zealand. The author would like to thank Elizabeth Rose and two anonymous referees for their helpful comments on earlier drafts of this chapter.

I. INTRODUCTION

The potential of foreign direct investment (FDI) to contribute to the welfare of host economies is of great interest to both academics and policy-makers, and is one reason FDI is increasingly sought after by both developing and developed economies. In fact, FDI has now become the most important source of external financing for many countries [*UNCTAD, 2000*]. The importance of FDI to host countries has been demonstrated by a literature that examines the relationship between economic development and levels of foreign investment at the level of the economy. Much of the research in this field has focused on FDI-led development in less-developed or emerging economies, rather than advanced nations. Emphasis given to the macro-level effects of inward FDI in previous research has been at the expense of our understanding of the process of upgrading of the capabilities of local firms.

This chapter adopts a different approach, assessing the impact of FDI at the level of the firm for a small, but developed, economy. The study uses a survey instrument to investigate the linkages and subsequent resource flows associated with inward FDI in New Zealand. The objectives of this chapter are twofold: first, to determine the impact of parent–affiliate resource flows on the competitiveness of the affiliate in the host economy; and second, to understand the relationship between parent–affiliate resource flows and affiliate–local firm resource flows that result from linkage formation between the affiliate and host country firms.

II. FDI AND DEVELOPMENT IN NEW ZEALAND

New Zealand is a developed economy of 3.95 million people, and has one of the most liberal trade and investment climates in the world [*Cremer and Ramasamy, 1996*]. FDI has played, and continues to play, an important role in the development and growth of local industry in New Zealand. Since widespread liberalisation and deregulation of the economy in the mid 1980s, inward FDI has become an even more important source of capital, assets and employment [*Enderwick, 1998*]. Through the second half of the 1990s, New Zealand was one of the developed countries most heavily dependent on inward FDI as a source of gross fixed capital formation [*UNCTAD, 1999*]. Currently, foreign-owned enterprises account for approximately three-quarters of employment in the finance and insurance sector, half in communication services, and one-third in the manufacturing, transport and storage, mining and wholesale trade sectors.

New Zealand's economy is heavily dependent on overseas trade and commodity production in agriculture, fishing and forestry. Although these sectors account directly for only around 8 per cent of gross domestic product (GDP), they provide a far greater share of export earnings and also supply inputs for processing industries. New Zealand's economic structure has relied heavily on income derived from pastoral exports since 1920, although there has been a shift in more recent years towards adding value to primary commodities, and gearing the domestic manufacturing sector towards exporting. In 2003, dairy products (milk powder, butter and cheese) accounted for 16 per cent of all merchandise exports, meat 14 per cent, logs and wood 8 per cent, and fish and fruit 8 per cent. In contrast, 47 per cent of imports comprise vehicles, mechanical and electrical machinery, and petroleum.

In comparison to other small, industrialised nations, New Zealand has fallen behind in the local development of technology [BCG, 2001]. Technology development is constrained locally by low domestic demand (due to the small domestic market size and the large geographic distance from key markets), few technological clusters and limited venture capital. In addition, spending on research and development is well below the OECD average. Research and development expenditure in New Zealand is ranked 23rd out of 28 OCED nations, largely as a result of low research and development spending by industry [BCG, 2001]. Although most local firms are small and under-resourced by international standards, many remain remarkably well-connected in the world, making them more likely to benefit from exposure to resources from international sources [Skilling, 2001]. In fact, inward FDI has already contributed to many areas of innovation and growth in New Zealand industry, such as pharmaceuticals, forestry development, paints and biotechnology. In contrast, the small size of indigenous firms, and their inability and unwillingness to make committed investments internationally, has meant that outward FDI has yet to make a noteworthy contribution to the local accumulation of skills and resources.

In part as a result of its continued reliance on the sale of commodity products in volatile international markets, New Zealand's living standards and competitiveness have fallen dramatically over the past 50 years. The country has failed to keep pace with other small, advanced nations, such as Sweden, Denmark and Ireland, and is even falling behind former developing nations such as Singapore. In 1950, New Zealand had the third highest standard of living in the world, measured by GDP per capita [Crocombe et al., 1991]. Today, it is ranked in 32nd place (or 56th place if measured by GDP per capita purchasing power parity). In 2002, New Zealand's GDP was just 15 per cent of Australia's total, and its GDP per capita was 73 per cent of Australia's and 41 per cent of the United States' (Statistics New Zealand). As of 2003, New Zealand ranked 14th in world competitiveness amongst small countries (populations less than 20 million), behind countries such as Belgium, Norway, Sweden and Singapore. New Zealand's closest neighbour, Australia, ranked 2nd behind the United States in the large country grouping (population 20 million +) [IMD, 2004].

For a small, open nation such as New Zealand, characterised by a heavy dependency on resource-based industries and the growing need to improve competitiveness in higher value added activities and to raise the level of outward

FDI by indigenous firms, inward FDI remains a vital part of the equation. Yet the extent of reliance on inward FDI in New Zealand has not been met by a corresponding level of research on its impact on the development of local firms. Despite New Zealand's historical reliance on FDI [*Akoorie, 1998*] – and a recent dramatic drop in net investment levels of 77 per cent in the 2000 to 2001 period, followed by a further drop of 50 per cent from 2001 to 2002 – a systematic analysis of the nature and extent of FDI's effects on local industry upgrading has not been attempted for over 30 years [*Deane, 1970*].

Since then, major shifts in government policy orientation (from import substituting and inward-looking, to export oriented and outward-looking), liberalisation and deregulation have substantially altered the receptor conditions for FDI and, consequently, the type of FDI in New Zealand [*Akoorie, 1998*]. Until recently, New Zealand adopted a neutral stance towards FDI policy, only limiting foreign ownership in a small number of 'sensitive' areas (such as certain tracts of land). Perhaps more importantly, and in sharp contrast to many of its neighbouring countries, including Australia, New Zealand has made little attempt to target or attract certain types of foreign investment, relying instead on 'market forces' rather than government-driven intervention. However, increasing competition for FDI, combined with concern over recent declines in inward investment flows to New Zealand, have led to recommendations by researchers that New Zealand policy-makers should actively encourage foreign investment in order to maintain growth and economic prosperity [*BCG, 2001*].

For a small, periphery economy such as New Zealand, FDI serves to extend the production possibilities and limited pool of resources available domestically, as well as improve access to international markets. An examination of recent research shows that FDI appears to be having a largely positive impact on the local economy, although the growing dominance of foreign-owned companies via acquisition of local firms, particularly in the service sector, has been cause for concern in the wider media [*Rosenberg, 1998; Scott-Kennel, 1998*]. A survey of selected foreign-owned firms in New Zealand [*KPMG, 1995*], and case studies of foreign investment from specific countries or regions, such as the United States [*Enderwick, 1995*], Japan [*Harper, 1994*] and Asia [*Cremer and Ramasamy, 1996*], found that local affiliates made positive contributions in terms of capital (financed largely offshore with low repatriation to foreign shareholders), technology transfer (new products, processes and techniques, and research and development for local adaptation), local employment and training, introduction of new management practices and enlarging market access for exports via international corporate networks [*see Enderwick, 1998 for a review*].

However, a major limitation of existing research with regard to our understanding of how FDI might contribute to growth and economic prosperity in New Zealand is its focus on impacts strictly at the macro-level of the economy such as output, employment and exports associated with flows of capital and technology from foreign ownership. This gives rise to a distinct gap in the extant literature regarding the longer-term impacts foreign-owned affiliates have on local industry.

Where previous studies have examined relationships between foreign and indigenous firms, they have typically been limited to the consideration of local sourcing or supply linkages. Enderwick's [*1995*] study of large US-owned multinationals indicated a high level of integration with the local economy, through an extensive network of local suppliers. A series of 20 case studies [*Duncan et al., 1997*] considered effects on the affiliate, such as investment capital, employment, and technology transfer, and also measured the extent of downstream benefits in terms of the amount of domestically sourced goods and services. Akoorie [*1996a*] investigated the process of upgrading at the firm level, through a longitudinal case study that showed how FDI acted as a catalyst for the development of a local firm. Such detailed case studies provide useful insights by examining the experiences of selected affiliates at the firm level. However, they are unable to present the wider view of how the overseas parent firms affect the locally based affiliates themselves and the local firms with which the affiliates interact. Thus, while they fall short of widely representative evidence, case studies do serve to indicate the types and extent of backward linkages formed by a selected group of foreign-owned affiliates.

To address the limitations inherent in the existing literature, this chapter reports on a large-scale study, aimed at understanding the impact of FDI on the capabilities and resources available to New Zealand industry.

III. FDI AND DEVELOPMENT

FDI can accelerate host countries' growth by contributing to domestic sources of capital, transferring and developing technology and expertise [*Barrell and Pain, 1997; Young and Lan, 1997; Lall, 2001*], generating employment [*Campbell, 1994; Lall, 1995; Zhao, 1998*] and exports [*Collis et al., 1994; Aitken et al., 1997; UNCTAD, 2002*], increasing competitive pressure in domestic markets, and creating externalities or spillovers [*Dunning, 1996*]. Many of the studies in this field have sought to examine the relationship between FDI and economic growth [*Doraisami and Leng, 1996; Dunning and Narula, 1996; Borensztein et al., 1998; Sun and Chai, 1998; Liu et al., 2002; Ram and Zhang, 2002*].

The majority of research in the area of FDI and economic development is concerned with developing countries [*for a review see Lall, 1996*]. This research offers a vast wealth of insights as to the determinants and externalities of multinational enterprise (MNE) behaviour on host economies, and we have drawn upon selected studies for this research. However, the focus of this chapter is on the experiences of a small, developed economy, albeit one that needs some of the types of resources frequently sought after by less-developed nations. Some applicable studies on the developmental impact of FDI on developed nations have focused on Canada and Australia; while they are larger economies, their histories and economic structures are similar to those of New Zealand [*Caves, 1974; Globerman, 1979*].

The relationship between inward FDI by foreign MNEs, eventual outward FDI by domestic firms, and a country's economic development has been formalised by Dunning's [*1981*] seminal work on the investment development path (IDP). Dunning [*1986, 1988*] developed the concept further, and it was extended to include a fifth stage by Narula [*1996*]. The IDP suggests that a country might progress through five stages of economic development, relative to the rest of the world. These stages may be identified by the country's net outward investment (NOI) position (the stock of outward FDI less the stock of inward FDI), where economic development is proxied by GDP per capita. Economic development through the stages can be associated with improvements to location-specific advantages, rising inward FDI and, from stage three onwards, rising outward FDI by indigenous firms, which eventually results in a positive net investment position.

Narula describes the FDI-development relationship as symbiotic: 'FDI activity is influenced by the structure of the economy, and at the same time influences its development' [*Narula, 1996: 11*]. Hence, the IDP provides a dynamic framework within which to examine the relationship between economic growth and FDI activity, where government acts as a catalyst to change. Each country's unique path is determined by: its resource structure; its market size; its strategy of economic development (economic system); and the role of government in the organisation of economic activity [*Narula, 1996*]. This suggests that it is important to consider the experiences of different countries when considering FDI-led development; in fact, researchers applying the IDP have found that countries follow different trajectories [*Dunning and Narula, 1996*].

For instance, despite its developed economy status, Akoorie [*1996b*] describes New Zealand as only being in the latter phases of stage three of the IDP. The reason for this, as with the IDP trajectories of other resource-rich economies, is that New Zealand's outward FDI has failed to meet, match or surpass its reliance on inward FDI, thus rendering it with a negative net outward investment position normally associated with earlier stage countries [*Narula, 1996*]. This scenario remains the same today, with stocks of outward FDI equal to 44 per cent of inward stocks, and New Zealand's net investment position at $-NZ\$100$ billion (2003 figures). As discussed earlier, the structure and policy framework of New Zealand's economy have had important implications for its IDP trajectory.

While previous research tends to support the relationship between FDI and economic development, it often fails to capture the impacts of FDI at the level of the firm. It is not surprising that these impacts receive less attention, particularly in empirical research, as they tend to be more diffuse and difficult to measure [*Enderwick, 1998*]. To address this issue, some authors have sought to quantify firm-level effects by measuring spillovers from FDI in selected industries. These studies report on the relationship between the presence of foreign capital and the effects on productivity and performance of the affiliate [*Figueroa, 1998; Williams, 1999; Khawar, 2003*] or the industry in which it operates [*Blomstrom, 1989; Kokko et al., 1996; O'Malley and O'Gorman, 2001; Sadik and Bolbol, 2001*]. However, the results of these studies are often mixed or inconclusive [*Aitken and Harrison, 1999; Bosco 2001*].

As with New Zealand-based research, case studies of inter-firm linkages provide useful perspectives on the extent of involvement of foreign firms in local industry, but are typically limited to particular industries [*Turok, 1993; Brown, 1998; O'Malley and O'Gorman, 2001*], local sourcing [*Ruane and Holger, 1997; Williams, 1999*] or single firms [*Barrow and Hall, 1995*]. Some studies have taken a more comprehensive approach in their examination of inter-firm interactions [*Rodriguez-Clare, 1996; Dunning, 1998; UNCTAD, 2001*], particularly with respect to affiliate–supplier/subcontractor linkages [*Poon, 1996; Raines et al., 2001*] and type of FDI [*Williams, 1997*].

The mixed findings of these studies reinforce the need to examine the experiences of FDI-led development for a range of different countries. Yet there has been limited research to date that examines the micro-level influence of FDI for a small, export-dependent economy. Specifically, little empirical work has been done that illuminates the extent of mutually beneficial interaction and subsequent capability building among local firms for such an economy. Although the literature offers strong support to the notion that FDI can contribute to economic development, it fails to elucidate the nature of inter-firm interactions between foreign-owned affiliates in a host country and local firms that can facilitate this development. While there is wide agreement that FDI has an impact on local industry different to that of local firms, the extant literature has not specifically considered the nature of resource transfer between foreign and indigenous firms. This gap leaves us without a clear understanding of how different types of firm-specific resources transferred from parent to affiliate might influence the upgrading of local firms. In this research, we address these limitations by examining the resource flows associated with FDI and affiliate activity in New Zealand.

IV. LINKAGES, RESOURCE TRANSFER AND FIRM DEVELOPMENT

We propose that, by examining the resource transfer from parent MNE to affiliate and from affiliate to local firms, we can better understand the firm-level impact of FDI. The transfer of a 'bundle' of resources from the parent is expected to improve the affiliate's performance relative to local competitors. In addition it has the potential to raise the capabilities of local firms through diffusion and transfer via linkages of the affiliates with local firms. From the host country's perspective, therefore, the impact of FDI may be translated into two main areas of impact at the level of the firm: the impact on the affiliate itself, and then the impact on local firms via linkages.

In the first instance, resources from the MNE will benefit the local affiliate. Traditional FDI theory holds that firm-specific advantages, such as property rights, intangible assets and the advantages of common governance, enable the MNE to overcome the disadvantages of operating in a foreign location [Hymer, 1960; Dunning, 1993]. MNEs typically enjoy efficiency advantages via the exploitation of company-wide resources over many markets, including product and production technology, human capital and accumulated knowledge, innovative management practices, established marketing networks and finance. In order to exploit these advantages internationally, the MNE must transfer them to its overseas affiliates. By doing so, the advantages remain internalised within the boundaries of the MNE. This also provides the affiliate with an opportunity to exploit market failure in the host economy by using its firm-specific advantages as a source of competitive advantage.

In the second instance, resources associated with FDI have the potential to benefit local firms. From the host country's perspective, if FDI is to have a wider impact, beyond that experienced by the affiliate, these resources need to disperse to local firms. There is some evidence to support the idea that firms may share, rather than strictly internalise certain resources. In order to remain competitive, firms may pursue the requisite flexibility and responsiveness by streamlining their operations, outsourcing, and undertaking collaborative agreements allowing them to augment, as well as exploit, existing assets [Teece, 1992; Buckley and Casson, 1998], while lowering the costs of research, development and technology [Hagedoorn and Narula, 1999]. Linkage formation via networked firms and collaborative partners is based on the perceived ability of the external firm to provide more net value, or more value than would be possible via sole reliance on internal markets within the MNE [Madhok, 1996]. Forming linkages with local firms may allow the MNE to concentrate on core activities, source inputs locally, take advantage of local firm experience and knowledge of the market, develop its assets in collaboration with other firms, and access unique resources created locally. Driffield and Love [2003] suggest that where FDI cannot acquire the advantages, such as technology, embodied in local firms, MNEs may undertake FDI in order to gain proximity to these firms of interest. This encourages linkage formation between foreign and local firms and offers the potential for upgrading of local capability.

The literature supports the notion that MNEs' offshore affiliates are able to overcome the liabilities of foreignness to successfully compete with their local counterparts [Hymer, 1960; Zaheer, 1995]. The resource-based view suggests that this can be attributed to the transfer of resources from parent to the affiliate [Wernerfelt, 1984]. Our first hypothesis is concerned with whether the 'bundle' of resources typically associated with foreign investment contributes to the competitiveness of the locally based affiliate.

H1:   Resources transferred from foreign parent companies to their locally based affiliates are positively related to the affiliates' competitive advantage in the host country.

Our second research hypothesis addresses the connection between parent-to-affiliate resource transfer and the transfer of resources to local firms via linkages with the affiliate. This is an issue that has received very limited attention in the existing literature. Table 1 shows a summary of the different types of linkages – the role of the foreign affiliate in the relationship, the affiliate's involvement (for example, sourcing or supplying, offering assistance or transferring resources), and the potential impact of the linkages on local firms.

Linkages between foreign affiliates and local firms may be indirect, direct or collaborative. Indirect linkages occur through competition or demonstration effects, and these are not addressed in this chapter. Direct linkages occur via transactional relationships between affiliates and local firms. They can be backward – sourcing inputs from local suppliers – or forward – supplying local firms with (intermediate) products or services that require further processing (or marketing).

Direct linkages may also involve inter-firm transfer of assistance and resources such as technical equipment, product specifications, and market information in order to help local firms raise the standard of their output [*Wong, 1992; Poon, 1996*]. Hence, direct linkages may do more than simply stimulate the level of business activity (demand); they may contribute to the productivity and competitiveness of local firms via ongoing relationships and assistance [*Turok, 1993*].

Collaborative linkages occur when affiliates and local firms engage in alliances, technology sharing or development agreements, or management contracts. Such linkages offer enormous potential for upgrading of both affiliate and local partner, via a reciprocal exchange of firm-specific advantages and resources. Yet, there have been few studies that investigate the existence or outcomes of affiliate–local firm collaborative linkages.

In the longer-term, linkages involving resource or assistance transfer may generate a stream of virtuous upgrading and economic development, including the creation of employment, and further downstream linkages between local firms and their buyer/supplier firms. Ultimately, the impact of these linkages is expected to be upgrading by indigenous firms.

Thus, our second hypothesis addresses the relationship between parent–affiliate resource transfer and the transfer of resources and assistance from affiliates to local firms via linkages.

H2:   Resources transferred from foreign parent companies to locally based affiliates are positively related to resources and assistance transferred from the affiliates to local firms.

TABLE 1
TYPES OF LINKAGE AND SUBSEQUENT IMPACT ON LOCAL INDUSTRY

Linkage	Role of the local firm	Affiliate involvement	Impact on industry
Backward (buy)	Supplier Subcontractor	Local sourcing of inputs	Demand for local products/ services increases Domestic and international competition to meet this demand may encourage local firms to improve standards
		Ongoing relationships	As above, plus increased incentives for local firms to meet standards required by foreign affiliates. Demonstration and emulation effects
		Assistance	As above, plus access to resources, inputs, skills and knowledge of foreign affiliates to improve standard of outputs
Forward (supply)	Customer Agent (for marketing, distribution etc.)	Provision of inputs	Supply of products/services and customer choice increases and (relative) prices decrease
		Ongoing relationships	As above, plus reliability/ quality of supply improves standard of outputs from local firms
		Assistance	As above, plus access to inputs, resources and knowledge related to products, marketing, distribution etc.
Collaborative	Alliance partner Technology development partner Management contract	One-off project Ongoing relationships Transfer of resources or assistance	Mutual upgrading of both local firms and foreign affiliates possible through sharing or developing complementary capabilities and/or resources

V. RESEARCH DESIGN

Data Collection

In order to overcome the lack of representativeness that has characterised previous research in this field in New Zealand, this study involved the construction of a database of foreign-owned firms. A survey questionnaire was selected as the main instrument for the research. There are two main limitations of this approach.

First, the survey provides a cross-sectional or 'snapshot' view. Second, the information obtained is limited to the affiliates' perspectives. Although confirmatory observations from local firms would be desirable, this is beyond the scope of this research. The survey instrument was subjected to three rounds of pre-testing and included a screening question that enabled the elimination of affiliates that were no longer 25 per cent or more foreign owned from the sample. This filter question enabled the database to be updated from an original figure of 1800 foreign-owned affiliates to a revised figure of 1554. The survey was administered in November 1999, and received 655 responses (36 per cent of the original figure), with 515 responses usable (33 per cent of the revised figure).

Measurement

In order to assess the effects of inward FDI on locally based affiliates, we asked respondents about the extent of their reliance on different types of resources from their foreign parent companies and the extent to which they rely on these different types of resources to afford them competitive advantage relative to other firms in New Zealand. The measures for 'extent of reliance on resources from parent' and 'extent of reliance as a source of competitive advantage for the affiliate in New Zealand' were measured on Likert scales where $1 =$ not at all, $2 =$ minor extent, $3 =$ moderate extent, $4 =$ major extent and $5 =$ completely (see Dunning [*1998*] for similar measures).

In order to address the effects of inward FDI on local firms, we are interested in whether different types of resources being transferred to the affiliate from the foreign parent are similar to those diffusing from the affiliate to local firms via inter-firm linkages. We can divide these linkages into two main groups. The first includes transactional linkages, such as forward linkages with customers and agents, and backward linkages with suppliers and subcontractors. The second group includes collaborative linkages with partners involved with strategic alliances, technology sharing or development, or managerial contracts. The reason for this distinction is the different nature of the two types of linkages. Transactional linkages are likely to involve payment in conjunction with the possible transfer of assistance and resources in areas relevant to the business relationship. In contrast, collaborative linkages are less likely to involve payment, but local firms are more likely to receive core resources from the affiliate in exchange for their own resource contributions. Hence it seems reasonable that the types and importance of resource transfer might differ between these two groups. To address this issue we modified our questions according to the type of linkage, and grouped resources into two broad categories: those relating to production and technology and those relating to management and marketing. We also allowed for possible overlap between the two categories. The different types of resources or assistance transferred from affiliate to local firms are coded as binary (yes/no) variables.

Respondent Profile

The majority of respondents (63.4 per cent) classified their firms as a New Zealand branch or affiliate of a foreign MNE, and 24.8 per cent are former New Zealand-owned companies, acquired by a foreign company. The primary reason for operating in New Zealand is to gain proximity to markets and customers domestically and in the Asia-Pacific region, with 54 per cent of the affiliates undertaking exporting from their New Zealand base. On average the affiliates in the survey have been operating in New Zealand for 27.6 years, and have been owned by their current foreign investors for 16.7 years. Fifty-five per cent of the affiliates were founded from 1981 onwards, reflecting the rise of foreign investment into New Zealand during the post-1984 reforms. On average the affiliates employed 166 full-time equivalent staff, had NZ$63 million in sales and spent 2.3 per cent on research and development, for the financial year prior to the survey. The respondents came from primary, secondary and tertiary sectors, and from all industries; including but not limited to manufacturing, transport and storage, property and business services, finance and insurance, wholesale and retail trade.

All affiliates relied on the transfer of resources from their foreign parent companies. The resources most frequently obtained from the foreign parent were product/service technology, access to information, experience and expertise (means = 3.4), research and development (3.2), production/service delivery technology, management practices and culture (3.0), and economies of scale or scope (2.8). Resources related to marketing systems (2.7), access to markets (2.6), distribution systems, employment practices, training, inputs (2.4) and human resources (2.3) were somewhat less likely to have come from the parent.

Competitive advantage of the affiliates in New Zealand came from many sources, including product/service technology (3.5), production/service delivery technology, management practices/culture, human resources (3.2), marketing systems (3.1), economies of scale or scope, access to markets (3.0), distribution systems (2.9) and favoured access to inputs (2.6).

Backward and forward linkages with local firms involving the transfer of resources or assistance were formed in the 12 months prior to the survey by approximately 52 per cent of the affiliates in the sample. Linkages with local partners, for alliances, technology sharing or management contracts had been established over the prior three years by 29 per cent of the respondents.

VI. RESULTS

A series of multiple regression models is used to test the first hypothesis. The dependent variables are the respondents' assessments of the extent to which particular types of resources give the affiliates competitive advantage relative to other New Zealand firms. The independent variables reflect the extent to which the respondents rely on different types of resources from their overseas parent companies. The results of the regression modelling are shown in Table 2; each column represents a separate regression. The variance inflation factors are all under 2.0, indicating there are no issues with multi-collinearity.

The results of the modelling provide considerable support for H1. Each resource type transferred from the parent is positively and significantly associated with its corresponding source of affiliate competitive advantage. For each area of resource-related competitive advantage held by affiliates in New Zealand, there is a corresponding positive relationship with the affiliates' reliance on this resource from the foreign parent companies. This finding provides very strong support for the association between the transfer of parent resources and affiliate advantage in the local context.

In addition to the highly significant relationship between reliance on parent resources and competitive advantage specific to those resources, we observe several cases in which sources of affiliate competitive advantage are also significantly associated with other parent resources. Production/service delivery technology from the parent is associated with higher competitive advantage with regard to economies of scale and scope (column seven in the table), and economies of scale and scope gained through parent companies are positively related to the affiliates' competitive advantage in production/service technology (column two). Product/service technology and economies of scale and scope from the parent are also linked positively to competitive advantage through access to inputs (column eight). Favoured access to inputs from the foreign parent also has a positive and significant relationship with the affiliates' access to markets (column nine). This is suggestive not only of the role the parent plays in the affiliate's activities in the local market, but also of the affiliate's role in the wider international corporate network.

Not all of the estimated relationships are positive. Controlling for affiliates' reliance on other resources from their overseas parents, heavier reliance on the parents' managerial practices and human resources are associated with lower levels of competitive advantage through product/service technology (column one). The extensive transfer of management practices and culture from the parent is also associated with less competitive advantage associated with favoured access to inputs (column eight).

These results suggest that, where inward FDI includes a 'bundle' of resources in addition to capital investment, the affiliate is able to gain competitive advantage from these resources in the local business environment. This is especially the case for resources associated with technology, products, production, economies of scale and inputs; higher levels of these resources are positively associated with competitiveness in more than just their own areas. The negative coefficients

TABLE 2
RELATIONSHIPS BETWEEN PARENT RESOURCE TRANSFER AND THE COMPETITIVE ADVANTAGES OF AFFILIATES

Parent resources (indep. variables)	Competitive advantages of affiliates (dependent variables)								
	(1) Product/service technology	(2) Production/service delivery technology	(3) Management practices/ culture	(4) Marketing systems	(5) Distribution systems	(6) Human resources and skills	(7) Economies of scale or scope	(8) Favoured access to inputs	(9) Access to markets
Product/service technology	0.408***							0.092*	
Production/service delivery technology		0.294***					0.103*		
Management practices/culture	−0.167**		0.189***					−0.092*	
Marketing systems				0.231***					
Distribution systems					0.276***				
Human resources and skills	−0.149*					0.219***			
Economies of scale or scope		0.123*					0.316***	0.111**	
Inputs (i.e. raw materials, products)								0.447***	0.172***
Access to markets									0.363***
F-statistic	13.806***	6.977***	3.506***	2.604**	6.515***	3.694***	12.604***	17.074***	9.829***
R^2	0.200	0.112	0.060	0.045	0.106	0.063	0.182	0.237	0.152
Adjusted R^2	0.186	0.096	0.043	0.028	0.089	0.046	0.167	0.223	0.136

Estimated coefficient significant at the $* = 0.05$, $** = 0.01$, $*** = 0.001$ level. Only significant coefficients are shown.

observed for the more intangible resources of management practices and human resources and skills may suggest that, while these resources are beneficial in helping the affiliate to develop resource-specific competitive advantage, over-reliance on the parent with regard to people and organisational culture may have negative effects in some other aspects of business.

The second hypothesis is tested using cross-tabulations, to assess the extent to which the resources transferred from overseas parent to the affiliate are related to whether or not the affiliate transfers different types of resources to local firms. The parent–affiliate transfer of resources is operationalised using a Likert scale (1–5 for transactional linkages and 1–3 for collaborative linkages, to accommodate the smaller sample size), and the inter-firm (affiliate to local) transfer is coded as a binary variable (yes/no). Significance is assessed using both the chi-square test and tests for the equality of proportions.[1]

Given the very different nature of transactional relationships between the affiliate and local agents, customers, suppliers and subcontractors, and collaborative relationships with local alliance partners, these relationships are analysed separately. The significant results, including the nature of the relationship, are shown in Tables 3 and 4 (transactional relationships) and Tables 5 and 6 (collaborative relationships). The results are broadly supportive of H2; that is, resources transferred from parent companies to their affiliates tend to be positively related to the transfer of similar, or related, resources from the affiliate to local firms.

Table 3 shows the results for production and technology related resources that are transferred by the foreign parent to the affiliate and the downstream transfer of similar resources to local firms via transactional relationships. There are many examples of positive relationships between parent–affiliate resource transfer and the probability of affiliate–local firm transfer. Affiliates receiving more resources related to product/service technology, research and development, inputs, and information and expertise from their foreign parents are more likely to transfer resources related to product/service components, samples and prototypes, technical assistance, and training to local firms through transactional linkages. In addition, affiliates that received research and development assistance from their foreign parents are more likely to share quality assurance and testing related resources with local firms. Higher parent–affiliate resource transfer related to inputs is also associated with a higher likelihood of the affiliates assisting local firms with the acquisition of inputs.

Affiliates capitalising on parent resources relating to economies of scale or scope are likely to pass on the benefits to local firms in the form of product samples, training, and assistance with inventory management and acquiring inputs. In addition, affiliates who rely heavily on production/service delivery technology from the foreign parent tend to transfer resources related to product samples and prototypes to local firms. Overall, subsidiaries receiving a broad selection of

TABLE 3

RELATIONSHIPS BETWEEN PARENT RESOURCE TRANSFER AND TRANSFER OF PRODUCT AND TECHNOLOGY RESOURCES TO LOCAL FIRMS VIA TRANSACTIONAL LINKAGES

	Resources and assistance transferred to local firms							
	Product/service components, specifications	Product samples, prototypes	Production/ service delivery technology	Technical assistance	Testing/quality assurance procedures	Inventory/ service systems management	Assistance with acquiring inputs	Staff training
Parent resources								
Product/service technology	+*	+*		+*				+*
Production/service delivery technology		+*						
Research and development	+**	+**	?*	+**				+***
Economies of scale or scope		+**			+*	+*	+*	+^
Inputs (i.e. raw materials, products)	+*	+***		+**			+*	+*
Information, experience and expertise	+*	+*		+*				+*

Chi-square statistic significant at the ^ = 0.1, * = 0.05, ** = 0.01, *** = 0.001 level.
+ = positive relationship, − = negative relationship, ? = relationship unclear (see Note 1).

TABLE 4

RELATIONSHIPS BETWEEN PARENT RESOURCE TRANSFER AND TRANSFER OF MANAGEMENT AND MARKETING RESOURCES TO LOCAL FIRMS VIA TRANSACTIONAL LINKAGES

	Resources and assistance transferred to local firms				
	Managerial assistance	Information about markets, suppliers, contacts	Trade or exporting assistance	Inventory/service systems management	Staff training
Parent resources					
Management practices/culture			−*		
Marketing systems					+*
Access to markets			+*		
Distribution systems	+^	+^		+*	+**
Employment practices		+*	−^	+*	
Training (or training systems)	+*		−*		+**

Chi-square statistic significant at the ^ = 0.1, * = 0.05, ** = 0.01, *** = 0.001 level.
+ = positive relationship, − = negative relationship, ? = relationship unclear (see Note 1).

TABLE 5

RELATIONSHIPS BETWEEN PARENT RESOURCE TRANSFER AND TRANSFER OF PRODUCT AND TECHNOLOGY RESOURCES TO LOCAL FIRMS VIA COLLABORATIVE LINKAGES[a]

	Resources transferred to local partners					
	Product/service technology	Production/service delivery technology	Research and development	Economies of scale or scope	Inputs (i.e. raw materials, products)	Information, experience and expertise
Parent resources						
Product/service technology	+***		+**			
Production/ service delivery technology	+**		+**			
Research and development		+*	+*			
Economies of scale or scope			+***	+**		
Inputs (i.e. raw materials, products)	+^		+**			
Information, experience and expertise						
Access to markets				+**	+*	?*

[a] Extent of reliance on parent resources has been collapsed from a 1–5 scale to a 1–3 scale owing to data considerations. In the revised scale, 1 = not at all/minor, 2 = moderate, 3 = major/complete.

Chi-square statistic significant at the ^ = 0.1, * = 0.05, ** = 0.01, *** = 0.001 level.

+ = positive relationship, – = negative relationship, ? = relationship unclear (see Note 1).

TABLE 6

RELATIONSHIPS BETWEEN PARENT RESOURCE TRANSFER AND TRANSFER OF MANAGEMENT AND MARKETING RESOURCES TO LOCAL FIRMS VIA COLLABORATIVE LINKAGES[a]

	Resources transferred to local partners						
	Management practices	Marketing	Distribution	Employment practices	Human resources, skills	Training	Research and development
Parent resources							
Management practices/culture						+^	+*
Marketing (systems)						+^	+*
Distribution (systems)			+**				
Employment practices		+*			+^		
Human resources, skills		+***	+**			+*	
Training (systems)		+*		?*	+^	+**	+^

[a] Extent of reliance on parent resources has been collapsed from a 1–5 scale to a 1–3 scale owing to data considerations. In the revised scale, 1 = not at all/minor, 2 = moderate, 3 = major/complete.

Chi-square statistic significant at the ^ = 0.1, * = 0.05, ** = 0.01, *** = 0.001 level.

+ = positive relationship, − = negative relationship, ? = relationship unclear (see Note 1).

resources from their parents are apt to transfer product and technology related resources to local firms, such as product samples and specifications, technical assistance, and staff training, through transactional linkages.

Relationships between parent–affiliate and affiliate–local firm transfer of resources relating to management and marketing via transactional relationships are shown in Table 4. Affiliates receiving more distribution systems resources from the parent are more likely to give managerial assistance, market-related information, help with inventory systems, and staff training to local firms with whom they have transactional linkages.

The transfer of market access and of marketing systems from the parent is translated into more assistance offered to local firms related to trade or exporting, and to staff training, respectively. More employment practices from the foreign parent are associated with a higher probability of more assistance being given to local firms, with respect to market information and contacts, and inventory management, but a lower probability of local help with trade and exporting. Affiliates with heavier reliance on their parents' training-related resources are more likely to pass those resources on to local firms; they are more likely to transfer resources associated with managerial assistance and staff training, but less likely to transfer trade/exporting resources. The acquisition of management practices and culture from the parent was also negatively associated with giving trade or exporting assistance to local firms.

Table 5 shows the significant relationships between parent–affiliate resource transfer and affiliate–local collaborative partner resource transfer for resources pertaining to production and technology. The results on the diagonal suggest that parent-supplied resources associated with product/service technology, research and development, and economies of scale or scope are likely to be passed on to local collaborative partners. Outflow related to research and development is also associated with inflows of product/service technology, economies of scale or scope, inputs and information. Affiliates that rely more on the parent for resources related to economies of scale are also more likely to transfer resources related to production or service delivery technology to their local partners. Collaborative linkages are more apt to result in the transfer of resources associated with product/service technology when there is more extensive parent–subsidiary transfer in the areas of research and development and information. Information-related resources received by the affiliates are positively associated with the transfer of input-related expertise to local partners. Access to markets does not appear to flow on to local firms, but is positively associated with resource transfer relating to economies of scale.

The relationships between resources relating to management and marketing are shown in Table 6. While there appears to be considerable sharing between affiliates and their local collaborative partners, particularly with respect to training, it is interesting to note that there is little one-to-one correspondence between management and marketing resources transferred from parent to affiliate and those transferred to local firms, aside from the areas of distribution and training.

Affiliates that rely on their parents for people-related resources seem more likely to share complementary resources with their local collaborative partners. Greater reliance on human resources and related skills from the parent companies is associated with more local sharing in marketing, distribution, training, and research and development. Parental training systems expertise also spreads to local firms, in terms of marketing, human resources, and research and development, and employment practices resources are positively associated with resource sharing in the areas of marketing, human resources, and research and development. Local partners also benefit, in terms of training resources, when the affiliates absorb resources related to management practices and marketing systems from their overseas parents.

Our results indicate a broadly positive association between the transfer of resources from foreign parent to affiliate and from affiliate to local firms, supporting H2. Although these results differ somewhat for different types of resources and between transactional and collaborative linkages, there is an overall positive relationship between parent–affiliate and affiliate–local firm transfers of technologies and resources relating to product/service, production/ service delivery, research and development, economies of scale and inputs. Surprisingly, there is not always a direct one-to-one correspondence between incoming resources and outgoing resources. For instance, no significant relationship is observed between parent–affiliate and affiliate–local firm resource transfer with regard to marketing systems or management. However, we find complementary resource transfers relating to human resources, employment practices, information, experience and expertise, and training.

This finding might be explained, in part, by consideration of the nature of the resources from the parent company. Affiliates responding to the survey reported relatively heavy reliance on their parent companies for product/ser- vice and production/service delivery technology, research and development, as well as management practices, information, experience and expertise. While we find evidence of direct affiliate–local firm transfer for the first set of resources, the latter set are more likely to be associated with the transfer of related or complementary assistance. In general, more intangible resources, particularly those relating to the human aspects of business, seem to lend themselves more readily to resource transfer in complementary areas such as assistance with marketing, trade and exporting, systems management and staff training.

Some types of resources originating from overseas parent companies are less location- (or firm-) bound. These types of resources may be easier to transfer to local firms. Survey respondents indicated that location-bound resources, such as local marketing and distribution networks, staff, employment practices, and training are more likely to be developed at the affiliate level rather than being transferred solely from the parent company. While we can observe relationships between the affiliates obtaining these resources, and complementary resources and assistance being transferred to local firms, levels of parent–affiliate transfer tend to be weaker. The interplay among human resources and associated skills, experience, practices and training has important implications for flows of similar resources to local firms. These results are strongly suggestive of the ability of outside ideas and capabilities to penetrate local business practices via the FDI medium. Although reliance on human resources from parent companies is relatively low, it seems that, where parent practices and experiences are transferred via staff, and where local linkages take place, there is a strong possibility that information, expertise and training are passed on to local firms. Although such resources may not be transferred directly to local firms, on a one-to-one basis, they are still positively associated with flows of other intangible, people-related resources. This may be the result of indirect flows from select foreign expatriate staff or overseas training programmes provided to the affiliate. This, in turn, improves affiliates' capabilities and performance through their local staff, who then transfer some of this experience to local business partners via inter-firm linkages.

VII. CONCLUSIONS

The principal contribution of this research is to offer a complementary perspective on the question of FDI and development. Our analysis takes a different approach to most previous research by considering the impact of inward FDI at the level of the firm, in the context of a small, developed economy that is heavily reliant on inward FDI and resource-based exports. While the obvious caveat regarding the extent of generalisability of these findings to other nations (developed and developing) must be raised, the results of this study do contribute to our understanding of FDI-led development issues. Specifically, this research offers useful insights into the interplay between foreign and local enterprises, which has strong implications for the upgrading of local capabilities in a small, periphery country looking to improve its capabilities beyond resource-based sectors.

Within the wider context of the FDI-led development debate, New Zealand occupies an interesting position. While the country is classified as a developed economy, it has certain characteristics (such as dependency on the primary sector for international revenue, low levels of outward FDI and local technological development, and declining living standards) typically associated with countries in earlier stages of the IDP. This suggests that even developed economies, particularly those whose competencies remain narrowly focused (such as resource-based economies) or who operate from a small domestic base at the periphery of global markets, have much to benefit from inward FDI, which can provide complementary resources, including capital, technology, labour-related skills, and access to international markets.

Previous research, which has focused on the more immediate effects of inward FDI pertaining to capital, technology and employment, has tended to underestimate the contribution of FDI towards local upgrading, by excluding the long-term effects that occur via linkages at the level of the firm. We have extended the literature as follows. First, we use a survey instrument to capture observations from a large sample of foreign-owned firms in New Zealand. Second, we incorporate a wide range of linkages that involve resource transfer into the analysis. Hence, our results reflect the nature of micro-level affiliate–local firm interactions within the New Zealand context, rather than the outcome in terms of aggregate measures of productivity or demand.

The main conclusion to be drawn from this study is that, via their foreign parents, affiliates introduce and exploit unique resources from offshore that contribute to, first, the affiliate's competitiveness in New Zealand and, second, the capabilities and resources available to local firms. At the affiliate level, our findings show that foreign affiliates are reliant on a wide range of parent resources, such as product technology, information and experience, management practices and production technology, and these can be associated with the affiliate's ability to compete against local competitors in the host economy. This result provides evidence of the importance of MNE-specific advantages for the affiliate's performance in the host country. From the host economy's perspective, this finding provides further support to the notion that foreign ownership differs fundamentally from domestic ownership, and thus exerts different developmental impacts. We find that the affiliate has access to firm-specific advantages and resources that are not available to locally based competitors. Combined with its own local adaptations and development, these firm-specific advantages give the affiliate a competitive edge in the local setting. Ultimately, superior capability and access to technology, knowledge and experience are expected to lead to better performance, output and productivity by the affiliate. These changes, in turn, lead to benefits for the host country, in the form of greater industry output and productivity, opportunities for employment, local supply and exports, and absorption of superior technologies.

This research found that half of the affiliates in the sample formed linkages that involved resource transfer with local firms. These relationships offer considerably more potential for upgrading and development of local firms than what would be expected solely from greater demand or supply. By incorporating resource transfer into the analysis, we provide insight into the nature of the upgrading and the process by which it might occur. Our results also imply that greater transfer of many different types of resources from the parent translates into a higher likelihood that similar or complementary resources will be transferred to local firms from the affiliate.

This finding provides evidence that inward FDI can be associated with indirect, but positive, impacts on local industry, where foreign affiliates engage in linkages with local firms. This is particularly apparent for collaborative linkages, and linkages that involve the transfer of product-related technologies, research and development, economies of scale, distribution systems and inputs. There are also spillovers from the parent–affiliate transfer of human resources, skills, training, information, experience and expertise. This lends support to previous research that reports a positive interplay between inward foreign direct investment and local capability building.

However, the overall positive relationship between parent–affiliate and affiliate–local firm linkages is tempered by the extent of linkage formation. Just over half of the affiliates in the sample formed transactional linkages with agents, customers and suppliers/subcontractors, and just under a third formed collaborative linkages. This means there is potential for much greater resource transfer and diffusion, given more extensive linkage formation. Because many foreign-owned affiliates in New Zealand do not engage in linkages associated with resource transfer, we can assume that their impact on local firms is limited to the effects associated with competition, emulation, demonstration, demand and supply. Previous studies have found these effects to be lower for foreign affiliates than local firms [*Barkley and McNamara, 1994; Barrow and Hall, 1995*].

Overall, our findings suggest quite strongly that local affiliates and, to a lesser extent, local firms are benefiting from resources that would otherwise be difficult to obtain within New Zealand. Thus, the research highlights the importance of inward FDI to upgrading in the New Zealand context. The political stance of New Zealand's non-interventionist government, the country's openness to trade and foreign investment, and its small domestic base, mean that New Zealand firms are increasingly having to confront, and to better, international competitors in order to survive. This suggests that the quality, rather than just the quantity, of foreign–local linkage formation must be of concern to New Zealand firms looking to compete internationally. The long-term value of linkages in a small, export-dependent nation such as New Zealand is not simply the extent of demand generated, but the extent to which local and foreign competencies and resources complement each other, so that foreign expertise and innovation can integrate into, as well as add to, local expertise and innovation. For example, linkages in which firms have the opportunity to share and develop complementary resources, such as ongoing supply relationships and collaborative linkages, should, in the long-term, have a far greater impact than transactional linkages that may be severed as 'spot' markets for goods and services fluctuate.

The notion of 'quality linkages' also raises an important point with regard to the results of this study in the context of the wider FDI-led development literature. This is not simply an issue for New Zealand. Quality linkages can be expected to bring favourable developmental effects in other small, industrialised countries, whose levels of local absorptive capacity and competence are sufficiently high to attract foreign firms seeking complementary skills, but who still experience major gaps in their knowledge and resource bases. This combination places local firms in the position to leverage their interactions with subsidiaries of overseas MNEs and benefit from inflows of foreign resources. In contrast to developing nations, where the benefits of FDI are not always forthcoming due to large technology 'gaps' and dominant foreign presence [*Kokko, 1994*], countries such as New Zealand have much to gain from FDI, because of the complementarities between local and foreign resources.

The main implications of our findings for future research and policy are twofold. First, there is a need to recognise the benefits of inward FDI as a catalyst for local upgrading, beyond changes to output, local sourcing, and capital flows. Consideration should also be given to potential benefits that arise from the inflow of unique advantages and resources from offshore. While the cross-sectional nature of this study precludes an evaluation of the extent to which foreign–local firm linkages have enhanced long-term firm-level competencies, future research might address this limitation by considering the question from the perspective of local suppliers, customers, agents and alliance partners. This approach would allow an evaluation of the contribution of FDI activity to local firm competitiveness, and provide insights into what local competence 'gaps' are being addressed by access to foreign resources and skills. It would also be useful to disaggregate the data by industry, in order to capture some of the different impacts on different sectors.

Second, the impact of the transfer of resources associated with inward FDI is important at the level of the firm in two distinct areas. For the affiliate, these resources contribute to competitiveness, productivity and output. For the local firm, they can contribute to capabilities and upgrading. Thus, a wider-ranging approach to considering the impact of FDI on a host economy needs to be incorporated in future research. It is also important for policy-makers to take this broader view; to avoid underestimating the extent of the impact of FDI, and to better target the types of FDI that are more likely to foster longer-term linkages in the local economy.

NOTE

1. Where the chi-square test implied significant differences, two-tailed tests of proportions were used to assess the nature of the relationships between reliance on parent resources (1 = not at all, 2 = minor, 3 = moderate, 4 = major and 5 = complete) and transfer of resources to the local firm. Where the observed proportion is significantly lower than expected for responses 1 and/or 2 (and/or higher than expected for responses 4 and/or 5), this implies that fewer parent resources are associated with fewer resources transferred to local firms (and/or more parent resources are associated with more resources transferred to local firms). This positive association between reliance on parent resources and the extent of resource transference is represented by + in the tables. In contrast if the observed proportion is significantly higher than expected for responses 1 and/or 2 (and/or lower than expected for responses 4 and/or 5), the negative relationship is represented by − in the tables. Unclear or inconsistent, but significant, directional relationships are represented by ? in the tables.

REFERENCES

Aitken, B.J. and A.E. Harrison, 1999, 'Do Domestic Firms Benefit from Direct Foreign Investment? Evidence from Venezuela', *American Economic Review*, Vol.89, No.3, pp.605–18.
Aitken, B., G.H. Hanson and A. Harrison, 1997, 'Spillovers, Foreign Investment, and Export Behavior', *Journal of International Economics*, Vol.43, pp.103–32.
Akoorie, M., 1996a, 'The Impact of Foreign Direct Investment and Government Policy on the Internationalisation Process of the New Zealand Firm', Unpublished DPhil Thesis, Hamilton: University of Waikato.
Akoorie, M., 1996b, 'New Zealand: The Economic Development of a Resource-Rich Economy', in J. Dunning and R. Narula (eds.), *Foreign Direct Investment and Governments: Catalysts for Economic Restructuring*, London and New York: Routledge, pp.174–286.
Akoorie, M., 1998, 'The Historical Role of Foreign Investment in New Zealand', in P. Enderwick (ed.), *Foreign Direct investment: The New Zealand Experience*, Palmerston North: Dunmore Press, pp.67–90.
Barkley, D. and K. McNamara, 1994, 'Local Input Linkages: A Comparison of Foreign-Owned and Domestic Manufacturers in Georgia and South Carolina', *Regional Studies*, Vol.28, No.7, pp.725–37.
Barrell, R. and N. Pain, 1997, 'Foreign Direct Investment, Technological Change, and Economic Growth within Europe', *Economic Journal*, Vol.107, No.445, pp.1770–86.
Barrow, M. and M. Hall, 1995, 'The Impact of a Large Multinational Organization on a Small Local Economy', *Regional Studies*, Vol.29, No.7, pp.635–53.
BCG, 2001, *Building the Future: Using Foreign Direct Investment to help Fuel New Zealand's Economic Prosperity*, Wellington: The Boston Consulting Group.
Blomstrom, M., 1989, *Foreign Investment and Spillovers: A Study of Technology Transfer to Mexico*, London and New York: Routledge.
Borensztein, E., J. De Gregorio and L.-W. Lee, 1998, 'How does Foreign Direct Investment affect Economic Growth?', *Journal of International Economics*, Vol.45, No.1, pp.1115–35.
Bosco, M.G., 2001, 'Does FDI Contribute to Technological Spillovers and Growth? A Panel Data Analysis of Hungarian Firms', *Transnational Corporations*, Vol.10, No.1, pp.43–68.
Brown, R., 1998, 'Electronics Foreign Direct Investment in Singapore: A Study of Local Linkages in "Winchester City"', *European Business Review*, Vol.98, No.4, pp.196–210.
Buckley, P.J. and M.C. Casson, 1998, 'Analyzing Foreign Market Entry Strategies: Extending the Internalization Approach', *Journal of International Business Studies*, Vol.29, No.3, pp.539–61.
Campbell, D., 1994, 'Foreign Investment, Labour Immobility and the Quality of Employment', *International Labour Review*, Vol.133, No.2, pp.186–204.
Caves, R.E., 1974, 'Multinational Firms, Competition and Productivity in Host-Country Markets', *Economica*, Vol.41, pp.176–93.
Collis, C., D. Noon and N. Berkeley, 1994, 'Direct Investment from the EC: Recent Trends in the West Midlands Region and their Implications for Regional Development and Policy', *European Business Review*, Vol.94, No.2, pp.14–19.

Cremer, R.D. and B. Ramasamy, 1996, *Tigers in New Zealand? The Role of Asian Investment in the Economy*, Wellington: Institute of Policy Studies.

Crocombe, G.T., M.J. Enright and M.E. Porter, 1991, *Upgrading New Zealand's Competitive Advantage*, Auckland: Oxford University Press.

Deane, R.S., 1970, *Foreign Investment in New Zealand Manufacturing*, Wellington: Sweet & Maxwell (N.Z.) Ltd.

Doraisami, A. and G.K. Leng, 1996, 'Foreign Direct Investment and Economic Growth: Some Time Series Evidence of the Malaysian Experience', *Asian Economies*, Vol.25, No.3, pp.45–54.

Driffield, N. and J. Love, 2003, 'Foreign Direct Investment, Technology Sourcing and Reverse Spillovers', in *The Manchester School: Manchester*, Vol. 71, No.6, pp.659–73.

Duncan, I., J. Yeabsley, M. Akoorie and P. Enderwick, 1997, *Foreign Investment Review*, Wellington: NZ Institute of Economic Research (Inc).

Dunning, J.H., 1981, 'Explaining the International Direct Investment Position of Countries: Towards a Dynamic or Development Approach', *Weltwirtschaftliches Archiv*, Vol.117, pp.30–64.

Dunning, J.H., 1986, 'The Investment Development Cycle Revisited', *Weltwirtschaftliches Archiv*, Vol.122, pp.667–77.

Dunning, J.H., 1988, *Explaining International Production*, London: Unwin Hyman.

Dunning, J.H., 1993, 'Trade, Location of Economic Activity and the Multinational Enterprise: A Search for an Eclectic Approach', in J.H. Dunning (ed.), *The Theory of Transnational Corporations*, London and New York: Routledge.

Dunning, J.H., 1996, 'Re-evaluating the Benefits of Foreign Direct Investment', in UNCTAD, *Companies without Borders: Transnational Corporations in the 1990s*, London: International Thomson Business Press.

Dunning, J.H., 1998, *Investment in British Manufacturing Industry*, London and New York: Routledge.

Dunning, J.H. and R. Narula, 1996, *Foreign Direct Investment and Governments: Catalysts for Economic Restructuring*, London and New York: Routledge.

Enderwick, P., 1995, *The Contribution of Foreign Direct Investment to the New Zealand Economy*, Auckland: American Chamber of Commerce in New Zealand.

Enderwick, P. (ed.), 1998, *Foreign Direct Investment: The New Zealand Experience*, Palmerston North: Dunmore Press.

Figueroa, A., 1998, 'Equity, Foreign Investment and International Competitiveness in Latin America', *Quarterly Review of Economics and Finance*, Vol.38, No.3, pp.391–408.

Globerman, S., 1979, 'Foreign Direct Investment and "Spillover" Efficiency Benefits in Canadian Manufacturing Industries', *Canadian Journal of Economics*, Vol.12, pp.42–56.

Hagedoorn, J. and R. Narula, 1999, 'Choosing Organizational Modes of Strategic Technology Partnering: International and Sectoral Differences', *Journal of International Business Studies*, Vol.27, No.2, pp.265–85.

Harper, D., 1994, *Teaming Up: A Study of Japanese-Affiliated Firms in New Zealand*, NZIER Research Monograph, No.62, Wellington.

Hymer, S.H., 1960, *The International Operations of National Firms: A Study of Direct Investment*, Cambridge, MA: MIT Press.

IMD, 2004, *World Competitiveness Yearbook*, International Institute for Management Development.

Khawar, M., 2003, 'Productivity and Foreign Direct Investment – Evidence from Mexico', *Journal of Economic Studies*, Vol.30, No.1, pp.66–76.

Kokko, A., 1994, 'Technology, Market Characteristics, and Spillovers', *Journal of Development Economics*, Vol.43, No.2, pp.279–93.

Kokko, A., R. Tansini and M.C. Zejan, 1996, 'Local Technology Capability and Productivity Spillovers from FDI in the Uruguayan Manufacturing Sector', *Journal of Development Studies*, Vol.32, No.4, pp.602–12.

KPMG, 1995, *Foreign Ownership – Cause for Concern?*, Wellington: KPMG.

Lall, S., 1995, 'Employment and Foreign Investment: Policy Options for Developing Countries', *International Labour Review*, Vol.134, No.4–5, pp.521–40.

Lall, S., 1996, 'Transnational Corporations and Economic Development', in UNCTAD *Transnational Corporations and World Development*, New York and Geneva: United Nations.

Lall, S., 2001, *Competitiveness, Technology and Skills*, Cheltenham: Edward Elgar.

Liu, X., P. Burridge and P.J.N. Sinclair, 2002, 'Relationships between Economic Growth, Foreign Direct Investment and Trade: Evidence from China', *Applied Economics*, Vol.34, No.11, pp.1433–40.

Madhok, A., 1996, 'The Organisation of Economic Activity: Transaction Costs, Firm Capabilities, and the Nature of Governance', *Organizational Science*, Vol.7, No.5, pp.577–90.

Narula, R., 1996, *Multinational Investment and Economic Structure: Globalisation and Competitiveness*, London and New York: Routledge.

O'Malley, E. and C. O'Gorman, 2001, 'Competitive Advantage in the Irish Indigenous Software Industry and the Role of Inward Foreign Direct Investment', *European Planning Studies*, Vol.9, No.3, pp.303–22.

Poon, T.S.-C., 1996, 'Dependent Development: The Subcontracting Networks in the Tiger Economies', *Human Resource Management Journal*, Vol.6, No.4, pp.38–49.

Raines, P., I. Turok and R. Brown, 2001, 'Growing Global: Foreign Direct Investment and the Internationalization of Local Suppliers in Scotland', *European Planning Studies*, Vol.9, No.8, pp.965–79.

Ram, R. and K.H. Zhang, 2002, 'Foreign Direct Investment and Economic Growth: Evidence from Cross-Country Data for the 1990s', *Economic Development and Cultural Change*, Vol.51, No.1, pp.205–16.

Rodriguez-Clare, A., 1996, 'Multinationals, Linkages, and Economic Development', *American Economic Review*, Vol.86, No.4, pp.852–73.

Rosenberg, B., 1998, 'Foreign Investment in New Zealand: The Current Position', in P. Enderwick (ed.), *Foreign Investment: The New Zealand Experience*, Palmerston North: Dunmore Press.

Ruane, F. and G. Holger, 1997, 'The Impact of Foreign Direct Investment on Sectoral Adjustment in the Irish Economy', *National Institute Economic Review*, Vol.160, April, pp.76–86.

Sadik, A.T. and A.A. Bolbol, 2001, 'Capital Flows, FDI, and Technology Spillovers: Evidence from Arab Countries', in *World Development*, Vol. 29, No. 2, pp.2111–26.

Scott-Kennel, J., 1998, 'Foreign Direct Investment and Privatisation in New Zealand', in P. Enderwick (ed.), *Foreign Direct Investment: The New Zealand Experience*, Palmerston North: Dunmore Press.

Skilling, D., 2001, *The Importance of being Enormous: Towards an Understanding of the New Zealand Economy*, Wellington: The New Zealand Treasury.

Sun, H. and J. Chai, 1998, 'Direct Foreign Investment and Inter-Regional Economic Disparity in China', *International Journal of Social Economics*, Vol.25, No.2, pp.424–47.

Teece, D., 1992, 'Competition, Cooperation and Innovation: Organisational Arrangements for Regimes of Rapid Technological Progress', *Journal of Economic Behaviour and Organization*, Vol.18, pp.1–25.

Turok, I., 1993, 'Inward Investment and Local Linkages: How Deeply Embedded is "Silicon Glen"?', *Regional Studies*, Vol.27, No.5, pp.401–17.

UNCTAD, 1999, *World Investment Report 1999: Foreign Direct Investment and the Challenge of Development*, New York and Geneva: United Nations.

UNCTAD, 2000, *World Investment Report 2000: Cross-Mergers and Acquisitions and Development*, New York and Geneva: United Nations.

UNCTAD, 2001, *World Investment Report 2001: Promoting Linkages*, New York and Geneva: United Nations.

UNCTAD, 2002, *World Investment Report 2002: Transnational Corporations and Export Competitiveness*, New York and Geneva: United Nations.

Wernerfelt, B., 1984, 'Resource-based View of the Firm', *Strategic Management Journal*, Vol.5, No.2, pp.171–80.

Williams, D., 1997, 'Strategies of Multinational Enterprises and the Development of the Central and Eastern European Economies', *European Business Review*, Vol.97, No.3, pp.134–8.

Williams, D., 1999, 'Foreign Manufacturing Firms in the UK: Effects on Employment, Output and Supplier Linkages', *European Business Review*, Vol.99, No.6, pp.393–8.

Wong, P.-K., 1992, 'Technological Development through Subcontracting Linkages: Evidence from Singapore', *Scandinavian International Business Review*, Vol.1, No.3, pp.28–40.

Young, S. and P. Lan, 1997, 'Technology Transfer to China through Foreign Direct Investment', *Regional Studies*, Vol.31, No.7, pp.669–79.

Zaheer, S., 1995, 'Overcoming the Liability of Foreignness', *Academy of Management Journal*, Vol.38, No.2, pp.341–64.

Zhao, L., 1998, 'The Impact of Foreign Direct Investment on Wages and Employment', *Oxford Economic Papers*, Vol.50, No.2, pp.284–301.

Where Do Foreign Direct Investment-Related Technology Spillovers Come From in Emerging Economies? An Exploration in Argentina in the 1990s

MARTIN BELL and ANABEL MARIN

Models underlying most research about foreign direct investment (FDI)-related spillovers suggest they originate in the centrally accumulated knowledge assets of multinational corporations (MNCs). From there a one-way 'pipeline' runs via a) international technology transfer to subsidiaries, b) 'leaks' into the host economy, c) varying degrees of absorption by domestic firms to d) those firms' productivity increases. We argue that this gives inadequate attention to knowledge-creating activities by MNC subsidiaries and domestic firms inside the host economy. These co-located and interacting activities are increasingly evident in knowledge-rich locations in advanced economies, reflecting location-specific advantages. We suggest here that such locally rooted and co-located knowledge creation may also lie between, but not necessarily causally connect, FDI and domestic firms' productivity growth in intermediate economies – as illustrated by the case of Argentina in the mid 1990s. Wider questions about policy are noted, with implications for future research highlighted.

Les modèles qui sous-tendent la majorité des recherches sur les excédents liés aux investissements directs étrangers (IDE) laissent supposer que ceux-ci sont le résultat des connaissances accumulées de manière centrale au sein des corporations multinationales (CMN). De ce centre, une conduite à sens-unique passe par a) le transfert international de technologies vers les filiales, b) des «fuites» bénéficiant le pays récepteur, c) différents degrés d'absorption par les entreprises domestiques, pour finalement arriver à d) une augmentation de la productivité de ces mêmes entreprises. Nous soutenons que ces modèles ne prêtent pas assez attention aux filiales des CMN et aux entreprises domestiques dont les

Martin Bell and Anabel Marin are at SPRU-Science and Technology Policy Research, University of Sussex, UK. The authors are very grateful to Valeria Arza, Rajneesh Narula and Nick Von Tunzelmann for comments on an earlier draft of this chapter.

activités produisent des connaissances à l'intérieur du pays d'accueil. Il devient de plus en plus évident que de telles activités interdépendantes et «co-localisées» existent dans des régions riches en connaissances á l'intérieur d'économies avancées, et qu'elles reflètent des avantages spécifiquement liés au lieu. Nous avançons qu'une telle création de connaissances locales et «co-localisées» peut tout à fait se situer entre – sans pour autant relier de manière causale – les IDE et la croissance de productivités des entreprises domestiques à l'intérieur d'économies moyennes – comme l'illustre les cas de l'Argentine au milieu des années quatre-vingt-dix. De plus vastes questions politiques sont mentionnées, ouvrant la voie à de futures recherches.

I. INTRODUCTION

The basic model underpinning studies of the economic significance of technological spillovers from foreign direct investment (FDI) in host economies has long been rooted in the ownership ('O') component of the eclectic Ownership–Location–Internalisation (OLI) paradigm. This O-centred element in the spillover model is linked to the 30- to 40-year-old I-related insights of scholars such as Caves [*1971, 1982*] and Hymer [*1960*], reinforced by Vernon's [*1966*] product life cycle model, that emphasised the importance of internalisation and hierarchical control in the exploitation of ownership advantages via FDI. Within that framework the answer to the question posed in the title to this chapter is obvious: spillovers originate in the generation and ownership of superior knowledge assets at the corporate centres of multinational corporations (MNCs) in their home countries. In association with FDI, components of these centrally controlled knowledge assets are transferred to affiliates in other economies, whence they leak out to be acquired and absorbed by domestic firms. These spillovers then yield economic gains (typically measured as productivity growth) to the absorbing firms in the domestic sector of the economy.

Location-specific factors, the 'L' component of the OLI framework, do come into play in the models of spillover processes, but only as mediating variables influencing the FDI-driven flow of knowledge from corporate centres to domestically owned firms in host economies. Local firms may not have an adequate base of existing knowledge to absorb effectively the new knowledge leaking from MNC affiliates [*e.g. Kokko, 1994*]; or wider characteristics of local economies may influence the scale or scope of knowledge that is transferred in the first place by MNC centres to affiliates [*Wang and Blomstrom, 1992*].

This framework has become well established as the basis of models used to estimate the economic significance of spillovers and the influence of various factors in shaping that significance. There are, however, three difficulties about this framework.

First, there is very little evidence of significant economic effects arising from FDI-related spillovers. Various kinds of knowledge spillover have been described in case studies and field surveys. However, systematic studies of the economic significance of such spillovers have suggested it is very limited in a wide range of situations [*Blomstrom and Kokko, 1997; Gorg and Strobl, 2001; Lipsey, 2002*].

Second, the framework typically takes very limited account of the steps and stages of the process lying between a) the FDI bringing with it superior knowledge at the 'input-end' of the process and b) the measured growth of productivity in domestic firms at the 'output-end'. One of those steps, the absorption of knowledge by domestic firms has been given attention in recent years – as noted above. But there is much more complexity in the process than that.

Third, the O- and I-centred model with its roots in the 1960s and 1970s is no longer an adequate basis for analysing the knowledge flows associated with FDI. Following the conceptualisation of MNCs in much more flexible terms during the 1980s [*e.g. Hedlund, 1986; Prahalad and Doz, 1987; Bartlett and Ghoshal, 1989, Ghoshal and Bartlett, 1990*], numerous studies have highlighted the significance of localised innovative activities of affiliates in host countries. Early explorations in that direction emphasised that these activities were merely adaptive adjuncts to the transfer of technology from parents, and that this was almost exclusively so in the case of MNC affiliates in developing countries [*Lall, 1979*]. Later studies have identified a much wider variety of roles for localised innovative activity in MNC subsidiaries [*e.g. Ghoshal and Bartlett, 1990; Kuemmerle, 1999; Zander, 1999; Pearce, 1999; Frost, 2001; von Zedtwitz and Gassman, 2002*], and various kinds of interaction between subsidiaries and local sources of new knowledge may be important in these roles, as recently emphasised in the European context by Cantwell and Iammarino [*2003*]. At the same time, the extent of independent initiative in affiliates may be much more significant than suggested in earlier centrally directed models of MNC activity [*Birkinshaw, 1997; Paterson and Brock, 2002; Birkinshaw and Hood, 1998*]; and local innovative activities, interacting with local knowledge sources, may be important elements in this 'dispersed entrepreneurship' at the affiliate level [*Jarillo andMartinez, 1990; Cantwell and Janne, 1999*]. More generally, it has been argued that, in the increasingly knowledge-based and globalised economy, there is an increasingly complex interdependence between ownership and location advantages [*Cantwell and Narula, 2001*].

Within these much more flexible and L-related perspectives on the technological roles of MNC subsidiaries, the answer to the question posed by this chapter is much less obvious. FDI-related spillovers will not necessarily originate from MNCs' centrally accumulated knowledge assets. They may instead be generated in knowledge-creating activities undertaken at the affiliate level. Indeed, knowledge flows may run in the opposite direction from that commonly presumed – i.e. from the host economy to the MNC subsidiary, and from the subsidiary to the parent or its other global affiliates. Alternatively, the knowledge flow may run both ways in a mutually reinforcing nexus, with bi-directional spillovers, rooted in local circumstances, resources and opportunities. In such a situation, productivity increases in domestic firms might well be statistically associated with high rates of FDI, but it is not at all obvious that this should be interpreted in terms of FDI and the associated transfer of technology being the source of spillovers that contributed to the productivity growth.

But there is one important limitation to these more L-centred studies of spillover generation. They almost all examine experience in the advanced economies, and even in those contexts the general presumption has been that these kinds of localised interaction will arise primarily in only more knowledge-rich locations where high skill levels, strong educational resources, an effective research infrastructure and a good science base provide the prerequisites for knowledge-interactions between affiliates and host economies.[1] With a few exceptions (e.g. in selected locations in India), less advanced economies have not been seen as contexts for these kinds of interaction.

In this chapter we question that limited view, drawing on the experience of Argentina in the mid 1990s. We explore whether, in this late-industrialising economy, a positive relationship between FDI and the productivity growth of domestic firms might originate not in knowledge that was originally delivered by MNC parents to their subsidiaries, but in localised knowledge-creation by MNC affiliates and domestic firms, and perhaps by knowledge-centred interactions between them. With this focus, we hope to push back a little the advanced country boundaries on research in this area that have been highlighted, for instance, by Molero and Alvarez [*2003*] in their work on the technological activities of MNCs in the 'intermediate' economy of Spain.[2]

The structure of the rest of the chapter is as follows. In the next section we elaborate on the three difficulties summarised above, briefly reviewing the empirical evidence about the economic significance of spillovers and noting some of the complexities in the process that links FDI and productivity growth in domestic firms. We highlight the importance of locally based knowledge acquisition and creation by both MNC subsidiaries and domestic firms – a 'black box' located between, but not necessarily linking, FDI and productivity growth in domestic firms. We explore that black box in this chapter.

In Section III we outline the methods used, and we present the results in Section IV. Extending beyond a previous chapter [*Marin and Bell, 2004*], we identify a significant industry-level co-location of innovative and knowledge-augmenting activities in both MNC subsidiaries and domestic firms. Our interpretation centres on the role of location-specific factors and the emergence of knowledge-augmenting interactions between local and domestic firms. We discuss conclusions in Section V.

II. PERSPECTIVES ON FDI-RELATED TECHNOLOGY SPILLOVERS

The Conventional View: A Centrally Driven Supply-side Model

Following from the work in the 1970s there is now a long history of empirical analysis of FDI-related technological spillovers. As noted above, a core element in the theoretical framework for this work is about the MNC's possession of unique technological assets. Spillovers to domestic firms in host economies are presumed to follow on from the centrally driven, intra-corporate exploitation of this technological advantage, as summarised recently by two of the more prolific contributors to the empirical analysis of FDI-related spillovers.

> It is well known that multinational corporations (MNCs) undertake a major part of the world's private R&D efforts and produce, own and control most of the world's advanced technology. When a MNC sets up a foreign affiliate, the affiliate receives some of the proprietary technology that constitutes the parent's firm-specific advantage and allows it to compete successfully with local firms that have superior knowledge of local markets, consumer preferences and business practices. This leads to a geographical diffusion of technology, but not necessarily to any formal transfer of technology beyond the boundaries of the MNC: the establishment of a foreign affiliate is, almost per definition, a decision to internalise the use of core technology. However, MNC technology may still leak to the surrounding economy through external effects or spillovers that raise the level of human capital in the host country and create productivity increases in local firms. [*Blomstrom and Kokko, 2003: 3*]

Some of the complexity of these steps and relationships that are claimed to link the research and development (R and D) of MNCs to productivity growth in local firms is illustrated in Figure 1.

The earlier studies within this perspective found positive associations between FDI (step 2) and productivity growth in local firms (step 9) [*e.g.Caves, 1974 or Globerman, 1979*]. However these studies relied largely on industry-level data and cross-sectional analysis and, as noted by Aitken and Harrison [*1999*], MNCs may locate in what are already the relatively high-productivity sectors in the host economy, rather than generating technology spillovers that contribute to that higher productivity. Consequently recent studies have generally used firm-level designs, typically combined with panel data analysis. Some studies still find positive spillover effects – for instance, Haskel *et al.* [*2002*] or Keller and Yeaple [*2003*]. But positive results are absent from a wide range of

FIGURE 1
SOME OF THE MULTIPLE STEPS LINKING FDI TO PRODUCTIVITY GROWTH IN HOST
COUNTRY FIRMS

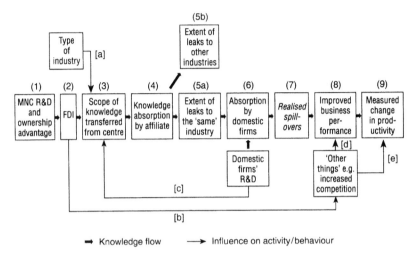

→ Knowledge flow   ⟶ Influence on activity/behaviour

studies cutting across advanced, transition and industrialising economies – for instance, Braconier *et al.* [*2001*], Chung [*2001*], Haddad and Harrison [*1993*], Djankov and Hoekman [*2000*], Aitken and Harrison [1999], and Konings [*2001*]. However, interpretation of these results is complicated by two common aspects of the method used.

First, most studies combine two different kinds of FDI-induced externality under the term 'spillovers'. One is the effect of knowledge flows running from the MNC and its subsidiary through the various steps in Figure 1 to influence productivity growth in domestic firms. The other is the consequence of competition from increased FDI – link [b] in Figure 1. Domestic firms may be stimulated by this to increase productivity, but they may do so in ways that draw little or nothing from knowledge that spills over from MNC subsidiaries. The distinction between 'genuine' knowledge spillovers and 'pseudo' spillover-like productivity effects of competitive pressure is very difficult to operationalise empirically, but the two processes may have very different implications for policy.

Second, because of the difficulties in estimating *inter*-industry spillover effects (5b in Figure 1), almost all studies use estimation methods that capture only *intra*-industry spillovers (5a). The significance of the omitted inter-industry effects is probably substantial. Numerous surveys and case studies have highlighted the importance of knowledge transfers running from MNC subsidiaries to suppliers and customers and, while some of these knowledge flows may occur within industry classification categories, a large and unknown proportion will not. The fraction that is captured by intra-industry studies is unknown and is likely to vary with differences in the level of industry aggregation used in the analysis. But it is likely in general to underestimate the effects of knowledge spillovers.

It is difficult to assess whether this helps to account for the mixed but largely negative results from econometric spillover studies, and research has moved in other directions to try to understand why, across such a wide range of circumstances, the assumed technological superiority of MNCs and their subsidiaries does not appear to diffuse to domestic firms. Given the core assumptions of the framework, few questions were initially asked about the centrally driven supply side of the process (steps 2–5 in Figure 1), and attention focused on step (6) on the demand side – the varying ability of domestic firms to absorb the (presumed to be) superior knowledge and skills originally delivered by MNCs to their subsidiaries.

Some studies have found such demand-side effects to be significant: for instance, Kokko [1994] for Mexico and Konings [1999] for Poland and Bulgaria. However, others have not – for example, Patibandla and Sanyal [2002], Sjoholm [1997]; Haskel et al. [2002], and Damijan et al. [2001].

The search for other possible influences on spillover effects turned later to step (3) in Figure 1, differences in the scope and type of knowledge transferred from the parent company. One view has emphasised the way in which inter-industry differences affect this aspect of the technological behaviour of MNCs – link [a] in Figure 1. Industries are presumed to differ in the levels of technological knowledge they use, the rates at which they develop it, and hence in their levels of technological opportunity.[3] So, for instance, some types of 'advanced' industry, such as the electronics or capital goods industries, are thought to possess greater potential for generating spillovers because they use more recent vintages of technology, employ greater numbers of skilled workers, undertake more R and D, etc. The scope of the knowledge transferred from the MNC parent will be relatively wide and 'advanced' in such industries. In contrast, more 'traditional' industries are presumed to involve more limited technology transfer, providing less potential for generating spillovers because they are in general less technology-intensive [Narula and Dunning, 2000].

Alongside arguments about the inherent technological characteristics of different industries and activities, other factors have been suggested as reasons for variation in the scope and depth of the technology transferred in association with FDI. Some studies have emphasised the role of host country conditions in attracting investment in particular kinds of industry. Narula and Dunning [2000] for instance have argued that limitations in host country infrastructure and capabilities help to shape traditional types of MNC investment in developing countries in low value-adding and labour-intensive industries that require limited technology transfer. Wang and Blomstrom [1992] also see a significant influence lying inside the host economy because international technology transfer emerges from parent company decisions in the light of expected strategic interaction between their foreign subsidiaries and the technological characteristics of host country firms. The speed of transfer and the vintage of technologies transferred depend, they argue, on the actions and capabilities of local firms. The higher the host country firms' investment in learning and R and D, the narrower is the future technology gap facing the MNC, and the greater is the propensity to transfer more advanced technology in order to ensure profitability in the face of more technologically capable competition – link [c] in Figure 1.

These views about variability in the scope of the technology transferred (supplied) by MNCs have added to the earlier interest in absorptive capacity on the demand side of the spillover process. But the dominant perception in both empirical and theoretical spillover studies continues to be about a one-way pipeline running from left to right in Figure 1. Attention still concentrates on the centralised technological assets of MNCs as the original source of the knowledge that may eventually give rise to productivity increases in domestic firms in host economies, and any variability on the supply side of the process is seen as arising from strategic corporate decisions about the scale and scope of knowledge to transfer from the centre of the MNC.

Correspondingly, subsidiaries in the host economy continue to be seen as playing only a passive role in the process, merely acting, at stage (5) in Figure 1, as a leaky section of the one-way conduit running from the creation of knowledge in the parent company to its absorption (or not) by domestic firms in the host economy. If they occur at all, R and D and other knowledge-creating activities in subsidiaries are merely reflections of parent company decisions. At the same time, the role of local firms in the process is typically seen as little more than one of absorbing knowledge delivered into the local economy by MNC parent companies. However, a wider literature, not yet well reflected in the spillover studies, suggests that a much greater role may be played by locally based and locally driven sources of spillovers and productivity growth.

An Alternative View: Locally Based and Locally Driven Sources of Spillovers

As noted earlier, research on business strategy and organisation long ago abandoned the homogeneous model of 'the MNC' as a centrally directed and closely integrated organisation. In a succession of developments in the field, wide-ranging heterogeneity between MNCs has been recognised, along with varying forms of organisational flexibility and internal heterogeneity in the roles of subsidiaries and their relationships with parents and other affiliates.[4]

Alongside this has emerged a large body of research about the extent, nature and strategic role of dispersed innovative activity among MNC subsidiaries. Until recently most of these studies have centred on the role of dispersed innovative activity within overall corporate technological strategy, what Ghoshal and

Bartlett [*1988*] referred to as 'local-for-global' innovation within the MNC structure. They include Pearce's [*1999*] discussion of increasingly interdependent roles for dispersed R and D within the corporation.[5] In similar vein, Zander [*1999: 195*] refers to the MNC's increasing 'integration of internationally dispersed technological capabilities'. Kuemmerle [*1999*] describes such strategically integrated patterns of R and D as 'home-base-augmenting' in contrast to the more traditional pattern of 'home-base-exploiting' R and D, while Dunning [2000] makes the similar distinction between the 'asset augmenting' and 'asset exploiting' activities of MNCs.

Nevertheless, various forms of 'local-for-local' innovative activity remain important, perhaps dominant, in most MNCs. And, as illustrated at step 5 in Figure 2, such localised innovation and knowledge creation in subsidiaries may play two roles in the spillover process.

First, they may contribute to the absorptive capacity of the subsidiary with respect to technology transferred from the parent – at step 4 in Figure 2. The extent to which FDI-driven technology transfer contributes to the potential spillover of superior knowledge depends not only on what is released by the parents, as discussed above, but also on the fraction of that which is absorbed

FIGURE 2
FDI, LOCAL KNOWLEDGE CREATION AND SPILLOVERS

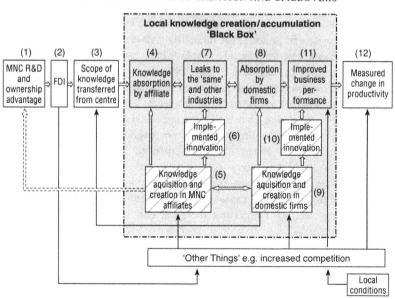

by the subsidiary.[6] Moreover, to act as locally superior technology with a potential for raising productivity in local firms, the transferred knowledge may well have to be substantially modified to embed its technological and wider organisational dimensions in a context with its own specific institutions, labour markets, skill structures and so forth – see for example the case of Volkswagen in Jurgens [*1998*].

Second, such localised knowledge-creation may involve more than merely enhancing the absorption of technology transferred from the centre and amplifying its spillover potential. It may become the source of more original innovation (at step 6 in Figure 2), knowledge about which leaks out to local firms (at step 7 in Figure 2) contributing to their productivity growth (at step 12).

The potential significance of such independent knowledge creation in subsidiaries has been highlighted by a growing body of recent research that has addressed issues about FDI from the 'bottom-up' – focusing primarily on the development of subsidiaries as organisational entities with significant degrees of autonomy in the direction and rate of their own development. Birkinshaw and Hood [*1998*], for instance, identify three interacting sets of drivers to explain differences between subsidiaries in their technological and other capabilities: not only a) the parent companies' strategic interests, control structures and delegated mandates and roles, but also b) the decisions and strategies of the subsidiaries, the degrees of autonomy they seek and the roles they negotiate within the corporation, together with c) aspects of the local environment that create constraints and opportunities for subsidiaries. One aspect of the heterogeneity across subsidiaries that arises from these interactions is the emergence among some of significant and substantially autonomous innovative capabilities – for instance, Frost [*2001*]; Patel and Vega [*1999*].

Even in industrialising economies domestic firms may also undertake their own knowledge acquisition and creation alongside the similar activities of MNC affiliates.[7] These too (as at step 9 in Figure 2) may contribute in two ways to productivity growth in local firms. First, as envisaged in the spillover literature, they may enhance the absorption of knowledge spilling over from MNC subsidiaries. Second, they may contribute more directly (via step 10) to improvements in local firms' business performance in ways that owe much less, and perhaps nothing at all, to knowledge derived from MNC subsidiaries.[8]

In summary, we are suggesting that, even in intermediate economies, a complex 'black box' incorporating knowledge-acquisition and knowledge-creating activities may lie between inward FDI and productivity growth in local firms. It is inherently difficult to separate the contributions to productivity made by the various activities and spillovers, but it is important to explore at least the possibility that the linkage between FDI and local firms' productivity growth does not consist exclusively of a one-way knowledge flow originating in FDI-related knowledge transfer, with the local activities of MNC subsidiaries or local firms contributing only to the amplification and absorption of that flow. In the advanced economies, evidence of the co-location of innovative activity of MNC subsidiaries and local firms is not interpreted in terms of a uni-directional relationship. Instead, as in Cantwell and Iammarino [*2003*] such evidence of co-location is taken as reflecting the existence of two partly independent and partly interconnected organisational structures of innovation, with the knowledge-centred interconnections between them probably running both ways.

In a previous chapter [*Marin and Bell, 2004*] we explored aspects of that 'black box' in the case of FDI and local firms' productivity growth in Argentina. Using a conventional, centrally driven supply side model,[9] expansion of FDI was as expected not significantly associated with productivity growth in domestic firms. We therefore explored some of the steps supposedly linking these two variables, as in Figure 2, concentrating in particular on two.

First, as is now common, we examined whether the absorptive capacity of domestic firms affected the relationship between FDI and those firms' productivity growth, using measures of knowledge creation and acquisition by domestic firms (step 9 in Figure 2) as indicators of their absorptive capacity. Contrary to common predictions, the effects were limited, with positive and significant spillover effects occurring only in connection with a small number of the indicators of absorptive capacity and even then only under restricted comparative conditions.

Second, going beyond previous work, we examined whether the local knowledge acquisition and creation activities of MNC subsidiaries (step 5 in Figure 2) affected the relationship between domestic firms' productivity growth and FDI. When we tested models incorporating measures of several different aspects of the local technological activities of subsidiaries, an array of strong, positive and significant results were generated. These might be explained in at least two ways: either i) the knowledge acquisition and creation undertaken by subsidiaries positively affected their own absorption of knowledge transferred from parent companies (step 4 in Figure 2), so enhancing the potential for spillover effects; or ii) the technological activities of the MNC subsidiaries were a source of externalities for domestic firms (running via steps 6 and 7, or perhaps 'leaking' directly between steps 5 and 9, in Figure 2).

In this chapter we seek to go beyond that analysis by examining in more detail two aspects of the technological behaviour of firms involved in those associations between expanding FDI and productivity growth in domestic firms. First, we aim to identify the extent to which knowledge acquisition and creation by MNC subsidiaries and domestic firms tends to vary in similar ways across industries, in particular whether high levels of these activities tend to be co-located in particular industries, creating conditions where knowledge spillovers are unlikely to run in only one direction from subsidiaries to domestic firms. Second, we try to identify some of the circumstances surrounding these patterns of technological behaviour and potential knowledge spillover. The aim is to assess the extent to which these are location-specific conditions in Argentina rather than O- and I-related conditions within conventional models of the relationship between FDI and technological development in intermediate host economies.

III. DATA AND METHODS

The Data Source and Key Indicators

The empirical analysis reported in this chapter uses information provided by the Innovation Survey in Argentina, 1992–1996. Following the framework of the Oslo Manual, this covers numerous aspects of the economic and technological behaviour of 1533 firms (283 multinational subsidiaries and 1250 domestic firms). The survey sample is representative of the universe of industrial firms in the country, and it includes 50 per cent of all industrial firms accounting for 53 per cent of total sales, 50 per cent of total employment, and 61 per cent of total exports.

Argentina provides a particularly appropriate context for our exploration of the knowledge-centred relationships between FDI and domestic firms in intermediate economies. First, it is a relatively FDI-intensive industrial economy. For example, in 2002 wholly owned MNC subsidiaries accounted for 50 per cent of the largest industrial firms with more than 500 employees [*Kulfas et al., 2002*]. Second, it is a relatively mature industrialising economy with substantial human resources and industrial experience.

The Innovation Survey provides basic economic information at firm level for 1992 and 1996 (size, age, value added, exports, imports, sales, employment, etc.). The Survey also provides information about a wide range of technological activities at the firm level.[10] These Survey data are used here to compute a total of nine indicators for both MNC subsidiaries and domestic firms: three measures of economic performance and six measures of technological behaviour. The indicators of economic performance are: value added per worker, export intensity, and investments per employee. The six indicators of technological behaviour are grouped in two broad categories covering investment in a) disembodied knowledge and skills and b) capital-embodied technology, as follows.

Expenditure on Disembodied Knowledge and Skills.   In principle, this potential source of locally driven knowledge spillovers covers the kinds of knowledge that are most mobile and likely to 'leak' from subsidiaries. Three variables are used.[11]

- R and D intensity: reported expenditure on R and D*
- Skill training intensity: reported expenditure on training*

- Skill intensity of employment: the number of engineers, other professionals and technicians employed in production (not in management) as a proportion of total employment.

Investment in Capital-embodied Technology. This kind of investment is likely to be an important source of productivity growth in the investing firms. However, it does not seem likely to be a significant driver of 'genuine' knowledge spillovers to other firms.[12] Although information about the introduction of capital-embodied assets in one firm may leak to another, the knowledge actually embodied in those assets is probably much more 'sticky'. Three variables are used.

- Investment in information technologies: reported expenditure specifically on information technology (IT) facilities and systems*
- Investment in equipment for innovation: reported expenditure on equipment required to introduce new products and processes*
- Investment in imported capital goods: reported expenditure on imports of capital goods.*

Exploring the 'Black Box'

As indicated earlier, the main aim of this chapter is to go beyond the analysis in our previous study in order to understand a little better the nexus of technological activities in MNC subsidiaries and domestic firms that lies between FDI growth and productivity increases in domestic firms. We do so in three steps.

First, descriptive information about the economic and technological behaviour of subsidiaries and domestic firms is reviewed to explore differences between the two groups of firms and the heterogeneity of behaviour within both groups.

Second, using only the six indicators of technological behaviour we examine the extent to which the various aspects of technological behaviour of subsidiaries and domestic firms are associated with each other at the industry level. Two types of equations are estimated for this purpose. First, we regress each aspect of technological behaviour in domestic firms against the same behaviour in subsidiaries in the same 5-digit industry. Then we repeat the same estimations, indicator by indicator, but with the reverse causality, that is subsidiaries' behaviour is regressed against domestic firms' behaviour. The two equations have the following general form:

$$\text{TBDF}_{ki-6} = f(\text{TBS}_{kl}; \text{ SDF}; \text{ Size, IND}) \qquad (1)$$

Where:

TBDF_{ki} is the k technological behaviour of the ith domestic firm and $k = 1, 2, \ldots, 6$, the six types of technological behaviour explained in Section III.a above;

TBS_{kI} is the k added technological effort of subsidiaries located in the same I 5-digit industry where $I = 1, 2, \ldots, 156$;

Size represents the size of the ith domestic firm and is measured by total sales or employment;

IND is an industry dummy, as explained below;

$TBDF_{ki}$, TBS_{kI} and Size are introduced in natural logarithm form.

Equation (2) is the same type of equation but we explain the technological behaviour of subsidiaries in relation to the behaviour of domestic firms. So:

$TBDF_{kj}$ is the k technological behaviour of the jth subsidiary;

TBS_{kI} is the k added technological effort of the domestic firms located in the same I 5-digit industry.

Equations (1) and (2) are estimated separately for each of the ($k = 6$) technology-related indicators described in Section III.a. The relationships are first controlled by size and then by broad industry groups at the 2-digit level.

We do not impose a specific direction of causality between the technological behaviour of the two groups of firms – for example, running from left to right in Figure 2. Instead we are interested in two kinds of preliminary exploration. First, are similar levels of investment by both groups of firms in disembodied and capital-embodied knowledge co-located in the same 5-digit industries? We take this as a step towards analysing whether common 'other' (location-specific) factors may be influencing the technological behaviour of both groups of firms. Second, we ask whether the co-location of those behaviours in the same industries might constitute a plausible basis for inferring the existence of two-way knowledge spillovers between the two groups of firms. So, while we do not use the regression estimates to identify whether the level of technological activity in one group influences the level in the other, we do take significant results in the two-way regression estimates as suggesting the probable existence of knowledge spillovers running both ways between the two groups of firms.[13]

Third, we move on to explore the particular circumstances within which any co-location of similar technological behaviour occurs, focusing in particular on the types of industries within which it arises. To simplify the analysis we shift the focus from the 5-digit to the 3-digit level of industry classification. Using eight of the nine indicators outlined earlier,[14] we identify the 3-digit industries in which both MNC subsidiaries and domestic firms are technologically active (or passive). Firms are classified as active (or passive) with reference to the median for each indicator. So, for example, firms with an R and D intensity higher (lower) than the median or that improved their training intensity more (less) than the median between 1992 and 1996, are classified as technologically active (passive). Each industry is then classified as characterised by a combination of technologically active (passive) MNC subsidiaries and domestic firms when more than 50 per cent of the subsidiaries *and* more than 40 per cent of domestic firms are active with respect to six or more of the eight indicators. Three types of 3-digit industries are therefore identified:[15]

- those characterised by relatively high levels and high rates of change of technological behaviour, labour productivity and export intensity on the part of both MNC subsidiaries and domestic firms – described as 'Joint Technologically Active Industries';
- those in which both groups of firms demonstrate relatively low levels and rates of change of the same types of behaviour – described as 'Joint Technologically Passive Industries';
- the other undefined industries.

The first two groups are then examined to assess whether differences between them appear to reflect global technological and other conditions or more locally specific advantages in Argentina.

IV. EMPIRICAL RESULTS

The Heterogeneity of Economic Performance and Technological Behaviour

We ask here whether subsidiaries clearly possess 'superior technology' that provides a basis for uni-directional flows of knowledge towards more technologically backward domestic firms. Table 1 presents descriptive data showing the levels of performance by both MNC subsidiaries and domestic firms with respect to the nine indicators explained above in Section III.a. Two broad patterns emerge from the table.

The first is about the general difference between MNC subsidiaries and domestic firms, as reflected primarily in the mean values for the two groups of firms. At first sight subsidiaries do appear to demonstrate a substantial 'superiority': on average, their labour productivity (value added per worker) is more than twice the level for domestic firms. However, this superiority is not matched by the other indicators. In a few cases these are similar for both groups of firms (export intensity and investment per employee), and in several they are higher for domestic firms: R and D intensity, training intensity, and all three indicators of investment in capital-embodied technology. Only in the skill intensity of employment do subsidiaries exceed domestic firms. This contrast suggests that either a) subsidiaries possess a very subtle form of technological superiority that enables them to achieve higher labour productivity with similar/lower levels of investment in R and D, training and various forms of fixed

TABLE 1
MNC SUBSIDIARIES AND DOMESTIC FIRMS: SELECTED INDICATORS OF ECONOMIC
PERFORMANCE AND TECHNOLOGICAL BEHAVIOUR (AVERAGE LEVELS 1992–96)

	Number of firms	Mean values	Quartiles			
			First	Second	Third	Fourth
1. Economic performance						
Added value per worker						
MNC subsidiaries	256	96,381	− 6,234	31,831	59,462	398,005
Domestic firms	1,173	38,877	2,513	18,916	33,179	147,433
Export intensity						
MNC subsidiaries	241	15%	0.2%	4%	12%	73%
Domestic firms	621	15%	0.1%	3%	12%	73%
Investment per employee						
MNC subsidiaries	270	13.0	0.21	3.2	8.5	75
Domestic firms	987	13.1	0.08	1.67	5.0	76
2. Investment in disembodied technology[a]						
R & D intensity						
MNC subsidiaries	166	3%	0.0%	0.1%	1%	14%
Domestic firms	377	5%	0.0%	0.0%	0.1%	13%
Training intensity						
MNC subsidiaries	187	1%	0.1%	0.2%	0.5%	18%
Domestic firms	406	4%	0.0%	0.1%	0.3%	24%
Skill intensity						
MNC subsidiaries	282	11%	1%	5%	10%	41%
Domestic firms	1,531	6%	0%	2%	5%	30%
3. Investment in capital-embodied technology						
In information technologies						
MNC subsidiaries	283	0.2%	0.0%	0.1%	0.2%	1%
Domestic firms	1,245	4%	0.0%	0.01%	0.09%	24%
In equipment for innovation						
MNC subsidiaries	143	4%	0.0%	0.0%	1%	18%
Domestic firms	404	6%	0.1%	2%	4%	46%
In imported capital goods						
MNC subsidiaries	192	4%	0.2%	0.9%	2%	18%
Domestic firms	407	5%	0.1%	1%	3%	26%

[a] Some of the reported data under these categories seem improbably high for a small number of domestic firms. However, omitting the most extreme outliers (20 cases) did not significantly alter the broad patterns shown here for the inter-quartile heterogeneity or the differences between the two groups of firms. In particular the apparent superiority of domestic firms in the fourth quartile remains unchanged, though it is slightly smaller in some cases. Consequently, and since we have as yet no clear basis for identifying probable reporting errors among the data, we have used the full reported data set for this table.

capital, or b) the distribution of subsidiaries and domestic firms across industries and product markets differs substantially, with the MNC subsidiaries occupying inherently higher value added segments of the economy. In either case, the potential for spillovers to domestic firms may be quite limited.

The second pattern is perhaps more important: the considerable intra-group heterogeneity. This is evident, for instance, in the case of the labour productivity of the MNC subsidiaries, where value added per head in the first quartile of firms is negative, while the level in the fourth quartile is more than ten times higher than in the second. Similarly, while the fourth quartile of subsidiaries invested the equivalent of 14 per cent of total sales in R and D, the first quartile did not invest anything at all. More strikingly, 50 per cent of the subsidiaries did not invest at all in equipment to implement product or process innovation, while 25 per cent of them invested the equivalent of 18 per cent of their total sales in this type of equipment.

Domestic firms demonstrate similar or greater heterogeneity and, even in the high performing fourth quartiles, the MNC subsidiaries do not appear to be consistently 'superior' to domestic firms. For example value added per worker in the fourth quartile of domestic firms was nearly eight times the level in the second. The first quartile invested nothing in training while the fourth spent the equivalent of 24 per cent of sales.[16] Similar wide differences are evident with respect to investment in capital-embodied technology. For example the intensity of investment in imported capital goods was 26 times greater by firms in the fourth quartile than by those in the second.

This wide diversity in technological behaviour suggests that the potential for generating spillover effects is unlikely to be pervasive across all MNC subsidiaries. On the contrary it is much more likely to be highly concentrated among only a proportion of MNC subsidiaries. As we suggested in our previous study, only those subsidiaries with relatively high levels of investment in creating and accumulating disembodied and capital-embodied technology (at steps 5 and 6 in Figure 2) are likely to be significant generators of knowledge spillovers. In contrast, their counterparts at the other end of the distribution have probably created and accumulated little or no 'superior' knowledge that could usefully be diffused to domestic firms.

At the same time, the heterogeneity among domestic firms implies the existence of two types of wide difference in their technological capabilities: not only a) differing capacities to absorb knowledge that is introduced or developed by MNC subsidiaries, as commonly discussed in the literature, but also b) differing capacities to act as *generators* of knowledge spillovers. In some circumstances the second type of capacity may be at least as great as it is in MNC subsidiaries, generating spillovers for other domestic firms and perhaps also for subsidiaries, so reversing the direction of knowledge flows from that typically assumed in the spillover literature.

The probability of such interaction would obviously be greater in industries where both groups of firms made similarly high levels of investment in knowledge creation and accumulation. We explore in the next section the extent to which this kind of association accompanies the heterogeneity presented in Table 1.

The Associated Technological Behaviour of Subsidiaries and Domestic Firms

The question addressed here is about whether the intensity of investment in disembodied and capital-embodied technology is similar for both groups of firms in particular industries, suggesting the possibility of bi-directional knowledge flows between them. Table 2 shows the results of regressions (1) and (2) described in Section III.b. Section (A) in the table (the top half) relates to the various types of expenditure on disembodied knowledge and skills, and section (B) covers investment in capital-embodied technology. Columns 1, 2 and 3 show the results of the estimations when the expenditure/investment of domestic firms was regressed against the added expenditure/investment by MNC subsidiaries (Regression 1). Columns 4, 5 and 6 show the results of the reverse relationship (Regression 2).

It is striking that all but one of the six estimations concerned with expenditure on disembodied knowledge and skills show significantly positive relationships, the only exception being when subsidiaries' R and D expenditure is identified as the dependent variable. Similarly, four of the six estimations concerned with investment in capital-embodied technology show significant positive relationships, the two exceptions arising with respect to investment in information technologies. We do not add a causal interpretation to these results about the scale of technology-related expenditure and investment in the two groups of firms. However, the fact that they appear to vary in close association with each other, and in particular that relatively high levels of expenditure and investment by both groups of firms tend to be co-located in the same 5-digit industries, suggests at the very least that there are some situations in which knowledge spillovers may run in both directions between them.

Some qualification to that is necessary. The control for size is significant in all the estimates in Table 2, but this does not mask the significance of the other relationships. However, this is not the case when control for broad (2-digit) industries is introduced – see Table 3.

The broad industry control makes little difference to the results for investment in capital embodied technologies. Four of the six relationships are still positive and significant, with investment in IC technologies again providing the exceptions. However, there is a substantial effect on the results concerned with expenditure on disembodied knowledge and skills. Only one of the six relationships remains positive and significant. In other words, in the areas that perhaps have the greatest potential for generating knowledge spillovers, the technological behaviour of both groups of firms in broadly defined (2-digit) industries appears to have common characteristics that mask the differences that were previously evident at the more detailed 5-digit level.

TABLE 2
THE ASSOCIATION BETWEEN DOMESTIC FIRMS' AND SUBSIDIARIES' TECHNOLOGICAL BEHAVIOUR

(A) Expenditure on disembodied knowledge and skill

MNC subsidiaries' behaviour (by 5-digit industries)	Domestic firms' behaviour			Domestic firms' behaviour (by 5-digit industries)	MNC subsidiaries' behaviour		
	R&D	Training	Skills		R&D	Training	Skills
	1	2	3		4	5	6
Control for size	63% (13)***	66% (13)***	−7.50% (−3.5)***	Control for size	75% (8.56)***	−5% (−0.6)	79% (25)***
R&D intensity	0.02% (3.39)***			R&D	0.0002% (0.32)		
Training intensity		0.0013% (2.61)***		Training		0.0012% (2.9)***	
Skills intensity			0.03% (4.76)***	Skills			0.12% (2)**
R2	22%	28%	3%	R2	22%	2%	61%
No. of observations	657	804	1662	No. of observations	302	372	540

(B) Investment in capital-embodied technology

MNC subsidiaries' behaviour (by 5-digit industries)	Domestic firms' behaviour			Domestic firms' behaviour (by 5-digit industries)	MNC subsidiaries' behaviour		
	Equipment for innovation	Imported capital goods	Information technologies		Equipment for innovation	Imported capital goods	Information technologies
	1	2	3		4	5	6
Control for size	90% (18)***	68% (12)***	15% (2.85)***	Control for size	93% (21.17)***	89% (10)***	54% (4.75)***
Equipment for innovation	0.000644% (2)**			Equipment for innovation	0.00096 (3.08)***		
Imported capital goods		0.00092% (1.74)*		Imported capital goods		0.0017 (3)***	
Information technologies			0.0016% (0.26)	Information technologies			(−0.02%) (−1.27)
R2	32%	18%	2%	R2	36%	27%	8%
No. of observations	713	745	899	No. of observations	971	333	283

Notes: The columns in the table include the dependent variables, with independent variables in the rows.
All standard errors, in parentheses, are corrected for heteroskedasticity.
×, Significant at 10% level; **, significant at 5% level; ***, significant at 1% level.

TABLE 3
DOMESTIC FIRMS' AND SUBSIDIARIES' TECHNOLOGICAL BEHAVIOUR – CONTROLLING BY INDUSTRIAL SECTOR

MNC subsidiaries' behaviour (by 5-digit industries)	Domestic firms' behaviour			MNC subsidiaries' behaviour		
	1	2	3	4	5	6
	R&D	Training	Skills	R&D	Training	Skills
(A) Expenditure on disembodied knowledge and skill						
Control for size	65% (12.23)***	69% (13.29)***	−0.05% (−2.43)**	85% (9.95)***	−11% (−1.39)	82% (25)***
R&D intensity	0.0020% (3.39)***			−0.0009% −1.45		
Training intensity		0.0008% 1.46			−0.0012% −1.21	
Skills intensity			0.005% 0.84			0.0041% 0.63
R2	30%	34%	19%	31%	11%	66%
No. of observations	657	804	1672	302	372	540

	Equipment for innovation	Imported capital goods	Information technologies	Equipment for innovation	Imported capital goods	Information technologies
(B) Investment in capital-embodied technology						
Control for size	92% (17)***	71% (11.43)***	14% (2.53)**	92% (19.3)***	80% (8.9)***	51% (4.18)***
Equipment for innovation	0.00067% (1.93)*			0.00% (3.42)***		
Imported capital goods		0.0016% (2.96)***			0.00% (2.64)***	
Information technologies			0.0021% (0.29)			−0.0040% (−0.028)
R2	36%	24%	3%	39%	36%	14%
No. of observations	713	745	899	971	333	283

Notes: The columns in the table include the dependent variables, with independent variables in the rows.
All standard errors, in parentheses, are corrected for heteroskedasticity.
*, Significant at 10% level; **, significant at 5% level; ***, significant at 1% level.

If one were to impose an FDI-centric perspective on these results, one might suggest that they reflect one or both of two sets of broad inter-industry differences. First, the intensity of FDI in host economies commonly varies across industries and, via the usual combination of competition-based inducements and spillover effects, such variation in the case of Argentina in the mid 1990s may have shaped the inter-industry pattern of technological behaviour in domestic firms. Second, broad industry groups vary widely in their inherent 'technological intensity', as with the inter-industry differences in R and D intensity that are common across OECD economies. The results in Table 3 probably constitute Argentinian reflections of global patterns of technological behaviour that are 'inherently' similar for both MNC subsidiaries and domestic firms in particular industries.

One might plausibly combine those perspectives along the following lines. Relatively high levels of FDI occurred in the more technology-intensive types of industry in Argentina during the early/mid 1990s, and at least in those industries the MNC subsidiaries brought with them the relatively 'active' patterns of technological behaviour required in such industries. The combination of high levels of FDI plus the subsidiaries' relatively high levels of local expenditure on knowledge creation and accumulation induced some of the domestic firms in those industries to match the patterns of technological behaviour.

In principle, however, one might also impose on the results in Tables 2 and 3 a perspective that is much less FDI-driven and much more sensitive to location-specific economic and technological advantages associated with particular industries in Argentina. We therefore move on to explore in more detail the characteristics of the industries where similar patterns of technological behaviour by domestic firms and subsidiaries are co-located.

The Characteristics of Industries Where Similar Technological Behaviours by MNC Subsidiaries and Domestic Firms are Co-located

We explore here the extent to which similar technological behaviours by both groups of firms are co-located in industries where global forces are likely to drive that behaviour or in industries that exploit specifically Argentinian economic and technological advantages.

As explained in Section III.b, we identified two contrasting groups of 3-digit industries in which both MNC subsidiaries and domestic firms were similarly 'technologically active' or 'technologically passive': 20 and 16 industries respectively. We examine here two other characteristics of these groups: their 'FDI intensity' during the period and their 'inherent' technology intensity.

The FDI Intensity of Industries. We distinguish between industries in which FDI during 1992–96 was:

- at a high initial level and rising during the period
- at a high initial level but falling during the period

• at a low initial level but rising during the period
• at a low initial level and falling during the period.

Table 4 cross-tabulates these categories and the distinction between technologically active and passive industries. Three quadrants in the table are of particular interest.

First, in nearly one-third of the technologically passive industries under (A), FDI was high but falling or high and rising during the period. In other words, as one might expect, in some industries FDI was high or high and rising where MNCs were able to exploit in local conditions their centrally accumulated technological advantages without engaging in much by way of complementary knowledge-creation and accumulation in those local conditions. Domestic firms in those industries matched the relatively inactive pattern of technological behaviour. Second, however, in a much larger proportion of the technologically passive industries (more than two-thirds) FDI was low and falling.

Third, and perhaps more surprising, 85 per cent of the technologically active industries under (B) had relatively high levels of FDI, with 55 per cent experiencing both high and rising levels. Put alternatively, more than three-quarters of the industries in which FDI was high or high and rising were also industries in which MNC subsidiaries achieved relatively high levels of labour productivity and export intensity *and* undertook relatively high levels of localised R and D, skill training, professional employment and investment in plant and machinery to implement innovation. Domestic firms in these industries matched those active patterns of technological behaviour.

From the perspective of the uni-directional pipeline model of FDI and spillovers in industrialising economies (Figure 1 earlier), one might interpret this third quadrant of Table 4 (accounting for nearly half of all the industries covered) along the following lines. MNCs entered these industries and came to undertake localised knowledge-intensive activities in order to augment their exploitation in Argentina of existing technological assets previously created centrally. The consequent competitive pressures induced technologically backward domestic firms to raise their investment in knowledge-creation and accumulation. Knowledge spillovers from the MNC subsidiaries facilitated that process.

But at least two other much less MNC-centric interpretations are also plausible.

• Domestic firms led the development of these relatively high-productivity and export-intensive industries, and they supported their operations with relatively high levels of R and D, training and skill employment, along with relatively high levels of investment in capital-embodied technology. Their success attracted high and rising levels of FDI and the MNC

TABLE 4
FDI INTENSITY AND JOINT TECHNOLOGICALLY ACTIVE/PASSIVE INDUSTRIES (NUMBER OF 3-DIGIT INDUSTRIES IN EACH CATEGORY)

FDI-intensity: 1992–96	A Subsidiary and domestic joint technologically passive industries		B Subsidiary and domestic joint technologically active industries		Total Both groups of industries	
	No. (%)	Column %	No. (%)	Column %	No. (%)	Column %
Low and falling intensity	11 (100%)	69%	0 (0%)	0%	11 (100%)	31%
Low but rising intensity	0 (0%)	0%	3 (100%)	15%	3 (100%)	8%
High but falling intensity	2 (25%)	12%	6 (75%)	30%	8 (100%)	22%
High and rising intensity	3 (22%)	19%	11 (78%)	55%	14 (100%)	39%
Total	16	100%	20	100%	36	100%

subsidiaries were able to supplement the knowledge resources they brought with them by drawing on an established local pool of knowledge and skills, with knowledge spillovers running primarily from the domestic firms to the MNC subsidiaries.

- The development of these industries was deeply rooted in local conditions in Argentina, and both groups of firms have exploited and built on these conditions. Competition, both domestic and international, has induced both groups to commit relatively high levels of investment in localised knowledge-creation and accumulation, and spillovers have flowed both ways between them.

To try to throw a little more light on these alternatives, we explore a second characteristic of the technologically active and passive industries: their generic technological intensity.

The Technology Intensity of Industries.   As noted earlier in Section II, it has been argued that, even in technology-following economies, more technology-intensive industries are likely to exhibit relatively high levels of labour productivity, skill, training, R and D, and so forth; and the results in Table 3 may constitute Argentinian reflections of such global industry differences. To explore this possibility, we distinguish here between broad groups of industries in a similar way to the common R and D-centred classification of industries in OECD countries. However, we use a taxonomy of industries devised by Ferraz *et al.* [*1991*] that is similar in principle to the OECD classification of industries in terms of their technology intensity,[17] but it is adapted for the particular context of Latin America. Ferraz *et al.* classify all 4-digit manufacturing industries into the six broad categories shown in Figure 3 – though we use a slightly collapsed version of the classification, merging durable goods and the automobile sector.

FIGURE 3
CLASSIFICATION OF INDUSTRIES IN LATIN AMERICA:
AS PER FERRAZ *ET AL.* [*1991*]

Broad Industry Groups	**Technological Intensity**
– Industry commodities	*Low* ⋀
– Agricultural commodities	
– Traditional sectors	
– Durable goods	
– Automotive and related sectors	
– Diffusers of technical progress	**High** ⋁

Table 5 shows the distribution of all the sample firms in the Survey across these categories. This indicates two broad patterns. First the MNC subsidiaries are not heavily concentrated in the more knowledge-intensive categories. Instead, a large proportion (70 per cent) are located in the traditional and commodity industries. Second, in most of the categories MNC subsidiaries are not a dominant presence, at least by the number of firms.

The cross-tabulation of these industry categories with the groups of jointly 'active' and 'passive' industries is shown in Table 6. Part of the picture fits what one might expect. Half of the technologically passive industries under (B) are in the commodity and traditional industries. Also six (30 per cent) of the technologically active industries under (A) are in the more technology-intensive categories (durable goods, automobiles and the diffusers of technical progress). Two other parts of the picture are more unexpected.

First, despite being more technology intensive, more than half (57 per cent) of the industries in the durables, autos and technology-diffusing categories are technologically passive. In other words, the technological characteristics of these industries at global/regional levels do not seem to be shaping the technological behaviour of firms in Argentina. Instead, in the particular context of Argentina, both MNC subsidiaries and domestic firms seem able to operate in these relatively 'high-tech' industries without significantly high levels of R and D, training, professional employment and innovation-related capital investment.

Second, the group of 14 industries in the top left-hand corner of the table, accounting for 70 per cent of the technologically active industries, are characterised by relatively high levels of local investment in disembodied and capital-embodied knowledge by both MNC subsidiaries and domestic firms. But these are not among the 'inherently' more technology-intensive industries; they fall into the commodity and traditional categories. The 14 industries are listed in Table 7. The most obvious characteristic of the majority of the group is that they are based on types of production where Argentina has natural resource and energy-related advantages.

But this does not seem to reflect a comprehensive industry effect. Several other commodity and traditional industries were among the technologically passive group of industries, and others fell into the intermediate category. We are led to suggest that the co-location of similarly active knowledge-creation and accumulation by MNC subsidiaries and domestic firms in this particular group of industries reflects specifically Argentinian location-specific advantages.

V. CONCLUSIONS

It is useful to bear in mind one simple characteristic of knowledge spillovers: they are barely visible to even the most diligent researcher, even in highly detailed case studies and surveys; and they are virtually impossible to measure in any

TABLE 5
DISTRIBUTION OF DOMESTIC FIRMS AND SUBSIDIARIES BY BROAD INDUSTRY GROUPS

Industry categories	Domestic firms		Subsidiaries		Total	
	No. (%)	Column %	No. (%)	Column %	No. (%)	Column %
Commodities	190 (77%)	15%	57 (23%)	20%	247 (100)	16%
Agro-based commodities	76 (85%)	6%	13 (15%)	5%	89 (100%)	6%
Traditional sectors	704 (85%)	57%	126 (15%)	45%	830 (100)%	54%
Durable goods and automobiles	103 (76%)	8%	32 (24%)	12%	135 (100%)	9%
Diffusers of technical progress	172 (76%)	14%	54 (24%)	19%	226 (100%)	15%
Total	1,245	100%	282	100%	1,527	100%

Source: Authors' calculations based on the Argentinean Innovation Survey.

TABLE 6

INDUSTRY GROUPS AND JOINT TECHNOLOGICALLY ACTIVE/PASSIVE INDUSTRIES (NUMBER OF 3-DIGIT INDUSTRIES IN EACH CATEGORY)

Industry groups	A Subsidiary and domestic joint technologically active industries		B Subsidiary and domestic joint technologically passive industries		Total Both groups of industries	
	No. (%)	Column %	No. (%)	Column %	No. (%)	Column %
Industrial commodities	5	25%	2	13%	7	19%
Agricultural commodities	4	20%	1	6%	5	14%
Traditional sectors	5	25%	5	31%	10	28%
Subtotal: Commodities and traditional	14 (64%)	70%	8 (36%)	50%	22 (100%)	61%
Durable goods and automobiles	3	15%	3	19%	6	17%
Diffusers of technical progress	3	15%	5	31%	8	22%
Subtotal: Durables, autos and technology diffusers	6 (43%)	30%	8 (57%)	50%	14 (100%)	39%
Total	20	100%	16	100%	36	100%

TABLE 7
TECHNOLOGICALLY ACTIVE BUT LESS TECHNOLOGY-INTENSIVE INDUSTRIES IN
ARGENTINA

Broad industry group	SIC code	Industry
Industrial commodities	241	Basic chemicals
	261	Flat glass and glass products
	269	Minerals and non-metallic products
	271	Iron and steel industries
	272	Primary metals: precious and non-ferrous metal
Agricultural commodities	152	Dairy products
	154	Miscellaneous food preparations
	202	Wood products
	210	Paper mills and paper products
Traditional sectors	222	Printing
	251	Rubber products
	252	Plastic products
	281	Fabricated structural metal products
	313	Wiring and wire equipment

direct way across populations of firms and industries.[18] Consequently, rather like astronomers trying to identify the existence and magnitude of non-observable planets, spillover researchers must infer the existence and magnitude of these FDI-related knowledge flows from data about other phenomena – primarily data about FDI and productivity.

So, perhaps to a greater extent than for many other social phenomena, knowledge spillovers are products of our imagination, though probably not just figments. In particular, in order to speculate about the magnitude, source and direction of FDI-related spillovers, we have to imagine a particular set of processes and interactions lying between the observations of FDI on the one hand and of productivity growth in domestic firms on the other.

The central argument of our chapter is simply that the imaginary system most commonly used (as elaborated in Figure 1) is unhelpful and probably misleading. This seems obvious enough in the context of advanced economies, where complex knowledge-centred interactions between MNC subsidiaries and domestic firms in host economies are well recognised. However, by drawing on innovation survey data we have suggested that the commonly used model is also misleading as a guide for drawing inferences about spillovers in intermediate economies which, like Argentina, have reasonably long-established industrial structures and human resource endowments. In particular, instead of imagining that FDI simply delivers spillovers of superior knowledge via a one-way pipeline to technologically backward domestic firms, we suggest it may be more helpful to imagine a much more complex and locally centred knowledge-production and diffusion system.

In the case examined here, our previous research [*Marin and Bell, 2004*] indicated that the observed association between FDI and productivity growth in domestic firms was mediated by the knowledge-creation and accumulation of MNC subsidiaries undertaken inside Argentina. In this chapter we suggest it is plausible to go further and suggest that local advantages, manifest at the level of detailed 5-digit industries, but reflecting broader characteristics of mainly resource-based industries in Argentina, led to the existence of co-located nuclei of technological activity on the part of both MNC subsidiaries and domestic firms, with the potential for spillovers running in both directions between them.

Others have highlighted the rapid growth of such resource-processing industries in post-liberalisation southern Latin American countries [*e.g. Cimoli and Katz, 2003*]. However, our findings do not seem consistent with associated views about the pattern of technological behaviour accompanying that shift in the pattern of industry specialisation. These have suggested that such inherently 'low technology' industries would be bereft of local innovative activity, particularly on the part of MNC subsidiaries which would source their key knowledge inputs from parent companies and other home country sources.

However, with our short period snapshot of the mid 1990s, we can only pose an unanswered question about how our findings map on to views about the longer-term dynamics associated with this concentration on resource-based industries. Cimoli and Katz [2003], for instance, suggest that, because these are mature and low-technology industries, countries like Argentina will be pushed in the longer run into a 'low development trap' [*p.387*] where 'most knowledge production will be localized outside of the Latin American production environment with a clearly deleterious impact upon accumulation of domestic technological capabilities' [*p. 403*]. On the other hand, it may be that the nuclei of active knowledge accumulation identified in this chapter will emerge as hubs of globally significant innovative activity and the sources of new areas of created comparative advantage. Unfortunately, however, we know little about the emergence and longer-term evolution of technological specialisation and advantage in late-industrialising economies.

Our findings also raise questions about the design of policy interventions intended to capture potential technology-related externalities associated with FDI – for example about the relative costs, efficiency and effectiveness of:

- measures intended to attract inward FDI versus measures designed to stimulate spillover-generating technological activities on the part of attracted MNC subsidiaries;

- measures that, presuming the superiority of the knowledge held by MNC subsidiaries, focus on stimulating one-way spillovers versus measures that foster the growth of, and interaction between, knowledge-accumulating and absorbing activities on the part of both MNC subsidiaries and domestic firms;

• measures that apply uniformly to all areas of economic activity versus those intended to focus selectively on fostering 'active' technological behaviour in industries with more pronounced location-specific advantages;

• measures that focus selectively on fostering active technological behaviour in areas of today's location-specific advantages versus those that seek to shape tomorrow's areas of advantage.

With the knowledge currently available about the relationship between FDI and technology-centred interactions with domestic firms in intermediate economies like Argentina, we can only leave those as questions. Answering them will require much more research within a framework that is much more like Figure 2 than Figure 1. It will also require such research to give much greater attention to the long-term evolution of areas of technological advantage in such economies. Fortunately, the growing availability of data derived from innovation surveys should make such work increasingly feasible.

NOTES

1. See, for instance, Cantwell and Narula [2001: 161]: '... it is where the ownership advantages of investing firms and the location advantages of the host region or country are strongest that we find the greatest potential scope for a process of mutual reinforcement of these advantages through the two-way spillover effects of internationalisation.'

2. See Molero and Alvarez [2003: 181]: ' ... a vast majority of the theoretical and empirical research has been carried out on the basis of statistical evidence provided by the most developed countries, including the US, Japan and the core of highly industrialized European countries. However, the experience of countries outside that cluster does not always fit easily within the same parameters...'.

3. Such differences are usually reflected in industry classifications based on R and D intensity indicators. They are also reflected in the differentiation between 'core' industries (that produce a large proportion of innovations) and 'others' (that absorb those innovations) [Robson et al., 1988; Baldwin and Hanel, 2003].

4. Kogut [2002] provides a useful survey.

5. 'Overseas R&D units now provide much more than an outlet for the effective application of centrally-created product technology. Instead they play increasingly powerful roles in the creative processes themselves' [Pearce, 1999: 160].

6. Teece [1977], for instance, showed that the cost of technology transfer within MNCs decreased with increasing size and R and D intensity of the affiliate recipient firm.

7. There is a large literature describing these kinds of learning and innovation activities in locally owned firms in emerging economies. Much of this was generated or inspired by the work of Jorge Katz and colleagues in Latin America in the early 1980s [Katz, 1987]. Other rich sources are the work of Linsu Kim on Korean firms [e.g. Kim, 1997] and of John Mathews and colleagues on a range of East Asian economies [e.g.Mathews and Cho, 2000]. See also Hobday [1995] or Lall and Urata [2003] on Asian firms and Figueiredo [2002] on Latin American firms.

8. It is interesting to note that much of the spillover literature captures this second type of contribution as an FDI-related spillover. This arises because spillovers are commonly defined as

including the productivity gains among local firms that are induced by increased competition arising from growing FDI – link [b] in Figure 1.

9. That is without taking into account the differences between types of industry or variations in the absorptive capacity of domestic firms.

10. More extensive information about the Survey, with some of the descriptive data summaries can be obtained from the authors.

11. When used as firm-level indicators, all the measures identified with an asterisk are normalised by the firm's total sales.

12. See the earlier comments about 'genuine' and 'pseudo' knowledge spillovers.

13. In other words, in seeking to identify whether similarly 'high' (or low) levels of technological activity in the subsidiary and local firm are co-located, we follow a similar approach to that used by Cantwell and Iammarino [2003]. However, instead of using patent-based indicators of innovation, we use the wider array of knowledge-acquiring, knowledge-creating and innovation activities indicated above. Also instead of identifying 'co-location' in terms of spatial regions, we identify it in terms of SIC 5-digit industries.

14. Investment per employee is dropped because of the strong overlap with the indicators of investment in capital embodied technology.

15. The first two of these groups are shown in Table 7.

16. Attention is drawn to the note attached to Table 1 about, first, the improbably high levels of the technological behaviour data reported by some domestic firms, and, second, the fact that plausible modification of the data still leaves very wide heterogeneity among domestic firms and considerable 'superiority' over subsidiaries in most aspects of their technological behaviour.

17. The distinctions are also similar to those between 'core' and 'other' industries as used by Baldwin and Hanel [2003] in the analysis of the Canadian Innovation Survey data – see Note 3 above.

18. Even the burgeoning industry of spillover estimation using citations recorded on patent front pages rests on the hope, not the demonstrated reality, that these are good indirect reflections of knowledge flows between actors in the innovation system.

REFERENCES

Aitken, B. and A. Harrison, 1999, 'Do Domestic Firms Benefit from Direct Foreign Investment?', *American Economic Review*, Vol.89, No.3, pp.605–18.

Baldwin, J.R. and P. Hanel, 2003, *Innovation and Knowledge Creation in an Open Economy: Canadian Industry and International Implications*, Cambridge: Cambridge University Press.

Bartlett, C.A. and S. Ghoshal, 1989, *Managing Across Borders: The Transnational Solution*, Boston: Harvard Business School.

Birkinshaw, J., 1997, 'Entrepreneurship in Multinational Corporations: The Characteristics of Subsidiary Initiatives', *Strategic Management Journal*, Vol.18, No.3, pp.207–29.

Birkinshaw, J. and N. Hood, 1998, 'Multinational Subsidiary Evolution: Capability and Charter Change in Foreign-owned Subsidiary Companies', *The Academy of Management Review*, Vol.23, No.4, pp.773–95.

Blomstrom, M. and A. Kokko, 1997, *How Foreign Direct Investment affects Host Countries*, Working Papers: International Economics, Trade and Capital Flows, 1745, Washington: World Bank.

Blomstrom, M. and A. Kokko, 2003, 'Human Capital and Inward FDI'', EIJS Working Papers Series 167, Stockholm: The European Institute of Japanese Studies.

Braconier, H., K. Ekholm and K. Midelfart, 2001, 'Does FDI Work as a Channel for R&D Spillovers? Evidence Based on Swedish Data', IUI Working Paper No. 553, Stockholm: The Research Institute of Industrial Economics.

Cantwell, J. and S. Iammarino, 2003, *Multinational Corporations and European Regional Systems of Innovation*, London and New York: Routledge.

Cantwell, J. and O. Janne, 1999, 'Technological Globalisation and Innovative Centres: The Role of Corporate Technological Leadership and Locational Hierarchy', *Research Policy*, Vol.28, No.3, pp.119–44.

Cantwell, J. and R. Narula, 2001, 'The Eclectic Paradigm in the Global Economy', *International Journal of the Economics of Business*, Vol.8, No.2, pp.155-72.

Caves, R.E., 1971, 'International Corporations: The Industrial Economics of Foreign Investment', *Economica*, Vol.38, pp.1-27.

Caves, R.E., 1974, 'Multinational Firms, Competition and Productivity in Host-country Markets', *Economica*, Vol.41, pp.176-93, May.

Caves, R.E., 1982, *Multinational Enterprise and Economic Analysis*, Cambridge: Cambridge University Press.

Chung, W., 2001, 'Identifying Technology Transfer in Foreign Direct Investment: Influence of Industry Conditions and Investing Motives', *Journal of International Business Studies*, Vol.32, No.2, pp.211-29.

Cimoli, M. and J. Katz, 2003, 'Structural Reforms, Technological Gaps and Economic Development: A Latin American Perspective', *Industrial and Corporate Change*, Vol.12, No.2, pp.387-411.

Damijan, J., M. Boris, K. Mark and M. Rojec, 2001, 'The Role of FDI, Absorptive Capacity and Trade in Transferring Technology to Transition Countries: Evidence from Firm Panel Data for Eight Transition Countries', Geneva: UN Economic Commission for Europe, mimeo.

Djankov, S. and B. Hoekman, 2000, 'Foreign Investment and Productivity Growth in Czech Enterprises', *World Bank Economic Review*, No.14(1), pp.49-64.

Dunning, J.H., 2000, 'Regions, Globalization, and the Knowledge Economy: The Issues Stated', in J.H. Dunning (ed.), *Regions, Globalization, and the Knowledge-Based Economy*, Oxford University Press: Oxford.

Ferraz, J.C., D. Kupfer and L. Haguenaver, 1997, *Made in Brazil: Desafios Competitivos Para a Industria*, Campus: Rio de Janeiro.

Figueiredo, P.N., 2002, 'Does Technological Learning Pay Off? Inter-firm Differences in Technological Capability-accumulation Paths and Operational Performance Improvement', *Research Policy*, Vol.31, pp.73-94.

Frost, T., 2001, 'The Geographic Sources of Foreign Subsidiaries' Innovations', *Strategic Management Journal*, Vol.22, No.2, pp.101-24.

Ghoshal, S. and C.A. Bartlett, 1988, 'Innovation Processes in Multinational Corporations', in M.L. Tushman and W.L. Moore (eds.), *Readings in the Management of Innovation*, New York: Harper Business, pp.499-518.

Ghoshal, S. and C.A. Bartlett, 1990, 'The Multinational Corporation as an Interorganizational Network', *Academy of Management Review*, Vol.15, No.4, pp.603-25.

Globerman, S., 1979, 'Foreign Direct Investment and Spillover Efficiency Benefits in Canadian Manufacturing Industries', *Canadian Journal of Economics*, Vol.XII, No.1, pp.42-56.

Gorg, H. and E. Strobl, 2001, 'Multinational Companies and Productivity Spillovers: A Meta-analysis', *The Economic Journal*, Vol.111, No.475, pp.723-39.

Haddad, M. and A. Harrison, 1993, 'Are there Positive Spillovers from Direct Foreign Investment? Evidence from Panel Data for Morocco', *Journal of Development Economics*, Vol.42, pp.51-74.

Haskel, J., S. Pereira and M. Slaughter, 2002, 'Does Inward Foreign Direct Investment Boost the Productivity of Domestic Firms?', NBER Working Paper No. 8724, Cambridge, MA: National Bureau of Economic Research.

Hedlund, G., 1986, 'The Hypermodern MNC: A Heterarchy?', *Human Resource Management*, Vol.25, pp.9-36.

Hobday, M., 1995, *Innovation in East Asia: The Challenge to Japan*, Aldershot: Edward Elgar.

Hymer, S., 1960, 'The International Operations of National Firms: A Study of Direct Investment', PhD Thesis, Massachusetts Institute of Technology, Cambridge, MA: MIT Press.

Jarrillo, J. and J. Martinez, 1990, 'Different Roles for Subsidiaries: The Case of Multinational Corporations in Spain', *Strategic Management Journal*, Vol.11, No.7, pp.501-12.

Jurgens, E., 1998, 'Implanting Change: The Role of Indigenous Transplants in Transforming the German Productive Model', in R. Boyer, E. Charron, U. Jurgens and S. Tolliday (eds.), *Between Imitation and Innovation – the Transfer and Hybridisation of Productive Models in the International Automobile Industry*, Oxford: Oxford University Press.

Katz, J.M. (ed.), 1987, *Technology Generation in Latin American Manufacturing Industries*, London: Macmillan Press.

Keller, W. and R.Y. Yeaple, 2003, 'Multinational Enterprises, International Trade and Productivity Growth: Firm-Level Evidence from the US', Centre for Economic Policy Research Discussion Paper No. 3805, Cambridge, MA: National Bureau of Economic Research.

Kim, L., 1997, *Imitation to Innovation: The Dynamics of Korea's Technological Learning*, Boston, MA: Harvard Business School Press.

Kogut, B., 2002, 'International Management and Strategy', in A. Pettigrew, H. Thomas and R. Whittington (eds.), *Handbook of Strategy and Management*, London: SAGE Publications.

Kokko, A., 1994, 'Technology, Markets Characteristics, and Spillovers', *Journal of Development Economics*, Vol.43, pp.279–93.

Konings, J., 2001, 'The Effects of Foreign Direct Investment on Domestic Firms: Evidence From Firm Level Panel Data in Emerging Economies', *Economics of Transition*, Vol.9, No.3.

Kuemmerle, W., 1999, 'Foreign Direct Investment in Industrial Research in the Pharmaceutical and Electronics Industries – Results from a Survey of Multinational Firms', *Research Policy*, Vol.28, pp.179–93.

Kulfas, M., F. Porta and A. Ramos, 2002, 'Inversion extranjera y empresas transnacionales en la economia argentina', Serie Estudios y Perspectives 10, Oficina de la CEPAL, Buenos Aires, Argentina.

Lall, S., 1979, 'The International Allocation of Research Activity by US Multinationals', in *Oxford Bulletin of Economics and Statistics*, Vol.41, November, pp.313–31.

Lall, S. and S. Urata (eds.), 2003, *Competitiveness, FDI and Technological Activity in East Asia*, Cheltenham: Edward Elgar.

Lipsey, R., 2002, 'Home and Host Country Effects of FDI', NBER Working Paper No. 9293, Cambridge, MA: National Bureau of Economic Research.

Marin, A. and M. Bell, 2004, 'Technology Spillovers from Foreign Direct Investment: An Exploration of the Active Role of MNC Subsidiaries in the Case of Argentina in the 1990s', SPRU Electronic Working Paper Series (SEWPS), No.118, Brighton, University of Sussex, SPRU–Science and Technology Policy Research.

Mathews, J.A. and D.S. Cho, 2000, *Tiger Technology: The Creation of a Semiconductor Industry in East Asia*, Cambridge: Cambridge University Press.

Molero, J. and I. Alvarez, 2003, 'The Technological Strategies of Multinational Enterprises: Their Implications for National Systems of Innovation', in J. Cantwell and J. Molero (eds.), *Multinational Enterprises, Innovative Strategies and Systems of Innovation*, Cheltenham: Edward Elgar.

Narula, R. and J. Dunning, 2000, 'Industrial Development, Globalisation and Multinational Enterprises: New Realities for Developing Countries', *Oxford Development Studies*, Vol.28, No.2, pp.141–67.

Patel, P. and M. Vega, 1999, 'Patterns of Internationalisation of Corporate Technology: Location vs. Home Country Advantages', *Research Policy*, Vol.28, No.3, pp.145–55.

Paterson, S. and D. Brock, 2002, 'The Development of Subsidiary-management Research: Review and Theoretical Analysis', *International Business Review*, Vol.11, No.2, pp.139–63.

Patibandla, M. and A. Sanyal, 2002, 'Foreign Investment and Productivity: A Study of Post-reform Indian Industry', Department of International Economics and Management, Copenhagen, Copenhagen Business School, mimeo.

Pearce, R.D., 1999, 'Decentralised R&D and Strategic Competitiveness: Globalised Approaches to Generation and Use of Technology in Multinational Enterprises (MNEs)', *Research Policy*, Vol.28, pp.157–78.

Prahalad, C.K. and Y. Doz, 1987, *The Multinational Mission*, London and New York: The Free Press.

Robson, M., J. Townsend and K. Pavitt, 1988, 'Sectoral Patterns of Production and Use of Innovations in the UK: 1945–1983', *Research Policy*, Vol.17, No.1, pp.1–4.

Sjoholm, F., 1997, 'Technology Gap, Competition and Spillovers from Direct Foreign Investment: Evidence from Establishment Data', *Journal of Development Studies*, Vol.36, No.1, pp.53–73.

Teece, D.J., 1977, 'Technology Transfer by Multinational Firms: The Resource Cost of Transferring Technological Knowhow', *Economic Journal*, Vol.81, June pp.242–61.

Vernon, R., 1966, 'International Investment and International Trade in the Product Cycle', *Quarterly Journal of Economics*, Vol.80, pp.190–207.

von Zedtwitz, M. and O. Gassman, 2002, 'Market versus Technology drive in R&D Internationalization: Four Different Patterns of Managing Research and Development', *Research Policy*, Vol.31, pp.569–88.

Wang, Y. and M. Blomstrom, 1992, 'Foreign Investment and Technology Transfer: A Simple Model', *European Economic Review*, Vol.36, No.1, pp.137–55.

Zander, I., 1999, 'How Do You Mean "Global"? An Empirical Investigation of Innovation Networks in the Multinational Corporation', *Research Policy*, Vol.28, pp.195–213.

Regulation of Foreign Investment in Historical Perspective

HA-JOON CHANG

Based on a historical survey, the chapter argues that during their early stages of development, now-developed countries systematically discriminated against foreign investors. They have used a range of instruments to build up national industry, including: limits on ownership; performance requirements on exports, technology transfer or local procurement; insistence on joint ventures with local firms; and barriers to 'brownfield investments' through mergers and acquisitions. We argue that, only when domestic industry has reached a certain level of sophistication, complexity, and competitiveness do the benefits of non-discrimination and liberalisation of foreign investment appear to outweigh the costs. On the basis of this, the chapter argues that the currently proposed multilateral investment agreement at the World Trade Organisation is likely to harm the developing countries' prospects for development.

Cet chapter basé sur une enquête historique argumente que, durant les premières étapes du développement, les pays actuellement développés prenaient systématiquement des mesures discriminatoires envers les investisseurs étrangers. Ils utilisaient une série d'instruments pour permettre à l'industrie nationale de se développer: limitations sur la propriété; conditions de performance touchant les exportations, transferts de technologies ou approvisionnement local; joint-ventures en participation avec les entreprises locales; limitations au rachat d'entreprises existantes (brownfield investments) à travers des fusions

Ha-Joon Chang is at the Faculty of Economics and Politics, University of Cambridge. The chapter draws on a joint research project with Duncan Green of the Catholic Agency for Overseas Development (CAFOD), whose result was published as an chapter titled, 'The Northern WTO Agenda on Investment: Do as we Say, Not as we Did' by the South Centre, Geneva, and CAFOD, London, in June 2003. While the material in the present chapter is from the author's contribution to the joint project, the author's intellectual interaction with Duncan Green during their joint work makes it difficult to separate neatly the individual contributions. The author thanks him very much for his partnership, intellectual and political. The author also thanks the South Centre and the Rockefeller Foundation for their support for the project. Also thanked is the Korea Research Foundation for research support through its BK21 programme at the Department of Economics, Korea University, where the author was a visiting research professor when the first draft was written. The author has benefited greatly from comments by Sanjaya Lall, Lynn Mytelka, Rajneesh Narula, and Rajah Rasiah in producing the final version of this contribution.

ou acquisitions. Nous soutenons que les bénéfices de la non-discrimination et de la libéralisation des investissements étrangers n'en dépassent les coûts qu'au moment où l'industrie domestique est arrivée à un certain niveau de sophistication, de complexité et de compétitivité. Sur la base de cette découverte, l'article argumente que l'accord multilatéral sur les investissements, proposé actuellement par l'Organisation Mondiale du Commerce, risque de léser les perspectives de développement des pays en développement.

I. INTRODUCTION

During the past several years, the developed countries have been stepping up their efforts to install a multilateral investment agreement (MIA) that prevents countries from controlling foreign direct investment (FDI), and possibly portfolio investments.

Initially, this was mainly pursued through the OECD, where it was proposed that the developed countries adopt an MIA to which willing developing countries are also allowed to sign up. When this move was thwarted in 1998, the main battleground on this issue was moved to the World Trade Organisation (WTO). As one of the 'Singapore issues', the possibility of an MIA comprising all member countries is now seriously discussed. While the push for an MIA at the WTO is in retreat for the moment following the collapse of the Cancún ministerial meeting, the issue is bound to come back in one way or another.

There are a number of well-known reasons for opposing an MIA. First, unlike what its proponents often argue, an MIA is unlikely to lead to increased flows of foreign investment, especially into developing countries. Second, it will merely add to, rather than replace, the patchwork quilt of over 2,000 bilateral investment treaties. Third, the WTO agenda is already overloaded, to the detriment of developing country participation. Fourth, the promises of flexibility for developing countries will be undermined by the realities of negotiations, where the developing countries are routinely subject to bullying and deceit. And last but not least, there is a lack of balancing obligations on home countries and investors.

This chapter adds another, rather compelling in our view, reason to this already long list. Based on a historical survey of the experiences of the US, the EU member states and the East Asian economies, it argues that during their early stages of development, now-developed countries systematically discriminated between domestic and foreign investors in their industrial policy. They have used a range of instruments aimed at foreign investors to build up national industry. These included: limits on foreign ownership; performance requirements on exports, technology transfer or local procurement; insistence on joint ventures with local firms; and barriers to 'brownfield investments' through mergers and acquisitions.

The main 'demandeurs' of investment negotiations, the EU and Japan, insist that non-discrimination, and in particular national treatment (there are fewer problems with most favoured nation treatment), should be a central aspect of any MIA. However, our historical survey shows that, only when domestic industry has reached a certain level of sophistication, complexity, and competitiveness do the benefits of non-discrimination and liberalisation appear to outweigh the costs. As a result, countries generally move towards a greater degree of non-discrimination and liberalisation as they develop. In that sense, non-discrimination is better seen as an *outcome* of development, not a cause. Therefore, an MIA founded on this principle is likely to harm the developing countries' prospects for development.

While the exact nature of the overall strategy and the exact mix of tools to be used can, and need to, vary across countries, and while the recent changes in global economic and political conditions have influenced the desirability and the feasibility of different strategies differently, history clearly shows the importance of the policy space for developing countries (of yesterday and today) to use a wide range of measures to regulate foreign investment.

II. FOREIGN INVESTMENT REGULATION IN HISTORICAL PERSPECTIVE

The United States

1. Overview

From its early days of economic development to the First World War, the US was the world's largest importer of foreign capital.[1] The eminent business historian Mira Wilkins states that during the 1875–1914 period, the US was 'the greatest debtor nation in history' despite its rise as one of the major lender countries in the international capital market at the end of this period [*Wilkins, 1989: 144*].

Given the country's position as a net importer of capital, there was naturally a lot of concern with foreign investment. While many Americans accepted the necessity of foreign investment and some sought it out enthusiastically, there was also a widespread concern with 'absentee management' [*Wilkins, 1989: 563*], and, further, foreign domination of the American economy.

The fear of foreign investment was not confined to the 'radicals'. For example, the *Bankers' Magazine* of New York remarked in 1884:

It will be a happy day for us when not a single good American security is owned abroad and when the United States shall cease to be an exploiting ground for European bankers and money lenders The tribute paid to foreigners is . . . odious . . . We have outgrown the necessity of submitting to the humiliation of going to London, Paris or Frankfort [*sic*] for capital has become amply abundant for all home demands. [*Bankers' Magazine, No. 38, January, 1884, cited in Wilkins, 1989: 565*]

According to the same magazine, the great majority of Americans believed it was 'a misfortune to have its [the country's] public, corporate, and private securities abroad' [*No. 33, April, 1879, cited in Wilkins, 1989: 915, note 67*].

Even Andrew Jackson (the seventh President of the US, 1829–37), a well-known advocate of small government and therefore something of a hero among American free-marketeers today, amply displayed anti-foreign feelings. He famously vetoed the renewal of the federal government charter for the country's second quasi-central bank, the (Second) Bank of the USA, largely on the grounds that 'many of its stockholders were foreigners' [*Wilkins, 1989: 61–2, 84; Garraty and Carnes, 2000: 255–8*].[2] When he exercised his veto in 1832, he said:

> . . . should the stock of the bank principally pass into the hands of the subjects of a foreign country, and we should unfortunately become involved in a war with that country, what would be our condition?. . . Controlling our currency, receiving our public moneys, and holding thousands of our citizens in dependence, it would be far more formidable and dangerous than the naval and military power of the enemy. If we must have a bank . . . it should be *purely American. [as cited in Wilkins, 1989: 84, italics original]*[3]

Others would go even further. On the eve of the de-chartering of the Second Bank of the USA (SBUSA), the Jackson government moved federal government deposits to other banks. One of these banks, the Manhattan Bank, was foreign owned but, not being a federally chartered bank like the SBUSA, it did not ban foreign shareholders from voting (which was the case with federally chartered banks – see below). Therefore, *Niles' Weekly Register*, one of the leading magazines of the time, found it scandalous that 'IN THIS BANK THE FOREIGN STOCKHOLDERS VOTE!' [*No. 45, 16 November, 1833, cited in Wilkins, 1989: 84, capitals in original*]. Another chapter that appeared two years later in this magazine [*No. 48, 2 May, 1835*] neatly sums up the dominant American feeling at the time: 'We have no horror of FOREIGN CAPITAL— if subjected to *American management*' [*cited in Wilkins, 1989: 85, italics and capitals original*].

One important point to note is that all these concerns about foreign investment were expressed despite the fact that the importance of foreign investment in the US at the time was far less when compared to that in today's developing countries. For example, inward FDI stock of the US in 1914 was 3.7 per cent of gross domestic product (GDP) [*Held et al., 1999: 275, Table 5.13*]. In contrast, the same figure for developing countries was 4.8 per cent in 1980, 10.5 per cent in 1990 and 19.9 per cent in 1995 [*Crotty et al., 1998: Table 3*].

In other words, if many people in the US in the nineteenth and the early twentieth century were concerned with the impacts of foreign investment, their counterparts in developing countries should be concerned way more.

In order to ensure that foreign investment did not lead to loss of national control in the key sectors of the economy, much federal and state legislation was enacted in the US since its independence until the mid-twentieth century, when it became the world's top economic nation. And as the main sectors that received foreign investments during this period were in finance, shipping, and natural resource extraction (agriculture, mining, logging), the legislation was concentrated in them.

2. Federal Legislation

Navigation. One of the first acts of the new Congress upon independence was an imposition in 1791 of differential tonnage duties between national and foreign ships [*Wilkins, 1989: 44*]. Similarly, a navigation monopoly for US ships for coastwise trade was imposed in 1817 by the Congress [*Wilkins, 1989: 83*]. This continued until the First World War [*Wilkins, 1989: 583*].

Finance. In the financial sector, legislative provisions were made in the charter for the country's first quasi-central bank, the First Bank of the USA (FBUSA) in 1791 to avoid foreign domination. Only resident shareholders could vote and only American citizens could become directors. And thanks to these provisions, the Bank could not be controlled by foreigners, who owned 62 per cent of the shares by 1803 and 70 per cent by 1811. Despite this, when its charter was up for renewal in 1811, the Congress did not re-charter the Bank 'in large part owing to fears of foreign influence' [*Wilkins, 1989: 38-9, 61, the quote is from p. 61*]. A similar provision against voting by foreign shareholders was made for the SBUSA, when it was given the federal charter in 1816 [*Wilkins, 1989: 61*].

In addition, the 1864 National Bank Act also required that the directors of national (as opposed to state) banks had to be Americans [*Wilkins, 1989: 455*] – this lasted even after the introduction of the Federal Reserve System in 1913 [*Wilkins, 1989: 583*]. This meant that 'foreign individuals and foreign financial institutions could buy shares in U.S. national banks *if* they were prepared to have American citizens as their representatives on the board of directors'. And therefore '[t]hat they could not directly control the banks served as a deterrent to investment' [*Wilkins, 1989: 583, italics original*].

Land. From the early days of independence, many state governments barred or restricted non-resident foreign investment in land [*Wilkins, 1989: 45*]. However, particularly strong feelings against foreign land ownership developed following the frenzy of land speculation by foreigners in the frontier areas in the 1880s. In 1885, the *New York Times* editorialised against 'an evil of considerable magnitude—the acquisition of vast tracts of land in the Territories by English noblemen' [*New York Times, 24, January, 1885, cited in Wilkins, 1989: 569*].

Reflecting such feelings, the federal Alien Property Act (1887) and 12 state laws were enacted during 1885–95 with a view to control, or sometimes even altogether ban, foreign investment in land [*Wilkins, 1989: 235*]. An 1885 resolution passed by the New Hampshire legislature read: 'American soil is for Americans, and should be exclusively owned and controlled by American citizens' [*Wilkins, 1989: 569*]. The 1887 federal Alien Property Act prohibited the ownership of land by aliens or by companies more than 20 per cent owned by aliens in the territories (as opposed to the states), where land speculation was particularly rampant [*Wilkins, 1989: 241*].[4] However, it must be noted that due to the lack of disclosure rule on ownership, it was practically not possible to check upon the identities of all the corporate owners and therefore the law was not totally effective [*Wilkins, 1989: 582*].

Natural Resources. There was less hostility towards foreign investment in mining than towards that in land, but still considerable ill-feelings existed [*Wilkins, 1989: 572–3*]. Federal mining laws in 1866, 1870, and 1872 restricted mining rights to US citizens and companies incorporated in the US.[5] In 1878, a timber law was enacted, permitting only US residents to log on public land [*Wilkins, 1989: 581*]. Similarly to the Alien Property Act, these laws were not totally effectual against foreign corporate investment, owing to the difficulty of checking company ownership [*Wilkins, 1989: 129*]. In 1897, the Alien Property Act was revised to exempt mining lands.

Manufacturing. Restrictions on foreign investment in manufacturing were relatively rare as such investment was not very important until the late nineteenth century, by which time the US had managed to build up a robust position in many sectors of manufacturing behind the world's highest tariff barrier.

However, there were still concerns about the behaviour of transnational corporations (TNCs) in manufacturing, especially transfer pricing. For example, a US government investigation in the wake of the First World War expressed grave concerns that the German TNCs were avoiding income tax payment by understating their net earnings by charging excessively for technology licences granted to their American subsidiaries [*Wilkins, 1989: 171*].

Interesting in relation to FDI in manufacturing was the 1885 contract labour law, which prohibited the import of foreign workers. This applied also to national companies, but it obviously affected foreign firms more, especially in relation to the import of skilled workers [*Wilkins, 1989: 582–3*]. Many TNCs did not like the law because it restricted their ability to bring in skilled workers from their headquarters.

3. State Legislation

Some of the state laws were even more hostile to foreign investment than the federal laws [*Wilkins, 1989: 579*]. In addition to the state laws that had existed from early independence banning or restricting non-resident foreigners' investment in land, 12 new state laws were enacted during 1885–95 to control, or even prohibit, foreign investment in land (see above) [*Wilkins, 1989: 235*]. In addition, there were a number of state laws that taxed foreign companies more heavily than American companies. There was also a notorious Indiana law in 1887 withdrawing court protection from foreign firms [*Wilkins, 1989: 579*].

The New York state government took a particularly hostile attitude towards foreign investment in finance, an area where it was rapidly developing a world-class position (a case of infant industry protection, one might say). A New York law in 1886 required foreign insurance companies to have 2.5-times the minimum paid-up capital of American companies [*Wilkins, 1989: 580*], while another law required all certified public accountants (CPAs) to be American [*p. 580*]. The New York state also instituted a law in the 1880s that banned foreign banks from engaging in 'banking business' (such as taking deposits and discounting notes or Bills). The 1914 banking law banned the establishment of foreign bank branches [*Wilkins, 1989: 456*]. These laws proved very burdensome on foreign banks. For example, the London City and Midland Bank (then the world's third largest bank, measured by deposits) could not open a New York branch, when it had 867 branches worldwide and 45 correspondent banks in the US alone [*Wilkins, 1989: 456*].

On the whole, federal government condoned anti-foreign state laws. Wilkins writes:

> The State Department and Congress did give an implicit green light to antiforeign *state* government laws. Neither was responsive to intermittent diplomatic inquiries from London, requesting the federal government to muzzle state legislators. The Secretary of State John Hay replied (in 1899) in a very standard manner to one such request that was related to discriminatory taxes against foreign fire insurers: "Legislation such as that enacted by the State of Iowa is beyond the control of the executive branch of the General Government". [*Wilkins, 1989: 584, italics original*]

4. Lessons from the US Experience

To sum up, in contrast to its strong support for foreign investment liberalisation today, when it was a capital-importing country, the US had all kinds of provisions to ensure that foreigners invested in the country but did not control its economy. For example, the US federal government had restrictions on foreigners' ownership in agricultural land, mining, and logging. It discriminated against foreign firms in banking and insurance, while prohibiting foreign investment in coastal shipping. It demanded that all directors of national banks be American citizens, while depriving foreign shareholders of voting rights in the case of federally chartered banks. It also prohibited the employment of foreign workers, thus implicitly disadvantaging foreign investors that wanted to import skilled labour from their home countries.

At the state level, there were even more restrictions. In addition to restrictions on land ownership, many states taxed foreign companies more heavily and some even refused them legal protection. Much state legislation in the financial sector was even more discriminatory. Some states imposed more strict capital base requirements on foreign financial institutions, and some even totally banned entry into certain financial industries (for example, New York state laws banning foreign bank entry). The federal government condoned such laws and refused to take action against state governments even when there were pressures from foreign investors and governments to do so.

What are the lessons that we can derive from the historical experience of the US in relation to foreign investment policy? The first important point to note is that, despite its often-draconian regulations on foreign investment, the US was the largest recipient of foreign investment. This questions the common contention that foreign investment regulation is bound to reduce investment flows. It should be mentioned that contemporary empirical evidence also shows foreign investment regulations to have only a marginal, if any, influence on the determination of foreign investment decisions [*for example, see the review in Kumar, 2001: 3,156*]. In particular, the large foreign investment inflow into China, with its numerous regulations on foreign investment, shows that regulations are not a major determinant of foreign investment. Therefore, it is simply erroneous to believe that an MIA will increase foreign investment.

The second, and more important, point is that, despite its strict regulations on foreign investment (as well as manufacturing tariffs that were the highest in the world), the US was the fastest-growing economy in the world throughout the nineteenth century up until the 1920s. This questions another common contention that foreign investment regulation will harm the growth prospect of an economy. When combined with the fact that many other developed countries that we shall review below also performed well despite strict regulations on foreign investment, it seems more reasonable to conclude that a well-crafted regime of foreign investment regulation can help, rather than hinder, economic development.

The More Advanced European Economies: the UK, France and Germany

1. Overview
Until the early twentieth century, the UK, France and Germany (together with the Netherlands and Switzerland) were mostly suppliers of capital to the less developed countries, including the US, Canada and Russia. Therefore, during this

period, the main concern for these countries, especially the UK from the late nineteenth century when it was rapidly losing its industrial supremacy, was how to control 'excessive' outward foreign investment rather than how to control inward foreign investment.

In the few decades following the end of the Second World War, however, controlling inward foreign investment became a major new challenge for these countries. If they were to close the newly emergent technological gap with the US, they had to accept American investment, especially FDI (Servan-Schreiber [1967] is the most prominent work of the time on this issue).

Until the 1980s, given that these countries did not adopt laws explicitly discriminating against foreign investors except in sensitive areas (for example, defence, cultural industries), the most important element in their control of foreign investment was their foreign exchange control, which gave their governments the ultimate say in foreign investment. Of course, this does not necessarily mean that their governments used the control to the same effect. For example, the UK, even before the adoption of its pro-FDI policy under Margaret Thatcher, took a more permissive attitude towards FDI and rarely used its foreign exchange control law (1947–79) to influence FDI, except in its early years [Young et al., 1988], whereas France was more active in the management of its FDI flows. However, there were also other mechanisms of control.

First, in all of these countries (except the UK after the 1980s), the significant presence of state-owned enterprises (SOEs) in key sectors in the economy has acted as an important barrier to FDI.[6] Also, while not technically SOEs, some of their key enterprises have had significant government ownership – for example, the state government of Lower Saxony is the biggest shareholder of Volkswagen, with a 20 per cent share ownership. Moreover, even when privatising some of the SOEs in the 1980s, the French government was careful to ensure that control of these enterprises remained French by reserving a significant proportion of shares for 'hard core' (noyau dûr) institutional investors close to the government [Dormois, 1999: 79].

Second, in the case of Germany, the barriers to hostile take-over, due to the presence of close industry–bank relationships as well as to the power of labour exercised through the supervisory board,[7] have acted as a significant obstacle to FDI. Given that in the UK, where hostile take-over is easy, the bulk of FDI has consisted of 'brownfield' investment based on take-overs rather than 'greenfield' investment, FDI in Germany could have been considerably higher without the above-mentioned defence mechanisms against hostile take-over.[8]

Third, all these countries, including the ostensibly FDI-friendly UK, have used informal performance requirements for key FDI projects. For example, in the UK, since the 1970s in certain industries, a variety of informal 'undertakings' and 'voluntary restrictions' were used to regulate foreign investment [Young et al., 1988]. These were mostly, although not exclusively, targeted at

Japanese companies, especially in automobiles and electronics. According to Young *et al.*,

> [i]t is widely believed that [all investments by Japanese electronics giants in the 1970s and the early 1980s – Sony in 1974, Matsushita in 1976, Hitachi and Mitsubishi in 1979, Sanyo and Toshiba in 1981] were subject to some form of voluntary restraint agreement with the Department of Industry on local sourcing of components, production volumes and exporting, but details are not publicly available. Several of the companies reported particular difficulties in implementing local procurement policies and in the slow build up of production which they were allowed. [*Young et al., 1988: 224*]

This prompted one observer to remark in 1977 that 'every Japanese company which has so far invested in Britain had been required to make confidential assurances, mainly about export ratios and local purchasing' [*Financial Times, 6 December, 1977, as reported in Young et al., 1988: 223*]. When Nissan established a UK plant in 1981, it was forced to procure 60 per cent of value added locally, with a time scale over which this would rise to 80 per cent [*Young et al., 1988: 225*]. Also '[t]here is much evidence that successive ministers in the Department of Trade and Industry have put pressure on [Ford and GM] to achieve a better balance of trade, although details in timing and targets are not available' [*p. 225*]. Young *et al.* observed in 1988 that 'limited use of performance guidelines (if not explicit requirements) are effectively now regarded as part of the UK portfolio' [*p. 225*].

2. Lessons from the Experiences of the UK, France and Germany
To sum up, the UK, France and Germany did not have to control foreign investment until the mid-twentieth century, as they were capital-exporting countries before that. However, when faced with the challenge of an upsurge in American investment after the Second World War, they used a number of formal and informal mechanisms to ensure that their national interests are not hurt. Formal mechanisms included foreign exchange control and regulations against foreign investment in sensitive sectors such as defence or cultural industries. At the informal level, they used mechanisms such as the SOEs, restrictions on take-over, and 'undertakings' and 'voluntary restrictions' by TNCs in order to restrict foreign investment and impose performance requirements.

The tightening of foreign investment regulation after the Second World War by these three countries reflected the changes in their status in the international investment game. As they switched their positions as net foreign investors with the US, they adopted restrictions on foreign investment that they had criticised when the US had used them.

This suggests that countries should use, and indeed have used, different policies towards foreign investment according to their status in the international investment flows. Given that developing countries are almost always at the receiving end of these flows, they need, and should be allowed to have, significantly more restrictive approaches towards foreign investment than do the developed countries.

The Less Advanced European Economies: Finland and Ireland

In this section, we examine Finland and Ireland – two countries that were among the poorest in Europe until a generation ago but have become star performers through very different policies towards foreign investment, the former very restrictive and the latter very permissive (although not as hands-off as many people believe).

1. Finland

Finland is often overlooked as one of the economic miracles of the twentieth century. Until the late nineteenth century, Finland was one of the poorest economies in the Europe. However, it is today one of the richest. According to the authoritative statistical work by Maddison, among the 16 richest countries of today, only Japan (3.1 per cent) achieved a higher rate of annual per capita income growth than that of Finland (2.6 per cent) during the 1900–87 period [*Maddison, 1989: 15, Table 1.2*].[9] Norway tied with Finland in the second place, and the average for all 16 countries was 2.1 per cent.[10]

What is even less well known than Finland's impressive growth performance is the fact that it was built on the basis of a regime of draconian restrictions on foreign investment – arguably the most restrictive in the developed world. As a country that had been under foreign rule for centuries[11] and as one of the poorest economies in Europe, Finland was naturally extremely wary of foreign investment and duly implemented measures to restrict it (all information in the rest of this sub-section is from Hjerppe and Ahvenainen [*1986: 287–95*], unless otherwise noted).

Already in 1851, Finland established a law prescribing that any foreigner, Russian nobles excepted, had to obtain permission from the Tsar, then its ultimate ruler of the country, to own land. Added to this were the 1883 law that subjected mining by foreigners to licence, the 1886 ban on banking business by foreigners, and the 1889 ban on the building and operation of railways by foreigners. In 1895, it was stipulated that the majority of the members on the board of directors of limited liability companies had to be Finnish. All these laws remained valid until at least the mid 1980s.

After independence from Russia, restrictions on foreign investment were strengthened. In 1919, it was stipulated that foreigners had to get special permission to establish a business and guarantee in advance the payment of taxes and other charges due to the central and the local states. In the 1930s, a series of laws were passed in order to ensure that no foreigner could own land and mining rights. It was also legislated that a foreigner could not be a member of the board of directors or the general manager of a firm. Companies with more than 20 per cent foreign ownership were officially classified as 'dangerous companies' and therefore foreign ownership of companies was effectively restricted to 20 per cent. As a result, while there was considerable foreign borrowing, there was little FDI during this period, a pattern that persisted at least until the 1980s.

There was some liberalisation of foreign investment in the 1980s. Foreign banks were allowed for the first time to found branches in Finland in the early 1980s. The foreign ownership ceiling of companies was raised to 40 per cent in 1987, but this was subject to the consent of the Ministry of Trade and Industry [*Bellak and Luostarinen, 1994: 17*]. A general liberalisation of foreign investment was made only in 1993, as a preparation for its EU accession.[12]

2. Ireland

Ireland is often touted as an example showing that a dynamic and prosperous economy can be built on the basis of a liberal FDI policy. Its impressive economic performance, especially during the recent period, earned it the titles of 'Celtic Tiger' or 'Emerald Tiger', following the 'miracle' economies of the 'East Asian Tigers' (Korea, Taiwan, Singapore and Hong Kong).

After the exhaustion of early import substitution possibilities and the ensuing industrial stagnation in the 1950s, Ireland shifted its industrial policy radically from an inward-looking to an outward-looking strategy (for further historical backgrounds, see O'Malley [*1989*]). The new policy regime focused on encouraging investment, especially in export industries, through financial incentives. The main incentive schemes used were: 1) capital investment grant, which required the recipient firms to be internationally competitive; 2) exemption of tax for profits earned from export sales above the 1956 level (the law had no new recipients since 1981 and was abolished in 1991); and 3) accelerated depreciation [*O'Malley, 1999: 224–5*]. In addition to encouraging investment, these schemes were also intended to reduce regional disparity by offering higher grant rates for investment in less developed regions. Additionally, the government established industrial estates in poor regions at its own expense [*O'Malley, 1999: 225*].

While this policy regime did not favour foreign enterprises *per se*, it had a certain degree of bias for foreign enterprises, as they typically had higher export orientation. The existence of this bias towards TNCs, however, should not be interpreted as the same as having a totally *laissez-faire* approach towards FDI. According to the 1981 US Department of Commerce survey, *The Use of Investment Incentives and Performance Requirements by Foreign Governments*, 20 per cent of US TNC affiliates operating in Ireland reported the imposition of performance requirements, in contrast to the 2–8 per cent in other advanced countries (8 per cent in Australia and Japan, 7 per cent in Belgium, Canada, France, and Switzerland, 6 per cent in Italy, 3 per cent in the UK, and 2 per cent in Germany and the Netherlands) [*Young et al., 1988: 199–200*].[13] However, it is true that the investment grants disbursed during this period were rather unfocused and therefore did not deliver the best value for money [*O'Sullivan, 1995; O'Malley, 1999*].

The post-1958 industrial policy ran out of steam by the late 1970s. FDIs continued to be mostly in low value added sectors, while they failed to create many linkages with indigenous firms. By the mid 1980s, there developed a sense of crisis in the country, when employment in indigenous firms experienced a rather sharp decline (about 20 per cent) since the peak of 1979, while employment in foreign firms had more or less stagnated since the late 1970s [*O'Sullivan, 1995; O'Malley, 1999; Barry et al., 1999*]. As a result, there was another policy shift in the mid 1980s towards a more targeted approach, especially towards the development of indigenous firms. The new policy regime was set out most clearly in the 1984 *White Paper on Industrial Policy* [*O'Malley, 1999: 228*]. According to O'Malley, the White Paper recognised that:

> ...there were limits to the benefits that could be expected from foreign investment and that the relatively poor long-term performance of indigenous industry called for a greater focus of addressing that problem. More specifically, policy statements since 1984 have referred to a need for policy towards indigenous industry to be more *selective*, aiming to develop larger and stronger firms with good prospects for sustained growth in international markets, rather than assisting a great many firms indiscriminately. *Policy was intended to become more selective*, too, in the sense of concentrating state supports and incentives more on correcting specific areas of disadvantage or weakness which would be common in indigenous firms (but not so common in foreign-owned firms), such as technological capability, export marketing and skills. It was intended to shift expenditures on industrial policy from supporting capital investment towards improving technology and export marketing. [*O'Malley, 1999: 228; emphasis added*]

As a result, after the mid 1980s,

> ...the award of [capital investment] grants was increasingly dependent on firms having prepared overall company development plans. With a view to obtaining better value for state expenditure, the average rate of capital grant was reduced after 1986, *performance-related targets were applied as conditions for payment of grants*, and there was the beginning of a move towards repayable forms of financial support such as equity financing rather than capital grants. [*O'Malley, 1999: 229; emphasis added*][14]

An increasing share of government grants was directed to capability-upgrading activities (for example, research and development, training, management development) rather than simple physical investment [*Sweeney, 1998: 133*]. Moreover, the government started explicitly targeting industries into which they wanted to attract FDI – emphasis was given to industries such as electronics, pharmaceuticals, software, financial services, and teleservices [*Sweeney, 1998: 128*].

Following the re-direction of FDI policy, there was a rise in high-quality FDI, with stronger linkages to indigenous firms. Largely as a result of this, the economy started to boom again. Manufacturing employment, which fell by 20 per cent during 1979–87, rose by 13 per cent during 1988–96, in large part due to the increase in FDI but also due to the improvement in the performance by indigenous firms [*O'Malley, 1999: 230*].

3. Lessons from the Experiences of Finland and Ireland
Finland and Ireland are arguably among the most impressive cases of industrial transformation in the second half of the twentieth century in Europe. However, their respective policies towards foreign investment could not have been more different, at least until Finland's accession to the EU in 1993 – Finland basically blocking any significant foreign investment, while Ireland aggressively seeking it out.

The comparison of these two polar cases raises two important points. The first is that there is no one-size-fits-all foreign investment policy that works for everyone. Finland built its economic miracle under arguably one of the world's most restrictive policy regimes *vis-à-vis* foreign investors, while Ireland benefited from actively courting and working with TNCs.

The second is that, however 'liberal' a country may be towards foreign investment, a targeted and performance-oriented approach works better than a hands-off approach, which is recommended by the developed countries today. Even in the case of Ireland, a combination of carrots and sticks has been used *vis-à-vis* the foreign investors since the early days, and it was only when it got the balance between the two right that the country started to truly benefit from FDI.

The East Asian Countries

1. Japan
Japan's restrictive stance towards FDI is well known. From the Meiji period on, it has tried its best to discourage FDI and go for technology licensing whenever feasible. Even during the first half of the twentieth century, when Japan took a more permissive stance towards FDI than either before or after – for example, the American TNCs dominated the automobile industry during the time – FDI remained small in scale and much of it remained joint ventures [*Yoshino, 1970: 346*].

Between the Second World War and the mid 1960s, when there was some liberalisation of FDI, the FDI policy regime remained extremely restrictive. In particular, before 1963, foreign ownership was limited to 49 per cent, while in some 'vital industries' FDI was banned altogether. Consequently, FDI accounted for only 6 per cent of total foreign capital inflow between 1949 and 1967 [*Yoshino, 1970: 347*].

There was some relaxation in policy over time, but it was a very slow and gradual process. After 1963, foreign ownership of over 50 per cent was allowed, even in some hitherto prohibited 'vital industries' [*Yoshino, 1970: 349*]. However, 'each investment application had to go through individual screening and was rigorously examined by the Foreign Investment Council' [*p. 349*]. And 'the criteria for screening foreign investment were stated with characteristic vagueness, giving the government officials and the Foreign Investment Council considerable latitude' [*p. 350*].

In 1967, FDI was further liberalised. However, even this was highly restrictive (the following details are from Yoshino [*1970: 361–3*]). The 1967 liberalisation 'automatically' allowed a maximum of 50 per cent foreign ownership in 33 industries (so-called 'Category I industries'), but this was on condition that: 1) the Japanese partner in the joint venture must be engaged in the same line of business as the contemplated joint venture, while one Japanese partner must own at least one-third of the joint venture; 2) the Japanese representation on the board of directors must be greater than the proportion of Japanese ownership in the venture; and 3) there should be no provision that the consent of a particular officer or a stockholder be required to execute corporate affairs – a hardly 'automatic' approval! And these were industries where the Japanese firms were already well established and therefore not attractive to foreign investors (for example, household appliances, sheet glass, cameras, pharmaceuticals, and so on), as proven by the fact that 'more than a year went by before the first joint venture was established' [*Yoshino, 1970: 363*]. In the 17 'Category II industries', 100 per cent foreign ownership was allowed, but these were industries where the Japanese firms were even more securely established (ordinary steel, motorcycles, beer, cement, and so on). And importantly, in both categories, 'brownfield' FDI was not allowed.

Further liberalisation in 1969 added 135 and 20 industries to Categories I and II respectively. This round of liberalisation deliberately included a number of attractive industries in order to diffuse foreign criticisms, but they were mostly unattractive to foreigners. Some strategic industries (especially, distribution, petrochemicals and automobiles) were considered as possible candidates for FDI liberalisation, but in the end the proposal was rejected. A hardly surprising decision, when the total output of Japanese industry (which was already the second largest in the world) was less than half that of General Motors, whose annual sales were larger than Japan's national budget, while the total outstanding shares of Toyota Motors at current market value were only about one-fifth of the annual profit of General Motors [*Yoshino, 1970: 366–7*].

The highly restrictive policy stance has been maintained in subsequent periods despite gradual liberalisation of FDI at the formal level. As in Germany and many other European countries, FDI was further constrained by the existence of informal defence mechanisms against hostile take-over, especially the cross-shareholding arrangements that lock up 60–70 per cent of the shares in friendly hands (major lending banks, related enterprises).

Consequently, Japan was arguably the least FDI-dependent country outside the socialist bloc. Between 1971 and 1990 (the post-1995 data are not available, but there is no indication that the situation has drastically changed), FDI accounted for only about 0.1 per cent of total fixed capital formation in the country (data from UNCTAD, various years). The developed country average was 3.5 per cent for the 15-year period before the late 1990s merger boom (that is, 1981–95).

2. Korea

While Korea has not by any means been hostile to foreign capital *per se*, it clearly preferred, if the situation allowed, for it to be under 'national' management, rather than relying on TNCs (the following heavily draws from Chang [*1998*]; for some more details, refer to *Koo [1993]*). According to Amsden, only 5 per cent of the total foreign capital inflow into Korea between 1963 and 1982 (excluding foreign aid, which was important until the early 1960s but not beyond) was in the form of FDI [*Amsden, 1989: 92, table 5*]. Even for the 1962–93 period, this ratio remained a mere 9.7 per cent, despite the surge in FDI that followed liberalisation of FDI policy in the mid 1980s [*Lee, 1994: 193, Table 7–4*].

The Korean government designed its FDI policy on the basis of a clear and rather sophisticated notion of the costs and benefits of inviting TNCs, and approved FDI only when they thought the potential net benefits were positive. The Korean government's 1981 *White Paper on Foreign Investment* provides a fine specimen of such policy vision [*see EPB, 1981*]. This White Paper lists various benefits of FDI such as investment augmentation, employment creation, industrial 'upgrading' effect, balance of payments contribution, and technology transfer, but is also clearly aware of its costs arising from transfer pricing, restrictions on imports and exports of the subsidiaries, 'crowding out' of domestic investors in the domestic credit market, allocative inefficiencies due to 'non-competitive' market structure, retardation of technological development, 'distortion' of industrial structure due to the introduction of 'inappropriate' products, and even the exercise of political influences by the TNCs on the formation of policies [*EPB, 1981: 50–64*]. It is interesting to note that this list includes more or less all the issues identified in the academic debates.

The policies towards TNCs employed by Korea have had a number of elements, but the most important was clearly the restrictions on entry and ownership. Initially, until the early 1970s, when the level of FDI was low, the government was quite willing to allow 100 per cent foreign ownership, especially in the assembly industries in free trade zones which were established in 1970. However, as the country tried to move into more sophisticated industries, where development of local technological capabilities is essential, it started restricting foreign ownership more strongly [*Lee, 1994: 187–8*].

To begin with, there were policies that restricted the areas where TNCs could enter. Until as late as the early 1980s, around 50 per cent of all industries and around 20 per cent of the manufacturing industries were still 'off-limits' to FDI [*EPB, 1981: 70–1*]. Even when entry was allowed, the government tried to encourage joint ventures, preferably under local majority ownership, in an attempt to facilitate the transfer of core technologies and managerial skills.

Even in sectors where FDI was allowed, foreign ownership above 50 per cent was prohibited except in areas where FDI was deemed to be of 'strategic' importance, which covered only about 13 per cent of all the manufacturing industries [*EPB, 1981: 70*]. These included industries where access to proprietary technology was deemed essential for further development of the industry, and industries where the capital requirement and/or the risks involved in the investment were very large. The ownership ceiling was also relaxed if: i) the investment was made in the free trade zones; ii) the investment was made by overseas Koreans; or iii) the investment would 'diversify' the origins of FDI into the country – that is, if the investment was from countries other than the US and Japan, which had previously dominated the Korean FDI scene [*for details, see EPB, 1981: 70–1*].

As a result, as of the mid 1980s, only 5 per cent of TNC subsidiaries in Korea were wholly owned, whereas the corresponding figures were 50 per cent for Mexico and 60 per cent for Brazil, countries which are often believed to have had much more 'anti-foreign' policy orientations than that of Korea [*Evans, 1987: 208*].

Policy measures other than the ones concerning entry and ownership were also used to control the activities of TNCs in accordance with national developmental goals. First, there were measures to ensure that the 'right' kinds of technology were acquired on the 'right' terms. The technology that was to be brought in by the investing TNCs was carefully screened and checked whether it was not overly obsolete or whether the royalties charged on the local subsidiaries, if any, were not excessive.

Second, those investors who were more willing to transfer technologies were selected over those who were not, unless the former were too far behind in terms of technology.[15] Third, local content requirements were quite strictly imposed, in order to maximise technological spillovers from the TNC presence. One thing to note, however, is that the targets for localisation were set realistically, so that they would not seriously hurt the export competitiveness of the country – in some industries they were more strictly applied to the products destined for the domestic market.

The overall result was that, together with Japan, Korea has been one of the least FDI-dependent countries in the world. Between 1971 and 1995, FDI accounted for less than 1 per cent of total fixed capital formation in the country (data from UNCTAD, various years), while the developing country average for the 1981–95 period (pre-1980 figures are not available) was 4.3 per cent.

FDI began to be liberalised since the mid 1980s and was drastically liberalised following the 1997 financial crisis. This was not only because of International Monetary Fund (IMF) pressure but also because of the decision, right or wrong, by some key Korean policy-makers that the country cannot survive unless it allows its firms fully to be incorporated into the emerging international production network. Whether their decision was right remains to be seen.

3. Taiwan

Taiwan took a similar attitude towards FDI to that of Korea, and has used all the measures that Korea used in order to control FDI [*see Wade, 1990: 148–56, and Schive, 1993, for further details*]. However, Taiwan's FDI policy has had to be somewhat more tempered than that of Korea for two reasons. First, due to the relative absence of large domestic private sector firms, which could provide credible alternatives to (or joint venture partners with) TNCs, the Taiwanese government had to be more flexible on the ownership question. Therefore, in terms of ownership structure of TNC subsidiaries Taiwan was somewhere in between Korea and Latin America, with 33.5 per cent of the TNC subsidiaries (excluding the ones owned by overseas Chinese) being wholly owned as of 1985 [*Schive, 1993: 319*]. Second, during the 1970s, when the diplomatic winds blew strongly in favour of China, Taiwan made efforts to host big-name TNCs, especially from the US, by offering them exceptional privileges (for example, guaranteed protection against imports) in order to strengthen its diplomatic position [*Wade, 1990: 154–5*].

Despite these constraints,

> '[f]oreign investment proposals have been evaluated in terms of how much they open new markets, build new exports, transfer technology, intensify input-output links, make Taiwan more valuable to multinationals as a foreign investment site and as a source for important components, and enhance Taiwan's international political support. [*Wade, 1990: 150*]

The 1962 guidelines on foreign investment, which were the backbone of Taiwan's FDI policies, limited FDI to 'industries which would introduce new products or direct their activities toward easing domestic shortages, exporting, increasing the quality of existing products, and lowering domestic product prices' [*Wade, 1990: 150, f.n. 33*]. This meant that, like in Korea, the favoured types of FDI kept changing with the changes in the country's economic and political conditions. For example, after an encouragement during the 1960s, FDI in labour-intensive industries was discouraged or prevented in the 1970s [*Wade, 1990: 151*].

First of all, although in a weaker form than in Korea, foreign ownership was restricted. There was, in particular, a restriction on the extent to which foreign investors could capitalise on their technology. In the case of a joint venture, the technology could not be valued at more than 15 per cent of the TNC's equity contribution [*Wade, 1990: 152*]. Second, local content requirements were extensively used, although, as in Korea, they were typically less tough for export products (see Wade [*1990: 151–2*] for details on the operation of local content requirements).[16] In some cases, the government gave approval for investment on the condition that the TNC help its domestic suppliers to upgrade their technology [*Wade, 1990: 152*].

Third, export requirements were also widely used [*Wade, 1990: 152*]. This was initially motivated by the foreign exchange consequences of FDI but it was kept even after Taiwan had no more foreign exchange shortage, because it was seen as a way to 'insure that the [foreign] company brings to Taiwan a technology advanced enough for its products to compete in other (generally wealthy Western) markets' [*Wade, 1990: 152*].

The overall result was that, although somewhat more dependent on FDI than were Japan or Korea, Taiwan was one of the less FDI-dependent countries in the world. Between 1971 and 1999, FDI accounted for only about 2.3 per cent of total fixed capital formation in the country (data from UNCTAD, various years), while the developing country average for the 1981–95 period (pre-1980 figures are not available) was 4.3 per cent.

4. Lessons from the East Asian Experience
Like the US in the nineteenth century, the three largest East Asian 'miracle' economies have tried to use foreign capital under national management as much as they can, and consequently have used extensive controls on foreign investment in terms of ownership, entry, and performance requirement, throughout their developmental period. Especially Japan and Korea (until recently) relied very little on FDI, while even Taiwan, the most FDI-friendly among the three countries, was below the international average in its reliance on FDI.

Their approach was decidedly 'strategic' in the sense that, depending on the role of the particular sectors in the overall developmental plan of the time, they applied very liberal policies in certain sectors (for example, labour-intensive industries established in free trade zones in Korea and Taiwan) while being very restrictive in others. It goes without saying that therefore the same industry could be, and has been, subject to relatively liberal treatments at some point but became subject to more strict regulations (and vice versa), depending on the changes in the external environment, the country's stage of development, and the development of the indigenous firms in the industries concerned. Especially the experiences of Korea and Taiwan, which provided extensive financial incentives to TNCs investing in their countries while imposing extensive performance requirements, show that FDI brings the most benefit when carrots are combined with sticks, rather than when either carrots or sticks alone are used.

III. IMPLICATIONS: LESSONS OF HISTORY

My recent book, *Kicking Away the Ladder*, shows that, when they were in 'catching-up' positions and trying to establish their industries against the competition from the more efficient producers of the more advanced countries, virtually none of today's developed countries pursued the free trade policies that they are so eager to impose on the developing countries today [*Chang, 2002: Ch. 2*]. An examination of their policies in relation to foreign investment reveals the same picture. In short, when they were net recipients of foreign investment, all of today's developed countries imposed strict regulation on foreign investment. Almost all of them restricted entry of foreign investment. Very often, the entry restrictions were directly imposed, ranging from a simple ban on entry into particular sectors to the allowance of entry on certain conditions (for example, requirement for joint venture, ceilings on foreign ownership).

However, in some cases the scope for foreign investment was also restricted through informal mechanisms that prevented hostile acquisitions and take-overs by foreign investors ('brownfield' investment). First of all, they achieved this through the presence of SOEs or by the government holding significant minority shares in enterprises in the key sectors – for example, the 20 per cent of Volkswagen shares owned by the state government of Lower Saxony. Even when privatising the SOEs, some of these governments, notably that of France, made sure that a controlling stake was held by friendly 'core' shareholders. Others, such as the US and Finland, restricted the entry of foreign investment by regulating the forms of corporate governance – they explicitly required, at least in some key sectors, that all members of boards of directors be citizens and that non-resident foreign shareholders could not vote, which obviously discouraged potential foreign investors, who were not given control commensurate to their ownership status.

When entry was allowed, governments placed numerous performance requirements on investors. Some of the requirements were put in place for balance of payments reasons, such as export requirements, foreign exchange balancing requirements, or ceilings on licensing fees. However, most were put in place in order to ensure that local businesses picked up advanced technologies and managerial skills from their interaction with foreign investors, either through direct transfer or through indirect spillover. Local content requirements and explicit requirements for technology transfer were the most obvious ways to ensure this. Some countries, such as Taiwan, took this logic further and explicitly required foreign investors to help their local suppliers to upgrade their technology. Bans on majority foreign ownership or the encouragement of joint ventures were also ways to encourage the transfer of key technologies and managerial skills. A ban on the employment of foreigners, as used in the US in earlier times, can also increase the chance that skills are directly transferred to the locals.

Even when there were no formal performance requirements, most developed countries used them informally, as we mentioned above. And even the local contents requirement, which was made 'illegal' by the trade-related investment measures (TRIMs) agreement, is still being used by the non-Asian developed countries, albeit under a different guise. The 'rules of origin' used by the EU and the North American Free Trade Agreement (NAFTA), by specifying the local contents of products that qualify for the preferential treatment in the regional free-trade agreements, effectively set local contents requirements for foreign investors in strategic industries (although 'local' here has been expanded beyond old national borders). The EU has strict rules of origin in automobiles, semiconductors, textiles and apparel, photocopiers, and telecom switching equipment, while the NAFTA has them in relation to colour televisions, computers, telecommunications equipment, office equipment, automobiles, machine tools, forklift trucks, fabricated metals, household appliances, furniture, tobacco products, and textiles [*for further details*, see *Kumar, 2001: 3,152, Box 1*].

As in the case of trade policy, the exact strategies that were used to regulate foreign investment varied across countries, ranging from the very welcoming (but not *laissez-faire* and increasingly selective over time) strategy of Ireland to the very restrictive strategies of Finland, Japan, Korea, and the nineteenth century US in certain sectors (especially finance and navigation). In other words, there was no 'one-size-fits-all' model of foreign investment regulation. However, one common factor is that they all took a *strategic approach* to the issue of foreign investment regulation. This meant that different sectors could be subject to different policies even at the same point in time. For example, Korea and Taiwan applied liberal policies towards FDI in labour-intensive industries while applying very restrictive policies towards FDI in the more technologically advanced industries, where they wanted to build local technological capabilities.

Also, over time, with changes in their economic structure and external conditions, their policy stances changed. After it had exhausted the benefits that it could gain from the inflow of export-oriented labour-intensive FDI, Ireland shifted from a rather permissive and unfocused foreign investment policy to a focused and selective one in the mid 1980s, in order to 'upgrade' the contents of FDI. As another example, Korea had a relatively open policy towards FDI in the automobile sector until the mid 1970s, but it tightened the policy afterwards in an attempt to promote domestic automobile producers. While such tightening led to the withdrawal of some foreign investors (Ford and Fiat), the policy resulted in the establishment of a spectacularly successful automobile industry.

To sum up, historical experiences of today's developed countries show that a strategic and flexible approach is essential if countries are to use foreign investment in a way that is beneficial for their long-term national interests. None of these countries pursued policies that were uncritically welcoming to foreign investment, in contrast to what many of them recommend to today's developing countries. In light of these lessons, we can conclude that the current proposals made by the developed countries in the WTO in relation to foreign investment regulation go directly against the interests of the developing countries.

IV. POSSIBLE OBJECTIONS

When criticised along the above line, the proponents of an MIA come back with a few objections that may seem plausible at first sight. However, their objections lack in logic and empirical supports.

'Times Have Changed' – The Irrelevance of History?

The most typical response to the historical criticism that we advanced above is to argue that 'times have changed'. It is argued that, thanks to globalisation in the recent periods, restrictive foreign investment policies that may have been beneficial in the past – say, in Japan in the 1960s or Korea in the 1970s – are no longer so. They argue that, with the increased mobility of capital, foreign investment is becoming more and more important in determining a country's competitive position in the world economy, and therefore that any regulation of foreign investment is likely to harm the potential host country.

One obvious problem with this argument is that there is no clear evidence that we are now living in such a 'brave new world' that all past experiences have become irrelevant. The world may have become much more globalised than, say, in the 1960s and the 1970s, but it is not clear whether globalisation has progressed so much that we have had a 'structural break' with the past. The fact that China has been able to attract a huge amount of foreign investment and benefit from it despite, or rather because of, its strategic regulation of foreign investment suggests that there has been no such clean break with past patterns. Also, in another era of high globalisation, that is, during the late nineteenth and the early twentieth century, when the world economy was as much, or even more in areas like immigration, globalised as that of today [*Bairoch and Kozul-Wright, 1996; Hirst and Thompson, 1999: Ch. 2*], the US attracted by far the largest amount of foreign investment at the time and grew the fastest in the world despite having a restrictive foreign investment policy regime.

Moreover, the current process of globalisation can be reversed, if it is not carefully managed. This is because under-regulated globalisation can lead to instability and stagnation, thereby leading to political discontents and policy reversals. This is exactly how the earlier phase of globalisation had been reversed between the First World War and the Second World War, and we have every sign that the world may be moving that way again.

We have suffered enough in the past from people who think they can transcend history and build a 'brave new world' that has an entirely new set of laws and rules. The Cambodian Communist leader Pol Pot, who declared 'year zero', may be the most extreme example of this, but the now-discredited gurus of the 'new economy' also suffered from the same delusion. We ignore history at our own peril.

'We Want to Protect the Developing Countries from Harming Themselves'

Some proponents of the MIA admit that in the past some countries have successfully regulated foreign investments for their benefits, although when they say this they are mainly thinking about the more recent examples such as Japan, Korea, and Taiwan in the post-war period, rather than the US in the nineteenth century or Finland since the mid-twentieth century. They argue, however, they still want to install an MIA because in many more cases, especially in the developing countries, foreign investment regulation has had negative effects. If left alone, they argue, many developing countries are likely to repeat the mistakes of the past, and therefore having constraints on their policy freedom will actually protect them from making mistakes.

This is a curious argument. Those who want an MIA tend to be free-market economists who criticise various interventionist policies at the domestic level for being 'paternalistic' and restricting the 'freedom of choice'. But when it comes to the choices for the developing countries, they seem to see no contradiction in taking that very paternalistic attitude that they so much criticise in other contexts. Even if strictly regulating foreign investment is likely to bring about 'wrong' outcomes – which we do not accept – one should allow countries 'the right to be wrong', if one is a consistent free-market economist who wants to preserve freedom of choice and who does not believe in top-down intervention.

'The Agreement Can Be Made Flexible Enough – We Simply Want Certainty'

Another typical response to our line of argument, which especially comes from the EU negotiators, is that the MIA need not harm the developing countries, as it can be negotiated in such a way that there is enough policy flexibility. Proponents of an investment agreement argue that developing country 'policy space' can be guaranteed by making the agreement extremely flexible. Especially emphasised is the General Agreement on Trade in Services (GATS)-style positive list approach that they propose, where the MIA would apply only to sectors that countries explicitly designate. This way, the proponents argue, countries can shut as many sectors as they like from foreign investment for as long as they want. For example, Fabien Lecroz, the EU negotiator, told non-governmental organisations at a Geneva seminar on 20 March 2003: 'you could be a WTO member, a signatory of an investment agreement, and keep your market completely closed to FDI, and with no national treatment. That is your policy choice.'

One immediate question that arises in one's mind is: if so much flexibility is allowed, why bother with an agreement? The proponents of an MIA say they still think an MIA is important because it gives certainty to foreign investors about the host country policies. They argue that enhanced certainty will help developing countries as well, because it will increase the flow of foreign investments into them.

However, when all empirical evidence shows that policy certainty is at best only a minor determinant of foreign investment flows, this is a rather curious attitude to take, given that whatever little additional investment a country attracts should come at the cost of reduced flexibility.

More importantly, the flexibility that is offered by the proponents of an MIA is a very curious sort of flexibility, as it is highly limited and one-way. It is highly limited because once you open up a sector, there is no flexibility within that sector. The only 'flexibility' that is available is regulation based on balance of payments considerations, but this is only a temporary arrangement. It is one-way, because once you open up a sector, it is going to be extremely difficult, if not completely impossible, to re-regulate that sector.

Moreover, when non-discrimination is a 'core principle' of the WTO and part of its institutional DNA, however much flexibility is initially provided, there will be an inevitable tendency for negotiators to chip away at developing countries' national policy space in this and successive rounds of negotiations, forcing them into a developmentally premature application of national treatment to FDI. The recent leak of the EU's requests under the GATS process amply justifies these fears [*World Development Movement, 2003, also see the appendix*].

'An MIA in the WTO is the Lesser of the Two Evils' – The Fears of Bilateral Investment Treaties and Regional Trade Agreements

Some developing country negotiators who are aware of the restrictions that an MIA is going to place on their countries' policy freedom still argue that they want an MIA because it is the lesser of two evils. They argue that, in the absence of an MIA, powerful countries, especially the increasingly unilateralist US, will put pressure on developing countries to adopt bilateral investment treaties (BITs), which are bound to be more restrictive than any MIA through the WTO. In addition, some countries worry that similar pressure will come through regional trade agreements (RTAs). In particular, the Latin American countries fear that they will be forced to adopt a NAFTA-style high-octane investment agreement through the negotiation for the Free Trade Agreement of the Americas (FTAA), if they are not protected by an MIA.

While it is true that BITs and RTAs can be more restrictive than an MIA, this is not a foregone conclusion. There are well-informed observers who think BITs can at least actually provide more flexibility. Kumar [*2001: 3,157*] argues that the existence of some 1,700 BITs as of 2000 is evidence that the greater flexibility that BITs give makes its conclusion easy. Also, BITs and RTAs, involving smaller numbers of parties, may be slightly more re-negotiable than an MIA.

Moreover, it is not as if the developed countries are going to give up existing BITs and RTAs or stop pushing for new ones, if an MIA is agreed in the WTO. The MIA will simply be an add-on, rather than a replacement for BITs and RTAs. Indeed, the experience with the trade-related intellectual property rights (TRIPS) agreement shows that, once adopted, a multilateral agreement tends to be interpreted as a 'floor' in bilateral negotiations, thereby raising the standards expected in bilateral agreements [*Kumar, 2003: 223*]. The likely result is that the MIA will form the floor and developing countries will be put under pressure to concede even more policy freedom in BITs.

V. CONCLUDING REMARKS

My historical examination shows that the developed countries did not use the liberal foreign investment policy that they ask of the developing countries, when they were developing countries themselves. Although there were important differences in terms of the overall strategies and the exact policy tools used across countries, most of today's developed countries used formal policy measures and informal restrictions in order to align the interests of foreign investors with their national interests, when they were mainly receiving FDI.

The US, now a champion for the rights of foreign investors, used to regulate foreign investment quite heavily until the early twentieth century. As another example, when the UK, France, and Germany became net capital-importers after the Second World War, they introduced a lot of formal and informal regulations on foreign investment. As members of the EU, they are now among the strongest advocates of MIA. Japan and Korea used to regulate foreign investment very heavily, although they are now strong advocates of MIA.

Of course, the changes in the global economic conditions make it neither feasible nor necessarily desirable for the developing countries to exactly replicate the strategies used by the developed countries in the past [*for a detailed discussion, see Lall, 2003*]. Technological changes have made the minimum entry requirements into industries higher. This means that the kind of 'autonomous' strategy pursued by countries like Japan, Finland, and Korea that did not welcome TNCs may be less feasible now. At the same time, with the emergence of global production networks in certain industries, there may be a higher chance than before that developing countries can develop through a tighter integration into the existing TNC networks.

Even considering these changes, however, restricting the measures of foreign investment regulation is likely to severely limit the development prospect of developing countries, as there is a clear limit to developing technological and organisational capabilities through 'non-autonomous' integration into the global production networks organised by TNCs [Lall, 2003]. Historical experiences of the developed countries also support this view.

Unfortunately, many of these measures have become 'illegal' due to existing agreements in the WTO such as the TRIMs agreement or the GATS. And already the review of TRIMs and the negotiation for GATS-2 are threatening to make illegal even more of those measures that are still available. If an MIA is added on top of this, virtually none of the measures used by now-developed countries in the past will be available for the developing countries. And even if countries can come up with some novel policy measures, they are likely to be thwarted by the all-powerful principle of 'national treatment' that is at the heart of the MIA proposal.

History never repeats itself. However, we ignore a pattern in history that has manifested itself over and over again at our peril – in our case, the need to regulate foreign investment in the earlier stage of economic development. The developed countries should stop pushing for an MIA and allow the developing countries a greater policy space in terms of the regulation of foreign investment. If the developed countries get their way in pushing for a comprehensive ban on foreign investment regulation, as well as a virtual elimination of industrial tariffs and subsidies, the developing countries will be condemned to low-productivity activities in the foreseeable future.

NOTES

1. Even until as late as 1914, when it had caught up with the UK and other leading nations of Europe, the US was one of the largest net borrowers in the international capital market. The authoritative estimate by Wilkins [1989: 145, Table 5.3] puts the level of US foreign debt at $7.1 billion, with Russia ($3.8 billion) and Canada ($3.7 billion) trailing in distance. Of course, at that point, the US, with its estimated lending at $3.5 billion, was also the fourth largest lending country, after the UK ($18 billion), France ($9 billion), and Germany ($7.3 billion). However, even after subtracting its lending, the US still has a net borrowing position of $3.6 billion, which is basically the same as the Russian and the Canadian ones.
2. However, the Second Bank of the USA was only 30% owned by foreigners, as opposed to 70% in the case of the First Bank of the USA, its predecessor (1789–1811) [Wilkins, 1989: 61].
3. Wilkins [1989: 84, n. 264] says that similar remarks were made by politicians in the debate surrounding the renewal of the charter of the First Bank of the USA.

4. At the time the territories were North Dakota, South Dakota, Idaho, Montana, New Mexico, Utah, Washington, Wyoming, Oklahoma, and Alaska. The Dakotas, Montana, and Washington in 1889, Idaho and Wyoming in 1890, and Utah in 1896 acquired statehood, and thus stopped being subject to this Act.

5. The 1866 law said that '[t]he mineral lands of the public domain ... are hereby declared to be free and open to exploration by all citizens of the United States and those who have declared their intention to become citizens, subject to such regulations as may be prescribed by law, and subject also to the local customs or rules of miners in the several mining districts' [*Wilkins, 1989: 128*].

6. According to the authoritative study by the IMF published in 1984, the average share of the SOE sector in GDP among the industrialised countries as of the mid 1970s was 9.4%. The share was 10.3% for West Germany (1976–77), 11.3% for the UK (1974–77), and 11.9% for France (1974) – all above this average.

7. In Germany, corporations are governed not simply by the board of directors, but also by the supervisory board, which contains an equal number of representatives from the workers and from the management (with the casting vote on the management side). This is called the co-determination system and has been a foundation stone of Germany's 'social market economy' after the Second World War.

8. During the 1970s and 1980s, Germany's FDI as a share of Gross Domestic Capital Formation (of course, the two numbers are not strictly comparable) was just 1–2%, whereas the corresponding figure ranged between 6 and 15% in the UK. The figures are calculated from various issues of the UNCTAD *World Investment Report*.

9. The 16 countries are, in alphabetical order, Australia, Austria, Belgium, Canada, Denmark, Finland, France, Italy, Japan, the Netherlands, Norway, Sweden, Switzerland, West Germany, the UK, and the US.

10. Despite the massive external shock that it received following the collapse of the Soviet Union, which accounted for over one-third of its international trade, Finland ranked at a very respectable joint-fifth among the 16 countries in terms of per capita income growth during the 1990s. According to the World Bank data, its annual per capita income growth rate during 1990–99 was 2.1% (the same as that of the Netherlands), exceeded only by Norway (3.2%), Australia (2.6%), and Denmark and the US (2.4%).

11. From the twelfth century until 1809, it was part of Sweden, then it existed as an autonomous Grand Duchy in the Russian empire until 1917.

12. See: www.investinfinland.fi/topical/leipa_survey01.htm, page 1. Interestingly, the government investment-promotion agency, Invest in Finland, emphasises that 'Finland does not "positively" discriminate foreign-owned firms by giving them tax holidays or other subsidies not available to other firms in the economy' [www.investinfinland.fi/topical/leipa_survey01.htm, page 2].

13. Interestingly, according to McCulloch and Owen [*1983: 342–3*] the same survey reveals that over one-half of all foreign subsidiaries in Korea and Taiwan benefit from some form of investment incentive. This is high even by the standards of the developed countries, which were in the 9–37% range as reported in table 6.1 of Young et al. [*1988: 200*] (Japan 9%, Switzerland 12%, Canada and France 18%, Germany 20%, Belgium 26%, Italy 29%, UK 32%, Australia 37%). Given that Korea and Taiwan are countries that were also infamous for imposing tough performance requirements (see below), this piece of evidence, together with the Irish example, suggests that both carrots and sticks are needed for a successful management of FDI.

14. In light of the fact that Ireland was already a country with a high level of performance requirement for TNCs before these changes (see above), it seems reasonable to conclude that performance requirements for the recipients of state grants (domestic or foreign) must have become even greater.

15. For example, the Korean government chose in 1993 the Anglo-French joint venture (GEC Alsthom) organised around the producer of the French TGV (high-speed passenger train), as the partner in its new joint venture to build the country's fast train network. This was mainly because it offered more in terms of technology transfer than did its Japanese and German competitors who offered technologically superior products [*Financial Times*, 23 August 1993, as cited in *Chang, 1998: 108*].

16. For example, the 1962 Guidelines subjected industries such as refrigerators, air conditioners, transformers, televisions, radios, cars, motorcycles, tractors, and diesel engines to local content requirements [*Wade, 1990: 150–51, f.n. 33*].

REFERENCES

Amsden, A., 1989, *Asia's Next Giant*, New York: Oxford University Press.
Bairoch, P. and Kozul-Wright, R., 1996, 'Globalisation Myths and Realities: Some Historical Reflections on Integration, Industrialisation and Growth in the World Economy', UNCTAD Discussion Paper, No. 113, Geneva: United Nations Conference on Trade and Development (UNCTAD).
Barry, F., J. Bradley and E. O'Malley, 1999, 'Indigenous and Foreign Industry: Characteristics and Performance', in F. Barry (ed.), *Understanding Ireland's Economic Growth*, Basingstoke: Macmillan.
Bellak, C. and R. Luostarinen, 1994, *Foreign Direct Investment of Small and Open Economies – Case of Austria and Finland*, Helsinki: Helsinki School of Economics and Business Administration.
Chang, H.-J., 1998, 'Globalisation, Transnational Corporations, and Economic Development', in D. Baker, G. Epstein and R. Pollin (eds.), *Globalisation and Progressive Economic Policy*, Cambridge: Cambridge University Press.
Chang, H.-J., 2002, *Kicking Away the Ladder – Development Strategy in Historical Perspective*, London: Anthem Press.
Crotty, J., G. Epstein and P. Kelly, 1998, 'Multinational Corporations in the Neo-liberal Regime', in D. Baker, G. Epstein and R. Pollin (eds.), *Globalisation and Progressive Economic Policy*, Cambridge: Cambridge University Press.
Dormois, J.-P., 1999, 'France: The Idiosyncrasies of Volontarisme', in J. Foreman-Peck and G. Federico (eds.), *European Industrial Policy – The Twentieth Century Experience*, Oxford: Oxford University Press.
EPB (Economic Planning Board), 1981, *Oegoogin Tooja Baeksuh* (White Paper on Foreign Investment) (in Korean), Seoul: The Government of Korea.
Evans, P., 1987, 'Class, State, and Dependence in East Asia: Lessons for Latin Americanists', in F. Deyo (ed.), *The Political Economy of the New Asian Industrialism*, Ithaca: Cornell University Press.
Garraty, J. and M. Carnes, 2000, *The American Nation – A History of the United States*, 10th Edn., New York: Addison Wesley and Longman.
Held, D., A. McGrew, D. Goldblatt and J. Perraton, 1999, *Global Transformation – Politics, Economics and Culture*, Polity Press: Cambridge.
Hjerppe, R. and J. Ahvenainen, 1986, 'Foreign Enterprises and Nationalistic Control: The Case of Finland since the End of the Nineteenth Century', in A. Teichova, M. Lévy-Leboyer and H. Nussbaum (eds.), *Multinational Enterprise in Historical Perspective*, Cambridge: Cambridge University Press.
Hirst, P. and G. Thompson, 1999, *Globalisation in Question*, 2nd Edn., Cambridge: Polity Press.
Koo, B., 1993, 'Foreign Investment and Economic Performance in Korea', in S. Lall (ed.), *Transnational Corporations and Economic Development*, London: Routledge.
Kumar, N., 2001, 'WTO's Emerging Investment Regime – Way Forward for Doha Ministerial Meeting', *Economic and Political Weekly*, Vol.36, No.33, 18 August, pp. 3151–8.
Kumar, N., 2003, 'Intellectual Property Rights, Technology, and Economic Development – Experience of Asian Countries', *Economic and Political Weekly*, Vol.38, No.3, 18 January, pp. 209–25.
Lall, S., 2003, 'Reinventing Industrial Strategy: The Role of Government Policy in Building Industrial Competitiveness', Paper prepared for the Intergovernmental Group on Monetary Affairs and Development (G-24).
Lee, H.-K., 1994, *Oegoogin Jikjup Tooja wa Tooja Jungchek* (Foreign Direct Investment and Investment Policy) (in Korean) Seoul: Korea Development Institute.
Maddison, A., 1989, *The World Economy in the 20th Century*, Paris: OECD.
McCulloch, R. and R. Owen, 1983, 'Linking Negotiations on Trade and FDI', in C. Kindleberger and D. Audretsch (eds.), *The Multinational Corporation in the 1980s*, Cambridge, MA: MIT Press.

O'Malley, E., 1989, *Industry and Economic Development – The Challenge for the Latecomer*, Dublin: Gill and Macmillan.

O'Malley, E., 1999, 'Ireland: From Inward to Outward Policies', in J. Foreman-Peck and G. Federico (eds.), *European Industrial Policy – The Twentieth Century Experience*, Oxford: Oxford University Press.

O'Sullivan, M., 1995, 'Manufacturing and Global Competition', in J. O'Hagan (ed.), *The Economy of Ireland – Policy and Performance of a Small European Economy*, Basingstoke: Macmillan.

Schive, C., 1993, 'Foreign Investment and Technology Transfer in Taiwan', in S. Lall (ed.), *Transnational Corporations and Economic Development*, London: Routledge.

Servan-Schreiber, J.-J., 1967 [1968], *The American Challenge*, translated from the French by Ronald Steel, New York: Atheneum (French original published in 1968, the English translation used published in 1979).

Sweeney, P., 1998, *The Celtic Tiger – Ireland's Economic Miracle Explained*, Dublin: Oak Tree Press.

Wade, R., 1990, *Governing the Market*, Princeton: Princeton University Press.

Wilkins, M., 1989, *The History of Foreign Investment in the United States to 1914*, Cambridge, MA: Harvard University Press.

World Development Movement, 2003, 'Whose Development Agenda: An Analysis of the European Union's GATS Requests of Developing Countries', April 2003, London: World Development Movement.

Yoshino, M.Y., 1970, 'Japan as Host to the International Corporation', in C. Kindleberger (ed.), *The International Corporation – A Symposium*, Cambridge, MA: MIT Press.

Young, S., N. Hood and J. Hamill, 1988, *Foreign Multinationals and the British Economy – Impact and Policy*, London: Croom Helm.

Will a Trade and Investment Link in the Global Trade Regime Be Good for Human Development?

KAMAL MALHOTRA

There is a long history of failed attempts to forge an international agreement on investment. The most recent attempt focuses on the multilateral trade regime. Both industrial country attempts and developing country opposition grew in the lead up to Doha in 2001 with investment becoming perhaps the most contentious issue at the World Trade Organisation (WTO) Cancun Ministerial in September 2003. Disagreement on it was both a proximate and significant cause for the Cancun meeting's collapse. This brief chapter traces the history of attempts to reach an international agreement on investment. Using a human development lens, it analyses both the experience of the Uruguay Round agreement on trade-related investment measures and the pros and cons of a future multilateral agreement focused on foreign direct investment. It concludes that such an agreement, especially one focused on the pre-establishment phase which has been under discussion at the WTO, is likely to constrain existing development policy space, without providing any predictable or significant development benefits.

Il existe une longue histoire de vaines tentatives pour arriver à un accord international sur les investissements. La tentative la plus récente vise le système multilatéral de commerce. Aussi bien les tentatives des pays industrialisés que l'opposition des pays en développement se sont intensifiées dans le contexte de Dauha en 2001, et les investissements sont peut-être devenus le point le plus controversé lors du sommet des ministres de l'Organisation Mondiale du Commerce (OMC) à Cancún, en 2003. Les désaccords à ce sujet sont une cause directe et significative de l'échec de la réunion de Cancún. Ce bref chapter retrace l'histoire

Kamal Malhotra is at the Bureau for Development Policy, United Nations Development Programme in New York. This chapter is based on material, especially Chapter 12, of a UNDP co-sponsored publication, *Making Global Trade Work for People* (published by Earthscan, 2003), of which the author of this chapter, Kamal Malhotra, was the lead author as well as author of Chapter 12. He is Senior Adviser on Inclusive Globalisation in the UNDP's Bureau for Development Policy in New York. However, the views in this chapter do not necessarily reflect UNDP or UN policy or the policy of the other co-sponsors of the book.

des tentatives pour arriver à un accord international sur les investissements. En choisissant une perspective de développement humain, il analyse les expériences de l'accord de la Ronde Uruguay sur les mesures d'investissements liés au commerce, ainsi que les avantages et désavantages d'un futur accord multilatéral sur les investissements directs étrangers. Il conclut qu'un tel accord – en particulier s'il s'agit de la phase préliminaire qui a été discutée au sein de l'OMC – risque de restreindre la marge de manœuvre de la politique de développement, sans pour autant offrir des avantages prédictibles ou significatifs pour le développement.

I. INTRODUCTION

Trade, investment and human development have a complex relationship. Understanding their interaction requires understanding the complexity of trade and investment policies, on the one hand, and human development as part of broader development policy, on the other. Discussing the human development implications of a trade and investment link in trade regimes remains urgent despite the impasse on the investment issue at the fifth World Trade Organisation (WTO) Ministerial Meeting in Cancun, Mexico in September 2003. This is because it still remains, although more tentatively than before Cancun, on the global trade regime's agenda. Moreover, despite the Cancun impasse and a clear recognition in May 2004 by the European Commission (EC),[1] the main proponent, that it is no longer tenable to have it as part of the Doha Round's 'single undertaking', it has not been totally abandoned by them. Partly because of this, it has also become an increasingly important part of the aggressive bilateral and regional trade negotiations or agreements being pursued with renewed vigour by major trading powers especially in Latin America and as part of the proposed Economic Partnership Agreements between the European Union (EU) and African, Caribbean and Pacific (ACP) states.

Among the many questions this chapter will attempt to address are the following: if all foreign direct investment (FDI) is sought to be brought under binding multilateral trade rules, does this mean that all FDI is good for human development? Many proponents argue for a multilateral investment agreement in the WTO because they believe it will provide security and predictability to foreign investors, thereby increasing FDI to developing countries. Is there empirical evidence to support this claim and is this likely? Will there be increased security and predictability for host governments in addition to foreign investors? Most importantly, will a multilateral investment agreement increase possibilities for achieving positive and enhanced human development outcomes?

Before I turn to these and other crucial questions, it is important to understand both the essence of human development and the history of attempts to reach international agreements on investment. These are briefly discussed in the first two sections that follow.

II. HUMAN DEVELOPMENT

People are the real wealth of nations, and the main goal of development is to create an enabling environment for people to enjoy long, healthy, creative lives. This may appear to be a simple truth. But for too long, development efforts have focused on creating financial wealth and improving material well-being. Forgotten in such pursuits is that development is about people. The preoccupation with economic growth has pushed people to the periphery of development discussions.

The ultimate aim of development is not to create more wealth or to achieve higher growth. It is to expand the range of choices and the opportunities to exercise those choices in the pursuit of poverty reduction and an enhanced quality of life for every human being. Thus, human development is concerned with enlarging choices and enhancing quality of life outcomes – and with advancing basic human freedoms and rights. Defined in this manner, human development is a simple notion with far-reaching implications.[2]

Though important, economic growth is only one means to development – not the ultimate goal. Economic growth is a necessary but not a sufficient condition for human development. It is the quality of growth, not its quantity alone, which is crucial for human well-being. Growth can be *jobless*, rather than job creating; *ruthless*, rather than poverty reducing; *voiceless*, rather than participatory; *rootless*, rather than culturally enshrined; and *futureless*, rather than environment-friendly. Economic growth which is jobless, ruthless, voiceless, rootless and futureless, is not conducive to human development [*Jahan, 2000*]. Economic growth must be equitable if its benefits are to be felt in people's lives.

The human development concept is broader than other people-oriented approaches to development. The human resource approach emphasises human capital and treats human beings as inputs into the production process, not as its beneficiaries. The basic needs approach focuses on people's minimum requirements, not their choices. The human welfare approach looks at people as recipients, not as active participants in the processes that shape their lives.

Human development treats people as the subject of development, not the object. It is both distinct from and more holistic than other approaches to development. Development of the people builds human capabilities. Development for the people translates the benefits of growth into people's lives. And development by the people emphasises that people must actively participate in the processes that shape their lives.

III. THE HISTORY OF ATTEMPTS AT REACHING INTERNATIONAL AGREEMENTS ON INVESTMENT[3]

Attempts to bring foreign investment under the discipline of international rules, which have a long history, largely failed till the early 1980s. However, efforts have been renewed with increased vigour over the past two decades starting with the Uruguay Round of trade negotiations. These have been accompanied by an increased focus on bringing investment under the discipline of the WTO which was created in 1995 as a result of the successful completion of the Uruguay Round in Marrakech, Morocco in 1994.

In the late eighteenth and the nineteenth centuries the European powers and the United States set standards for the protection of foreign investment that were superior to national treatment. Furthermore, host countries were not permitted to interfere with or expropriate foreign assets.

Latin American countries were the first to challenge the favourable treatment of foreign investors. The 1868 Calvo Doctrine established the same rights for foreigners and nationals and prohibited countries from intervening to enforce the claims of their citizens in other countries. Between the First and the Second World Wars, the League of Nations was stalemated on this issue, and since the Second World War industrial countries have been unsuccessful in their efforts to establish an international regime for the protection of international investment.

The 1947–48 United Nations Conference on Trade and Employment considered investment in its discussions on the expansion of international trade. Investment measures formed part of a wider discussion on restrictive business practices, and the Havana charter for an International Trade Organisation (ITO) contained provisions on such measures. But the negotiations leading to the charter and eventually to the General Agreement on Tariffs and Trade (GATT) showed that governments were not prepared to subject their investment policies to international rules and disciplines.

Following the failure to establish the ITO, industrial countries implemented policies bilaterally through investment promotion and protection treaties and agreements. Such treaties were intended to ensure that investors' properties would not be expropriated without prompt, adequate and effective compensation, non-discriminatory treatment, transfer of funds and dispute settlement procedures. In addition, in the late 1950s an evaluation of restrictive business practices was carried out by a GATT group of experts, focusing on activities of international cartels and trusts that could hamper the expansion of world trade and interfere with GATT objectives.

Later the issue of international investment surfaced at the United Nations, where developing countries sought international approval for their sovereign aspirations and tried to alter the international investment standards that had prevailed in the colonial period. One outcome was the UN General Assembly's

Charter of Economic Rights and Duties of States, passed in 1974. Article 2 of the charter provided for the rights of every state to regulate and exercise authority over foreign investment in conformity with its national objectives and stated that no state would be compelled to grant preferential treatment to foreign investment. The draft Code of Conduct for Transnational Corporations, issued by the United Nations Center on Transnational Corporations, addressed a range of additional issues – almost all of which remain unresolved because most industrial countries opposed a legally binding status for the code. In addition, the Set of Multilaterally Agreed Equitable Principles and Rules for the Control of Restrictive Practices, negotiated under the United Nations Conference on Trade and Development, covered investment and competition policy issues – and suffered the same fate.

After the conclusion of the GATT's Tokyo Round in 1979, renewed attempts were made to bring a limited number of performance requirements imposed on foreign investors by host countries under its purview, particularly two trade related investment measures (TRIMs), local content and export performance requirements. Though many developing countries continued to maintain that foreign direct investment was beyond the GATT's purview, the US and some other industrial countries argued that such performance requirements affect trade and should be addressed by the trade regime.

A 1982 dispute over administration of the Foreign Investment Review Act, brought by the US against Canada, significantly boosted its efforts to bring investment under the purview of multilateral trade disciplines. While many delegations were sceptical about bringing such a dispute to the GATT, its council finally decided to allow a panel to investigate the US claim. Among other things, the panel ruled that Canada's practice of requiring foreign direct investors to purchase Canadian goods was inconsistent with GATT article III:4, though not with article XI:1. The US-Canada dispute set the stage for a more effective challenge of TRIMs at the multilateral level. The ruling also appears to have led to an amendment in US trade legislation to address investment issues more directly.

Investment was a major issue in the GATT Uruguay Round, featuring in and affecting discussions and agreements on trade in services (GATS), TRIMs, Trade-Related Aspects of Intellectual Property Rights (TRIPS), government procurement and subsidies. The 1988 Omnibus Trade and Competitiveness Act, which provided the US with negotiating authority for the Uruguay Round, had explicit language on investment. TRIMs were viewed by the US as preventing its transnational corporations from designing coherent global strategies, and their removal became a main negotiating issue for the US and some other industrial countries during the Uruguay Round.

During the negotiations, attempts were made to go beyond TRIMs to develop a regime for investment in general, including the right of establishment and national treatment. Industrial countries also argued for the elimination of all

TRIMs, rather than just minimising and avoiding their adverse affects on trade. Most developing countries differed from the US, Japan and other industrial countries on two main counts: whether multilateral disciplines should be limited by existing GATT articles or expanded to develop an investment regime; and whether some or all actionable TRIMs should be prohibited or dealt with case by case, based on a clear demonstration of their direct and significant restrictive and adverse effects on trade. The US and Japan favoured an all-encompassing investment regime, with TRIMs as one part of it. Developing countries, on the other hand, called for strict adherence to the GATT mandate and for limiting negotiations to investment measures with direct and significant adverse effects on trade. While developing countries managed to limit the scope of the TRIMs agreement during the Uruguay Round, article 9 called for a review of the agreement's operation within five years of its entry into force – with a view to determining whether it should be complemented with provisions on investment and competition policy.

In addition, the General Agreement on Trade in Services (GATS), which takes a 'positive list' approach,[4] covers investment liberalisation since it includes commercial presence as one of the modes of service supply (mode 3 which is foreign commercial presence, covering services supplied 'by a service supplier of one Member, through commercial presence of any other Member' – such as the establishment of branches of banks in host countries or the acquisition of foreign companies). In fact, it is believed by many that the term 'trade in services' was coined as a way of bringing investment within the scope of Uruguay Round agreements in a more forceful way than the TRIMs agreement would allow due to opposition from developing countries. Most developing countries opposed bringing trade in services under the purview of multilateral disciplines and agreed only on the condition that it be kept separate from negotiations on trade in goods. Thus while TRIMs were discussed during negotiations on goods, the GATS was discussed in separate negotiations on services. Nevertheless, the US and transnational private sector actors devoted substantial efforts to ensuring that 'trade in services' was defined to include investment and that it would become acceptable terminology.

Thus it is no surprise that the maximum market access commitments under the GATS have been achieved under mode 3, especially in financial services and telecommunications.

Regional agreements such as the North American Free Trade Agreement (NAFTA) go further than the TRIMs agreement and the GATS, providing national and non-discriminatory treatment to foreign investment. NAFTA also prohibits a number of performance requirements. For this reason services are clearly differentiated from investment in NAFTA. In addition, by January 1997 there were 1,330 bilateral investment treaties in 162 countries – up from fewer than 400 treaties in the early 1990s and these continue to grow significantly each year.

Major differences remain on the issue of bringing investment under multilateral trade disciplines. Not satisfied with the TRIMs agreement, industrial countries have, till the collapse of the WTO's Ministerial Meeting in Cancun in September 2003, maintained intense pressure for the inclusion of four new issues (investment, competition policy, trade facilitation, government procurement) ever since the first WTO Ministerial Conference, held in Singapore in 1996. Of these, investment was probably the most important to them. Despite most developing countries' resistance to the inclusion of these issues in Singapore, members agreed that all four (subsequently dubbed the 'Singapore issues') should be studied further in working groups, with a view to recommending whether negotiations should take place on them at a future ministerial conference. The scope of the government procurement discussion was limited to transparency, not market access. At the same time, the Organisation for Economic Co-operation and Development (OECD) began trying to reach a Multilateral Agreement on Investment among its members – only to fail, indicating how difficult it is to agree on investment issues even among countries at relatively similar levels of human development.

The 2001 WTO Ministerial Conference in Doha, Qatar, remained deadlocked on investment and the three other 'Singapore issues'. Most industrial countries, especially EU members insisted that they were part of the Doha Round's 'single undertaking'. They wanted to start negotiating an agreement on these four issues after Cancun while many developing countries wanted to continue studying them. The Doha declaration agreed to continue studying the issues until the 2003 WTO Ministerial Conference in Cancun, Mexico. Investment was perhaps the highest profile 'new' issue in Cancun in September 2003 and clearly the most contentious. Disagreement on whether to include it in the Doha Round's negotiating mandate was both a proximate and major cause for the collapse of the Cancun Ministerial Meeting, largely because of North–South differences.

As indicated in the introduction to this chapter, the inclusion of investment in the Doha Round is much less likely after Cancun. Nevertheless, while it can be considered to be on the backburner for the present, it is not exactly off the agenda, even though the US has, in January 2004, come out openly against its inclusion while the EC has at least accepted that it needs to be de-prioritised in the Doha Round. Indeed, significantly, on 9 May 2004, the EC, the main but not the only proponent, offered new flexibility on investment issues, accepting that each of the four Singapore issues should be treated on their respective merits but on the understanding that those members who wished to pursue investment outside the Doha Round's 'single undertaking' would be able to do so. The EC, in this communication to Trade Ministers of WTO member countries also clearly recognised in writing that there was no consensus to start multilateral negotiations on investment in the WTO.

In analysing these recent post-Cancun developments, it must, however, be understood that the US has never been an enthusiastic proponent of a multilateral investment agreement (since its coverage was at best going to include FDI, not portfolio and other capital flows which the US has successfully pushed for inclusion in many of its bilateral agreements including recent ones with Chile and Singapore). The EC and Japan, the main proponents of a multilateral investment agreement in the WTO, while recognising the post-Cancun political and negotiating reality, have also only reluctantly put the issue on the backburner for now. There appears little doubt, therefore, that investment as an issue will re-surface in due course in the multilateral discussions. In the meanwhile, it is both alive and being actively pursued by its proponents as well as the US in bilateral and regional trade agreements, including in the proposed Economic Partnership Agreements (EPAs) between the EU and the ACP group of countries.

Notwithstanding the above, it is perhaps safe to assume that after the débâcle at Cancun, any future discussion on including investment in a multilateral trade agreement in the foreseeable future will, of necessity, have a restricted definition. Given this chapter's predominant focus on the multilateral global level, it therefore makes eminent sense for it to focus only on foreign direct investment. The attempt of some WTO members to have a broader definition of investment agreed, one which would include portfolio and other capital flows, is probably now fatally crippled post-Cancun, at least in the context of multilateral negotiations.

IV. THE IMPLEMENTATION EXPERIENCE OF THE TRIMs AGREEMENT IN THE POST-URUGUAY ROUND PERIOD

Governments use two primary measures to attract and regulate foreign direct investment: performance requirements (such as local content, local manufacturing, export performance and technology transfer requirements) and investment incentives (such as loans and tax rebates). When these are related to trade in goods, they are called Trade-Related Investment Measures (TRIMs). Some TRIMs entail performance requirements. Implementation measures have been extremely important for many developing and some industrial countries, often serving as part of broad strategies aimed at achieving economic growth, industrialisation and technology transfer. TRIMs have also been used to guard against and counter anti-competitive and trade-restrictive business practices – particularly those of transnational corporations.

Many developing countries contend that, on the basis of the implementation experience so far, the TRIMs agreement in the WTO which prohibits the use of certain performance measures has not taken into account their development requirements. They are particularly concerned about the agreement's negative effects on employment and value added, because it prohibits late-industrialising countries from pursuing domestic content polices. Such policies were crucial to the successful development strategies of many of today's industrial countries and East Asia's newly industrialised countries.

Developing countries have put forward a number of reasons in the WTO for maintaining TRIMs. Among these are ensuring the fullest, most efficient contribution of investment to their economic development. For example, TRIMs may allow small firms to expand to full competitive scale and can be used to channel FDI to bring potentially strategic infant industries to maturity. In doing so, such enterprises are likely to increase domestic employment and valued added. TRIMs can also mitigate the problems of disadvantaged regions and enhance the contribution of investment to building and upgrading domestic technological capacity and increasing the value added share of exports. In this context, the TRIMs agreement is viewed by many developing countries as a major impediment to upgrading technology and increasing value added.

Developing country governments have also argued that TRIMs counter the trade-restrictive and distorting strategies of transnational corporations. For example, local content requirements can be used to increase employment, protect the viability of local firms and avoid overpricing by transnational corporations. Local content requirements can also be a necessary and effective response to vertically integrated transnational corporations that dominate the market.

The electronics industry for example, appears to be a case of missed opportunity. It derives little local content from developing countries despite having significant operations in them. This is because many of the corporations that dominate the industry prefer to source components and parts vertically or horizontally from parent companies or foreign affiliates – even if parts of comparable quality are available domestically in developing countries. As a result most of the value added from the industry goes to transnational corporations.[5]

Implementation of the TRIMs agreement has posed a number of challenges for developing countries. These include the difficulty of identifying TRIMs covered by the agreement and ensuring their timely notification to the WTO, the inadequacy of the transition period for phasing out prohibited TRIMs and disputes arising from the lack of clarity between the GATT, the TRIMs agreement and the Agreement on Subsidies and Countervailing Measures. Of greatest concern, however, are dispute settlement rulings involving prohibitions on local content requirements – rulings that many developing countries view as running counter to their interests.

Although a number of countries have de-emphasized the use of local content in recent years, such requirements continue to be used in both developing and industrial countries – particularly in the automotive sector, where they are most widespread in developing countries.[6] Accordingly, since the TRIMs agreement came into force, this sector has seen the largest number of disputes lodged by industrial against developing countries. Between 1995 and February 2002, 11 complaints in the automotive sector (involving not just local content requirements but also subsidies, incentives and foreign exchange balancing) were brought by Japan, the European Communities and the US against four developing countries with large actual or potential automotive markets: Brazil, India, Indonesia, and the Philippines. Rulings had been made on six of these complaints by late 2002 – four against Indonesia and two against India. Japan's complaint against Indonesia (and similar subsequent complaints against Indonesia by the EU and US) illustrate a number of development concerns.[7]

A positive response to some of the implementation concerns of developing countries was the July 2001 decision of the WTO Council for Trade in Goods to extend until the end of 2001 the transition period for the TRIMs notified under chapter 5:1. Another two-year extension was made available upon request and upon the fulfilment of certain conditions, such as the presentation of a phase-out plan for TRIMs.

Though useful in the short run, these extensions do not deal with the fundamental problem of the TRIMs agreement: they do not provide developing countries with the policy space they need to freely use certain development policy instruments as they choose – such as local content and other performance requirements – that could enhance their value added, employment and trade competitiveness.

The TRIMs agreement, as currently designed, may not be in the best interests of developing countries and human development. Thus it should be reassessed, with a view to rolling back its prohibition on the use of instruments that enhanced the development prospects of today's industrial and newly industrialised countries. In addition, TRIMs and the WTO's GATS' provisions on performance requirements should be made consistent: the GATS allow them while the TRIMs agreement prohibits many.

If a rollback is not possible, it will be necessary to rethink the parameters of the TRIMs agreement through the application of special and differential treatment exemptions for local content requirements, especially in the automotive and electronics industries of developing countries. These industries should be prioritised because they are dynamic, with significant potential for contributing to human development outcomes. As some have argued, there may also be value in rethinking the TRIMs agreement to focus it on trade related investment measures with direct and negative implications for trade, as opposed to the current outright prohibition of certain measures. In addition, any discussions on bringing other investment measures under multilateral disciplines should be approached with caution, keeping in mind the experience with TRIMs so far.

V. INVESTMENT AS A 'NEW' ISSUE IN THE POST-URUGUAY ROUND PERIOD

OECD discussions on the Multilateral Agreement on Investment were all-encompassing, reaching beyond traditional notions of foreign direct investment to cover nearly every type of tangible and intangible asset [*OECD, 1997*]. Thus in addition to FDI the proposed agreement included both intellectual property and portfolio investment.

The motivations for the failed OECD discussions and the initial phases of the investment discussions in the WTO appear to have a lot in common, even if the discussion of the types of investment covered by the WTO Working Group on the Relationship Between Trade and Investment (the Group has not been reconvened after the 2003 Cancun collapse) were more limited. The common motives seem to be the strategic interests of transnational corporations to ensure uniform global rules that will reduce both their transactions costs and the uncertainty surrounding their investment decisions while simultaneously giving them secure property rights. Since the vast majority of transnational corporations are based in OECD countries, it is not surprising that reaching a multilateral agreement on investment with such an emphasis has been and remains a high priority for OECD governments.

But from a developing country perspective these motivations imply an inherent asymmetry in the discussions, because so far the discussions have focused on the rights of foreign investors in host countries – not their obligations. From a human development perspective, key issues include whether FDI is supportive of human development and whether a multilateral agreement on investment in the WTO will give developing countries the policy flexibility and autonomy they need to pursue their human development goals. Given the implementation experience of the TRIMs agreement over the past decade, it will be important to take this experience into account while making such an assessment.

While the 2001 Doha declaration does not explicitly define what is meant by investment for WTO discussion purposes, the relevant paragraph reads: 'recognizing the case for a multilateral framework to secure transparent, stable and predictable conditions for long-term cross-border investment, particularly foreign direct investment, that will contribute to the expansion of trade'. This suggests that any proposed future agreement in the WTO can be expected to focus on long-term foreign direct investment, not short-term portfolio capital flows even though some industrial countries have indicated their desire to see it cover all types of capital flows.

The more limited interpretation is consistent with the frequent reminders of developing countries since the 1996 Singapore Ministerial Conference that the working group in this area was established with the understanding that its work would be limited to foreign direct investment [*cited in Correa, 1999*]. Given the Doha emphasis, the Singapore understanding and most importantly, the Cancun disagreements and impasse on the issue of investment, it can be reasonably expected that future discussions, if any, will focus exclusively on FDI.

The Changing Nature of Foreign Direct Investment

There is growing recognition that in the context of financial globalisation, some of the long-standing characteristics of FDI (such as its stability and long-term nature) that have differentiated it from portfolio investment may be eroding, making the distinction between the two increasingly blurred. This has complicated the debate about the nature of FDI and its potential and real benefits for human development. More than a decade ago a World Bank study illustrated the changing nature of FDI in the context of financial liberalisation [*Claessens et al., 1993*]. It argued that 'bricks and mortar' investments can easily be converted into liquid assets and remitted out of a country. The study stated that

> Because direct investors hold factories and other assets that are impossible to move, it is sometimes assumed that a direct investment inflow is more stable than other forms of capital flows. This need not be the case. While a direct investor usually has some immovable assets, there is no reason in principle why these cannot be fully offset by domestic liabilities. Clearly a direct investor can borrow in order to export capital, and thereby generate rapid capital outflows. [*cited in Singh, 2001*]

In such situations there is no documentation that distinguishes foreign direct investment from other financial capital. Retained profits, repatriated out of the host country, now account for a significant portion of foreign assets – as much as 50 per cent in the case of US-based foreign investors.

Clearly, FDI in this form cannot be equated or compared with domestic capital accumulation. As a result, Singh argues that in the context of financial globalisation, a first-order issue is understanding what FDI comprises. He indicates that the past decade probably saw the largest volume of cross-border mergers and acquisitions in world history. While most took place between industrial countries, mergers and acquisitions also greatly expanded in developing countries in the second half of the 1990s. Excluding China, the share of mergers and acquisitions in the combined FDI of developing countries rose from an average of 22 per cent during 1988–91 to 72 per cent during 1992–97 [*UNCTAD, 1999b*]. Moreover, most of this was in the form of acquisitions, not mergers.

This trend accelerated during and after the 1997 East Asian financial crisis. Singh argues that the implications of this trend are troubling for developing countries because, unlike 'greenfield' investment (which represents a net addition to the capital stock of developing countries), FDI in the form of an acquisition may not represent any addition in terms of capital stock, employment or even output. But as others note, such investment could lead to positive effects in terms of subsequent investment, technology transfer and short-term balance of payments effects. While there is no conclusive evidence on the human development impacts of this form of FDI, on balance it appears less likely to create value added in developing countries, at least in the short run, compared with traditional greenfield investment in productive assets that add to the host country's capital stock.

Finally, it is important to bear in mind that, contrary to a widespread view, not all foreign direct investment is in the form of equity. Much is in the form of high-interest-bearing loans and of an intra-firm nature. Sometimes these loans are even government guaranteed.

Foreign Direct Investment and Development

The potential contribution of FDI to development is covered extensively in other chapters in this volume. Hence, this chapter will not address this issue except as it relates to the potential inclusion of investment as an area for multilateral trade rules.

Proponents of FDI and its inclusion in the multilateral trade regime argue that, on balance, FDI has a positive impact on human development, especially through its technology transfer and domestic productivity spillover effects [*WTO, 1996*]. Over the past two decades such optimism about the economic growth, technology transfer and productivity spillover consequences of FDI has led most developing countries to unilaterally lower barriers to foreign investment, including portfolio capital.

Given the emphasis placed by proponents on technology transfer, it is instructive to see how the existing WTO agreement which has emphasised this has fared in terms of this crucial issue which is one of the most widely acknowledged potential benefits of FDI.[8] Provisions for such transfers currently exist in the TRIPS agreement and while TRIPS consolidates knowledge ownership and reduces opportunities for learning and imitation for new entrants,[9] it, at the same time, has provisions that offer opportunities and challenges for technology acquisition and use. Among them are articles 66 and 67 as a result of which industrial countries are expected to provide incentives to their enterprises to encourage technology transfer to least developed countries to help them create a 'sound and viable technological base'. However, articles 66 and 67 have not been implemented even as symbolic measures. Technology transfer has not occurred in any recorded, coherent or consistent manner through TRIPS.

More broadly, while there is little disagreement that certain types of FDI can play an important role in enhancing human development, proponents of a multilateral agreement on investment appear to assume that all foreign direct investment is good for human development. Is this true?

There have been numerous studies on the impact of greenfield FDI in different countries, sectors and settings. The results have been mixed at best, with no conclusive evidence in any one direction. Such investment has been used for different purposes. For example, Latin American countries have often relied on FDI to finance balance of payments deficits, while Asian countries have used it more for technology transfer. FDI can be expensive and unsustainable if used for balance of payments purposes. It is also much harder to differentiate from financial capital if used in this manner.

In a number of cases FDI has not realised its human development potential. Firm-level evidence from a large sample of manufacturing plants in developing countries fails to indicate the existence of productivity spillovers related to FDI. Indeed, the presence of transnational corporations appears to depress the productivity of domestic plants in some countries - with negative consequences for employment and other human development variables [*Hanson, 2001*].

In addition to the failed promise of the TRIPS agreement in this area, lost opportunities for technology transfer through FDI, more generally, are also well documented. In fact, successful, sustainable technology transfer through FDI has been more the exception than the rule. Moreover, FDI may be an expensive way of achieving technology transfer. This is because, given the many risks associated with FDI, investors need to ensure high rates of return – exceeding the interest rates that typically apply on foreign loans for imports of capital goods.

Foreign direct investment can also have negative development effects through its balance of payments impact, especially in the context of financial liberalisation. An important argument [*Kregel, 1996*] is that

> FDI may have both a short and a longer-term structural influence on the composition of a country's external payment flows. While financial innovation allows FDI to have an impact in the short run which is increasingly similar in terms of volatility to portfolio flows, the more important aspect is the way it may mask the true position of a country's balance of payments and the sustainability of any combination of policies.... Accumulated foreign claims in the form of accumulated FDI stocks may create a potentially disruptive force that can offset any domestic or external policy goals.

So, whatever the potential merits of some types of FDI for human development – and there are many – it is by no means always a positive influence on key variables that are important for advancing human development in developing countries: employment, productivity and technology transfer. A comprehensive review of experiences with FDI perhaps summed up the evidence best when it concluded that 'in terms of the impact of FDI on different parameters of development ... FDI promises more than it delivers' [*Kumar, 1996: 40*].

A major lesson that emerges from the empirical evidence is that some kinds of foreign investment are preferable to others. Because not all types of FDI are equally desirable, less may be better than more unless all of it is of the desirable kind. Moreover, FDI in certain sectors may be preferable to others. In other words, developing countries need to both attract FDI selectively and govern it effectively if it is to play a positive role in human development.

VI. KEY CONSIDERATIONS FOR A MULTILATERAL AGREEMENT ON INVESTMENT IN THE WTO

It is now time to turn to an analysis of key issues for consideration if there were to be a multilateral agreement on investment in the WTO. This analysis will need to be particularly informed by the previous analysis in this chapter, especially the implementation experience of the TRIMs agreement in the post-Uruguay Round period and the analysis and lessons summarised in the immediately preceding section. This section is divided into a number of sub-sections, with each considering a specific important issue in the ongoing debate on whether, on balance, investment should be brought under multilateral trade rules and disciplines.

Would a Multilateral Investment Agreement Limit Development Policy Space?

Some critics have questioned whether the notion of a multilateral framework on investment is compatible with the need to preserve flexibility in development policies and strategies. By its nature, a multilateral framework aspires to a one-size-fits-all approach – which, while recognising some differences between countries, allows few lasting exceptions. Such a framework appears unlikely to provide the policy autonomy and flexibility that developing countries need for another important reason: investment discussions in the WTO have so far focused on the pre-establishment phase of investment, that is which sectors are open to investment and to whom [*Winters, 2002*].

A focus on the pre-establishment phase will not increase foreign direct investment because the factors most essential to attracting and sustaining FDI are domestic in nature and come into play only in the post-establishment phase. Moreover, a preoccupation with the pre-establishment phase will reduce – and possibly eliminate – a government's ability to be selective and allow only FDI that promotes its development interests and has a positive impact on human development.

More specifically, a multilateral investment agreement focused on the pre-establishment phase will mean that countries will no longer be able to restrict the types of assets that may be acquired by foreigners, specify the structure of ownership and lay down requirements for the future operations of foreign investors (such as employment of local workers, use of local raw materials and export requirements). All these policies were crucial elements in the pre-WTO policy arsenals of the East and Southeast Asian countries who, as a group, have been most successful in enhancing human development outcomes since the Second World War.

Moreover, in negotiations on any multilateral investment agreement, industrial countries will emphasise their market access ambitions and seek to reduce the choice of development instruments available to developing countries – such as performance requirements currently allowed under the TRIMs agreement (see the US Trade Act of 2002, title XXI, section 2102). A multilateral investment agreement, even one based on a GATS-style 'positive list' approach as intended by the Doha declaration, will nevertheless be binding. Acceptance of the national treatment principle, for example, would limit the ability of host governments to restrict or exclude investment in certain sectors and require that local ownership clauses and other currently permitted performance requirements be specified in country schedules. This would also limit the ability of governments to control and direct domestic investment for development purposes, including by reducing the flexibility provided by certain bilateral investment treaties. Moreover, transgressions of the agreement will invite disputes and retaliatory sanctions.

The Need for Domestic Competition Policies in Developing Countries

Another risk is that socially beneficial domestic competition is likely to be reduced. Inward foreign direct investment can spur competition among domestic firms and move them to an internationally competitive level of productivity. But in the absence of an appropriate and effective domestic competition policy, foreign firms can crowd out domestic investment, stifle domestic competition, reduce domestic productivity growth, raise domestic prices and diminish prospects for industrialisation.

Domestic competition laws and their enforcement should be designed to restrain anti-competitive behaviour by large domestic private corporations, limit or pre-empt abuses of monopoly power by large transnational corporations and support human development objectives. This is where the experience of Japan and other East Asian countries is likely to be most useful for developing countries. For example, as was the case in many of these countries, it should be permissible for a developing country to allow domestic corporations to merge or establish a minimum critical mass of research and development activity, to enable them to compete more effectively with large transnational corporations, while at the same time denying such merger opportunities to foreign transnational corporations. But this would violate the WTO's national treatment principle [*Singh, 2002*]. It could also bring cross-retaliation against the developing country in another area as part of the WTO's dispute settlement procedure.

It is also worth noting that even the most effective competition policy will be unable to constrain the global anti-competitive behaviour of large transnational corporations. That will require the co-operation of industrial countries, where most such corporations are based. And it will require an appropriate framework for international co-operation on competition issues, similar to those embodied in the failed proposals put forth by developing countries two decades ago. While the need for such a framework remains urgent, the possibility of this happening appears even less likely than it was two decades ago and the WTO is an unlikely forum for agreement on such a framework.

Reconciling the Most Favoured Nation Principle

Another concern that will need to be addressed is reconciliation of the most favoured nation principle, which is basic to all multilateral trade agreements, with the special treatment conferred under bilateral investment treaties and regional agreements to ethnic overseas investors in countries such as China and India. This issue is important because evidence suggests, for example, that in a number of cases ethnic overseas investment is more development-friendly. There is also the question of whether application of the most favoured nation principle will imply that the terms in regional agreements (such as the NAFTA chapter 11 investor-state arbitration procedure) will be incorporated in a multilateral investment agreement.

Will the Smallest and Most Vulnerable Countries Benefit from a Multilateral Investment Agreement?

Advocates of a multilateral investment agreement make some important arguments. One is that the smallest, most vulnerable countries are always better off in multilateral than in bilateral agreements because of the unequal power relationships between countries.

This is a valid argument, but only if the multilateral agreement can be guaranteed to be more flexible and to increase development policy autonomy. As the previous analysis shows, this is unlikely if the current emphasis on the pre-establishment phase of investment serves as the basis for a multilateral agreement in the future: an investment agreement based on such a principle will likely considerably limit many developing countries' policy autonomy. Moreover, it cannot be assumed that a multilateral investment agreement will negate the need for bilateral investment treaties. Both types of agreement coexist in trade and other areas; one is not a substitute for the other. A new multilateral investment agreement, in addition to adding another layer that may reduce developing country policy autonomy, will likely also drain their limited human resources, especially those of the least developed, smallest and most vulnerable among them.

Once in, especially as part of the 'single undertaking', it will also be harder for such countries to withdraw from a multilateral agreement. Such action would be met by threats of dispute claims and retaliatory sanctions or by demands for further unilateral concessions.

Are Lower Transaction Costs Inevitable?

Another argument for a multilateral agreement is that it should lower transaction costs, especially for the poorest and most vulnerable developing countries, as a result of one agreement replacing the multitude of bilateral ones. While this may be true for multilateralism over bilateralism in some areas, it has not proven to be the case in the trade area and it is doubtful that a multilateral investment agreement will replace bilateral investment treaties, at least in the short term – especially if a number of bilateral agreements continue to offer more favourable terms and more flexibility to some developing countries. Rather than reducing transaction costs, a multilateral agreement may actually increase them for developing countries, especially the poorest.

Equally importantly, a multilateral agreement is unlikely to reduce transaction costs for foreign investors. It has been convincingly argued that

> the major proportion of the transactions costs associated with foreign direct investment is likely to arise from differences in language, culture, politics and the general business climate of a host country. Familiarizing oneself with the investment laws of a country seems trivial in contrast to these more daunting challenges that exist regardless of whether the country is a signatory to a multilateral or bilateral investment agreement. [*Hoekman and Saggi, 1999: 16*]

Can the Higher Opportunity Costs be Justified?

Finally, it is questionable whether policy-makers in developing countries can justify the opportunity costs of diverting scarce human and other resources to negotiating and administering new issues such as investment. This is because of the questionable development value of such an agreement and their arguably more pressing domestic and poverty reduction priorities.

Indeed, experts have argued that taking high-quality human and other resources away from such domestic priorities is unlikely to be their best possible economic use [*Rodrik, 2001; Winters, 2002*]. Even if confined to the trade area, developing country priorities and those of poverty reduction lie much more in the traditional 'border' areas (agriculture and textiles) – where they should logically invest their limited resources if they wish to maximise their gains.

VII. FIVE KEY CONCLUDING POLICY MESSAGES

1) Domestic resource mobilisation has been much more critical to the successful pursuit of human development strategies than a reliance on foreign capital flows including FDI. At best, FDI can supplement domestic

resources and play a modest role in contributing to positive human development outcomes. It cannot and should not supplant the need for developing country governments to concentrate on generating domestic resources, including those from trade, if sustainable human development is the goal. A country's first priority should therefore be to maximise the generation of domestic savings and resources and develop the absorptive capacity to put such resources to maximum human development benefit, rather than the pursuit of foreign direct investment.

2) To the extent that FDI can be a useful supplement, it needs to be understood and internalised that the key determinants of successfully attracting FDI are not the nature of the trade regime or international legal regime, but a country's post-establishment conditions and characteristics, including human development related ones such as the quality of the work-force, the quality of institutions and infrastructure, and political and social stability. As a result, if the objective is to attract human development-friendly FDI, it will be more important for developing countries to invest their scarce resources on 'inside the border' areas such as health, education, the creation of labour-intensive employment schemes, agrarian reform and physical and institutional infrastructure than in negotiating a multilateral, regional or even bilateral trade regime on investment. Indeed, it is hard to convincingly argue that investing scarce human and financial resources in negotiating a multilateral agreement on investment is more important than their use in the pursuit of the aforementioned domestic priorities.

3) It is important that countries invite FDI selectively and govern it effectively if they wish to maximise its contribution to poverty reduction and human development outcomes. FDI quality and its strategic investment as part of a coherent national development strategy, not its volume and indiscriminate use should be the focus. This lesson is based on the experience of many successful Asian countries, including the Republic of Korea and Malaysia. The latter, in particular, is widely seen to have benefited greatly from FDI but is among the most visible leaders in the now vociferous opposition to an investment agreement in the multilateral trade regime. This is because Malaysia recognises that many of the investment strategies it has pursued so successfully over the years would most likely be foreclosed if there were to be a multilateral agreement on investment. This lesson must be even more seriously internalised by late industrialisers for whom such an agreement would really be akin to 'kicking away the ladder' [*Chang, 2002*]. Moreover, the idea that foreigners should be allowed to exercise property rights in their countries through the threat of the use of trade sanctions remains political

anathema in Malaysia and many other countries, including many newly industrialised ones.

4) It is unlikely that a multilateral agreement on investment will reduce the plethora of bilateral agreements, thereby reducing transaction costs for both the host country and foreign investors. If anything, such an agreement could dramatically increase opportunity costs for the poorest countries without reducing their transaction costs.

5) Bilateral agreements on investment which have focused on the post-establishment phase, allowing countries to attract FDI selectively and govern it effectively, have probably more to offer developing countries than a multilateral agreement.

NOTES

1. See European Commission letter dated 9 May 2004 from Pascal Lamy, EU Trade Commissioner and Franz Fischler, EU Agriculture Commissioner to Trade Ministers of all WTO member countries.
2. For a more detailed discussion of the concept of human development, its implications and its measurement see annual UNDP *Human Development Reports* since 1990 [*see specifically Jahan, 2001*]. For a discussion of the relationship between trade and human development, see Chapter 1 of the UNDP co-sponsored publication *Making Global Trade Work for People* [*UNDP et al., 2003*].
3. See Chapter 12 of the UNDP co-sponsored publication *Making Global Trade Work for People* [*UNDP et al., 2003*] and Gibbs and Mashayekhi [*1998*].
4. In an international agreement, a positive list is a list of items, entities, products and the like which will apply, with no commitment to apply the agreement to anything else. This is in contrast with a negative list which defines that which does not apply to the agreement. See glossary of *Making Global Trade Work for People* [*UNDP et al., 2003*].
5. UNCTAD [2002a] discusses the role of Japanese foreign direct investment in the international networks of the electronics industry and their policies towards local parts and suppliers. The analysis also highlights how little of the value added from these networks remains in developing countries.
6. Local content requirements also occur in tobacco, audiovisual, pharmaceutical, computer equipment and food processing industries.
7. See Chapter 12 of *Making Global Trade Work for People* [*UNDP et al., 2003*] for details on the WTO complaint about Indonesia's car programme brought by Japan to the WTO Dispute Settlement Mechanism. The EU and US reserved third party rights to the case. A more detailed analysis can be found in Tang [*2002*].
8. Developing countries acquire technology in four broad ways: through embedded technology in capital goods imports, through foreign direct investment, through purchase or foreign technology licensing, or through technology transfer through assistance. Empirical evidence shows that the relative importance of intra-firm technology flows has increased since the mid 1980s as a way of transferring technology. This was spurred by the emergence of new technologies in information, electronics and biotechnology. Companies see these technologies as key to long-run competitiveness and are keen to preserve their monopoly.
9. In some cases, capacity constraints are the impediment. The *sui generis* regime on integrated circuit designs under TRIPS does not prevent reverse engineering. However, few developing countries possess the requisite knowledge or resources to do so.

REFERENCES

Chang, Ha-Joon, 2002, *Kicking Away the Ladder: Development Strategy in Historical Perspective*, London: Anthem Press.

Claessens, Stijn, Michael Dooley and Andrew Warner, 1993, 'Portfolio Capital Flows: Hot or Cold?', in *Portfolio Investment in Developing Countries*, Discussion Paper 228, Washington, DC: World Bank.

Correa, Carlos, 1999, 'Preparing for the Third Ministerial Conference of the World Trade Organisation (WTO): Issues for the Member States of the Islamic Development Bank in the Built-In Review of the Agreement on Trade-Related Investment Measures (TRIMs) of the WTO', Study for the Islamic Development Bank, University of Buenos Aires, Argentina.

Gibbs, Murray and Mina Mashayekhi, 1998, 'Uruguay Round Negotiations and Investment: Lessons for the Future', Geneva: United Nations Conference on Trade and Development.

Hanson, Gordon, H., 2001, 'Should Countries Promote Foreign Direct Investment?', G-24 Discussion Paper 9. Geneva: United Nations Conference on Trade and Development, and Cambridge, MA: Harvard University, Center for International Development.

Hoekman, Bernard and Kamal Saggi, 1999, 'Multilateral Disciplines for Investment-Related Policies?', Paper presented at the Institutional Affari Internazionali Conference on Global Regionalism, 8–9 February, Rome.

Jahan, Selim, 2000, 'Economic Growth and Human Development', Human Development Report Office, New York: United Nations Development Programme, mimeo.

Jahan, Selim, 2001, 'Human Development Paradigm: Some Thoughts', *Journal of Social Science*, The Hague, Vol.IX, No.2, pp.41–55.

Kregel, Jan, A., 1996, 'Some Risks and Implications of Financial Globalisation for National Policy Autonomy', Geneva: United Nations Conference on Trade and Development.

Kumar, Nagesh, 1996, 'Foreign Direct Investments and Technology Transfers in Development: A Perspective on Recent Literature', Discussion Paper 9606, Maastricht: United Nations University and Institute for New Technologies.

OECD (Organisation for Economic Co-operation and Development), 1997, 'Main Features of the MAI', Paper presented at the OECD symposium on the Multilateral Agreement on Investment, 3–4 April, Seoul.

Rodrik, Dani, 2001, 'The Global Governance of Trade As If Development Really Mattered', Background paper for Trade and Sustainable Human Development Project, New York: United Nations Development Programme.

Singh, A., 2001, 'Foreign Direct Investment and International Agreements: A South Perspective', T.R.A.D.E. Occasional Paper, Geneva: South Centre.

Singh, A., 2002, 'Competition and Competition Policy in Emerging Markets: International and Development Dimensions', Revised version of a paper prepared for a G-24 Technical Group meeting, March, Beirut.

Tang, Xiaobing, 2002, 'Experience of Implementation of the WTO Agreement on Trade-Related Investment Measures: Difficulties and Challenges Faced by Developing Countries', Geneva: United Nations Conference on Trade and Development.

UNCTAD (United Nations Conference on Trade and Development), 1994, 'Assessment of the Outcome of the Uruguay Round', Geneva: UNCTAD.

UNDP (United Nations Development Programme) *et al.*, 2003, *Making Global Trade Work for People*, London: Earthscan.

Winters, L. Alan, 2002, 'Doha and the World Poverty Targets', Paper presented at the Annual World Bank Conference on Development Economics, 29 April, Washington, DC.

WTO (World Trade Organisation), 1996, *WTO Annual Report: Trade and Foreign Direct Investment*, Vol. 1, Geneva: WTO.

WTO (World Trade Organisation) and UNCTAD (United Nations Conference on Trade and Development), 2002, 'Trade-Related Invesment Measures and Other Performance Requirements', Geneva: Council for Trade in Goods.

INDEX

Abrenica, J.V. 167
absorptive capacity 8–11, 14, 207, 214, 216–17, 288
aerospace 23–4
Africa 9, 86, 271, 277
Agreement on Subsidies and Countervailing Measures 278
Agreement on Textiles and Clothing 58
agriculture 11, 94, 98, 102–3, 117, 179, 245, 247, 287
Ahvenainen, J. 251
Aitken, B.J. 143, 211
Akoorie, M. 182–3
Alabama 87
Alien Property Act 245
Allied Signals 24
Alvarez, I. 210
Amsden, A. 256
Andean Community 55
Aoki, M. 146
apartheid 23, 26
apparel industry 55–8
apprenticeships 97
Argentina 7, 64, 88, 207–40
Arrow, K. 147
ASEAN Supporting Industry Database (ASID) 129
Asia 2, 4–5, 12, 15, 27, 54, 57–8, 64, 67, 76–8, 117–18, 143, 157, 189, 242, 252, 254–60, 278, 281, 283–5, 288
assembly and testing plants (ATPs) 61–2, 64–5
assets 4–5, 7–8, 12, 44, 47, 179, 185, 207–9, 211, 214–15, 228, 281–2, 284

Association of South East Asian Nations (ASEAN) 125, 129–30
Atlantic LNG 102
Atlas Methanol 99
Audretsch, D. 149
Australia 29, 44, 180–1, 183, 253
automotive industry 6, 19–52, 55, 57, 66, 73, 76, 87, 124, 126–7, 129, 231, 250, 254–5, 261–2, 278–9

BANCOMEXT 77
Bangladesh 68
Bankers' Magazine 243–4
banking 243–8, 251–2, 256
Barclay, Lou Anne 6, 9, 12, 14, 85–114
Barnes, Justin 6, 9, 19–52
Bartlett, C.A. 215
Belgium 180, 253
Bell, Martin 7–9, 144, 149, 207–40
Benchmarking Club 30–1
bilateral investment treaties (BITs) 73, 77, 264–5, 275, 289
Birkinshaw, Julian 21, 216
Blomstrom, M. 4, 91, 213
Board of Investment (BoI) 125–30, 134, 137
BoI Unit for Industrial Linkage Development (BUILD) 127–30, 134, 137
Borensztein, E. 8
Bosch 24
Braconier, H. 211
Brazil 5, 14, 24, 26, 64, 68, 87–8, 257, 279
Bretton Woods 131
Brimble, P. 167

291

brownfield investment 241–2, 249, 255, 260
Bulgaria 213
Bureau of Supporting Industries Development (BSID) 131

CAATEC Foundation 107
Calvo Doctrine 273
Cambodia 263
Canada 26, 68, 72–3, 78, 183, 248, 253, 274
Canada-US Free Trade Agreement 73
Cancun Ministerial 242, 270–1, 276–7, 281
Cantwell, J. 209, 217
capabilities 149–72, 254, 272
Caribbean 6, 55–6, 58–9, 64, 86, 95, 271, 277
Caribbean Industrial Research Institute (CARIRI) 94, 98
Caves, R.E. 91, 144, 208
Center on Transnational Corporations 274
Central America 55–6, 58–9, 64
Central America and Caribbean (CAC) see Caribbean; Central America
certified public accountants (CPAs) 247
Chart Pattana Party 131
Charter of Economic Rights and Duties of States 274
Chile 55, 64, 89, 277
China 14, 46, 58, 61–2, 64, 88, 248, 258, 262, 281
Chrysler see DaimlerChrysler
Chuan Leekpai 131
Chung, J. 211
Cimoli, M. 235
CL Financial 99, 101
clothing industry 89, 104
Coalicion Costaricense de Iniciativas para el Desarrollo (CINDE) 65, 103–4, 107, 109
Code of Conduct for Transnational Corporations 274
Colombia 89
commodity chains 118–19
competitiveness 66–7, 73, 76, 78, 86–93, 104, 107, 117–18, 122, 135–8, 144, 146–9, 163, 178–80, 182, 185–6, 188–90, 192, 200, 211, 214, 227–8, 230, 241, 243, 258, 262, 278, 285–6

complementary factors 2–3, 12, 104
completely built up vehicles (CBUs) 27–8
completely knocked down components (CKD) 27
computer-assisted design (CAD) 105
Conference on Trade and Employment 273–4
Congress 245, 247
constraints 3–8
Cook-Weisberg test 164
Coordinating Task Force (CTF) 94
Costa Rica 4, 12–13, 55, 59–66, 77–8, 85–6, 93, 102–9
Council for Scientific and Industrial Research (CSIR) 42
Council for Trade in Goods 279
Craig, Steven 26

Daewoo 67
Daimler-Benz 88
DaimlerChrysler 39, 67
Damijan, J. 213
Davy Corporation 99
debt 87, 91, 124, 131, 136, 243
DeGregori, Thomas 26
Dell 146, 162
Delphi 24
Democrat Party 131
Denmark 180
Department of Commerce 252
Department of Industrial Promotion (DIP) 130–1, 133
Department of Industry 250
Department of Trade and Industry (DTI) 250
development stages 5
Djankov, S. 211
Doha Round 270–1, 276, 280–1, 285
Doner, R. 146
Dorbyl Automotive Technologies 30
Driffield, N. 185
Dunning, John 21, 183, 213, 215
dynamics 24–6, 30, 37–8, 46, 48, 57, 59, 68

Eastern Europe 26, 29
Economic Partnership Agreements (EPAs) 9, 271, 277
education 9–10, 21, 23–4, 41–2, 47, 64, 104, 148, 167, 210, 288

electronics industry 5, 55, 57, 64, 78, 86–7, 92–3, 102–7, 126–7, 130, 141–77, 213, 250, 254, 278
Enderwick, P. 182
engineering 41–2, 47, 96–7, 101–2, 104
Engineering Institute 98–9
entrepreneurs 4, 11, 21, 44, 48, 54, 132, 136–8, 209
Ernst, D. 144, 149
Europe 38–9, 42, 62, 66–8, 72, 78, 119, 209, 243, 248–54, 256, 273
European Commission (EC) 271, 276–7
European Community 279
European Environmental Award 39
European Union (EU) 73, 109, 242–3, 252, 254, 261, 263–5, 271, 276–7, 279
export processing zones (EPZ) 58, 141, 143, 173
export-oriented industrialisation (EOI) 120, 125–6, 128, 131, 143, 157, 168, 181, 184

FDI Assisted Development 91
Federal Reserve System 245
Federation Chemicals 95
Federation of Thai Industries (FTI) 128–9, 132, 135, 137
Ferraz, J.C. 230
Fiat 262
finance 243–8, 251, 254, 272, 281, 283
Findlay, R. 8
Finland 251–2, 260–1, 263, 266
First Bank of the USA (FBUSA) 245
First World War 243, 245, 263, 273
fishing 89, 179
flower industry 89
follow design/source 25, 42, 47, 136
Follow-up Study on Supporting Industries Development 131–2
Ford 39, 44, 67, 88, 250, 262
Foreign Investment Council 255
Foreign Investment Review Act 274
forestry 89, 103, 179
Forfar 109
France 248–51, 253, 260, 265
Free Trade Agreement of the Americas (FTAA) 265
free trade agreements (FTAs) 73, 77
Frost, T. 216
furniture industry 89

Gachino, G. 143
gas industry 86, 92–102, 107–8
General Agreement on Tariffs and Trade (GATT) 73, 77, 273–5, 278
General Agreement on Trade in Services (GATS) 77, 264, 266, 275, 279, 285
General Assembly 273
General Motors (GM) 24, 39, 67–8, 250, 255–6
Germany 38, 99, 245, 248–51, 253, 256, 265
Ghoshal, S. 214
globalisation 12–13, 15, 25–6, 28, 30, 44, 53–4, 59–64, 66–73, 79, 86, 116, 209–10, 227, 230, 262–3, 266, 281
Globerman 91
government policy 10–12, 24, 53–4, 64–7, 73–8, 87, 90, 94–6, 98, 100, 102–3, 106–9, 115–40, 146–7, 154–5, 172, 181, 247–8, 263, 266, 277, 285–6
greenfield investment 249, 281–2
gross domestic product (GDP) 24, 27, 57, 64, 76, 93, 107, 126, 136, 179–80, 183, 244

Ha-Joon Chang 13, 241–69
Haddad, M. 143, 211
Hamilton, A. 146
Harrison, A. 143, 211
Haskel, J. 211, 213
Havana Charter 273
Hay, John 247
Hirschman, A. 144, 165
historical perspectives 241–69, 273–7
Hitachi 250
Hjerppe, R. 251
Hoekman, B. 211
Hong Kong 88–9, 252
Hood, N. 216
host country policy 59–77
human development 270–90
Humphrey, John 26
Hymer, S. 208

Iammarino, S. 209, 217
ICI 99
Import Rebate Credit Certificates (IRCCs) 28
Import-Export Complementation (IEC) Scheme 27

Import-substitution industrialisation (ISI)
73, 76–7, 120
India 5, 7, 14, 26, 64, 210, 279
Indigenous technology 21–6, 47–9
Indonesia 64, 68, 279
Industrial Development Corporation (IDC)
94
Industrial Plant Services 101
Industrial policy (IP) 144, 146–7
Industrialisation 9–15, 53–84, 94–5,
115, 117–18, 120, 123–7, 148, 179,
202, 210, 216, 218, 227–31, 235, 253,
255–7, 260, 266, 278, 285, 288
Information and communications
technology (ICT) 60, 147, 165, 167
Information technology (IT) 23–4, 105,
149, 219
Innovation 2, 8–10, 19–52, 60, 66,
85–114, 142, 144, 146, 201, 209–10,
215–17, 219, 235–6
Innovation Fund 23
Innovation Survey 218
Institute of SME Development (ISMED)
132–3
institutions 10–11, 13, 42, 89–90, 95–6,
99, 102, 108, 122–3, 131, 137, 142,
146–7, 153, 167, 169, 171–2
Instituto Technologico de Costa Rica
(ITCR) 104
Intel 4, 55, 59–66, 93, 104–6, 143, 146
intellectual property rights 39, 43, 47, 89,
265
Inter-American Development Bank 103,
107
International Labour Organisation 132
International Monetary Fund (IMF) 108,
258
international systems of integrated
production (ISIP) 54, 56, 59–77, 79
International Trade Organisation (ITO)
273
investment development path (IDP) 183,
200
investment promotion agencies (IPAs) 109
Ireland 61–2, 65, 109, 142, 180, 251–4,
261
Israel 61
Isuzu 67
Italy 253

Jackson, Andrew 244
Jansen, Karel 126
Japan 26, 38–9, 42, 54, 66–8, 76–7, 89,
119, 125, 129–34, 142–3, 146–7, 243,
250–1, 253–6, 258–9, 261–3, 265–6,
275, 277, 279, 285
Japan International Cooperation Agency
(JICA) 130–1
Japanese Institute for Small Business
Management and Technology (JSBC)
132–3
JETRO 131
Joint Technologically Active/Passive
Industries 221, 231
Jurgens, E. 216

Kaldor, N. 147
Kaplinsky, Raphael 26
Katrak, H. 7
Katz, J.M. 235
Keller, W. 211
Kellogg Brown & Root 99
Kenya 89
Kogut, B. 13
Kokko, A. 4, 9, 213
Konings, J. 211, 213
Korea 54, 66–7, 76–7, 89, 125, 142, 252,
256–63, 265–6, 288
Kuemmerle, W. 215
Kumar, N. 265

Lada 25
laissez-faire 252, 261
Lall, Sanjaya 1–18, 144, 149
land 245–7, 251–2
Latin America 54–9, 64–5, 77–9, 106,
230, 235, 258, 265, 271, 273, 283
Lauriden, Laurids S. 12, 14, 115–40
League of Nations 273
Lecorz, Fabien 264
Lewis, W. Arthur 86
light commercial vehicles (LCVs) 28, 44
Likert scale 188, 192
linkages 3–7, 10, 54, 57–9, 65, 79, 89–91,
102, 105, 107–8, 115–40, 178, 182,
184–6, 201–2, 253, 270–90
liquefied natural gas (LNG) 95–9, 101
List, F. 146
local content requirements (LCRs) 120,
124, 129, 133

local firms 21–2, 28, 30–1, 39, 46–9, 58, 99, 101–7, 109, 116–24, 127–32, 134–7, 141–206, 213–31, 234–6, 241–2, 253–4
London City and Midland Bank 247
Lorentzen, Jochen 6, 9, 19–52
Love, J. 185
Lung, Yannick 26
Lurgi Oel Gas Chemie GmbH 99

macroeconomics 13, 21, 26–30, 73, 117, 127, 131, 134, 179, 181
Maddison, A. 251
Malaysia 12, 25, 29, 61–2, 65, 68, 88, 124, 141–77, 288–9
Malhotra, Kamal 14, 270–90
Manhattan Bank 244
Manu Leopairote 131
manufacturing 7, 24–5, 29, 40–1, 46, 48, 57, 66, 73, 87, 105, 117, 131, 134, 179, 189, 245, 254, 257
maquiladora 56–7, 76, 105
Marcos, Ferdinand 143
Marin, Anabel 7–9, 207–240
Massachusetts Institute of Technology (MIT) 42
Master Plan for the Development of Supporting Industries 130–1, 134
matchmaking 121, 127–9
Matsushita 250
Mauritius 149
Mazda 67
Meiji period 254
Memedovic, Olga 26
Mercedes-Benz 87
Mercosur 55
Metair 30
methyl tertiary butyl ether (MTBE) 100
Mexican Automotive Decrees 76
Mexico 4, 6, 12, 25–6, 55–9, 64, 66–77, 88, 213, 257, 271, 276
microeconomics 21, 26–30, 135, 184, 200
Microsoft 60
military 23, 41, 47
Mill, J.S. 146
minimum efficiency scale (MES) 148–9
mining 245, 247, 251–2
Ministerial Restructuring Act (MRA) 137
Ministry of Industry (MoI) 127–8, 130–4, 137

Ministry of International Trade and Industry (MITI), 130, 132
Ministry of Trade and Industry 252
Mitsubishi 250
Miyazawa fund 131–2, 134
Mizutani 132
Molero, J. 210
Morocco 273
Morrison, A. 21
Mortimore, Michael 4, 6, 13–14, 53–84
Most Favoured Nation (MFN) 77, 243, 286
motivation 4–6, 23
Motor Industry Development Programme (MIDP) 27–8
multilateral investment agreement (MIA) 242–3, 248, 262–6, 276, 280, 284–9
multinational corporations (MNCs) 31, 39–40, 44, 46, 97, 207–11, 213–24, 228, 230–1, 234–6
multinational enterprises (MNEs) 1–9, 12–13, 15, 21, 27, 30, 178, 182–5, 189, 200, 202, 258
Murray and Roberts 30
Mytelka, Lynn K. 6, 9, 12, 14, 85–114

Narula, Rajneesh 1–18, 21, 183, 213
National Bank Act 245
National Biodiversity Institute (INBio) 103
National Competitiveness Committee (NCC) 137
National Economic and Social Development Board (NESDB) 137
National Energy Skills Centre (NESC) 96–7
national innovation system (NIS) 22–4, 30, 41–2, 47–48, 144, 146–7, 149, 163
National Institute for Higher Education (NIHERST) 94
National Supplier Development Programme (NSDP) 128, 134
National Treasury 57
Natural Gas Company (NGC) 95–6, 98
Natural Gas Export Task Force 95
neo-classicism 146–7
net outward investment (NOI) 183
Netherlands 248, 253
New United Motor Manufacturing Inc (NUMMI) 68, 72
New Zealand 7, 179–82

newly industrialised countries (NICs) 118,
    126, 143, 278, 289
newly industrialised economies (NIes) 2,
    12
Nissan 67, 78, 250
North America 39, 66–8, 72–3, 76, 78
North American Free Trade Agreement
    (NAFTA) 57–8, 66–7, 73, 76, 78, 261,
    265, 275, 286
Norway 180, 251

OEMs 38–40, 42–4, 46
oil 94–5, 97, 99, 107
O'Malley, E. 252–3
Omnibus Trade and Competitiveness Act
    274
Organisation of Economic Cooperation
    and Development (OECD) 37, 73, 77,
    87, 90, 179, 230, 242, 276, 280
Oslo Manual 218
outsourcing 24, 59
ownership 6, 31, 39, 43, 47–9, 76, 104–5,
    135, 146–7, 152, 156–7, 159, 165, 169,
    172, 181–2, 184, 200, 209, 241–53,
    255–7, 259–61, 284
Ownership-Location-Internalisation (OLI)
    paradigm 208–10, 218
Ozawa, Terutomo 21

Pacific 189, 271, 277
Patel, P. 216
path dependency 41–2, 47
Patibandla, M. 213
Pavit, K. 144, 149
PCS Nitrogen 101
Pearce, R.D. 215
Perez, C. 8
Petrochemical Company of Saskatchewan
    (PCS) 98
Petroleum Company of Trinidad and
    Tobago (PETROTRIN) 99–100
pharmaceuticals 103, 179, 254–5
Philippines 61–2, 65, 89, 141–77, 279
Phoenix Park Gas Processors 99
Plaza Accord 125, 143
Point Lisas Industrial Estate 94, 100
Pol Pot 263
Poland 213
Portelli, B. 8
Portugal 68

poverty 272
power relations 121
primary sector 7
printed circuit boards (PCBs) 157, 159,
    162
Process Plant Services Co 101
PROCOMER 107
productivity 207–11, 216–17, 219, 221,
    223, 235, 266, 282–3
Proton 25
Public Administration Act (PAA) 137
public goods 147
Public Sector Development Commission
    137
Pyke, F. 148

Qatar 276
quality of life 272

Ramstetter, Eric D. 124
Rancher 44
Rasiah, Rajah 9, 12, 141–77
recession 57, 60, 95
regional trade agreements (RTAs) 265
Renault 87
Rodriguez-Clare, A. 7
Rodrik, D. 10
Russia 25, 248, 251
Rutherford, T.D. 26

Sabel, C. 148
Samsung 67
Sanyal, A. 213
Sanyo 250
Saxenian, A.L. 146
Schumpeter, J.A. 147
science 23, 48, 58, 98–9, 103, 108, 210
Science, Engineering and Technology
    Institutions (SETIs) 23–4
Scott-Kennel, Joanna, 7, 178–206
SEAMICO 128
Second Bank of the USA (SBUSA) 244
Second World War 249–50, 255, 263, 265,
    273, 284
semiconductors 60, 106, 148, 159, 162–3,
    172
Sengenberger, W. 148
Set of Multilaterally Agreed Equitable
    Principles and Rules for the Control of
    Restrictive Practices 274

Shell 97
Silicon Valley 146
Singapore 64–5, 87–9, 124, 142, 180, 242, 252, 276–7, 280–1
Singh, A. 281
Sjoholm, F. 213
small and medium-size enterprises (SMEs) see local firms
SME Development Bank 136
SME Financing Advisory Center (SFAC) 133
SME Master Plan 132
SME Promotion Office (SMEPO) 132
Smith, A. 144, 146
social capital 10
Soete, L. 8
Solectron 146
Sony 250
South Africa 6, 19–52
South African Bureau of Standards (SABS) 42
South America 55
Southern Cone 55
Soviet Union 13
Spain 210
State Department 247
state-owned enterprises (SOEs) 249–50
strategy 42–7, 54–5, 59–73, 76–9, 85–114, 118–19, 214, 243, 259, 261–2, 278, 288
structural adjustment programmes 87, 95
Study on Industrial sector Development 130
Subaru 67
subsidiaries 4–5, 7–8, 21, 30–1, 39–40, 44, 46–7, 61, 67, 72, 120, 125, 192, 197, 207, 209–11, 213–30, 234–6, 245, 256–7
Subsidies and Countervailing Measures Agreement (SCM) 3, 14
supplier development 115–40
supply-side models 211–14, 217
Suwat Liptapallop 131
Sweden 180
Switerland 248, 253
systems view 9–11

Taiwan 54, 77, 89, 125, 142, 252, 258 61, 263
Tambunlertchai Somsak 124, 126

targets 53–84
tariffs 27, 58, 76, 120, 124, 134, 169, 245, 248, 266
technical agreements (TAs) 39
Technology for Human Resources Programme (THRIP) 24
technology transfer 2–3, 6, 8–9, 12, 20, 38, 54, 57–9, 65, 79, 87, 89, 91, 118, 120, 129, 132, 149, 157, 178, 182, 189, 192, 197–8, 207, 209–11, 213–16, 241–2, 256–8, 261, 277, 282–3
Tecson, G.R. 167
Texaco 97
textiles industry 89, 104, 261, 287
Thai Rak Thai (TRT) Party 131, 136
Thailand 12, 64, 68, 89, 115–77
Thaksin Shinawatra 115, 131, 136–8
Thammasat University 133
Thatcher, Margaret 249
tiger economies 252
Titan Methanol 99, 101
Tobit regression 165, 168
Tokya Round 274
Toshiba 250
Tourism and Industrial Development Corporation (TIDCO) 95, 102
Toyota Motor Corporation (TMC) 4, 38, 55, 66–78, 256
Toyota Motor Manufacturing Alabama (TMMAL) 68, 72
Toyota Motor Manufacturing Baja California (TMMBC) 68, 72
Toyota Motor Manufacturing Canada Inc (TMMC) 68, 72
Toyota Motor Manufacturing France (TMMF) 72
Toyota Motor Manufacturing Indiana (TMMI) 68, 72
Toyota Motor Manufacturing Kentucky (TMMK) 68, 72
Toyota Motor Manufacturing Poland (TMMP) 72
Toyota Motor Manufacturing Texas (TMMTX) 68, 72
Toyota Motor Manufacturing Turkey Inc (TMMT) 72
Toyota Motor Manufacturing UK (TMUK) 68
Toyota Motor Manufacturing West Virginia (TMMWV) 68, 72

Toyota Peugeot Citroen Automobile Czech
   (TRCA) 72
trade unions 148, 152, 165, 169, 171, 173
Trade-related Aspects of Intellectual
   Property Rights (TRIPs) 3, 14, 77, 265,
   274, 282–3
Trade-related Investment Measures
   (TRIMs) 14, 77, 122, 261, 266, 270,
   274–9, 284
transfer pricing 245, 256
transnational corporations (TNCs) 54–9,
   64–7, 76–9, 85–8, 90–1, 95, 98, 103,
   107, 109, 115–21, 123, 127–9, 133,
   135–7, 142–3, 245, 252, 254, 256–60,
   266, 277–8, 285
Trinidad and Tobago 6, 13, 85–6, 92–102,
   105, 107–8
Trinidad and Tobago Institute of
   Technology (TTIT) 97–8
truncation 5, 11, 59, 146

United Kingdom (UK) 88, 99, 248–51,
   253, 265
United Nations Industrial Development
   Organisation (UNIDO) 132
United Nations (UN) 78, 92, 256, 258–9,
   273–4
United States (US) 26, 38–9, 57–9, 61–2,
   64, 66–8, 72–3, 76, 78, 88, 95, 99, 101,
   104–5, 119, 143, 146, 149, 180, 242–5,
   249–50, 252, 254, 259–63, 265, 273–7,
   279, 281
universities 11–12, 23, 41–2, 89, 94, 97,
   102–3, 133, 171
upgrading 19–52, 57, 79, 102, 104–7, 109,
   115, 117, 120, 127, 129–30, 132, 136,
   144, 149, 178–9, 184–6, 199–201, 254,
   256, 259, 261, 278
Urata, S. 143
Uruguay Round 270, 273–5, 277–84

Vega, M. 216
Vendors Meet Customers (VMC) 129
Venezuela 68
venture capital 24, 106, 179
Vergara, Sebastian 4, 13–14, 53–84
Vernon, R. 208
Visteon 24, 44
Volkswagen (VW) 25, 78, 87, 216, 249,
   260

Wade, R. 12
Wang, Y. 213
Washington 3, 11, 15, 73
weaponry 23
Western Europe 29, 39
Westphal, L.E. 144, 149
White Paper on Science and Technology
   23
Wignaraja, G. 144, 149
Wilkins, Mira 243, 247
Wilkinson, F. 148
Working Group on the Relationship
   Between Trade and Investment 280
World Bank 108, 131, 137, 281
world car 25
World Trade Organisation (WTO) 1, 3, 14,
   58, 96, 241–2, 262, 264–6, 270–1, 273,
   276–80, 282, 284–7

Xu, B. 9

Yeaple, R.Y. 211
Yoshino, M.Y. 255
You, J.I. 148
Young, A. 144
Young, S. 250

Zander, I. 215

Printed in the United States
by Baker & Taylor Publisher Services